ECONOMICS AND ECONOMIC CHANGE

macroeconomics

DD202 COURSE TEAM

Paul Anand, Lecturer in Economics

Suma Athreye, Deputy Course Team Chair and Lecturer in Economics

Brenda Barnett, Course Secretary

Penny Bennett, Project Leader

Pam Berry, Compositor

Karen Bridge, Software Designer

Michael Brogan, Course Manager

Vivienne Brown, Senior Lecturer in Economics

Stephen Clift, Editor

Lene Connolly, Print Buyer

Neil Costello, Associate Director, SQW

Sarah Crompton, Graphic Designer

Graham Dawson, Course Team Chair and Lecturer in Economics

Sue Dobson, Cartoonist

Christopher Downs, Software Course Team Chair and Lecturer in Economics

Wilf Eynon, Audio Visual

Ian Fribbance, Staff Tutor

Phil Gauron, Series Producer, BBC

Janis Gilbert, Graphic Artist

Richard Golden, Production and Presentation Administrator

Mark Goodwin, Editor

Celia Hart, Picture Researcher

Martin Higginson, Staff Tutor

Susan Himmelweit, Professor of Economics

Steve Hoy, Producer, BBC

Andrew Law, BBC

Damian Lewis, Software Developer, BBC

Avis Lexton, Secretary

Maureen Mackintosh, Professor of Economics

Ione Mako, BBC

Paul Manners, BBC

Mariana Mazzucato, Lecturer in Economics

Vicki McCulloch, Graphic Designer

Judith Mehta, Lecturer in Economics

David Morris, Software Developer

Jonathan Owen, Graphic Artist

Anne Paynter, Course Secretary

Carlton Reeve, BBC

Roberto Simonetti, Lecturer in Economics

Hedley Stone, Temporary Lecturer in Economics

Andrew Trigg, Lecturer in Economics

Tutor consultants

Michelle Jenkins

Maureen Le Roi

Alistair Young

External authors

Gavin Cameron, Lecturer in Economics, University of Oxford

Nick Crafts, Professor of Economic History, University of Warwick

Guiseppe Fontana, Lecturer in Economics, University of Leeds

Francis Green, Professor of Economics, University of Kent at Canterbury

Diane Perrons, Senior Lecturer in Economics, London School of Economics and Political Science

Malcolm Sawyer, Professor of Economics, University of Leeds

David Spencer, Lecturer in Economics, University of Leeds

Anthony J. Venables, Professor of Economics, London School of Economics and Political Science

External Assessor

John Vint, Professor of Economics, Manchester Metropolitan University

ECONOMICS AND ECONOMIC CHANGE

macroeconomics

Edited by Graham Dawson, Suma Athreye, Susan Himmelweit and Malcolm Sawyer

The Open University

This publication forms part of an Open University course DD202 *Economics and Economic Change*. Details of this and other Open University courses can be obtained from the Course Information and Advice Centre, PO Box 724, The Open University, Milton Keynes MK7 6ZS, United Kingdom: tel. +44 (0)1908 653231, e-mail ces-gen@open.ac.uk

Alternatively, you may visit the Open University website at http://www.open.ac.uk where you can learn more about the wide range of courses and packs offered at all levels by The Open University.

To purchase this publication or other components of Open University courses, contact Open University Worldwide Ltd, The Open University, Walton Hall, Milton Keynes MK7 6AA, United Kingdom: tel. +44 (0)1908 858785; fax +44 (0)1908 858787; e-mail ouwenq@open.ac.uk; website http://www.ouw.co.uk

The Open University
Walton Hall, Milton Keynes
MK7 6AA

First published 2003

Edited, designed and typeset by The Open University.

Printed and bound in the United Kingdom by The Bath Press, Glasgow.

ISBN 0 7492 5370 3

1.3

CONTENTS

PREFACE

Economics and Economic Change is a new introductory economics text. The book contains the core teaching of an Open University course of the same title, which consists of *Microeconomics* and *Macroeconomics*. More and more students in higher education are studying independently, in part because part-time and distance provision are expanding and in part because large classes create difficulties in providing adequate individual attention. Economics principles texts can be hard going for students without the support of seminars and discussion. In contrast, *Economics and Economic Change* mixes critical debate, ethical reflection and discussion of current economic issues with the exposition of theoretical analysis. Together with the interactive style of teaching drawn from The Open University's long experience of open supported distance education, the text offers, we believe, an engaging introduction to an important social science.

Economics and Economic Change is one of a 'new generation' of economics courses that reflects the economic and social impact of information and communication technologies. While the text teaches students how to analyse the effects of new technologies on the economy, the accompanying CD-ROMs enable students to see themselves as taking part in the economic processes they are learning to understand. In presenting a range of teaching materials in this way – real-world case studies, 'test your understanding' quizzes, a statistical package, and 'virtual tutorials' on diagrammatic analysis – *Economics and Economic Change* 'enacts' the changes that are taking place and enables students to develop ICT skills.

Economics and Economic Change forms a series with *Microeconomics: Neoclassical and Institutionalist Perspectives on Economic Behaviour*, edited by Susan Himmelweit *et al.* (2001, Thomson Learning/The Open University). These two texts comprise the core discipline-specific courses of the Open University Economics Discipline and are designed as a coherent whole, providing a progression of skills and learning outcomes and a continuity of style and approach.

Like all Open University courses, this book is a product of collective working. The course team, listed on p.ii, includes both Open University academics and outside contributors. The academic editors are grateful to our external contributing authors for giving the considerable time this enterprise requires. We would particularly like to thank Malcolm Sawyer for his collaboration in planning and editing *Macroeconomics*.

An Open University course team also includes many essential contributors besides academic authors. The academic editors of this book are very appreciative of the outstanding professional effort and expertise contributed by the course manager and project leader, the secretarial staff, the publishing editors, the designers and artists, the software designers, and the BBC producers. The external assessor for the course as a whole, John Vint, has been a source of wise advice on structure, content and the accessibility of the course. Finally, the members of our panel of Open University tutors have put a great deal of effort into trying to ensure that the course content is appropriate for students and have always contributed to the conviviality of course team meetings.

February 2003

INTRODUCTION

Graham Dawson ● ● ● ● ● ● ● ● ● ● ● ● ● ● ● ● ● ● ●

Macroeconomics, the second book of *Economics and Economic Change*, develops further the twin 'storylines' of economic change and economic analysis that ran through the first book. We have chosen three main themes for the economic change strand in this book. Why do capitalist economies tend to go through booms and slumps, and how do policy makers try to cope with the resulting inflation and unemployment? What do we know about the economic outcomes of globalization? Why have some economies grown so much bigger than others, and is their growth environmentally sustainable?

Macroeconomics is the branch of economics that analyses the economy as a whole, or the 'aggregate economy', by looking at the relationship between key aggregates such as the overall level of output, unemployment and inflation. The idea of analysing the economy as a whole in this way was the core theoretical innovation of *The General Theory of Employment, Interest and Money*, published in 1936 by John Maynard Keynes, probably the most influential economist of the twentieth century.

Before the *General Theory*, the prevailing belief among economists was that markets work automatically in a self-adjusting manner. According to this view, the price mechanism works by allocating resources to where they are most needed. If a good is in short supply, then its price is too low and it will rise; if a good is in oversupply, then its price is too high and it will fall. In so far as aggregates were thought about at all, they were assumed to behave similarly to the particular goods whose markets were analysed using the techniques of microeconomics. So, according to this view, unemployment must be the result of wages – the price of employing labour – being too high, and a labour market free from interference would in time see a reduction in wages to balance demand and supply at full employment. Keynes argued that this view was wrong and that the labour market is not able to adjust automatically to eliminate unemployment.

According to Keynes, the aggregate markets of the macroeconomy are fundamentally interconnected, so that it is inappropriate to use the methods that one would use for analysing demand and supply in a single unconnected market. For this reason, the fault with the argument that the labour market is self-adjusting is that it ignores the relationship between employment and the aggregate economy, between the labour market and the goods market. Widespread unemployment can emerge because there is a problem at the level of the aggregate economy that prevents the labour market from adjusting. In particular, Keynes focused on the role of 'aggregate demand' – the total demand for goods and services in the aggregate economy – as a key determinant of the level of unemployment. If aggregate demand for goods is low and firms cannot sell all their output, they will cut back production and workers will lose their jobs.

Keynes's *General Theory* was revolutionary in providing economic analysis with this new notion of the 'aggregate economy'. The aggregate economy refers to the national economy as a structured set of economic relations between economic agents. Chapter 11 builds on the model of the circular flow of income (Chapter 8) to explain some of the interdependencies in a national economy where one agent's expenditure is another's income. To analyse this flow, it is necessary to group economic agents into different aggregate types. There are *workers* who sell their labour. There are *firms* that produce the national output and *households* who consume it. There is also the *government*; and there is the *rest of the world*. Understanding the outcome of these different types of agents' planned expenditures enables us to clarify the conditions for equilibrium of the aggregate economy.

Thinking of the aggregate economy in this way also implies a process of aggregating across markets. Chapter 12 analyses the three aggregated markets that comprise the aggregate economy: the goods market, the labour market and the money market. The chapter examines the components of aggregate demand in the goods market, in terms of the different types of economic agents and the type of demand they provide. There is consumption demand from consumers and investment demand from firms. Government expenditure provides another source of demand, as does the rest of the world in the demand for exports. All these different types of demand have different causes and therefore depend on a different set of factors, some of which can be influenced by policy. Adding up the demand for final goods and services in all the markets in the economy gives aggregate demand. If supply, the capacity to produce output, is not a problem, the level of aggregate demand determines the equilibrium level of national output. Relating this level of output to the labour needed to produce it shows that aggregate demand may be lower than is required to ensure full employment. If so, the government may intervene to raise aggregate demand, perhaps by changing its tax and spending plans, to influence consumer demand and government demand, or perhaps by changing interest rates in the money market, to influence investment demand.

Chapter 13 examines the limitations of government policy to boost aggregate demand in order to reduce unemployment. In the Keynesian model examined in Chapter 12, there are no supply constraints because it is assumed that there are unemployed workers and unused capacity and resources. Inflation in the 1970s persuaded many policy makers to temper their commitment to adjusting aggregate demand to reduce unemployment in the short run. The experience of the deleterious effects of inflation suggested that greater weight should instead be given to considerations of price and financial stability as necessary conditions for long-run growth.

Analysis of the aggregate economy requires a notion of the national economy. In the analysis of Chapters 11 to 13 the aggregate or macroeconomy is defined by national boundaries. The government that intervenes to reduce unemployment is the national government, which has a particular responsibility for the performance of its own national economy. Thus, Keynesian macroeconomics also helped to identify the national economy as composed of a distinct set of economic relationships that is amenable to systematic analysis, and which is the particular concern of the national government.

Chapter 16 considers the macroeconomics of open economies, that is, national economies that are open to international trade. First, Chapter 14 makes a return to microeconomic theory and Chapter 15 examines empirical evidence on the application of this theory to globalization. The return to microeconomics is necessary because the microeconomic analysis of international trade between particular industries in different national economies provides an important foundation for understanding international trade and its effects on the performance of national economies. The analysis of international trade used in this chapter is microeconomic because it looks at the gains from trade in markets for two specific goods, where the industries supplying the market may be located in different national economies. The economic relationships between national economies as such, mediated by the exchange rates of national currencies, are examined in Chapter 16.

Chapter 14 considers how international trade arises from the differential endowments of resources among national economies. It shows how international trade can improve the consumption possibilities of economies, increase world output and make everyone better off. There are substantial benefits from participation in international trade. However, there are losers as well as winners. Although the consumers in a national economy may benefit from international trade, the theory of international trade suggests that this may be at the expense of some producers who cannot compete with foreign producers. This leads once again to a consideration of policy issues, in particular the circumstances in which the imposition of a tariff may be preferable to allowing completely free trade.

In considering the population's well-being, therefore, much depends on the distribution of the gains from trade. The acceleration of international trade and production is usually referred to as 'globalization'. Chapter 15 investigates the extent to which theoretical predictions about the gains from trade, and who the winners and losers are, can be observed in the contemporary global economy. This largely empirical chapter finds that globalization has in practice been confined to a relatively small number of economies. Some low-income countries appear to have benefited from globalization to the extent of catching up with living standards in high-income countries. However, globalization seems also to be associated with increasing inequality both between and within national economies.

Chapter 16 examines 'open economy macroeconomics', the macroeconomic analysis of economies that are open to trade, by bringing together Chapters 14 and 15's discussion of economic relations between national economies with the macroeconomics of Chapters 11 and 12. This involves integrating a new element into the analysis, the exchange rate, and investigating how it is determined under fixed and floating exchange systems. The chapter examines the impact of the exchange rate on macroeconomic variables including inflation, interest rates and aggregate demand. It finds that, in a world economy with a high degree of international capital mobility where funds can be moved easily across national borders to buy and sell national currencies, fixed exchange systems are unsustainable. However, floating exchange rates bring a risk of volatility and unexpected impacts on the national economy. The alternative is for a group of countries, most of whose trade is with each other, to set up a single currency, as some European Union member states have done by adopting the euro.

Chapters 17 to 20 develop the theme of long-run growth prospects, introduced in Chapter 13, in the context of the performance of national economies established by Chapters 14, 15 and 16. What are the determinants of economic growth? Why have some economies grown so much more quickly than others? Is economic growth sustainable, or is it using up environmental and other resources faster than it replaces them? Chapter 17 puts the groundwork in place with a discussion of investment, picking up the link between interest rates and investment and hence aggregate demand that Chapter 12 established. The importance of the level of investment to policy makers derives from both its role in achieving and sustaining economic growth and its volatility. Investment is the most volatile element of aggregate demand, yet it is also the one with the greatest significance for the rate of economic growth in the long run.

The determinants of growth are analysed in Chapter 18, which reviews several models of economic growth that give a progressively more central role to technological change. New growth theories have refined this general insight to identify three broad sources of growth: research, human capital formation and openness to ideas. One reason for investigating the causes of economic growth is to understand why some countries have grown rapidly over a long period of time to attain high average living standards for their populations, while others have not 'developed' so that their populations remain in poverty.

Having investigated some theoretical models of investment and growth, Chapter 19 takes a more reflective look at some of the issues raised by economic growth. Using climate change as a case study, the chapter discusses the limits to growth. Ecological economists argue that the physical environment sets limits to growth and that economic activity should be redirected towards sustainable development. The chapter also discusses ethical or social limits to growth, building on Chapter 8's analysis of theories of human well-being that go beyond the material standard of living. The policy dimension is again prominent in a discussion of emissions trading, an attempt at the international level to use markets to achieve environmental objectives set through the political process.

Chapter 20 reviews the macroeconomic performance of selected economies in the light of the theoretical insights that have been developed in this book. The aim is to clarify the relationship between long-run growth and the use of macroeconomic policy designed to stabilize the economy in the short run. Comparisons of macroeconomic policy and performance in different national economies suggest that policy can influence outcomes, although a major factor in explaining growth, namely technological change, is not controlled by policy makers. The chapter argues that macroeconomic policy making has improved in recent years, in part through the delegation of monetary policy to the central bank (such as the Bank of England in the UK). Nevertheless, the performance of any national economy is always potentially at risk to 'shocks' from elsewhere in the world, such as the oil price rises of the 1970s.

Welcome to *Macroeconomics*. We hope you enjoy this introduction to the study of national economies and their constantly changing interrelationships.

macroeconomics

NATIONAL ECONOMIES

CHAPTER 11 THE CIRCULAR FLOW OF INCOME, NATIONAL INCOME AND MONEY

Malcolm Sawyer ●

Objectives

After studying this chapter you should be able to:
- appreciate the difference between *ex ante* (plans) and *ex post* (outcomes)
- appreciate the difference between an equality and an identity
- understand the nature of the circular flow of income
- appreciate the nature of financial flows between the various sectors of the economy
- understand the role of money in a modern economy
- understand the creation of money through the loan process, and the relationship between loans and deposits.

Concepts

- *ex ante*
- *ex post*
- circular flow of income
- loans and money creation
- money
- base money
- measures of money supply

1 INTRODUCTION ●

The economy and society in which we live are highly complex. There are numerous economic interactions between people. You may buy goods and services from others and as you do so that provides income for those from whom you have bought the goods and services. You may sell your labour to an employer that provides your income which, in turn, enables you to buy goods and services you need from other producers, who may then employ others. Such market exchange creates interdependence between the economic agents involved: if one person does not spend, another does not receive an income. Some economies have much less market exchange and interdependence than others. These are, or were, subsistence economies where families produce much of their own food and clothing with limited exchange of goods with others. However, in industrialized economies each of us produces little of what we need; we buy goods and services from a wide range of other people. What does this interdependence mean for the working of the economy as a whole? This chapter explores that question and finds that this interdependence is intimately connected to the level of national income at which the economy will settle.

Another feature of market exchange economies is the extensive use of money. Almost all transactions involve the use of money. The interdependence between people and the use of money is connected in that it is difficult to believe that an economy could be so interdependent without the use of money (or some close equivalent). When we buy and sell we use money, and the more we buy and sell the more money we use. It is usually necessary to have money in order to be able to buy things. I also consider in this chapter what the role of money is and how money is created, notably by the banking system. The banking system provides loans which are used to finance expenditure and, in the process, banks also create money.

The plan of this chapter is as follows. I start with a simple depiction of an economy using the device of the circular flow of income which you have met earlier in Chapter 8. In order to simplify and explain the relationships between different agents I classify them into different sectors of the economy. A starting point is to think of households as consumers who buy goods and as workers who sell their factor services, and firms as principally engaged in production by buying factor services from households and in turn selling goods and services to households. What can we say about the equilibrium level of income in such a simple economy? This model is then gradually made more complex, first, by adding in more sectors to encompass the activities of foreign trade and the government, which is so important in modern economies and, second, by considering the role of money in this economy. I explain the need for finance and how money is created by the banking system in the economy.

2   THE CIRCULAR FLOW OF INCOME   • • • • • • • • • • • • • • • •

2.1   PLANS AND OUTCOMES

We all know that we can have plans and intentions but that those plans cannot be carried out as we would wish for a variety of reasons. When interaction with others is involved in our plans (which is usually the case), then the plans of all those involved will in general not be mutually consistent. Hence, not all the plans can be carried through simultaneously. But when the plans are mutually consistent (say after some negotiation between those involved) they can all be realized in practice. When all the plans and intentions are fulfilled, there are no endogenous forces causing the outcome to change. Thus, it could be said that there is some form of equilibrium when the plans of economic agents are mutually consistent.

The close relationship between mutually consistent plans and equilibrium of the system implies that it is useful to make a clear distinction between plans (or intentions) and actual outcomes. To do so I use a terminology widely used in economics: I refer to plans (intentions) as the *EX ANTE* position and the actual outcomes as the *EX POST* position. I will use the terms plans and intentions interchangeably and contrast them to the actual outcomes.

The simplest example of the difference between the two can be seen from the analysis of demand and supply that you have studied in *Microeconomics*. The demand curve (function) relates the amount individuals would wish (plan, intend) to buy at each price. The demand curve is the *ex ante* position of consumers in any one market and indeed is something of a thought experiment, for the demand curve says for each price how much would individuals wish to buy. Notice that although the demand curve asks the question of how much would be bought for each price, most of those prices are not observed in practice. In a similar vein, the supply curve (function) relates the amount that firms would wish (plan, intend) to sell at each price. Hence, the supply curve also refers to an *ex ante* position: that of producers in the same market. In general the demand intentions and the supply intentions are not consistent, that is they are not equal to each other. The only case where those two sets of intentions are equal is at the equilibrium price where the demand curve and the supply curve intersect (Chapter 5).

However, whether or not there is equilibrium, it must be the case that the amount of the product bought is equal to the amount of the product sold: it is not possible for someone to sell without someone else buying. If the demand plans of consumers do not match the supply plans of producers there are either unsatisfied customers or unsold stocks. In either case the *ex post* situation is that the amount bought (the demand) is the same as the amount sold (the supply). This is a clear indication as to why the distinction is drawn between *ex ante* (planned) and *ex post* (outcome). An equality in *ex post* terms is assured, but equality in *ex ante* terms is required for a position of equilibrium. If the *ex ante* demand and supply are not equal (in a perfectly competitive setting), then the expectation is that the price in that market will change, and continue to do so until there is an equality. Unsold stocks will induce producers to drop prices and more consumers may then want to buy the product. The idea which is implicit in that statement is that if there are differences between *ex ante* demand and supply, then that will lead to changes (in this example through changes in market price) in the *ex ante* demand and supply until they are brought into equality.

2.2 THE CIRCULAR FLOW OF INCOME AGAIN

The general idea of the circular flow of income was introduced in Chapter 8 which demonstrated the equivalence of measuring national income (GDP) in terms of output, of expenditure and of factor incomes. The figures recorded in the tables of Chapter 8 are drawn from the national income accounts and refer to actual outcomes, which, to use the language of the previous sub-section, is the *ex post* situation. Those figures record what actually happened in a given time period (all the figures used in Chapter 8 relate to the year 2000).

EX ANTE

An *ex ante* position refers to 'before the event', and to the plans and intentions of individuals.

EX POST

An *ex post* position refers to the actual outcome.

Figure 11.1 The circular flow of income with savings and investment

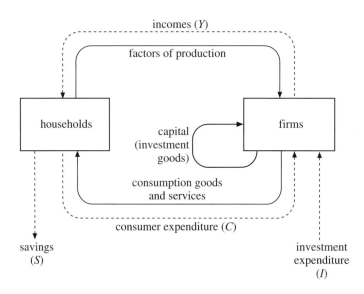

THE CIRCULAR FLOW OF INCOME

THE CIRCULAR FLOW OF INCOME

The circular flow of income is the flow of income circulating around the economy as income and expenditure transactions between individuals, firms, the government and the rest of the world.

THE CIRCULAR FLOW OF INCOME can be given a planned (*ex ante*) interpretation or an outcome (*ex post*) interpretation. In Chapter 8 the circular flow was considered in *ex post* terms. In this chapter, however, I also refer to the *ex ante* flow of incomes.

The magnitude of *ex post* flows in the circular flow of income is always equal. In order to understand why this is so, consider savings and investment expenditure (Figure 11.1). Households do not typically spend all their income but save some of it, depositing their savings with banks and building societies. These financial institutions collect up savings and lend them on to firms to help to finance investment (Section 3). Savings (*S*) have the effect of reducing consumption expenditure below household incomes and are a leakage out of the circular flow (Figure 11.1). The result is that firms' production of consumption goods and services is less than total production. Firms also produce capital or investment goods to purchase from each other, shown by the small capital (investment) goods circuit in Figure 11.1. The monetary flows injected into the circular flow when firms purchase capital goods are shown by the investment expenditure (*I*) dashed line (Figure 11.1).

In each period when the circular flow is not in equilibrium, it would still be the case that *ex post* savings equal *ex post* investment. But some of the savings and investment being made will be unintended, and the outcome in terms of savings and investment will differ from the plans which households had for savings and firms had for investment. Thus if firms produced more than households wish to consume then they would accumulate unsold stocks that would be counted as investment, even though it is not planned. It would be considered investment in accounting terms, as it is income not consumed by households. For this reason, *ex post* equalities are referred to as identities and denoted by the sign ≡ as shown below:

$$Y \equiv C + S \equiv C + I$$

The above identity says that total income of the economy (*Y*) is identically equal to consumption expenditures (*C*) and savings (*S*) of households. It is also by construction identically equal to the value of goods and services sold to households (*C*) plus the investment expenditure of firms (*I*). In general, the identity sign is used when two entities are always equal.

This is not generally the case when the *ex ante* circular flows are considered. An *ex ante* interpretation of the circular flow would lead to words such as 'planned' or 'intended' to be placed in front of each of the flows in Figure 11.1. This would then mean that the consumer expenditure by households is the planned level of consumption, and the consumption goods and services being supplied by firms correspond to firms' desired output levels. It would also mean that the households are supplying the factors of production (including labour time) that they would wish to provide, and in turn receiving income for those factors of production at rates firms wish to pay. However, unlike *ex post* flows, in general, the magnitude of *ex ante* flows between firms and households would not be equal to one another, except in the special case when the plans of households and firms are mutually consistent. That is, when households want to buy exactly those amounts of goods that firms in the economy want to sell. When there is such an equality between the magnitudes of the flows, then the circular flow of income would be in equilibrium. Not only do households receive their desired incomes which cover their spending and firms receive revenues which cover their expenditure on the factors of production, but these all fit in with their plans and intentions.

Consider Figure 11.1 where households do not wish to spend all of their income, and hence wish to save some of it. These savings which households wish to make represent a leakage from the circular flow of income. Initially, it could be expected that households would be accumulating money – income would be coming into the household but not all of the money would be returned to the circular flow in the form of expenditure. More money would be flowing into the households than is flowing out. Savings create a potential imbalance between the flows of income and the flows of goods and services around the system.

Savings also imply the production of consumption goods and services will be less than total production. On the other side, firms are paying out more on the factors of production (which forms the income of households) than households plan to spend. Money would be flowing out of firms. But there is an injection into the circular flow in the form of investment expenditure by firms (Figure 11.1).

The equilibrium condition for the circular flow to be maintained at a constant level is that the injections from the circular flow are balanced by the leakages. In this simple case, that is achieved when there is equality between investment (as the form of injections) and savings (as the form of leakages). That conclusion has something of an intuitive appeal: any flow, say of water around a system, which is subject to leaks, can only continue at the same rate if the leakages are compensated by injections of water. Denoting consumption expenditure by C, savings by S and investment expenditures by I, we can write this condition for equilibrium mathematically as:

$$Y = C + S = C + I$$

or

$$I = S \tag{1}$$

Notice that we now use the equality sign to denote the condition for equilibrium. This indicates that $I > S$, or $S > I$, are both possible in *ex ante* terms.

QUESTION

What would happen if there were a difference between savings and investment?

This question refers to a difference in *ex ante* terms, as there would always be equality in *ex post* terms. The difference between the *ex ante* position and the *ex post* outcome could arise in a number of ways. For example, households may actually save more than they wanted to if there were not enough output on sale by firms to meet their consumption plans. Firms could find that they have produced more than they can sell and accumulate inventories of the products, and this counts as investment. In our simple circular flow, this would mean that in terms of outcomes, savings would be equal to investment, but there may be (and in general would be) differences between the *intended* savings and *intended* investment.

If there is indeed a difference between *ex ante* savings and investment then we could consider two possibilities: $S > I$ or $I > S$. Let us consider a situation where there has been an equilibrium in the circular flow of income, but then households plan to spend less on consumption and plan to save more. As the households carry out their plans, firms would find that they are selling less, and their income has declined. Firms would then be likely to cut back on production, as firms cannot sell what they would like to produce. As firms cut back on production, they would hire less factors of production, and hence pay out less so that households receive less income. There would be an element of a vicious circle in the circular flow: households spend less than their income, expenditure falls, firms cut back on production, factor payments fall, household income falls leading to further falls in expenditure. This downward spiral would then continue until a point is reached where there is again equality between *ex ante* savings and *ex ante* investment. In this example, *ex ante* investment plans were unchanged, but *ex ante* savings declined to match the levels of investment intended by firms. How did that happen? The level of income in the new equilibrium is lower, and hence it could be expected that households will plan to spend less and to save less since their income is lower.

In this example, the plans of households (in terms of savings) and the plans of firms (in terms of investment) have been reconciled through changes in the level of income which in turn has led to revision of plans and intentions, until there is equality between the levels of planned savings and planned investment. This conclusion, that it is changes in income which bring about the equality between planned leakages and planned injections, is an important one. It clearly implies that if, for example, planned injections fell, then income would continue to fall until the revisions of plans lead eventually to an equality of planned savings and investment.

Work out in a similar way what would happen when *ex ante* investment plans were higher than the level of savings planned by households. How would income levels adjust in this case?

Equilibrium between *ex ante* injections and *ex ante* leakages (which may or may not be reached) merely says that those injections and leakages are equal. It does not, however, tell us two important things. First, it does not tell us by how much income must change in order to match the leakages with the injections. Second, it does not tell us how good or bad that equilibrium is. It could be, for example, that the equilibrium occurs where the flow of income is relatively low and as a consequence the levels of output and employment are relatively low. Both these questions are answered more fully in the next chapter; here I am just indicating the questions. Intuitively, however, it could be expected that if the injections into the circular flow are relatively low, then the leakages will have to be correspondingly low, and the overall flow of income small.

Before concluding this simple circular flow model, you should note a couple of things. First, what form do the savings of households take? The immediate form which savings take is the build up of the holding of money: more money is coming into the household in the form of income than is leaving in the form of expenditure. The next stage is often that the money is used to acquire financial assets; this may take the form of making deposits with financial institutions (e.g. banks), the purchase of new equity issued by firms or the purchase of assets from other households. Note that the sale of an existing asset (say existing equity or house) by one household to another does not constitute higher net savings by households: one household is saving (acquiring an asset) but another is dissaving (selling an asset). Overall consumption, adding over both households, is unchanged and so overall saving too is unchanged. Financial institutions such as banks and building societies collect savings of households, consolidate them and then lend the savings on to firms to help fund their physical investment. Financial institutions thus act as intermediaries between savings (by households) and investment (by firms).

Second, investment undertaken by firms means the acquisition of new capital assets, whether of the form of buildings, machinery, plant or equipment. An extensive discussion of the forms of investment and why firms undertake investment is to be found in Chapter 17. The point to note here is that in economic analysis 'investment' is given a rather specific meaning that differs considerably from everyday usage of the term investment. The depositing of household savings in the bank, while often called investment, is not the same as physical investment which is the acquisition of directly productive assets. Economists would regard the latter as investment but not the former.

2.3   ADDING MORE SECTORS: THE GOVERNMENT AND THE REST OF THE WORLD

There are clearly numerous financial and real flows taking place in an economy. To analyse the behaviour of the macro economy it is often useful to think in terms of broad sectors rather than about individual agents. For this purpose three sectors are usually identified, namely the private domestic sector (comprising households and firms), the public (government) sector and the overseas sector. Note, however, that there are four major forms of expenditure: consumers' expenditure, investment expenditure, government expenditure, and the net foreign expenditure (exports minus imports). Furthermore, expenditure by consumers, firms and the government now include both expenditure within the country and expenditure abroad. External expenditures can be measured in net terms, that is net exports are exports minus imports. Government expenditure refers to what is spent on the purchase of goods and services, and does not include transfer payments (such as pensions and unemployment benefits). The expenditures that are included here are those which relate to the production of goods and services, and which, therefore, use up resources in the course of production. The effect of transfers on expenditure comes into play through their effect on consumers' expenditure in that those who receive transfer payments spend them.

Table 11.1 reports the relative magnitudes of these four components of expenditure for the UK economy in 2000. It can readily be seen that consumer expenditure accounts for nearly two-thirds of total expenditure with government expenditure and investment each accounting for under 20 per cent. In 2000 imports exceeded exports (hence leading to a deficit on the balance of trade). Imports and exports each amounted to the equivalent of almost 30 per cent of gross domestic product, with a net balance of −1.7 per cent in that year.

Table 11.1 Composition of GDP of the UK, 2000 (£ million and %)

Expenditure method	£ million	%
Consumers' expenditure	617 648	65.5
Gross investment	167 099	17.7
Government expenditure	174 791	18.5
Exports	265 305	28.1
Imports	281 024	29.8
Net exports	−15 719	−1.7
Statistical discrepancy	−407	
GDP at market prices	943 412	

Note: figures do not necessarily sum to 100 due to rounding.

Source: *United Kingdom National Accounts (The Blue Book)*, 2001

QUESTION

Do the figures in Table 11.1 refer to *ex ante* flows or *ex post* flows?

Recall from the earlier discussion that these figures refer to *ex post* expenditures as they are accounting categories. In Chapter 8, the distinction was made between GDP – that which is produced within a country – and gross national product (GNP) – the income of those within a country. The difference arises from the income produced within a country but received by those outside the country, and in the other direction income received by those within a country but generated outside the country. As the figures in Table 11.1 indicate, there are very substantial inflows and outflows of income in the case of the United Kingdom: exports account for 28.1 per cent of GDP while imports account for a higher 29.8 per cent of GDP.

How would the circular flow of income look with these expenditures considered in *ex ante* terms? The circular flow illustrated in Figure 11.2 is a more complex version of Figure 11.1 with the government and the foreign sector added. Government expenditure is an injection into the circular flow while government taxation is a leakage; similarly, exports are an injection and imports are a leakage. The equilibrium condition is again that planned injections equal planned leakages.

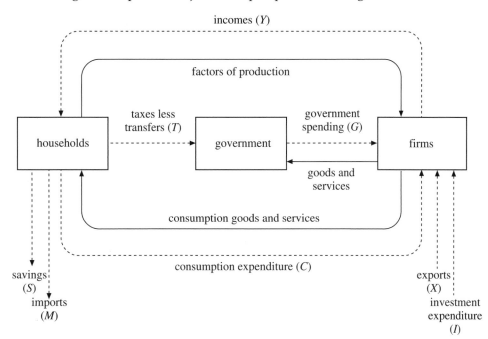

Figure 11.2 The circular flow of income with the government and the rest of the world

The expenditure (on domestic production) is now equal to $C + I + G + (X - M)$ where C is total consumer expenditure whether on domestic or foreign output, and I and G similarly for investment and government expenditure, X is exports and M is imports. Hence, expenditure by a country's residents on domestic production is $C + I + G - M$, to which is added the expenditure by foreign residents on domestic production. The income of households is used on consumers' expenditure, savings and taxation so that

$Y = C + S + T$. The equality of expenditure flows and income flows indicate consistent plans. So for equilibrium this yields:

$$C + I + G + (X - M) = C + S + T$$

which can be written as:

$$S + T + M = I + G + X$$

This is the equality between leakages and injections in the circular flow of income. It can again be given an *ex post* interpretation, that is, this equality is satisfied in the outcome and, as we saw in Table 11.1, in the national income accounts. But when considered in *ex ante* terms it is the equilibrium condition for the circular flow of income. The *ex ante* interpretation would be that if for any level of planned savings, taxation, government expenditures, imports and exports the equality just described held, then the expenditure and income plans of households, firms and the government are mutually consistent and the circular flow is in equilibrium.

The equation given above can be further rearranged as follows:

$$S + (T - G) = I + (X - M)$$

Government expenditure, G, includes current expenditure on goods and services (C_g) and capital expenditure on investment (I_g) which leads to the further re-arrangement:

$$S + (T - C_g) = I + I_g + (X - M) \tag{2}$$

The left-hand side is the sum of private savings plus government savings (excess of tax revenue over current government expenditure) and can be labelled total domestic savings. The right-hand side is the sum of investment plus the current account surplus which is equal to investment plus the capital account deficit (recall the current account surplus is equal to the capital account deficit). The right-hand side can then be seen as the sum of domestic investment plus (net) foreign investment (equal to the capital account deficit). The (net) foreign investment may be positive or negative. Equation (2) can then be summarized by saying that total savings is equal to total investment, when investment includes that undertaken by government, and savings includes taxation net of government expenditure.

2.4   SURPLUS SPENDING AND DEFICIT SPENDING SECTORS

The three-sector model also tells us something more fundamental about the surpluses and deficits of sectors in the macro economy. Recall from Chapter 8 that the difference between GDP and GNP relates to the net flow of income from abroad. If we denote by R the net income earned from the rest of the world or the external sector, then $\text{GNP} \equiv \text{GDP} + R$ and $\text{GDP} \equiv C + I + G + (X - M)$. The uses of income equation can be written $\text{GNP} \equiv \text{GDP} + R \equiv C + S + T$, hence $\text{GDP} \equiv C + S + T - R$. Putting the two equations for GDP together yields:

$$(S - I) + (T - G) + (M - X) - R \equiv 0 \tag{3}$$

The significance of this equation is that overall there is no deficit and no surplus, and so at any time at least one sector will be in deficit and at least one in surplus (unless all three sectors are in balance). A budget surplus by the government (hence $T - G > 0$) would mean the government sector is making net savings and so at least one of the other two sectors must be in deficit. Either the private domestic sector is spending more than it is saving ($S - I < 0$), or the overseas sector is spending more on domestic output than it is saving by acquiring domestic capital assets ($M - X - R < 0$), or both.

Within the private sector individuals and firms lend and borrow to each other, but the net flow from the private sector is the balance between savings (by households and by firms, S) and private investment (I). The net flow for the government is the difference between its expenditure (G) and its receipts (largely from taxation, T). The net flow for the overseas sector is the current account, this is a combination of the trade balance, namely exports (X) minus imports (M) (that is net exports), and the net income flow from factor services exported abroad. The net flow for the government is financed by government borrowing, this is predominantly undertaken by the government selling bonds and bills to the private sector but can also include the issuing of money which, as we shall see below, is a particular kind of borrowing.

QUESTION

What would happen if instead of a deficit there were net surpluses for the government sector?

When there is a net inflow with the government (that is a budget surplus) then there is net repayment of debt by the government. Similarly, the net flow for the overseas sector requires a corresponding capital flow in the opposite direction; that is, a current account deficit requires a capital inflow (borrowing from overseas) and a current account surplus involves a capital outflow.

This three-sector model illustrates a more general point. Within the circular flow of income some are spending less than their income whilst others are spending more than their income. The former can be referred to as 'surplus units' and the latter as 'deficit units'. But it is an accounting identity that the sum of surpluses and deficits must be zero. What the circular flow then enables us to infer is that one sector's lending is another sector's borrowing. This is because, at the sectoral level, there is the requirement that the net lending or borrowing between sectors sum to zero.

It is also generally the case that any economic unit cannot be a 'deficit' unit forever. Each period's deficit adds to the debt of the individual or firm and the interest payments required to finance the debt increase. A continuing deficit would mean rising debt and more interest payments. The person concerned would find it increasingly difficult to meet the interest payments on their accumulating debt and to find others to lend money to them.

The national income accounts provide data which can be used to statistically illustrate the relationship between the three sectors identified in equation (3) above. Table 11.2(a) indicates the financial flows in terms of net lending or borrowing between sectors where the private sector has initially been further disaggregated into non-financial corporations, financial corporations, and households. The net lending or borrowing of, say, the private sector does not completely correspond to the difference between savings and investment. There are, for example, transfers received by and paid out by the private sector that lead to a difference between savings and investment on the one hand and what the private sector borrows or lends on the other. The net lending or borrowing across the three main sectors add up to zero (apart from the statistical discrepancy). The flows involved appear to be large, amounting to several billions of pounds, but they can be compared with the figure for GDP given in Table 11.1 to give some perspective. It can be seen that for the UK there were considerable swings in the net lending or borrowing by sectors with the government budget position swinging from a deficit of some £39 billion in 1992 to a surplus of over £18 billion in 2000. Over this period the borrowing from the rest of the world changed relatively little (by some £4 billion) but the position of the private sector moved from a surplus of over £26 billion to a deficit of £35 billion. These figures illustrate that when one sector is in surplus at least one other sector must be in deficit.

Table 11.2(a) Financial flows between sectors for selected years, UK (£ million)

Net lending/borrowing	1992	1996	2000
Non-financial corporations	−7906	6957	−4839
Financial corporations	1975	−2086	−27 943
Households	32 449	20 818	−2689
Private sector (total of above)	26 518	25 689	−35 471
General government	−39 071	−33 662	18 367
Rest of the world	12 553	7973	16 452
Statistical discrepancy	−	−	652

Table 11.2(b) Financial flows between sectors for selected years, UK (£ million)

	1992	1996	2000
Savings (S) − investment (I)	20 302	20 520	−38 520
Taxation (T) − government expenditure (G)	−33 276	−29 229	19 443
Current account deficit	12 974	8709	18 425
Statistical discrepancy			−652

Source: calculated from *United Kingdom National Accounts (The Blue Book)*, 2001

Rearranging the financial flows in terms of equation (3) leads to the figures in Table 11.2(b) in terms of the three elements of the equation. Note, however, that I refers to private investment, while government investment is included in general government expenditure G. It can be seen that for 2000 in the UK, private savings fell short of private investment to the extent of £38 520 million, whereas there was a budget surplus $(T - G)$ of £19 443 million and a current account deficit of £18 425 million, and these three figures sum to zero, apart from the statistical discrepancy of £652 million. This statistical discrepancy arises from measurement errors – difficulties of recording some types of income etc. In effect, in 2000, the deficit of private savings (over private investment) was matched by government savings (excess of tax revenue over expenditure) and borrowing from overseas (the other side of the current account deficit). The net lending and borrowing figures for 2000 were relatively unusual in that it has been the norm for governments to run budget deficits and for the private sector to run surpluses (to some degree reflecting an excess of savings over investment). In the context of the UK borrowing from the rest of the world, corresponding to a current account deficit, has been the more usual position. Figures for the earlier years of 1992 and 1996 are also given in Table 11.2. These figures also suggest large swings in the size of the balance of each sector.

EXERCISE 11.2

Fill in the blank cells for Table 11.3 which records the transactions of different sectors in a hypothetical economy. Assume that net income from overseas is zero.

Table 11.3

Variable	Amount
Savings (S)	20 000
Investment (I)	25 000
Savings (S) – Investment (I)	– 5 000
Exports (X)	40 000
Imports (M)	45 000
Balance of trade	– 5000
Government expenditure (G)	50 000
Taxation (T)	50, 000
Budget deficit	

Let us now look at the net flow of each sector in some detail. The third term in equation (3), $(M - X)$, represents the economy's current account with the rest of the world. Since one country's imports are another country's exports, the worldwide level of exports and the level of imports are equal to one another. Similarly, one country's income inflow is another country's outflow. While some countries have a balance of trade (or current account) deficit, others must necessarily have a surplus.

The net payments $(X - M)$ are a monetary measure of the *balance of trade* on the international account. There is no particular need or reason why X and M should balance in any period, so there may be a trade surplus $(X > M)$ or a trade deficit $(X < M)$. The trade balance of $(X - M)$ in the circular flow model forms a major part of the current account (that with the rest of the world). Another significant part of the current account is the net income received from abroad (that is the difference between income flowing in and income flowing out of the country). There is also a capital account (with the rest of the world) which records the borrowing and lending activities of the economy with the rest of the world. Together with the current account it forms a country's overall *balance of payments* which is further discussed in Chapter 16.

A country with a current account deficit must finance that deficit in some way. One way would be that the reserves of foreign currency (held by the government or central bank) are used to finance the difference. There are some obvious limits to how far that can continue. The other, and dominant, way is that the deficit on the current account is matched by a surplus on the capital account. In other words, the country is borrowing from other countries. This borrowing can take a variety of forms, it would include foreign direct investment, the sale of existing assets to foreigners, and the sale of government and other bonds to nationals of other countries. When a country is running a trade surplus (so that exports exceed imports), then it can either accumulate reserves of foreign currency and/or lend abroad.

The second term in equation (3) is $(T - G)$ and this is the excess of tax revenue over government expenditure. It is generally the case that this term is negative (that is the government runs a budget deficit), though that is not universally the case (at the time of writing governments in both the UK and USA are running budget surpluses). The budget deficit can be financed in two ways, and usually by some combination of the two. The government can borrow from the public and pay interest on its borrowing. Much of that borrowing takes the form of the sale of government bonds to the public. These bonds will pay a fixed yield to the holders which is set when the bond is sold. The bonds usually have a redemption date, that is the date at which the government will repay the sum advanced. Borrowing by the government can take other forms, such as the sale of Treasury Bills (which are redeemed after 90 days) and directly from the public in the form of national savings. The second way the budget deficit can be financed is that the government, or more accurately the central bank on its behalf, 'prints money'. Then the amount of 'base money' in the economy increases. 'Base money' is that part of money which is supplied directly by the government (central bank) and consists of notes and coins and reserves held by the banking system with the central bank.

The final element to be considered from equation (3) is $(S - I)$, that is the excess of private savings over private investment (sometimes called net private savings). It could be thought of as savings available to finance other sectors of the economy (the public sector and the foreign sector). Financial intermediaries such as banks, building societies and insurance companies play an important role in collecting these individual savings and making them available to deficit spenders in the economy, such as private sector firms, the government or economic agents in the rest of the world.

3   MONEY AND THE ECONOMY

In terms of outcomes, the lending of 'surplus' units is identically equal to the borrowing of 'deficit' units, and at the sectoral level this equality was reflected in the identity $(S - I) + (T - G) + (M - X) \equiv 0$. Recall that the first term is the private sector's surplus, the second the government's surplus and the third the rest of the world's surplus. The surpluses sum to zero, which means that some of the surpluses are negative, that is, were actually deficits. But what happens when there are plans to increase expenditure, for example when firms want to undertake investment or when the government plans to increase expenditures on health and education? Where do the resources required for these planned increases in expenditure come from? If these injections take place, then there will be changes in the circular flow of income which will give rise to increased leakages. But how can the planned increase in injections be initially financed, which it has to be if the expenditures are to be undertaken?

3.1   FINANCE AND MONEY CREATION

If one individual wants to spend more than her income (so that her expenditure exceeds her income) then she must be able to fund the difference. She would then become a 'deficit' unit since there is a deficit of income compared with expenditure. This individual has to cover the deficit in some way, maybe through borrowing or through running down their wealth. But if one individual is running a deficit, the *ex post* identities of the circular flow indicate that there must be another individual who is running a surplus (a 'surplus' unit), that is an individual whose income exceeds expenditure. In effect, the deficit units are (directly or indirectly) borrowing from the surplus units. Adding together all the 'deficit units' and all the 'surplus units' must lead to the outcome that overall there is a balance between (*ex post*) income and expenditure.

This is also true at the global level. In particular, it means that one country's trade deficit (imports greater than exports) has to be balanced by another country's trade surplus (exports greater than imports). It is also the case that one country's imports must be another country's exports. You will study more about international finance in Chapter 16; here we concentrate on any one national economy.

QUESTION

How are the individuals who are running deficits matched with the individuals who are running surpluses?

This could happen directly or indirectly. Let us consider the direct ways first. Some matching may be done through individual contact: you are running a surplus, your friend is running a deficit, and you are willing to lend to your friend. Or, you might acquire an existing financial asset, for example an equity share sold by a firm that needs funds for investment. A financial asset has been created and sold to you. The financial asset (an equity share) enables the 'deficit' unit (in this case the firm issuing the equity) to acquire finance from a 'surplus' unit. Similarly, the government may borrow from surplus units by the issue of bonds.

The matching between surplus and deficit units happens indirectly through financial institutions such as banks, building societies and insurance companies. It is likely that if you are running a financial surplus, you will accumulate financial assets: your bank balance may be increasing, your building society account being added to, you may be acquiring shares and bonds, etc. The main way by which the additional finance will be provided to deficit units is through loans from the banking system. When a bank provides a loan, it immediately adds to the borrower's bank account, and enables the borrower to sign cheques, and to pay others for the expenditure. The borrower pays money in exchange for the goods and services to be purchased, and the supplier receives that money. In turn the supplier is likely to spend that money.

Thus, financial intermediaries such as banks, building societies and insurance companies perform a very important function in industrialized economies. However, they can only perform this function due to the widespread use of money. The surplus income of households is held in *money* form, and firms receive *money* with which they buy plant and machinery. We now proceed to consider the nature of money and how money is defined and measured, before returning to elaborate on the ways in which banks are able to grant loans and create money.

3.2   WHAT IS MONEY?

To appreciate the role of money we could try to envisage an economy without money, this is generally labelled a barter economy. In such an economy, people would be exchanging goods directly for other goods, and for exchange there would have to be the *double coincidence of wants*. What that means is clear from the following example. A person with apples who wanted pears would have to find another person who, at the same time, had pears but wanted apples in order to make the exchange (and they would have to agree on the rate of exchange between apples and pears). There are occasionally reports of some direct barter between companies, but these are relatively rare. We may ourselves be involved in some elements of direct barter – we may swap something we have with goods (or services) from our friends and neighbours.

The overwhelming majority of exchange transactions involve money. We sell something (such as our labour) for money, and then use that money to buy something else (such as food or clothes). In common parlance the word money is often used to denote wealth, such as saying 'he is loaded with money' or 'she left all her money to her children'. Economists, when they talk of money, mean that which is widely used in the exchange of goods and services: a commodity or token which you will accept when you sell something. Through history, physical items have served as money, the best known examples are the use of gold and silver. These physical items often have an intrinsic value themselves: gold may be used as money and it is also valued for its other attributes. But in most economies (particularly in all industrialized ones) what serves as money has become either a physical item with little intrinsic value (e.g. a £5 note) or a book keeping entry with no physical existence (e.g. a bank deposit). In the UK, at one time, money would have largely taken the form of coins (based on silver or gold) and notes (similarly backed by gold or silver). While use is still made of notes and coins, these are no longer backed by gold or silver, and the notes and coins are of little value in themselves. For example, a £5 note has little intrinsic value, but is of value to any individual because some other individual will accept the note in exchange for items of value. Increasingly, even paper money is becoming redundant as most transactions are now financed by the exchange of bank deposits: payment by cheque/debit card is authorization to a bank to reduce one person's bank deposit and increase another's. The authorization to move funds from one bank account to another is increasingly taking the form of electronic transfer.

These recent forms of money are financial assets so far as the holder of the money is concerned, but for the body that has issued the financial asset it represents a financial liability. Notes and coins issued by the central bank (on behalf of the government) represent a liability (they are part of the national debt). Bank deposits, in a similar way, are assets for the public but are liabilities for the banks. A characteristic of money is that it is a *financial asset*. But the financial assets which are used as money also have the property of being transferable from one person to another and are widely accepted as a means of payment.

The changing forms of MONEY suggest that we need to define money in terms of its characteristic functions rather than by the commodity that happens to be money today. Defining money in terms of its functions recognizes that the physical form money can take can vary. Thus the commonly accepted definition of money is that it is any commodity that performs the following functions in the economy. The first is that it is a *unit of account*. That is, prices, wages, rent, etc. are measured in terms of the units of money; in the UK in terms of pounds, in most of the European Union in terms of euros, in the USA in terms of dollars, etc. Contracts will generally be specified in terms of this unit of account. Further, these financial assets have a fixed nominal price: the price of money in terms of itself can always be thought of as 1. Other financial assets (e.g. shares and bonds) have prices which vary and cannot be regarded as money.

electronic transfer a means of payment

Money is a financial asset

MONEY
Money is a means of payment, store of value and unit of account.

① Unit of
    account
② Mean of
    payment
③ Store of value

The second function is that money is a generally accepted *means of payment*. When we wish to acquire some good or service the person selling the item will generally accept money and we will usually expect to offer money for the purchase of the item. There may be exceptions: we may, for example, directly exchange goods and services with our neighbours without any money being involved. Money facilitates exchange and it is often referred to as a *medium of exchange*. However, the term *means of payment* is used here as money is also used to settle debts, notably tax obligations to the state, which do not arise from exchange.

A third function of money is that it serves as a *store of value*. This means that at minimum money should retain its value between the time of receipt to the time of disbursement. As individuals, we may well receive our income in the form of money once a month or once a week and gradually spend the money during the course of the month or week. We would be unwilling to accept money if it was to lose a significant part of its purchasing power before its actual use to purchase items. In times of high levels of inflation, money does lose value quickly (in terms of the goods and services which it can buy) and hence it performs less well its function as a store of value. More generally, the store of value function implies money is a significant form in which individuals hold part of their wealth.

3.3   MEASURES OF MONEY

Money has been defined above in terms of three functions and one of those functions is that money is a generally accepted means of payment. Translating that definition of money into a measure of what actually constitutes money at a particular place and time faces some difficulties. For example, a cheque will not usually be accepted as payment for a bus fare, but trying to buy a house for cash is likely to raise suspicion.

The narrowest form of money, labelled M0 and often referred to as the monetary base, is money issued by the central bank (the Bank of England in the case of the UK) and consists of notes and coins and reserves held by the banks with the central bank. This form of money is part of the national debt as it is a debt of the central bank and appears to be the form of money directly under the control of the central bank.

The measure M1 is current account (demand) deposits with banks as well as notes and coins (M0). Current account deposits can be readily transferred to another person through cheque or electronic transfer and are a generally accepted means of payment. But they are not a universally accepted means of payment, as you would find if you sought to pay your bus fare by cheque. So many small day-to-day transactions are paid in cash, whilst larger transactions will be paid through cheque or electronic transfer.

M2 includes deposit account (time) deposits with banks as well as M1. A deposit account deposit cannot be immediately transferred to another person but it can be readily moved to a current account deposit (held by the same person with the same bank) and then used as a means of payment. There may be some delay in being able to move money from one account to another (e.g. a period of notice has to be given) and/or some financial penalty involved. As a financial asset, a deposit account deposit has a fixed price in terms of the monetary unit of account. A share or a bond as a financial asset has a variable price, but £100 put into a deposit account will be returned as £100 (plus the interest accruing, and provided that the financial institution holding the deposit remains solvent).

Sometimes another measure of money supply, M3, is used which includes M2 plus repurchase agreements and money market fund shares. Another broad measure of money is M4. This includes deposits with building societies and most financial assets which have a fixed nominal price.

Table 11.4 gives figures for some of the widely used measures of money, along with their official definitions. It can be seen that for the UK, the narrow definition of money (M0) is around 8 per cent of M1. Recall that M1 is the measure of money supply that most closely corresponds to money as the main means of payment. In turn, M1 is around half of the broader money measures such as M3 or M4. These broader moneys are financial assets with values fixed in terms of the unit of account; they can be readily and with little cost changed into M1.

Table 11.4 Stock of money in the UK

Measure of money	Definition	Stock of money, December 2001 (£ million)
M0	Notes and coins in circulation plus reserves held by banks with the central bank: sometimes called 'base money'	37 317
M1	M0 plus non-interest bearing bank deposits	502 164
M2	M1 plus other bank retail deposits	884 600
M3	M2 plus repurchase agreements, money market fund shares and paper	1 017 354
M4	Holdings by the private sector, other than monetary financial institutions, of sterling deposits including certificates of deposit, commercial paper, bonds, liabilities arising from repurchase agreements and sterling bank bills, notes and coins	942 496

Source: Bank of England, http://www.bankofengland.co.uk/mfsd/ms/020830/, accessed January 2002

It can be seen that most measures of the money supply include the value of bank deposits which are created by banks. Thus, as these financial intermediaries carry out their finance functions in modern economies through granting loans, they also create money. This is not, of course, intuitively obvious. The next section considers how this happens.

3.4   BANKS, LOANS AND MONEY CREATION

In a Western industrialized economy the vast majority of transactions (measured in value terms) are financed by money as measured by M1. Within that most transactions are by the transfer of bank deposits from one person to another. Although many transactions will be paid for by cash, those transactions will be small in value relative to the transactions which are paid for through the transfer of bank deposits. These may involve the writing of a cheque to transfer a deposit from one person's bank account to another person's. Or else the transfer may be accomplished by an instruction to the bank in the form of a standing order, a direct debit arrangement, a written instruction, or an electronic instruction. Thus, most of what is used as money are bank deposits.

A bank deposit represents an asset as far as the person holding it is concerned: it adds to their wealth. But a bank deposit is a liability so far as the bank is concerned: it has an obligation to pay (generally on demand) the depositor. A bank deposit is something of a liability to the bank in a more general sense because the bank may pay some interest on the deposit (although in the case of M1 the interest rate is generally small or often zero) and it has the costs associated with the transfer of deposits from one person to another.

Besides accepting and holding deposits, another major function carried out by banks is the provision of loans to the public. Banks, of course, charge interest on loans and it is a major way by which they make a profit. Loans are part of the assets of the banks since they yield interest to the banks and the loan holders are under an obligation to repay the loan. The loans outstanding are assets for the banks since they represent money that is owed to them and, provided the loans are 'performing', banks will receive interest on those loans and the repayment of the sum owed at the end of the loan period. It serves as a reminder that what is an asset for one (this case the bank) is a liability for another (in this case those who have taken out loans from the bank). The banks also hold reserves with the central bank and some notes and coins, and these are included in the term reserves in the balance sheet.

A highly simplified version of the balance sheet of a bank is shown in Table 11.5. This balance sheet is simplified in two particular respects. First, the assets of the bank only include loans and reserves, the bank's ownership of other financial assets such as government bonds, buildings, land, etc. is ignored. Second, the two sides of the balance sheet are assumed to be equal, and hence the net worth of the bank is taken to be zero. These simplifying assumptions are made so that we can focus on the roles of loans and deposits.

Table 11.5 Simplified balance sheet of a bank

Assets	Liabilities
Loans	Deposits
Reserves	

The deposits which appear in the balance sheet of banks are generally seen as part of the stock of money. The transfer of those deposits (e.g. by cheque) is a main way by which payments are made. In Table 11.4, bank deposits would clearly be part of M1. It can now be seen from this balance sheet of the banks that when loans increase then there must be some corresponding changes in reserves and in deposits. But, conversely, an increase in deposits (and that is in the amount of money) would go along with some corresponding changes in loans and reserves. Since Table 11.5 represents a balance sheet, the expansion on one side must be accompanied by an expansion on the other side. In this context two particular questions arise. First, which side of the balance sheet tends to be the cause of the expansion: is it more likely to be deposits or loans? Second, since an expansion of the balance sheet may involve an expansion of reserves, can the availability of reserves limit any expansion? The reserves in the balance sheet of the banks are the reserves held with the central bank and holdings of notes and coins issued by the central bank; if the central bank restricts the availability of those reserves would that constrain the expansion of the balance sheet?

The way in which the banks expand their balance sheets and the consequences for the creation of money have been analysed in two rather different ways and from which rather different conclusions can be drawn. One view is that the expansion of the balance sheet comes from an expansion of the available reserves. For example, consider what would happen if the central bank expanded the amount of notes and coins in circulation. This could arise from, for example, the government financing some of its expenditure through the printing of notes and the minting of coins. Some of the individuals who receive the increased amount of notes and coins are likely to deposit some of it with the banks. The banks may hold some of those notes and coins as their reserves, and may place some of them with the central bank as reserves. But the banks find that they have more reserves and more deposits than before, and are then in a position to extend more loans. The extension of loans requires that there are businesses and households who wish to take out loans (at the price being charged). The further extension of loans, and hence the expansion of the banks' balance sheet, also requires that the banks are willing to make the loans. This requires that the banks can find credit-worthy borrowers to whom they wish to lend. But banks may feel that they should (or be legally required to) keep a particular ratio between their reserves and the overall amount of deposits. People may withdraw their deposits from banks (in the form of notes and coins) and banks have to be in a position to meet those withdrawals. But others are depositing notes and coins with the banks. The banks keep some reserves to meet the possible differences between withdrawals and deposits, and those differences fluctuate from day to day, sometimes positive, sometimes negative.

How far the expansion of the banks' balance sheet can proceed can be illustrated as follows. The amount of base money (sometimes called high-powered money) is taken as B, and this can be either held by the public as notes and coins C, or held by the banks as their reserves R. Hence:

$$B = C + R \tag{4}$$

The deposits held by the public with the banks are labelled D, and if we further assume that the banks wish to (or have to, by law) hold reserves which amount to a proportion r of the deposits, then we can write:

$$R = rD$$

or

$$D = \frac{R}{r} = \frac{B - C}{r}$$

The stock of money M is held either in the form of notes and coins or in the form of bank deposits. We can write this as:

$$M = C + D$$

The extent to which the public wish to hold cash or to hold bank deposits would depend on payment practices that differ from economy to economy. For example, the ease of using cheques or electronic transfer to make payments would reduce the amount we wished to hold as cash. Let us call the proportion of money held as cash c, then:

$$C = cM$$

Substituting the values of C and D in $M = C + D$ from equation (4), we get the alternative expression for money supply (M):

$$M = cM + \frac{R}{r}$$
$$= cM + \frac{(B-C)}{r}$$
$$= cM + \frac{(B-cM)}{r}$$

This can be written as:

$$M(c + r - cr) = B$$

or

$$M = \frac{B}{(1-(1-c)(1-r))}$$

The term $\dfrac{1}{(1-(1-c)(1-r))}$ is often referred to as the money multiplier or the credit multiplier. Since the denominator is less than 1, it suggests that the stock of money is a multiple of the base money. This approach suggests that the amount of money is not directly under the control of the central bank but may be indirectly so. If the central bank controls base money B, then it sets the limits on M.

EXERCISE 11.3

1   Look at Table 11.4. Which of the measures corresponds to the total quantity of base money (B) in the economy?

2   Is the total money supply in the economy greater than base money?

3   Consider some likely values of c and r. If c is 0.10 and r is 0.01, what is the value of the money multiplier?

The other view on the relationship between money and loans starts from an emphasis on the taking out of loans. Since for individuals and firms wanting to take out loans there are costs involved – notably the rate of interest to be paid on the loan – it is presumed there is some purpose in taking out the loan. The purpose will usually be to acquire the finance to undertake expenditure. Thus the financing of expenditure is closely linked with the creation of loans. The expansion of the loans outstanding (that is new loans being granted in excess of those being repaid) generates an increase in bank deposits, and thereby in the stock of money. When a loan is taken out it creates a deposit in the bank account of the person to whom the loan is made. In turn, it can be expected that the person receiving the deposit (created by the loan) will spend it and pass it on to someone else. The newly created deposit thereby circulates through the economy. The stock of money has increased. But someone receiving the deposit has a number of options on what to do with the bank deposit. They can spend it on goods and services, and then it is passed on to someone else. They may decide to acquire a financial asset, and again the bank deposit is passed on to someone else, in this case as payment for a financial asset. Another option for someone who has an outstanding loan is to pay off part of the loan. In the case of someone with an overdraft this would in effect operate automatically – as the deposit is received it serves to reduce the outstanding amount. In other words, loans can be extinguished and paid off as well as created. Further, how much of the bank deposit remains in circulation depends on how far individuals use deposits to pay off loans.

The banks will meet the demand for loans provided that they think it will be profitable to do so. The profitability for banks of loans will depend on the interest rate which is charged for loans, and on the risk of default on the loans. It is often observed that the rate of interest on loans is closely related to the rate of interest charged by the central bank, with the loan interest rate a mark-up over the central bank interest rate. The rate of interest charged by the central bank is the rate of interest which banks would have to pay the central bank if the banks sought to borrow reserves from the central bank.

The central bank acts as the 'lender of last resort', that is, the central bank will provide reserves to the bank system (at a price). The central bank stands ready to supply reserves when required. Thus, it is argued, banks can expand their balance sheets provided that the public wish to take out loans (at the price charged by the banks) and the public are prepared to hold the deposits which are generated. When this expansion requires more reserves, these will be augmented by the central bank.

Plans to undertake spending can only be made effective if they are backed by purchasing power: that is, we can only spend if we have the money. In many cases the money we spend in, say, a month has come to us as our income. If our expenditure is equal to our income then we may have some timing problems – we have to receive the money from income before we can spend it – but we can finance our own expenditure. If our expenditure exceeds our income then we have to find some way to bridge the gap between expenditure and income. We have to borrow from others to finance the difference. The particular importance of bank loans is that they permit an increase in expenditure over and above income and without drawing on the savings of others.

EXERCISE 11.4

Consider a hypothetical economy, Utopia, with several firms and households but only one bank. Households deposit 10 per cent of their incomes with the bank and the bank has a policy of keeping 10 per cent of its deposits as cash reserves, but lending out the remaining 90 per cent of deposits as loans to firms. The government of Utopia has printed currency notes and coins worth 1000 units.

1   What is the total money supply in this economy?

2   Suppose Utopia's neighbour Warlike declares war on Utopia and the government is forced to finance new military spending by printing additional currency of 500 units. What will be the total money supply in the economy now?

3.5   THE DEMAND FOR MONEY BY HOUSEHOLDS

The demand for money by households and firms in the economy is closely related to the two main functions of money, namely as a means of payment and as a store of value. Any individual is continually receiving and paying out money, but the receipt of income and the payment on expenditure are not completely co-ordinated. If they were completely co-ordinated there would be little requirement to hold money: in effect if income and expenditure were perfectly co-ordinated, immediately income was received, expenditure would then be undertaken. But, in reality, at any moment, an individual is likely to hold some money which is to some degree held in anticipation that the money will be spent in the relatively near future. The average amount of money held by an individual for use in the settlement of exchange activities is often referred to as that person's transactions demand for money. This demand is for holding money for the purpose of financing transactions: it is holding money between receiving it as income and making use of it to finance expenditure. We do not generally hold money because we like the pictures on the bank notes but rather because we anticipate spending it in the near future, though we may not have a precise plan as to what money will be spent on.

As an example, consider an individual who receives income on a monthly basis and usually spends all of their income over the month on an even basis. This person would have a holding of money as illustrated in Figure 11.3. On pay day, this person's holding of money would rise to equal the monthly income, and that holding would gradually run down over the month as expenditure takes place. In this example, the individual would have a transactions demand for money equal to half of their monthly income. This transactions demand would be the average amount of money held; for this individual the money held at the beginning of the month would be considerably more than the money held at the end of the month. As this individual spends money, others, of course, receive it, and their holding of money would also fluctuate.

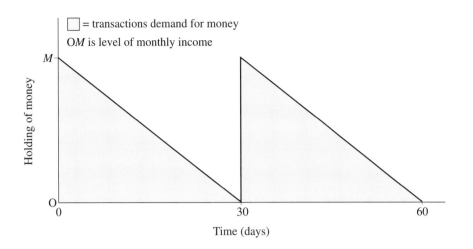

Figure 11.3 The transactions demand for money

The average amount of money which an individual holds is likely to depend on a range of factors. One could be expected to be the frequency with which the individual is paid: a person paid weekly may hold less money, on average, than one who is paid monthly. If the holding of money by the person paid weekly follows a similar pattern to that in Figure 11.3, then their average holding of money would approximate to half a week's pay. It could also be expected that the average holding of money depends on the alternatives available. If there are other financial assets available which yield a significant rate of interest and the costs of switching from money into that financial asset are low, then it may be worthwhile, say for the person paid monthly, to switch, briefly, from money into that financial asset.

It could also be envisaged from Figure 11.3 that if an individual's income increased, then the transactions demand for money (Md) would also increase, and in roughly the same proportion. The transactions demand for money may then be written as $Md = kY$ where Y is the level of (nominal) income. The factor k could be expected to depend on the interest rates on other financial assets for reasons indicated in the previous paragraph. It could also be expected to depend on matters such as the frequency with which a person is paid.

The transactions demand for money relates to money held for subsequent use as a means of payment. Income that we did not plan to spend or to keep as a precaution to meet emergencies, that is income which we planned to save for interest or any other form of reward, would often not be kept in the form of money. Cash and notes may be held as wealth when there are few financial institutions which are accessible (e.g. to the relatively poor), and when there is suspicion of financial institutions (whether for reasons of lack of confidence in them or to avoid the record keeping which goes with the use of financial institutions). But cash and notes will usually be a poor way of holding wealth; there are many alternatives, whether financial assets or real assets which yield a rate of return. However, what may be termed broad money, such as deposit accounts with banks, does yield a positive rate of interest. That rate of interest may be below the rate of return which could be obtained on, say, bonds, but broad money has some advantages over bonds. For example, broad money is relatively liquid, it can be turned into narrow money which can be spent quickly. A simple instruction to the bank will move money from a deposit account into a current account, and the latter can be spent. Further, the price of bonds can vary, whereas the price of money remains constant (although the value of money overall goes down when there is inflation).

There is then what may be termed a portfolio demand for money; that is, money held as part of the wealth portfolio. This demand for money depends on two sets of factors. The first is the total wealth of the economy: as wealth rises it will be held in different forms, one of which would be money. The second is the rate of return on different assets including on money itself. The relevant rate of return on money is the rate of interest on deposits such as those held in deposit accounts. The rates of return on other assets would include the expected rate of return on bonds (which would be the rate of interest and anticipated gains or losses on the price of bonds) and the expected rate of return on equity (which would be based on the expected dividends and price changes).

4   CONCLUSION

The chapter began with re-introducing the idea of the circular flow of income and introduced the distinction between *ex ante* and *ex post* circular flow. The circular flow serves as a reminder of some of the interdependences in an economy whereby one person's expenditure is another person's income. The *ex ante* circular flow can also be used to set out conditions for the equilibrium of the whole economy.

We also observed that one person's deficit is another person's surplus, and that one sector's deficit has to be balanced by a surplus in another sector of the economy. This general idea was applied to the financial relationship between the private sector, the government and the rest of the world.

Expenditure has to be financed, and that requires that money is available to those who want to spend. This stresses the role of money as a means of payment, which is one of the three functions usually associated with money. Money is also a unit of account and a store of value. Most money takes the form of bank deposits and the creation of money mainly comes through the extension of loans by the banking system. We also studied some commonly used measures of money supply.

CHAPTER 12 AGGREGATE DEMAND

Guiseppe Fontana ● ● ● ● ● ● ● ● ● ● ● ● ● ● ● ● ● ●

Objectives

After studying this chapter you should be able to:
- appreciate the difference between Say's Law and Keynes's theory of aggregate demand
- explain the determinants of aggregate demand
- understand the multiplier process
- explain how national income and employment are determined
- understand the elements of macroeconomic policy.

Concepts

- Say's Law
- aggregate demand
- autonomous expenditure
- paradox of thrift
- transitory and permanent income
- multiplier

1 INTRODUCTION ●

In an article published in the *New York Times* (21 February 1998) it was claimed that Say's Law had become American capitalism's guiding aphorism. The 'law' bears the name of Jean-Baptiste Say (1767–1832), a well-respected French businessman and scholar. Like the British economist Adam Smith (1723–1790), Say advocated the benefits of free markets. Say's most famous work is his *A Treatise on Political Economy* (1803) where he outlines his controversial 'law of markets', better known as 'Say's Law'.

In summary form, SAY'S LAW states that aggregate demand, the total value of goods and services demanded in an economy, could neither exceed nor fall below aggregate supply, the total value of goods and services supplied in that economy. This later became encapsulated in the idea that 'supply creates its own demand' for the economy as a whole. In a famous passage from *A Treatise on Political Economy*, Say spells out his idea:

SAY'S LAW
Say's Law is usually expressed as the idea that supply creates its own demand.

When the producer has put the finishing hand to his product, he is most anxious to sell it immediately, lest its value should diminish in his hands. Nor is he less anxious to dispose of the money he may get for it; for the value of money is also perishable. But the only way of getting rid of money is in the purchase of some product or other. Thus the mere circumstance of creation of one product immediately opens a vent for other products.

(Say, 1803, pp.138–9)

In effect, products can be sold because the people producing them want to spend the proceeds from what they sell, and that money creates an equivalent amount of demand for other products. The implication of this 'law' is that any shortage of demand which causes workers to be laid off because products cannot be sold will always be balanced somewhere else by excess demand. So any fluctuations in the levels of output and employment in the economy should be only temporary and self-reversing. The economy is 'self-correcting' and any situation of unemployment should quickly revert to full employment.

Say's 'law' and its economic implications were criticized by a well-known British economist, John Maynard Keynes (1883–1946), who revolutionized the economic profession with the publication of his book *The General Theory of Employment, Interest and Money* (1936). Great economists are all products of their times. Whereas Say and Smith were the spokesmen for the nascent capitalistic system, the work of Keynes was the product of the Great Depression. The Depression of the 1930s was one of the most disruptive economic crises in history. All the major Western countries experienced mass unemployment and greatly reduced levels of GDP. For instance, in 1933, one-quarter of the US labour force was unemployed and real GDP was more than 40 per cent below its 1929 level (Chapter 20). Economists appeared to be powerless in the face of this terrible reality. According to Say's Law, the economy was self-righting, and yet the Depression continued year after year across all industrialized economies.

To explain why economists had little to offer against the problems of the widespread depression of the inter-war period we need to understand what, according to Say's Law, should happen when there is unemployment; that is, when the supply of labour exceeds the demand for labour. In that situation the basic law of demand and supply (Chapter 5) would suggest that the price of labour (wages) would decline until it reaches a level at which the supply of labour services is just equal to the demand by firms for labour services. Thus, excess of supply in the labour market (unemployment) should force down wages and this reduction in the cost of labour services would encourage firms to produce more output and employ more labour.

But why should firms be able to sell this increased output? According to Say's Law, workers would offer their services and employers employ them because they both want to use the income they gain from the increased production to purchase other goods and services. This creates additional demand of a monetary value exactly equal to that of the increased output. In this way, the higher level of output should raise the level of aggregate demand just to the level needed for all the increased output to be sold, that is, up to the point where there would be full employment in the labour market. In short, taking those two 'laws' together, there is no reason for aggregate demand, and hence production, to stop short of the full employment level. In this framework then, unemployment can exist only as a transitory phenomenon. In equilibrium the economy would always be at full employment.

The persistently high levels of unemployment in the inter-war period led many economists to question the validity of Say's Law. Keynes was thus stimulated to propose a new theoretical approach because the available economic tools of his time could not explain, let alone solve, one of the most dramatic problems of modern capitalism: the coexistence of mass unemployment and excess capacity with economies producing at a level of output well below what should have been possible.

Keynes presented a new way of analysing the economy, the theory of aggregate demand, which would allow for the possibility of under-employment equilibrium. In Keynes's vision there was no self-correcting property in the economy that would solve economic downturns. In his theory, the level of employment depends on the level of aggregate demand, which he claimed could settle at any level. As a result, the equilibrium level of employment in the economy could also be at any level between zero and full employment. As the dramatic events of the 1930s showed, there was no guarantee that a level of aggregate demand would prevail in which the economy's resources of labour and capital were fully utilized. In this way, Keynes concluded that full employment represents just one particular outcome of an economic system, and that other levels of employment could also result and could coexist with unused productive capacity.

In this chapter, I shall develop the simple Keynesian model of aggregate demand for goods and services which underlies the determination of total income and employment in the economy. First, I shall look at what determines two of the main components of planned aggregate demand, namely consumption and investment (Section 2). This will allow us to see why the level of income and the interest rate are key determinants of the level of aggregate demand in the economy. Section 3 explains the relationship between aggregate demand and national income through the 'multiplier', and extends the model of national income determination to include the rest of the world and the government sector. A consideration of the implications of the level of national income for labour demand allows us to determine whether there is full employment or unemployment.

Section 4 then extends this simple model to examine the scope for government intervention in the economy. Two main forms of intervention are considered: government spending and taxation (fiscal policy) and government control of the money supply and/or interest rates (monetary policy). In the simple model developed in Sections 2 and 3, I assume that there is under-utilized capacity and that prices do not change. This was a reasonable assumption in the context of the Great Depression when Keynes formulated the model. Later, in Chapter 13, this assumption is relaxed and the relation between aggregate demand and price inflation is examined.

2 THE DETERMINANTS OF AGGREGATE DEMAND IN A CLOSED ECONOMY WITH NO GOVERNMENT SECTOR

In the previous chapter a distinction was made between plans or intentions of economic agents, the *ex ante* position, and the actual outcomes of those plans or intentions, the *ex post* position. That distinction was used to discriminate between two different ways of interpreting the circular flow of income. We also saw that we could use statistical estimates to see the actual amounts of *ex post* flows.

QUESTION

Look again at Table 11.1. What is the main component of aggregate expenditure?

We can see from Table 11.1 that 65.5% was spent by households on consumer goods and services such as clothes, food, and cars; 17.7% was spent by firms for buying capital goods such as factories, machines, and land; 18.5% was spent by the government in providing public services such as health, defence, and education.

Whilst Table 11.1 can provide some insights into the size of the contributions of the different components of expenditure to national income, it does not tell us why the level of national income is what it is in each period. If we are interested in knowing why the economy has settled at a particular equilibrium level of income and employment we need to spell out the causal mechanism involved in arriving at that level of income. Since in equilibrium total income equals total planned expenditure, the level of income depends on expenditure plans. This means that we have to look at what determines the spending plans or intentions of households, firms and the government, that is the *ex ante* positions of our circular flow, and then see what level of income results. This is not just a simple adding-up procedure because plans may depend on income as well as the other way around. This is why, as you saw in Chapter 11, the outcome in terms of income and expenditure may be rather different from what was planned or intended.

For example, consider again what happens when households plan to save more than firms plan to invest. After reading Chapter 11, you know that in such a situation (assuming government does not change its expenditure) firms will face increased inventories and therefore are likely to cut back on production and use less labour. Households will then have less income and will tend to reduce their expenditure. As households reduce their expenditure, less output can be sold by firms who may then cut back further on production. Eventually, an equilibrium may be reached, but it will be one where expenditure and income will be lower than they would have been if households had not planned to save so much of their income.

A causal explanation of what determines national income and employment must thus start with a study of what determines the planned level of expenditures in an economy. In other words, it should begin with an analysis of aggregate demand.

AGGREGATE DEMAND is the total value of goods and services demanded in an economy. Four major components of aggregate demand are usually identified, namely: consumption demand, investment demand, government demand and net foreign demand (that is export demand minus import demand). Figure 11.1 looked at domestic demand alone, so ignored net foreign demand. In this section, I shall do the same, assuming what is called a 'closed' economy, one with no foreign trade. I shall also not consider government expenditure. Both these assumptions will be relaxed later. Initially, I concentrate on examining the determinants of the first two components of the aggregate demand, consumption and investment demand. This requires understanding how households and firms make their spending plans.

AGGREGATE DEMAND
Aggregate demand is the sum total spending plans of the different sections of the economy.

2.1   CONSUMPTION DEMAND

We saw in Table 11.1 that consumer spending by households is the major component of total aggregate expenditure. Consumption demand consists of the expenditures that households plan to make on both durable and non-durable goods, and on services. Durable goods are those commodities, such as cars and computers, that generate benefits for their owners over a substantial period of time. Non-durable goods are commodities, such as food and clothes, which are consumed or used over a relatively short time period. An individual will generally purchase non-durable goods frequently, whereas she will generally purchase durable goods infrequently. Finally, services are those commodities, such as a medical check-up or the teaching of a class, that have the characteristic of having to be consumed at the same time as they are produced.

Consumption demand and its fluctuations are an essential part of the explanation of booms and recessions. There are different theories to explain what determines the level of consumption demand by households. Keynes conjectured that planned consumption demand C depended on Y, the level of current disposable income of households. Disposable income is simply income that households can spend, that is total income plus transfers less taxes. Since, for the moment, we are assuming a simple model with no government expenditures or taxation, disposable income is just the same as total income. This may seem like a rather obvious proposition – that our demand for consumption goods depends on how much income we receive – but it was in fact a very different way of thinking about demand from existing views in the 1930s.

To appreciate this, just stop and think for a moment about how it compares with the notion of market demand that you encountered in *Microeconomics*. In *Microeconomics*, market demand was a function principally of relative prices, while in the Keynesian model consumption demand is a function principally of current incomes. This idea that (planned) consumption depends on income can be summarized by equation (1) which gives the *consumption function*, presenting consumption as a function of income:

$$C = C_0 + bY \qquad\qquad (1)$$

Here C_0 is 'autonomous consumption', that is expenditure which does not depend on households' income, so it is expenditure that households will undertake even if they have no income.

Writing the consumption function as in equation (1) makes the assumption that each additional increment to income has the same effect on consumption. So households plan to spend a fixed proportion of each increment in income. This proportion b is known as the MARGINAL PROPENSITY TO CONSUME. Its value is assumed to be positive but less than unity, on the grounds that people will spend some but not all of any increment in their income. So

MARGINAL PROPENSITY TO CONSUME

The marginal propensity to consume tells us the extent to which a marginal change in income is associated with a marginal change in consumption.

$$0 < b < 1$$

Anything that the household does not spend is saved, and hence the consumption function in equation (1) also indicates that some part of any additional pound of income is saved. If S denotes the level of saving, then

$$S \equiv Y - C$$

So equation (1) implies that the saving function of the economy is

$$S = Y - (C_0 + bY) = -C_0 + (1-b)Y \tag{2}$$

MARGINAL PROPENSITY TO SAVE

The marginal propensity to save tells us the extent to which a marginal change in income is associated with a marginal change in savings.

The coefficient $(1 - b)$ is sometimes called the MARGINAL PROPENSITY TO SAVE of the economy; it gives the proportion of each additional increment of income that is saved. It should also lie between 0 and 1 because some, but not all, of any additional income is saved.

A graphical illustration of the consumption function is shown in Figure 12.1. The marginal propensity to consume b is the slope of the consumption demand function: a consumption function with a higher marginal propensity to consume would be more steeply sloped than one with a lower marginal propensity to consume. The constant term C_0 is autonomous consumption and is represented by the intercept of the consumption function on the vertical axis (Figure 12.1).

Figure 12.1 The consumption function

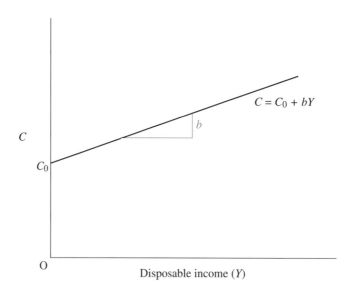

The consumption function given above in equation (1) is clearly a rather simple one, and many have argued that it provides too simplistic a view of consumption behaviour. It claims that individuals immediately spend a proportion of any increase in current income. However, would you respond to a rise in your income which you expected to be temporary in the same way as you would to what you expected to be a permanent increase in your income? When making decisions on what to spend and what to save, do you just pay regard to your present income or do you think more broadly about the longer-term prospects for your income? It is reasonable to suppose that the consumption plans of two people each receiving, say, £200 a week may be different depending on whether they think that £200 a week is the most they will ever earn or whether they think that their future income prospects are much better.

The Nobel prize winning economist Franco Modigliani pointed out that: (a) income varies over a person's life and (b) people use saving and borrowing to smooth their consumption over their lifetimes. Thus, consumption demand should depend not only on current income but also on their future prospects for income. This view forms the basis of Modigliani's *life-cycle hypothesis* that individuals will pay regard to their lifetime income prospects when making consumption and saving decisions. In those periods of their lives when their income is relatively high, people will save; in those periods when their current income is relatively low, people will dissave (and run down their past savings or borrow).

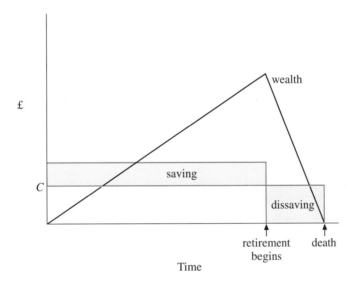

Figure 12.2 The life-cycle hypothesis

Figure 12.2 illustrates an interesting implication of the life-cycle hypothesis. It shows a plausible pattern of income, wealth and consumption of an individual over her adult life. The amount of £s is represented on the vertical axis and time is measured on the horizontal axis. Modigliani argued that most people do not want a major decline in the standard of living when they retire. This means that during her working years this individual would save part of her income and accumulate wealth. After retirement she would then use the income saved (dissaving) and wealth to keep enjoying her pattern of consumption. As drawn in Figure 12.2, the individual knows not only her income but also the time of her demise. Her wealth falls to zero at exactly the time of death. However, it can be noted that individuals often place their savings with pension funds or with other financial institutions, and those funds and institutions provide pensions that do indeed cease with the individual.

The life-cycle hypothesis suggests that people will tend to save little over the full course of their lifetime, but that savings are used to shift consumption from periods when income is relatively high to periods when income is expected to be relatively low. If this is the case then the amount of net savings being undertaken in any economy would depend on the balance between relatively young people (assumed to be saving) and relatively old people (assumed to be dissaving).

Another Nobel prize winning economist, Milton Friedman, proposed a similar theory of consumption. He suggested distinguishing between 'TRANSITORY' AND 'PERMANENT' INCOME, where the former is the part of income received in one period that is not expected to recur in the future, whereas permanent income is, as its name suggests, the part of income that is expected to go on year after year. He maintained that only permanent income should enter in the consumption function since saving and borrowing are used to smooth the effects of changes in transitory income. Thus, transitory income (which may be positive or negative) would, Friedman argued, be ignored in the demand for consumption since the long-term prospects for permanent income are not changed. This is the core of his 'permanent-income' hypothesis.

These theories of consumption based on the life-cycle hypothesis and the permanent-income hypothesis suggest that consumption demand may be sensitive not only to current income but also to future prospects for (permanent) income and wealth. However, note that they do not differ on the fundamental proposition itself, namely that planned consumption depends on income. They only differ on whether knowledge of current income alone is enough to explain planned consumption.

TRANSITORY AND PERMANENT INCOME

Transitory income is the part of income received in one period that is not expected to recur in the future. Permanent income is the part of income that is expected to recur every year.

2.2   INVESTMENT DEMAND

Investment consists of spending by firms and households to increase their capital. Firms make two types of investment spending: (a) fixed investment, when they buy capital inputs such as equipment and buildings to use in production, and (b) inventory investment, which consists of finished output in storage or work in progress that has not yet been sold. Households' investment spending consists mainly of new residences.

The demand for investment is usually seen as the most volatile component of aggregate demand. This volatility derives from the fact that investment decisions are always forward-looking and based on expectations. When firms make investment decisions they have to forecast the flow of future income that a project is likely to generate. Whether based on guesses or careful calculations those expectations are inherently unstable and capable of sudden and sharp reversals. Thus, most of the changes in the level of income when a country experiences a boom or recession are thought to be due to a decline in, or a recovery of, investment demand.

Figure 12.3 plots the growth of the different components of UK expenditure over the period from 1970 to 2000. The graph shows quite clearly that investment expenditure is much more volatile than the other components of domestic expenditure. Thus, investment expenditure grew over 20 per cent per annum in 1972 and 1987, whereas it declined by over 15 per cent in 1974 and in 1979. This volatility alone makes

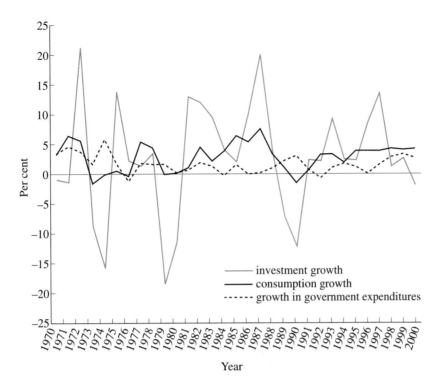

Figure 12.3 Rates
of change of
components of
UK domestic
expenditure,
1970–2000

investment demand difficult to predict in the aggregate. Anyone who has been involved in real investments also knows that no two people would assess a risk in the same way; neither might the same person consider the implications of a risk to be the same at two different points in time. What this means is that the level of investment depends heavily on the gut feelings and expectations of the managers of firms in the economy. Keynes wrote that in the main it was determined by the 'animal spirits' of the investing firms!

Despite the large role of uncertainty there are two factors that firms are likely to consider when they plan investments. These are: (a) the cost of financing investment, including the interest rate they could have to pay on bank loans r, and (b) the expected returns on the projects they plan to invest in.

Most firms have to borrow money from banks to pay for investment. Thus, the interest rate on bank loans is the financial cost to firms of making additional investment. The link between investment demand and the rate of interest on bank loans r can be expressed as an investment function

$$I = I(r) \tag{3}$$

in which investment depends on the rate of interest, and we would expect the relationship to be a negative one. When firms decide to make an investment, such as buying a new machine or a new factory, they compare the additional profit that they may expect to earn from using the new machine or factory with the interest that they would have to pay to borrow the money to finance that investment. If the interest rate, or the cost of borrowing, is low relative to the returns they expect from the investment, firms will go ahead with the investment. If interest rates rise, however, and the expected return from the investment stays the same, firms will be reluctant to proceed. For a given expected return, an increase in the interest rate on loans raises the financing cost of investment and so lowers the demand for investment. How a firm decides whether an investment project is profitable will be explained in Chapter 17, Section 3.

3 THE BASIC MODEL OF INCOME DETERMINATION ••••

If we are interested in knowing why the economy has settled at a particular equilibrium level of income, we need to analyse the *ex ante* positions of our circular flow in order to spell out the causal mechanism involved in arriving at that particular level of income. If we knew this, then we would be able to reduce the determinants of national income to just a few key variables, those that affect firms and households in making their expenditure plans. With this information and an understanding of the process involved, we could say how the economy arrived at the equilibrium level of income. We would then have a full causal explanation of the determination of the level of national income rather than a mere *ex post* description of its components.

In constructing a model of income determination, we distinguish between exogenous and endogenous variables. Exogenous variables are those variables that in the context of a particular model are considered fixed, that is, determined outside the model. By contrast, endogenous variables are those variables that are determined within that particular model. Variables are not intrinsically endogenous or exogenous; it is only in a particular model or theory that a variable is either endogenous or exogenous. In an economic model the exogenous variables determine the endogenous variables.

3.1 INCOME DETERMINATION IN A CLOSED ECONOMY WITH NO GOVERNMENT SECTOR

We have studied the two main components of aggregate demand: consumption demand C and investment demand I. Assuming, for simplicity, that we are considering a closed economy, that is net foreign demand is zero and that investment demand is a function of the interest rate alone, we can then write aggregate demand AD in this simple economy as a sum of its components:

$$AD = C + I$$

where, using equations (1) and (3)

$$C = C_0 + bY \tag{1}$$

$$I = I(r) \tag{3}$$

or

$$AD = C_0 + bY + I(r) \tag{4}$$

This equation states that the *ex ante* level of aggregate demand depends on a constant or exogenous term C_0 and the value of two other variables, namely the interest rate r and the level of current income Y. This is an important result since it tells us the variables that are directly capable of influencing the level of aggregate demand.

We can now use this information to find the equilibrium level of income in this simple closed economy. Note that I am assuming in the short run there is plenty of unutilized capacity in the economy, so that whatever is demanded can in fact be supplied. The equilibrium position arises when the plans for aggregate demand can be fulfilled, so that the level of output (and income) is equal to the level of aggregate demand, or

$$Y = AD$$
$$Y = C_0 + bY + I(r) \tag{5}$$

We can now ask how much income changes when a component of aggregate demand changes. To do this let us simplify equation (5) and assume investment is at some predetermined constant level $\bar{I}$. We say investment is now exogenous or autonomous to indicate that it is not determined inside the model so $I = \bar{I}$. Collecting the terms with Y in them on the left-hand side, we get:

$$Y - bY = C_0 + \bar{I}$$
$$Y = \frac{(C_0 + \bar{I})}{(1-b)} = \left(\frac{1}{1-b}\right)(C_0 + \bar{I}) \tag{6}$$

This means that when either of the exogenous elements of expenditure, C_0 or $\bar{I}$, changes by a certain amount, income changes by $\dfrac{1}{1-b}$ times that amount. This is a bigger change in income than the original change in exogenous expenditure because $1 - b$ is the marginal propensity to save, which is between 0 and 1, so $\dfrac{1}{1-b}$ is greater than 1. You can see this more easily when the simple model is shown diagrammatically as in Figure 12.4.

The lower line in Figure 12.4, $C + I$, is the sum of the consumption function, from Figure 12.1, and the predetermined level of investment $\bar{I}$. This line gives aggregate demand in the economy plotted against the level of income. Its slope is the same as that of the consumption function because investment does not vary with income, it just adds a fixed amount to consumption demand. The equilibrium condition is to have equality between aggregate demand and aggregate supply (or total national income). In Figure 12.4, this is given by the diagonal 45° line through the origin.

QUESTION

Why does this diagonal 45° line show equality of income and aggregate demand?

Along the diagonal 45° line every point is the same distance from the X-axis as it is from the Y-axis. (You can check this for yourself.) Here our X-axis variable income is total (national income) and the Y-axis indicates the levels of aggregate demand. So for every point on that line the equilibrium condition that income is equal to aggregate demand holds.

Figure 12.4 The determination of national income and the multiplier

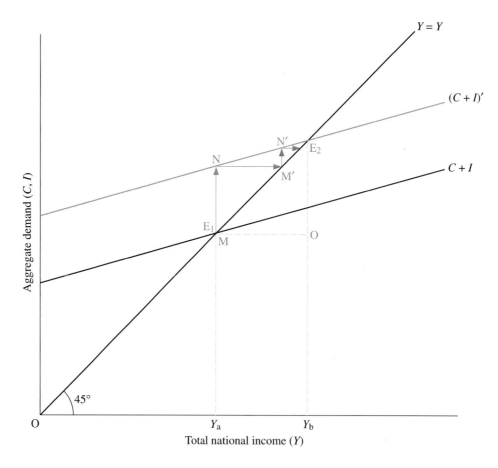

The equilibrium level of income in this simple model is Y_a where planned aggregate demand equals planned aggregate supply at point E_1. Check for yourself that at any point before Y_a and any point after Y_a the economy will be driven back to Y_a. If this is not clear read Section 2.2 of Chapter 11 again.

Now suppose that investment expenditure increases by MN. The aggregate demand schedule shifts upward by the extent of the increase in investment expenditure and is now represented by the upper line in Figure 12.4, labelled $(C + I)'$. The equilibrium level of income increases from Y_a to Y_b. The total increase in income is the distance MO (which is equal to $Y_b - Y_a$). Notice that MO > MN, which is what we would have expected; income has changed by *more* than the change in investment expenditure. The next section explains that the difference between MO and MN is the additional consumption expenditure induced by the initial increase in income via the multiplier process.

3.2   THE MULTIPLIER PROCESS

AUTONOMOUS EXPENDITURE

Autonomous expenditure is expenditure on consumption, investment or by the government that happens independent of the level of national income.

The ratio MO/MN (the increase in income divided by the increase in investment expenditure) is referred to as the 'Keynesian multiplier'; it measures by how much you have to multiply an increase in AUTONOMOUS EXPENDITURE to work out the corresponding increase in income. In fact, the multiplier is $\dfrac{1}{1-b}$ the inverse of the marginal propensity to save.

Why is MO > MN? After the initial increase in investment demand, aggregate demand is greater than aggregate supply. Since there is unutilized capacity, income in the economy rises to NM′ in the first instance (Figure 12.4). Due to this increase in incomes there will be an increase in consumption. From the consumption function we know that the increased consumption is a proportion b of the increase in income MN, where b is the marginal propensity to consume. This increased consumption adds to aggregate demand which is now higher by M′N′. So aggregate demand is now

$$MN + M′N′ = MN + bMN$$

Since there is still unutilized capacity this increase in aggregate demand again creates new incomes for the suppliers of goods and services who will consume a proportion b of these increased incomes. Aggregate demand increases yet again, and so on. Since b is less than 1, each successive addition to aggregate demand is smaller than the first one. This process continues until we reach point E_2 in Figure 12.4 where the total increase in aggregate demand and incomes is OE_2 = MO. So MO is the total increase in aggregate demand in the economy:

$$MO = MN + bMN + b(bMN) + b(bbMN) + ...$$
$$MO = MN(1 + b + b^2 + b^3 + ...)$$

This means that the multiplier $\dfrac{MO}{MN}$ is $1 + b + b^2 + b^3 + ...$

We can work out how much this is by looking at it another way. At E_2, since the economy is back in equilibrium, MO is both the increase in income and the increase in aggregate demand. The increase in aggregate demand has two components. First, there is the increase in autonomous investment, MN, and, second, there is the increase in consumption bMO, as a result of the increase in the level of income, MO.

So

MO = increase in income

= increase in aggregate demand

= MN + bMO

So

$$(1 - b)MO = MN$$

So the multiplier

$$\frac{MO}{MN} = \frac{1}{(1-b)} \tag{7}$$

The multiplier thus tells us by how much the total amount of goods and services demanded changes after a change in some autonomous component of demand, here investment expenditure. Firms are assumed to accommodate changes in demand through a corresponding change in output as there is unutilized capacity.

There is an important point to note about this conclusion. The multiplier is based on the assumption that all changes in aggregate demand are translated into corresponding changes in the level of output. In other words, the supply of output expands (or contracts) in response to changes in the level of aggregate demand. This may be a good assumption to make when there is under-utilized labour and capital in the economy, but not when there is full employment of labour and capital.

Although you may have followed the algebra, and/or appreciated the diagrammatic exposition, a niggling thought may persist: how does it all happen? What is the economic process that underlies the multiplier result?

Consider, for example, what happens if Marks & Spencer decides to open a new shop. Investment expenditure in the UK economy rises by, say, £10 million. It wants to spend this money on the construction of a new shop, the hiring of more staff, and the purchase of merchandise in order to accommodate this new demand. Building and merchandise companies may hire new workers or ask current employees to work longer hours. In any case, the amount of money allocated to workers increases and so do the profits made by the companies involved. Note that this extra income (profits and wages) is equal to the monetary value of the initial spending. That initial £10 million becomes the wages of builders, shop assistants and workers in clothing factories and the profits of their employers. Therefore, £10 million extra income in the form of wages and profits now enters the economy. An expansion in investment spending of £10 million would therefore produce an initial increase in income of £10 million. This is the first-round effect of the new investment. But this is not the end of the story. Further increases in income occur when that £10 million income increment starts to circulate in the British economy.

These workers and employers will now plan to spend some of their newly acquired income. They will not plan to spend it all, as we know, because they will plan to save some of it. But assuming a marginal propensity to consume b equal to 0.6, the £10 million extra income leads to a rise in planned consumption and in real GDP of £6 million. This £6 million new income is the second-round effect of the multiplier process. It represents the monetary value of the extra amount of goods and services demanded by the workers and the owners of building and merchandise companies when they plan to spend a portion (0.6) of their increased income. After this second round, aggregate demand has thus increased by £16 million: £10 million on the first round and £6 million on the second round. The cumulative change in real GDP as well as the changes in these two individual rounds in real GDP is shown in the first two rows of Table 12.1. However, the multiplier process does not stop after two rounds. Goods and services bought by these workers and employers are commodities produced by other firms. The workers and owners of those firms would now enjoy larger sales and higher income. As a result, their consumption spending would increase.

QUESTION

As a consequence of this third round of spending in the economy, total income increases by £3.6 million. Can you explain why?

According to the basic aggregate demand model, consumption and income increases by b times the additional income, that is 0.6 times £6 million or £3.6 million. This £3.6 million increase in income is what economists call the third-round effect of the multiplier process. Taken together with the effects of previous rounds, the cumulative change in real GDP is now £19.6 million.

Table 12.1 A numerical illustration of the multiplier (£ million)

Round	Change in real GDP	Cumulative change in real GDP
First round	10.000	10.000
Second round	6.000	16.000
Third round	3.600	19.600
Fourth round	2.160	21.760
Fifth round	1.296	23.056
...	...	...
...	...	...
After an indefinite number of rounds	0.000	25.000

The process continues. Another £3.6 million consumption spending in goods and services means £3.6 million in income for workers and owners of companies who produce those commodities. The basic aggregate demand model tells us that consumption and income would again increase by b times this additional spending, that is 0.6 times £3.6 million. This £2.16 million increase in income is the fourth-round effect of the multiplier process. The cumulative change in real GDP is now £21.76 million. After an indefinite number of rounds the cumulative change in real GDP gets closer and closer to £25 million as indicated in the last row of Table 12.1. In practice, all the rounds of the multiplier process occur rapidly, usually over the course of a year. Note that the size of the multiplier depends on the assumptions we made about the marginal propensity to consume b which captures how consumers react to an increase in their income: how much of it they decide to spend and how much to save.

In this case the multiplier is

$$\frac{£25 \text{ million}}{£10 \text{ million}} = 2.5 = \frac{1}{0.4} = \frac{1}{(1-0.6)} = \frac{1}{(1-b)}$$

EXERCISE 12.1

1   What would be the effect on national income of a decrease in investment spending of £10 billion when the marginal propensity to consume b is 0.9?

2   How would this change if b drops to 0.4?

We are now in a position to define the multiplier more formally.

The MULTIPLIER is the ratio of the change in real GDP to the change in any autonomous or exogenous component of aggregate demand (for example, investment demand or autonomous consumption expenditure):

$$\text{multiplier} = \frac{\text{change in real GDP}}{\text{change in autonomous component of } AD}$$

MULTIPLIER

The multiplier measures the change in aggregate income (GDP) resulting from a change in an autonomous (exogenous) component of the aggregate demand (AD).

A component of aggregate demand is 'autonomous' if it is not influenced by the level of income, that is, it is an exogenous variable in the context of the economic model being used. Thus, in the model we have used above, consumption demand is influenced by the level of income, whereas investment expenditure is not influenced by income.

In my examples so far, I have considered only the expansionary effect of the multiplier since I have only considered increases in spending. Should autonomous spending decrease, the multiplier predicts a contraction effect on national income well below the initial contraction of expenditure. To illustrate this we have briefly to consider the paradox of thrift.

QUESTION

What will be the effect on aggregate demand of an increase in autonomous savings?

An increase in autonomous savings entails a fall in autonomous consumption. If people save more in preference to immediately spending, this will cause problems for firms who will not be able to sell some of their output. Faced with lower demand for their output and lower sales revenue, the likelihood is that firms will cut back on production. In so far as any increase in saving causes aggregate demand to fall, which, in turn, leads to lower output and lower employment, people saving more of their income becomes a serious problem for the economy as a whole.

PARADOX OF THRIFT

The paradox of thrift refers to the negative effects of increased savings on aggregate demand and therefore national income.

Keynes puts this idea in terms of the PARADOX OF THRIFT. The paradox is that though individuals may save more to enhance future consumption, collectively their actions may reduce future income and therefore consumption. An individual wanting to increase consumption in the future should save more now. Both the money saved and the interest gained as a result can be used to increase future expenditure. Higher saving at an individual level can also provide additional funds for investment. On the other hand, however, if everyone chooses to save more, then the aggregate intended increase in saving, because it will come at the expense of aggregate consumption, will lead to a lower level of aggregate demand. This fall in aggregate demand will lead to lower levels of output, and in the context of falling sales, firms will be inclined to reduce investment and eventually shed workers.

The paradox of thrift also highlights the 'fallacy of composition' in that what holds at the individual level (the individual desire for increased savings as a means to higher consumption) does not hold at the aggregate level (increased savings across the economy as a whole reduces aggregate demand and lowers output and employment). Actions favourable at the individual level can have profound negative implications at the aggregate level. Drawing on the discussion of the circular flow of income in Chapter 11, we can see that if households save more than firms plan to invest (that is, if 'leakages' exceed 'injections') there will be a fall in the level of income, the extent of this fall in income being determined by the value of the multiplier. The fall in income will, in turn, result in lower levels of saving and investment.

QUESTION

If you believed in Say's Law what would you predict about the effect on aggregate demand of an increase in savings?

An increased desire to save by households must come at the expense of a desire to consume: if more is to be saved then less has to be consumed (for a given level of household income). The consumption component of aggregate demand falls and the level of aggregate demand will then fall, unless investment expenditure rises to take the place of consumer expenditure. Supporters of Say's Law would argue that a change in the rate of interest will bring about such a counterbalancing rise in investment expenditure. If the interest rate falls, investment is stimulated and (to some degree) savings inhibited. A sufficient fall in the rate of interest will bring about a sufficient rise in investment to compensate for the initial fall in consumption. The level of aggregate demand will be maintained; it will just be for different goods, for more investment goods and fewer consumption goods.

The higher level of saving thus allows firms to increase investment with equality between savings and investment being brought about through adjustment in the rate of interest. Total income will remain constant, though now more income will be spent on investment and less will be spent on consumption. On this basis, supporters of Say's Law argue that changes in aggregate demand (whether in the form of changes in consumption or investment) exert an entirely neutral effect on the overall level of income and output. They will, however, affect its composition, so that if people decide to save more, fewer consumer goods and more investment goods will be produced.

So as a consequence of the increased desire to save, economists who believe in Say's Law would predict that the rate of interest changes to bring about equilibrium in the market for loanable funds. Followers of the Keynesian argument, however, believe that it is the level of income that changes (contracts) to bring about a new equilibrium.

3.3   EXTENDING THE MODEL: GOVERNMENT SPENDING AND AN OPEN ECONOMY

Government purchases are another important component of aggregate demand. The government pays for the building of roads, schools and hospitals and it pays for the services of teachers and doctors etc. All those transactions make up government demand G. In most Western industrialized countries, government expenditure on goods and services represents around one-fifth of the total expenditure (Table 11.1). In the aggregate demand model presented here government demand is taken to be an exogenous policy variable, that is the value of the variable is taken as a fixed value $\overline{G}$ determined, by policy makers, outside the economic model. So

$$G = \overline{G}$$

Governments finance these expenditures through the imposition of taxes, T. They may also print more money or borrow more from households in the economy. Taxes reduce disposable income with households, but government spending adds to aggregate demand. If the level of taxes is exogenous, we can write $T = \overline{T}$. Note this is not a very realistic assumption since the level of taxes in practice often depends on Y, the level of income.

If the government taxes households then consumption demand depends on disposable income, that is income minus taxes, and instead of equation (1) above we should write the consumption function as:

$$C = C_0 + b(Y - \overline{T}) \tag{1a}$$

where $\overline{T}$ is taxes minus transfers, so that $Y - \overline{T}$ is disposable income.

QUESTION

Can you work out what the level of equilibrium income would be in this case?

Equilibrium in the economy now occurs when

$$Y = AD \equiv C + I + G$$

So

$$Y = C_0 + b(Y - \overline{T}) + \overline{I} + \overline{G}$$
$$(1 - b)Y = C_0 - b\overline{T} + \overline{I} + \overline{G}$$
$$Y = \left(\frac{1}{1-b}\right)(C_0 - b\overline{T} + \overline{I} + \overline{G}) \tag{8}$$

QUESTION

Compare the multiplier in equation (7) with that in equation (8). Is the multiplier larger or smaller? Why do you think this is the case?

The multiplier is the same, $\dfrac{1}{1-b}$, as it was for investment. Government spending at the level $\overline{G}$ increases national income by $\dfrac{\overline{G}}{1-b}$. This is the same as the effect of an increase in autonomous investment. Again because $\dfrac{1}{1-b} > 1$ an increase in government spending has an effect on national income greater than the original increase in spending. Taxation at the level $\overline{T}$ reduces national income by $\dfrac{b\overline{T}}{1-b}$.

An interesting feature of equation (8) is that when taxation is used to finance government spending completely, so that $\overline{T} = \overline{G}$, the net result is an increase in national income. This is because $b < 1$ so that the reduction in income due to the increased taxation $\dfrac{b\overline{T}}{1-b}$ is less than the increase due to the government spending $\dfrac{\overline{G}}{1-b}$. The reason is that all government spending is spent, while some of the income taxed to pay for it would have been saved if it had not been taxed.

We can also extend the multiplier analysis further to the case of an open economy (with imports and exports) as additional influences on aggregate demand. Imports are taken to depend on the level of income, so that $M = m(Y - T)$ where m is the marginal propensity to import, meaning that a certain proportion of a change in national income $Y - T$ is spent on imports M instead of being part of domestic aggregate demand. The level of exports, X, is treated as exogenous, as it depends not on domestic levels of income but on levels of income of overseas nationals. Aggregate demand is now:

$$AD = C_0 + b(Y - \overline{T}) + I + \overline{G} + \overline{X} - m(Y - \overline{T})$$

In equilibrium $Y = AD$:

$$Y = AD = C_0 + b(Y - \overline{T}) + I + \overline{G} + \overline{X} - m(Y - \overline{T})$$

or

$$Y(1 - (b - m)) = C_0 + I + \overline{G} + \overline{X} - (b - m)\overline{T}$$

or

$$Y = \left(\frac{1}{1 - (b - m)} \right)(C_0 + I + \overline{G} + \overline{X} - (b - m)\overline{T}) \qquad (9)$$

QUESTION

Compare the multiplier in equation (9) with that in equation (8). Is the multiplier smaller or larger? Why do you think this is the case?

There is an extra leakage (imports) from the circular flow of income, so the multiplier is now $\dfrac{1}{1 - (b - m)}$ which is smaller than in the case of the closed economy (since m is positive, the denominator of the multiplier formula is larger, and the value of the multiplier smaller). However, a stimulus to the circular flow of income could now arise from an increase in any of the components on the right-hand side of this equation. These are the autonomous components of aggregate demand, investment, government expenditure, exports and the autonomous component of consumption. A £1 million increase in exports would have the same impact as a £1 million increase in government expenditure or a £1 million increase in autonomous investment.

3.4   EMPLOYMENT, UNEMPLOYMENT AND THE REAL WAGE

The level of aggregate demand was seen above to determine the amount of goods and services that firms produce. Of course, firms have to use inputs to produce those commodities. As you know from Chapter 3, economists use the device of the production function to infer how much of an input is needed to produce a given level of output. Letting K and L represent the amount of capital and labour used to produce commodities, we can write:

$$Y = f(K, L)$$

QUESTION

Recall the discussion of the production function in Chapter 3. How would the production function be modified if we were interested only in the short run?

The short run is the period of time for which the amount of at least one factor is fixed. Usually this is capital, in which case firms can vary only the amount of labour to change the level of output and to accommodate any variation in the aggregate demand. Thus, in the short run, the production function is written as:

$$Y = f(L)$$

Firms in the economy will make hiring decisions according to this production function, assuming their capital stock is fixed. Once the quantity of goods and services is known, the production function will tell firms how much labour they should hire. In Chapter 7, Section 2, you learnt that when the labour market is competitive firms demand labour up to the point when the marginal revenue product of labour is equal to the wage rate. Put differently, the marginal physical product (*MPP*) must equal the real wage rate $\dfrac{W}{P}$. So if firms already know how much labour they need they will also have a real wage rate in mind that will maximize the returns from employing that quantity of labour.

Algebraically,

$$P . MPP = W$$

and

$$MPP = \frac{W}{P}$$

For a given state of technology, as more labour is employed in production its marginal product eventually starts to diminish so that firms will employ more units of labour only at a lower real wage rate. This equation, therefore, is the demand for labour by firms. The supply of labour, on the other hand, increases as the real wage increases.

QUESTION

From Chapter 7, what is the key variable that determines unemployment in the labour market?

The key variable in determining labour market unemployment is the real wage rate. If the real wage rate moves freely then the labour market will clear so that labour demand is equal to labour supply. The real wage rate is, however, determined by two separate components: the nominal wage rate and the price level in the economy. Keynes suggested two reasons why the real wage rate may not move freely.

Nominal wages in the labour market are often set by the bargaining power of unions based on their notion of what constitutes a 'fair wage', rather than the marginal productivity of labour. The price level in the economy, on the other hand, depends on how close the economy is to full capacity. If there is under-utilized capacity there is no reason for the price level to change. For both these reasons the real wage rate may actually be inflexible.

This inflexibility means that the labour demanded by firms may be at odds with that supplied in the labour market. In the absence of some mechanism that changes real wages, or else changes the demand for or supply of labour, it is difficult to see why labour markets should clear. From the Keynesian perspective of aggregate demand, changes in the demand for labour are particularly important in explaining why labour markets may fail to clear. The Keynesian model of aggregate demand implies that the equilibrium level of national income could coexist with unemployment. In that case firms could cut back production and still produce the output that is needed to satisfy aggregate demand. The production function tells us that the lower level of output requires less labour to produce it and so redundancies and unemployment will rise.

There are two ways of explaining unemployment from a Keynesian perspective. First, real wages are inflexible in response to a fall in the demand for labour. Second, the level of aggregate demand is so low that firms would have no reason to take on unemployed workers even if real wages were to fall. Both of these explanations are shown diagrammatically in Figure 12.5.

Once the aggregate demand for commodities is known, the production function allows us to infer the derived demand for labour – based on the technology in use and the factor prices at that time – by firms in the economy. Corresponding to Y_a, the equilibrium level of income from equation (1), from the upper half of Figure 12.5 the production function allows us to read the corresponding level of demand for labour and therefore employment in the economy. This is L_d units of labour.

QUESTION

Is L_d units of labour the full employment level of labour demand?

Full employment usually means the absence of unemployment; that is, the level of employment when all the labour supply offered is absorbed by firms that need labour to produce goods and services. This depends on the labour market and how much labour is supplied at the prevailing real wage rate. If all the labour that is supplied is absorbed by labour demand then we have no unemployment. If labour supplied is greater than the labour demanded then there would be unemployment.

Returning to Figure 12.5, the lower half of the figure represents the labour market. L_s units of labour are supplied at the prevailing wage rate $\dfrac{W}{P}$. At this real wage L_s units of labour are supplied in the labour market, but only L_d units of labour are demanded by firms. So the distance from L_d to L_s represents units of unemployed labour.

Figure 12.5
National income,
employment and
wages

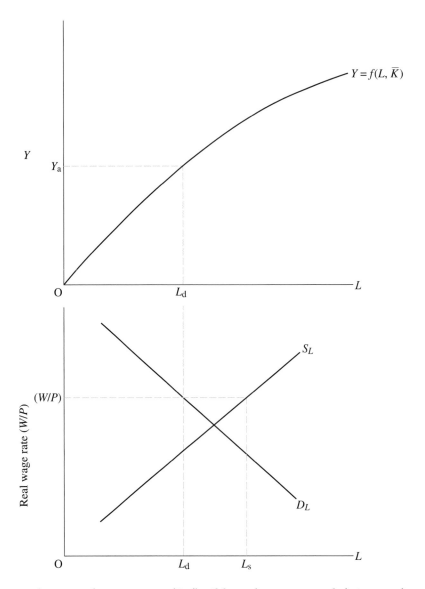

Is this unemployment the outcome of inflexible real wages or a deficiency of aggregate demand? First, inflexible real wages would be responsible if the unemployment persisted even though an increase in national income were to increase the demand for labour to the notional equilibrium level at the intersection of D_L and S_L. If it were not for the inflexibility of the real wage rate at $\dfrac{W}{P}$, firms would be willing to move down the labour demand curve D_L and workers down the labour supply curve S_L until the labour market cleared.

Second, the unemployment might persist even if the real wage rate were to fall because the level of aggregate demand and hence national income remains too low. Given the equilibrium level of national income of Y_a, it follows that L_d is the quantity of labour that firms demand *regardless of how far the real wage rate falls below* $\dfrac{W}{P}$. In effect, the labour demand curve below $\dfrac{W}{P}$ is perfectly inelastic at L_d. The explanation is that at this equilibrium level of national income Y_a the employment of labour in excess of L_d would result in the production of goods that could not be sold. There is no profit to be made employing such labour even if the workers taken on worked for nothing. The implication is that a fall in real wages, while it would reduce unemployment by reducing the supply of labour, would do nothing to increase employment. What is needed is an increase in the equilibrium level of national income and hence the demand for labour.

How might governments go about increasing employment in labour markets? Expenditures by the government sector can stimulate demand in the economy and increase the demand for labour directly at the existing wage rates. Interest rates can also be lowered with the aim of stimulating aggregate demand. Section 4 discusses these policy instruments.

3.5   SUMMARIZING THE BASIC MODEL

We are now in a position to sum up the main points of the aggregate demand model presented in Sections 2–3. Firms make production plans based on the amount of goods and services demanded in the market by other firms and households. This means that in order to understand the equilibrium level of output in an economy we have to know the level of aggregate demand and its components. The multiplier is a simple way to show how increases in the different components of aggregate demand, namely consumption, investment and government demands, affect the equilibrium level of output by more than the initial increase in aggregate demand. An important assumption that underlies this result is that the economy has under-utilized capacity in the short run.

Once firms know the level of output demanded in the market, they can hire workers and start production plans. Economists represent this process in terms of a production function relating the aggregate supply of commodities to the amount of labour units used. The production function also determines the marginal physical product of labour (MPP); that is, the additional amount of output that firms get from an extra unit of labour services. Firms will employ units of labour as long as its marginal product is greater than or equal to the real wage rate they pay for this labour. If the resulting amount of labour employed is less than the amount of labour supplied at that real wage rate there will be unemployment.

How can full employment be restored without cutting real wages to reduce labour supply? Government expenditures can raise the level of aggregate demand in the economy and so increase the demand for labour.

4   THE SCOPE FOR GOVERNMENT POLICY   • • • • • • • • • • •

A role for government intervention in the economy is suggested in this simple model to secure full employment because aggregate income and employment ultimately depend on the level of aggregate demand. Governments can intervene to increase or decrease aggregate demand directly by their spending actions, or indirectly by trying to influence interest rates in the economy. The taxation and spending activities of governments are its fiscal policies, while its interventions to influence interest rates (and therefore money supply) are its monetary policies. In this section I will briefly discuss these two chief instruments of macroeconomic policy available to policy makers.

4.1   FISCAL POLICY

It is evident from equation (8) that government spending is a source of aggregate demand which has the effect of increasing national income and therefore employment. By raising the level of aggregate demand in the economy the government would in effect be increasing the demand for labour in the economy. As a consequence, employment and income in the economy can increase as a result of an expansion of government expenditure.

It would then appear that since government expenditure is policy determined, it can be used to stabilize the level of aggregate demand in the economy, and to compensate for the volatility of investment. So in periods when investment expenditure is low, government spending can stimulate aggregate demand and restore employment. What are the limits on this? There are three which I want to outline here. The first is that it takes time to decide on and implement changes in the level of public expenditure. The statistics on which the decision is based have to be collected and processed. Approval for changes in public expenditure may have to be secured through parliament. In sum, there may be considerable lags between, say, a downturn in investment expenditure and a response from government expenditure to offset that downturn.

The second limit arises from the funding of an increase in government expenditure which would generally involve an increased budget deficit (or smaller surplus). Recall the formula from the previous chapter that $(S-I)+(M-X)+(T-G) \equiv 0$, which can be re-written as $(G-T) \equiv (S-I)+(M-X)$. In other words, the funding of a government deficit $(G-T)$ comes from a combination of net domestic savings $(S-I)$ and borrowing from overseas (recall that $M-X$ is the current account deficit which is equal to the capital account surplus). In so far as an increase in government expenditure leads to a higher level of income (through the multiplier process) then tax revenue also rises and the size of the budget deficit is not as large as the initial increase in government expenditure. The rise in income will also increase savings and imports; in effect the increase in private savings and in the capital account surplus fund the budget deficit. But the budget deficit does mean that the government is borrowing and is then committed to making future interest payments on its borrowing.

The third limit is the concern that an increase in government expenditure stimulates demand to a level which exceeds the capacity of the economy to supply. When demand is high relative to capacity, there can be problems of inflation developing; this is further discussed in Chapter 17. Like any other increase in expenditure, an increase in government expenditure at a time when demand was in balance with capacity would be seen as inflationary.

4.2   MONETARY POLICY

Monetary policy, in the form of changing interest rates, can be used to influence the level of aggregate demand in the economy. It has been postulated above that investment expenditure is influenced by the rate of interest and other forms of expenditure (such as consumer expenditure) may also be sensitive to the rate of interest.

Banks usually set the price of providing finance, that is the interest rate on loans r, as a mark up m over the nominal short-term interest rate i set by the central bank. This is the interest rate that banks pay to each other for overnight loans of reserves held in the central bank. For banks, the nominal short-term interest rate is the cost of obtaining the necessary liquidity for their lending activity. Thus banks add a mark-up to cover their overheads and profits with respect to the short-term interest rate to arrive at the interest rate on loans r.

As the banker to the government and the banking system, the central bank oversees the circulation of money between the accounts of the government and banks and tries to smooth out any imbalance that may result. For instance, when the flow of money from banks to government is higher than the flow of money from government to banks, there can be a shortage of liquidity in the money market. This shortage of cash would be damaging to the level of economic transactions, if there was not enough money to buy commodities, and this could have adverse effects on the level of income and employment. The central bank seeks to prevent problems such as this by supplying the extra cash – so-called monetary reserves – that the banking system needs to balance its accounts. But as the final provider of liquidity to the economic system the central bank can choose the nominal interest rate i at which the extra cash is provided.

QUESTION

Why would the provision of extra reserves by the central bank increase liquidity in the economic system?

Recall from Chapter 11 that liquidity is the extent of money supply in the economy which is available for the purchase of goods and services. An increase in reserves increases the base money in the economy. It thus increases the ability of banks to create new money through loans. In turn, this expands the effective money supply in the economy.

In practice, the central bank does not directly control the nominal short-term interest rate i which is determined by the supply and demand of reserves. The central bank can expand or contract the supply of monetary reserves in another way. This is by undertaking open market operations (OMO) which in turn determine the nominal short-term interest rate i. For instance, when the central bank wishes to lower the short-term interest rate it buys government assets such as Treasury securities from banks in exchange for cash. This purchase increases the quantity of monetary reserves in the money market and lowers the interest rate i.

QUESTION

If the central bank wishes to increase the interest rate should it sell or buy Treasury securities?

When a central bank wishes to increase the short-term interest rate i, it reduces the quantity of monetary reserves in the money market by selling government assets such as Treasury Bills to the banks. Thus, by choosing to supply the relevant amount of reserves to the banking system, the central bank can effectively keep the nominal short-term interest rate near its desired level.

The interest rate i corresponds to what in the USA is called the federal funds rate and in the UK the repo rate. The federal funds rate and the repo rate are set, according to the process described above, by the Federal Reserve System and the Bank of England, the central banks of the USA and the UK, respectively. In modern economies the nominal short-term interest rate i represents a tool central banks use to affect aggregate demand, and hence the level of output and employment.

The sequence of events through which a change in monetary policy eventually affects the level of income is called the monetary transmission mechanism. Figure 12.6 shows how the mechanism works. The operations of the central bank (the first box) in buying government assets and supplying bank reserves leads to a fall in the short-term rate of interest i which feeds through into a fall in the rate of interest on loans r (which is shown in the second box). The fall in the rate of interest on loans tends to encourage investment demand (leading to the third box) and the additional investment demand adds to the level of aggregate demand which leads to a rise in GDP (fourth box).

Figure 12.6
The monetary
transmission
mechanism

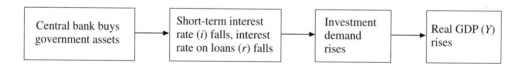

The mechanism would also operate in reverse for a sale by central banks of government assets. When the central bank sells government assets, monetary reserves fall, the interest rate i and the interest rate on loans r rises. This means that, for a given expected return, the cost of investment is higher. Investment demand falls and, in that way, the level of real GDP and employment declines. Monetary policy is often used to target the rate of inflation. Hence, when the rate of inflation rises (or is expected to rise), interest rates are increased; this reduces the level of aggregate demand in the expectation that the lower level of aggregate demand will restrain inflation.

5 CONCLUSION

In this chapter I have developed the simple Keynesian model to explain the determination of aggregate income and employment in the economy. I have shown that aggregate demand determines the level of income in the economy through the multiplier process. The level of income in turn determines labour demand via the production function.

There are two main conclusions from the aggregate demand model presented here. First, the particular level of output and employment at which the economy would finally settle is determined by the complex interactions of individuals on the labour market, the money market and the commodity market. Second, and related to the first conclusion, the economy could potentially settle at any level between zero and full employment. The level of aggregate demand determines the final equilibrium level of output and employment, but that equilibrium is not necessarily a good one since expenditures and income may be lower than they could have been.

The above model also suggests a role for government policy in stabilizing the level of aggregate demand in the economy, in order to maintain stability in national income generation and full employment. The government can intervene directly to raise aggregate demand in the economy through the use of fiscal policies. Alternatively, it can use monetary policies to change interest rates and intervene indirectly to change aggregate demand.

CHAPTER 13 UNEMPLOYMENT AND INFLATION

Graham Dawson ●

Objectives

After studying this chapter you should be able to:
- discuss different estimates of the costs of unemployment and inflation
- understand different interpretations of the relationship between unemployment and inflation
- understand changes in the policy response to unemployment and inflation.

Concepts

- unemployment
- inflation
- the Phillips curve
- adaptive and rational expectations
- the long-run vertical Phillips curve
- monetary policy rule
- the aggregate demand/inflation curve

1   INTRODUCTION ●

In the late 1970s and early 1980s, policy makers throughout the large OECD economies abandoned the goal of full employment that had guided macroeconomic policy throughout the 1950s and 1960s and made their first priority the elimination of inflation. They did so because they believed that inflation does more damage to the economy than unemployment, in part because they became convinced that inflation itself caused unemployment. This change in macroeconomic policy was taken a step further in the 1990s as first the European Union and then the UK government delegated the control of interest rates, the crucial weapon in 'the battle against inflation', to their respective central banks. Thirty years earlier, UK finance ministers and their economic advisers had made short-run adjustments in interest rates (and other macroeconomic policy instruments affecting aggregate demand) with the aim of reducing unemployment by allowing inflation to rise, or curbing inflation at the cost of higher unemployment. Today, finance ministers throughout the European Union set a strategic objective of price stability (in practice, an inflation rate very close to zero) and leave it to their central banks to decide on the level of interest rates that will achieve it. The aim of this chapter is to examine the reasons for this change in policy regime.

Section 2 examines the underlying principle of much macroeconomic policy making in the 1950s and 1960s: that there was an inverse relationship between unemployment and inflation. The issue for policy makers was to achieve an appropriate balance between them, for example by trading off higher inflation for lower unemployment. In these circumstances it is important to decide which is the more serious problem – inflation or unemployment? Why does getting inflation down matter? What price is paid for getting inflation down when unemployment increases – and who pays it? Section 3 assesses the costs of unemployment and inflation. The outcome of this inquiry is that the costs of high rates of inflation are substantial. Section 4 examines theoretical developments that have influenced macroeconomic policy from the 1970s onwards, based on the argument that there is a risk that moderate inflation will accelerate into high inflation. The policy implications are discussed in Section 5, using current UK macroeconomic policy as a case study. In this way the chapter seeks to explain why, in 1997, the UK government granted the central bank a greater degree of independence in operating monetary policy and why the focus of policies for economic stabilization has shifted from the management of aggregate demand to the reform of the supply side.

2   THE TRADE-OFF BETWEEN INFLATION AND UNEMPLOYMENT ●

The fundamental dilemma confronting economic policy makers is to decide whether government intervention in the economy will improve its performance or make things worse. Whatever the area of economic policy under consideration, there is no escape from the disturbing thought that any policy intervention itself might do more harm than good. The idea of a trade-off between unemployment and inflation is directly relevant to this dilemma in the macroeconomic field. This trade-off, expressed in the Phillips curve analysis outlined below, was developed in the 1960s into a guide for policy makers whose main objective was full employment: 'one could achieve and maintain a permanently low level of unemployment merely by tolerating a permanently high level of inflation' (Mankiw, 1990, p.1647). The aim of this section is to examine the relationship between UNEMPLOYMENT and INFLATION that informed macroeconomic policy making in many countries during the 1960s.

2.1   THE PHILLIPS CURVE

The first step in answering the question of whether there is a trade-off between unemployment and inflation is to inspect the annual rates of inflation and unemployment over a reasonably long period of time and see if unemployment comes down when inflation goes up and vice versa. This is almost what Phillips (1958) did for the British economy, initially for the period from 1861 to 1913. It is not *exactly* what he did, because, while we think of inflation as a rise in the general level of *prices*, Phillips plotted the rate of *wage* inflation (that is, the rate of increase of the general level of wages) against the unemployment rate. The result of fitting a curve through these data points was an initially steep curve becoming gradually flatter – THE PHILLIPS CURVE (Figure 13.1). The same curve fitted the data for the years 1948–57 almost as well, suggesting that there was indeed a trade-off between unemployment and inflation over the previous hundred years.

UNEMPLOYMENT

An unemployed person is someone who is actively seeking work but unable to find it. The total of those working and seeking work constitutes the labour force. The unemployment rate expresses the number of unemployed people as a percentage of the labour force.

INFLATION

Inflation is a rise in the general level of prices. The rate of inflation measures the annual percentage increase in the general level of prices.

THE PHILLIPS CURVE

The Phillips curve is a graph showing a trade-off between unemployment and inflation: the lower the rate of unemployment, the higher the rate of inflation.

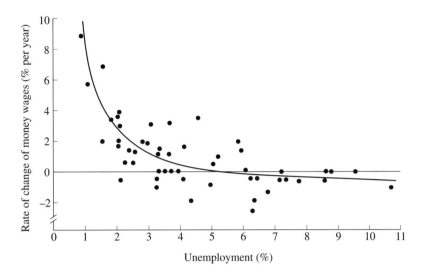

Figure 13.1 The original Phillips curve for the British economy 1861–1913

Source: Phillips, 1958

The next question is: what does this empirical relationship mean? How is it to be explained? The interpretation offered by Phillips is an application of supply and demand analysis to the labour market. Suppose initially that wages are stable (the rate of wage inflation is zero) and the labour market is in equilibrium. If the demand for labour falls, unemployment above equilibrium in the form of an excess supply of labour drives down its market price or, in other words, leads to a fall in the general level of wages, the rate of wage inflation is negative. If, instead, the demand for labour rises, excess labour demand brings unemployment below its equilibrium level and initiates wage rises, the rate of wage inflation is positive.

Phillips's (1958) paper stimulated further research into the relationship between unemployment and inflation. Price inflation as distinct from wage inflation was also found to be negatively correlated with unemployment and it became customary to think of the Phillips trade-off in these terms. This was more useful for policy makers because unemployment and (price) inflation were in the 1960s, as in the 2000s, two of the central macroeconomic problems they faced. The Phillips curve now presented policy makers with a range of options from which to choose the optimal, or least undesirable, combination of inflation and unemployment. For example, the inflation rate that would have to be tolerated to achieve full employment could simply be read off a Phillips curve diagram such as the one shown in Figure 13.2. The popularity the Phillips curve quickly won with policy makers is shrewdly commented on by Humphrey (1986):

> the Phillips curve appealed to policy makers because it provided a convincing rationale for their failure to achieve full employment with price stability – twin goals that were thought to be mutually compatible before Phillips' analysis. When criticized for failing to achieve both goals simultaneously, the authorities could point to the Phillips curve as showing that such an outcome was impossible and that the best one could hope for was either arbitrarily low unemployment or price stability but not both.

(Humphrey, 1986, p.15)

Figure 13.2 An expansionary movement along the Phillips curve

Source: *OECD Economic Outlook* (various years)

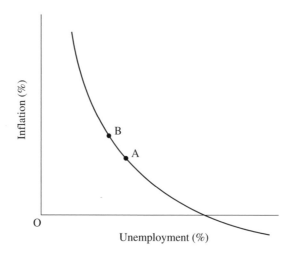

2.2   DEMAND-PULL AND COST-PUSH INFLATION

This section will introduce two theories of inflation, demand pull and cost push, using the Phillips curve analysis to distinguish them. Let us start by considering the case of a government which wants to reduce unemployment and is prepared to live with an increase in inflation to do so. A set of expansionary monetary and/or fiscal policy measures is therefore introduced and the economy duly moves along its Phillips curve in a 'north-westerly' direction – from A to B in Figure 13.2. Inflation has indeed risen and unemployment fallen. When inflation is caused in this way, by an expansion of aggregate demand, it is known as *demand-pull* inflation.

The aggregate demand expansion is reflected in a rise in prices which, if money wages are fixed by contractual agreements, leads to a fall in real wages. Firms therefore hire more labour and use it to increase output. So an expansion of aggregate demand raises the price level and output and reduces unemployment. The Phillips curve relates inflation (the rate at which the price level is changing) and unemployment.

Not much more than a decade after Phillips had reported his discovery of a trade-off between unemployment and inflation going back almost a century, it appeared to break down. Plotting the time path of inflation against unemployment for the UK economy in the 1970s reveals a relationship that cannot be depicted by the downward sloping Phillips curve and cannot readily be explained in terms of demand pull (Figure 13.3).

QUESTION

Did the Phillips curve simply cease to exist in the 1970s or do traces of it continue to be observable?

The first and second oil price shocks of the 1970s are quite clearly visible, in the almost vertical movements of the curve in Figure 13.3 for 1973–74 and 1979–80. The increase in inflation of the years 1973–75 and 1978–80 was not associated with a fall in unemployment.

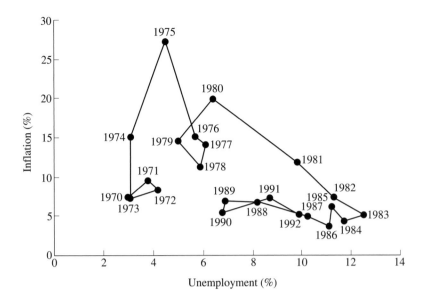

Figure 13.3
Inflation and unemployment in the UK, 1970–92

Source: *OECD Economic Outlook* (various years)

The empirical relationship between unemployment and inflation had become more complex than that observed by Phillips for the British economy from 1861 to 1913. The Phillips curve analysis could easily be modified to reflect the more complex unemployment–inflation relationship now observed throughout the industrial world. Basic supply and demand analysis has shown you that curves shift if there is change in the conditions we hold constant in drawing the original curve. Perhaps all that had happened was that the Phillips curve had shifted outwards or to the right? For example, the oil price rise of 1979 could be seen as shifting the UK Phillips curve in this direction; higher oil prices fed through into higher prices in general, so that any given unemployment rate was associated with a higher inflation rate, as noted in the discussion of Figure 13.3. An increase in oil prices raises transport costs throughout the economy. Producers will attempt to pass on some of the cost increases to consumers in the form of higher prices and in this way the oil price increase leads to an economy-wide increase in the costs of production. When inflation occurs in this way, it is classified as *cost-push* inflation.

However, there are two segments of the time path plotted in Figure 13.3 that slope downwards like a Phillips curve, one only briefly in 1975–77, the other over the years 1980–83. These Phillips curve remnants may reflect the response of policy makers to the cost-push inflationary episodes which shifted the Phillips curve outwards.

QUESTION

What policy measures might have initiated these south-easterly movements on Figure 13.3?

It seems that policy makers wished to reverse the inflationary consequences of the increases in oil prices. Certainly, the south-easterly movements are consistent with their using monetary and/or fiscal policies to reduce aggregate demand (Chapter 12, Section 3). The reduction in aggregate demand would cause inflation to fall and unemployment to rise. The following exercise asks you to consider what will happen if policy makers are more concerned with unemployment than inflation.

EXERCISE 13.1

Explain how the UK Phillips curve shown in Figure 13.3 might have looked if policy makers had sought to reduce unemployment a little following the oil price rise in 1979.

3   THE COSTS OF UNEMPLOYMENT VERSUS THE COSTS OF INFLATION •

One possible reason for policy makers prioritizing the defeat of inflation over the achievement of full employment is that the costs, or adverse effects, of inflation are much greater than those of unemployment. This section surveys theoretical arguments and empirical research on the costs of unemployment and inflation, with the intention of discovering whether inflation is more damaging to economic activity than unemployment.

3.1   THE COSTS OF UNEMPLOYMENT

I received ten minutes notice on being made redundant.

I felt better – money in the bank – less tired – plenty of fresh air – an opportunity to do things with my life without the frustrations and claustrophobia of factory life ... [a couple of years later] depressed and insecure, no success in finding even part-time work to supplement savings.

Whenever I get a sufficient amount or come into money I spend it fast, mostly on drink. I seem to panic when I have money to spend.

To survive this unwanted gap in one's life one has to be drunk or half-crazy most of the time it seems.

I feel like an autistic child in relation to other working folk.

For many people, those words, spoken by interviewees taking part in a research project (Dawson, 1992), may be enough to convince them that full employment is the only objective of macroeconomic policy worth pursuing. Would policy makers not do better to listen to unemployed people talking about their experiences rather than just analyse tables of economic statistics?

THE HUMAN COST OF UNEMPLOYMENT

The costs of unemployment are incurred mainly by the unemployed people themselves and concern health, current income and future income and employment. It is clear that many unemployed people and their families experience a deterioration in their psychological well-being, ranging from anxiety and boredom to severe depression and despair. Even if the majority of unemployed people are still able to get a lot out of life, this may mean not that unemployment is only a trivial setback but that considerable moral strength has been invested in coming to terms with the major crisis. There is a greater incidence of physical ill health among unemployed people, although the degree to which this reflects a previous record of poor health continues to be a matter of academic dispute.

It is not easy to generalize about the degree of financial hardship imposed on unemployed people and their families, because national benefit systems vary both in their conditions of eligibility and in the 'replacement ratio', which expresses unemployment benefit as a percentage of previous earnings (Chapter 9, Section 5). In the USA during the high unemployment of the early 1980s, for example, married couples where the previously employed partner was paid close to average US earnings were likely to face a replacement ratio somewhere between 45 per cent and 66 per cent. For the UK during that same period of high unemployment, most unemployed people – single or married couples with no children – were looking at replacement ratios of less than 60 per cent unless earnings when last in work had been very low. The only group likely to be 'better off on dole' comprised married couples who have four or more children and were previously on less than half average male manual earnings (about four per cent of unemployed people came into this category). A replacement ratio as high as 80 per cent still means the loss of a fifth of income from work, typically from an already low income. So unemployment has a severely regressive effect on the distribution of income.

There is, however, much more to the impact of unemployment on the people who are unemployed than the effect it has on current income. Unemployment inflicts 'a longer-term "scar" through the increased future incidence of unemployment and lower subsequent earnings in employment' (Arulampalam *et al.*, 2001, p.F577). Unemployment scarring captures the idea that the worst effects of unemployment are concentrated on the unemployed people themselves in two ways: the first period of unemployment tends to bring further periods of unemployment and re-engagement tends to be associated with a lower earnings profile.

Arulampalam *et al.* (2001) offer two explanations of why unemployment scarring occurs, which can be understood in terms of labour market concepts introduced in Chapter 7. Leaving a job has been found to lead to a permanent loss of human capital that is specific to the firm but the effects of unemployment on human capital are wider (human capital was explained in Chapter 7, Section 2). At the very least, for the duration of unemployment, the unemployed person is denied opportunities to gain further work experience, develop existing skills and acquire new ones. The effects are likely to be more far-reaching, particularly for long-term unemployment, in that skills may deteriorate or even be lost. The concept of efficiency wages, also introduced in Chapter 7, sheds further light on unemployment scarring. The assumption underlying efficiency wage theory is that the worker's productivity is unobservable. Prospective employers may interpret periods of unemployment as an indication of a worker's low productivity and either refuse job offers or link job offers to lower wages.

In a symposium on unemployment scarring, the *Economic Journal* (*EJ*) in 2001 published three papers attempting to estimate its importance for unemployed men in Britain. The focus on unemployed *men* is explained by the different unemployment experience of men and women in the early 1980s. A large number of skilled and less skilled manual jobs that had traditionally been occupied by men were lost in manufacturing and mining, while the number of women entering the labour market to take (often part-time) jobs in service industries increased. Unemployment scarring in the 1980s and 1990s was in this sense a largely male phenomenon. The papers in the *EJ* symposium sought to address a weakness in the methodology of early studies of unemployment scarring, which failed to include information on workers who kept their jobs during the years of high unemployment. The consequence was that there was no 'control group' against which to compare the experience of unemployed people. Suppose for example that men lost their jobs in a declining industry and were subsequently re-employed in the same industry at lower real wages. This does not necessarily amount to unemployment scarring, because real wage cuts might have been experienced by workers retained in employment in the declining industry. The possible effect of industry decline on real wages can only be taken into account by comparing the real wage profiles of unemployed individuals with those of people who remained in work throughout the period.

All three *EJ* papers use very large data sets, covering the labour market experience of large numbers of men during the 1980s and 1990s and enabling comparisons to be made between 'workers with unemployment histories as well as those with no interruptions to the employment experience' (Arulampalam *et al.*, 2001, p.F578). The results confirm the importance of unemployment scarring as a consequence of the mass male unemployment of the 1980s in Britain. According to Arulampalam (2001, p.F585) a 'spell of unemployment is found to carry a wage penalty of about 6 per cent on re-entry in Britain, and after three years, they are earning 14 per cent less compared to what they would have received in the absence of unemployment'. Gregory and Jukes (2001) reach a broadly similar conclusion once allowance is made for an important distinction. This is the distinction between the effect on 're-engagement' wages of the incidence of unemployment, that is, its occurrence among the individuals being studied, and the duration of unemployment. Incidence, or the fact that someone has experienced a spell of unemployment, is found to have only a temporary impact –

'an average earnings setback of 10 per cent on initial re-engagement largely eroding over two years' (Gregory and Jukes, 2001, p.F607). By contrast, the effect of unemployment duration is permanent, 'a one-year spell adding a further penalty of 10 percentage points' (ibid.). Combining these two elements brings the results of the two studies broadly into line. The fact that Arulampalam (2001) did not find any effect from duration is in part explained by differences in the data that reflect changes in the administration of unemployment benefits. Gregory and Jukes (2001) covered the 1980s (as well as the 1990s) when long-term unemployment was high, while Arulampalam (2001) focuses on the 1990s when many long-term unemployed men had been transferred onto sickness benefits.

The third paper in the *EJ* symposium examines the further effects of unemployment scarring on inequality and poverty. Gregg (2001) undertakes a long-term analysis to try to discover whether there is a correlation between 'cumulated' experience of unemployment (adding up separate spells of unemployment) in the 16–23 age range and that in the 28–33 age range. The result is that there is such a correlation, implying that unemployment is concentrated on a minority of the workforce. This minority is characterized by low educational attainment, financial deprivation and childhood behavioural problems. There are clear policy implications: 'attacking low educational achievement, and preventing the build-up of substantial periods in unemployment as youths, may reduce the extent to which a minority of men spend a large part of their working lives unemployed' (Gregg, 2001, p.F626).

THE OUTPUT COST OF UNEMPLOYMENT

The principal cost which unemployment imposes on society as a whole is the loss of output that would have been produced if resources, including labour, had been fully employed. The simplest approach to measuring this output loss is to assume that everyone who is out of work would, if found a job, produce as much as the average person already in employment. But unemployed people tend to be less skilled than the labour force as a whole, so that, other things being equal, the average product method may exaggerate the scale of output loss.

On the other hand, there are reasons why the average product method might underestimate the output loss. When recorded unemployment rises, other symptoms of spare capacity emerge. Part-time work falls (without adding to the officially recorded unemployment figures) and so too does overtime working. There is usually a decline in the participation rate, that is, the percentage of the population of working age who declare themselves to be part of the labour force by seeking work, because the poor prospects of finding a job discourage some people from trying. An increase in hidden unemployment occurs when firms 'hoard' labour even though there is nothing for the workers concerned to do, with the aim of retaining skilled workers who might be difficult to replace when demand picks up.

A more promising approach is therefore to extrapolate the trend rate of output growth under full employment through the years of unemployment, and to measure the 'output gap', the amount by which actual output during the years of high unemployment falls short of full employment output. Using an output gap method, Okun (1970, p.140) concluded that 'a reduction in unemployment ... has a much larger than proportionate effect on output'. Okun's method takes into account the hidden spare capacity associated with recorded unemployment. The estimate of the output loss using this method is sensitive to the level of unemployment chosen as an approximation to feasible full employment.

Empirical estimates applying Okun's methodology to periods of historically high unemployment suggest that the output costs of unemployment are substantial. For example, in 1983 the output of the German economy was estimated to be up to a fifth lower than it would have been if the economy had been running at full capacity (Junankar, 1985). For the German, UK, Italian and French economies in 1983, the output gap was more than 10 per cent, or, in other words, each economy produced 10 per cent less output than it was capable of producing at full employment. Nevertheless, you might feel that the loss of goods that might have been produced but were not and never will be is a somewhat intangible, hypothetical deprivation. But this loss of potential output has serious effects on people's well-being. In the circular flow model of the economy, output equals income (Chapters 8 and 11). So everyone bears some of the output costs of unemployment in the form of a reduction in income. People's incomes are lower on average than they would be if there was full employment.

The *incidence* of output loss, or the impact of unemployment on the distribution of income, falls disproportionately on unemployed people, because of the limited extent to which social security benefits compensate unemployed people for the loss of earned income (see the section 'The human cost of unemployment' above). The fiscal cost of unemployment represents that part of the incidence of output loss that is in principle placed on taxpayers, as public spending on unemployment benefits rises and income tax revenues fall. For most OECD economies, each one per cent increase in unemployment raises unemployment benefits paid out by 0.2 or 0.3 per cent of GDP (OECD, 1993, p.39). Then there is the loss of income tax revenue when people lose their jobs. The rise in unemployment in the early 1990s did in fact lead to a deterioration in the public finances of many OECD countries.

There is no doubt that unemployment seriously damages the health of the economy and the well-being of unemployed people. But governments in many industrial nations seem to believe that inflation carries an even more alarming health warning. What are the economic arguments for this position?

3.2   THE COSTS OF INFLATION

After twenty years of variable, if moderate, inflation, *The Economist* proclaimed that 'the best inflation rate ... means zero because anything higher interferes with the fundamental function of prices – their ability to provide information about relative scarcities' (22 February, 1992). The elimination of inflation or the lasting achievement of price stability has been, and in many economies remains, the principal objective of macroeconomic policy. During the past ten years central banks throughout the world have adopted long-run price stability as their primary goal (Temple, 2000). Does inflation inhibit output growth? Are there other costs that inflation imposes on people?

THE COSTS OF ANTICIPATED INFLATION

Inflation may be anticipated by economic agents if their expectations about the future rate of inflation are correct and they are free to adjust their economic activity in the light of those expectations. There are two reasons for believing that even perfectly anticipated inflation might impose welfare costs on society: 'shoe leather' (or monetary) costs and menu costs.

'Shoe leather' costs

One way of anticipating, or guarding against, inflation is for people to economize on cash balances and demand deposits in favour of time deposits (Chapter 11, Section 3.3), so that the interest earned will protect the purchasing power of their income. The 'shoe leather' used up in making frequent trips to the bank is a metaphor for all the productive resources consumed in this way, including fuel and lost output as workers leave their jobs to queue at banks. 'Shoe leather costs' probably contributed to economic collapse under hyperinflation in Germany during 1922–23. Empirical studies on the shoe leather costs of moderate inflation are highly sensitive to the assumptions made in the theoretical models underlying them. In a survey of theoretical models of shoe leather costs, Orphanides and Solow (1990) found a variety of outcomes, depending mainly on the interest elasticity of the demand for cash and on the definition of money, given that cash (or 'narrow money') is a relatively small proportion of the broader money supply.

Menu costs

The menu costs of inflation are the sum of the costs of changing prices and adjusting wages. Resources are used up in revising not only menus but catalogues, price tags, vending machines and so on. Adjusting nominal wage rates may involve a potentially lengthy process of negotiation and hence the costs of the management time devoted to it.

During inflation the price of a good may rise either as part of the inflationary process or as the consequence of a change in market conditions (in this case an increase in demand or a decrease in supply). So menu costs include the costs of gathering information about market conditions. Assuming that firms operate in imperfectly competitive markets and are therefore price makers, they may choose to delay a price rise in response to an acceleration in inflation. Firms may be assumed to change nominal prices only at regular intervals or only when actual prices diverge too far from their optimal level (Blanchard, 1983; Ball and Mankiw, 1994). The costs of changing prices – the menu costs – deter firms from constant monitoring and immediate revision. The irregularities of price changes during inflation may disturb the pattern of relative prices. So relative price variability may be the outcome of the inflationary process itself, even when the inflation is perfectly anticipated (Briault, 1995, p.36). If so, menu costs reinforce the 'inflationary noise' argument that inflation leads to inefficiency and low growth (see below).

THE COSTS OF UNANTICIPATED INFLATION

The most serious costs of inflation are experienced when inflation is unanticipated. Unanticipated inflation is thought to impose costs on society in two main ways: through the unplanned redistribution of income and wealth and through the reduction in economic growth.

Estimating the redistributive effects of inflation is complicated because there are many different routes along which the inflationary process might affect income distribution, making some individuals or groups better off while making others worse off. In class terms, inflation has sometimes been seen as redistributing income away from the capitalist class towards the working class. If rising wage awards are driving inflation, then inflation is associated with an increase in the share of wages in national income at the expense of profits. Inflation also erodes the value of non-indexed financial assets that are disproportionately held by the upper middle class. So inflation can have a progressive impact on income distribution. On the other hand, inflation can undermine the living standards of low income groups relying on state benefits. In many economies, social security benefits such as unemployment benefits and old age pensions are indexed to rise with inflation by earnings. However, if such benefits are tied to the consumer price index when average wages are rising more rapidly, pensioners and other recipients will experience a decline in their standard of living relative to that of the employed population. The redistributive effects of a period of inflation reflect not only inflation itself but also the bargaining power of different social groups. In general it has proved difficult to disentangle the redistributive impact of inflation from the forces of supply and demand, such as changes in the pattern of demand for goods and services and hence changes in the derived demand for different kinds of labour.

The difficulty of making general statements about the redistributive effects of inflation, such as that they always benefit a particular group or are always progressive, does not imply that they are unimportant. Far from it – it is precisely the unpredictability of the redistributive effects of inflation that are sometimes claimed to be responsible not only for its unpopularity but also for much of the real damage that it causes. Baumol and Blinder exemplify this view: 'Why, then, is the redistribution caused by inflation so widely condemned? Because its victims are selected capriciously ... The gainers do not earn their spoils, and the losers do not deserve their fate. This is the fundamental indictment of inflation' (Baumol and Blinder, 1988, p.104).

The 'inflationary noise' argument states that without price stability markets cannot allocate resources efficiently. Inflation distorts the transmission of price signals, so it is said to resemble the 'noise' or background interference that distorts the transmission of radio signals. If you think back to Chapter 5 on perfect competition, you will recall that changes in the conditions of supply and demand – changes in the relative scarcity of resources and in the relative popularity of products – cause price changes that act as signals to consumers and producers. Friedman (1977, p.466) argued that as the inflation rate rises so does its volatility, with the consequence that 'an additional element of uncertainty is, as it were, added to every market transaction'. Economic agents might confuse a price rise that is merely part of the general inflationary background with a price rise that signals a real change in relative scarcity. For example, suppose that a firm buying copper as input to a production process observes a price rise in a highly inflationary environment. If the price rise genuinely signals a change in relative scarcity but the firm dismisses it as 'noisy', it will waste this newly scarce material. If, on the other hand, the price rise is purely inflationary or noisy but the firm misinterprets it as a scarcity signal, it will incur extra costs in needlessly economizing on copper, perhaps by searching for a substitute or a possible alternative supply.

The implication is that high inflation will slow down economic growth. Hence we can evaluate the inflationary noise argument by asking an apparently straightforward factual question: is inflation positively associated with low economic growth? A substantial amount of empirical research on the possible links between inflation and growth has been carried out in recent years. The methodologies used in this research vary considerably. For example, there are different models of economic growth, some of which assume technological change to be endogenous while others take it as given (Chapter 18). Again, some models use time series analysis to test for a correlation between inflation and growth for a single country over many years; others employ cross-country analysis to test for a correlation between inflation and growth at a given point in time.

Two main results emerge from this large and diverse body of empirical work. First, as Friedman (1977) predicted, the variability (or volatility) of relative prices increases as inflation accelerates (Fischer and Modigliani, 1978; Clare and Thomas, 1993). Does this correlation lead to the further link between inflation and growth? The answer is a significantly qualified 'yes'. The result of most studies is that there is a significant negative correlation between inflation and growth at higher rates of inflation. For example, Temple (2001, p.419) concludes from an exhaustive survey of empirical studies that there is 'general agreement that high inflation, say above 100 per cent a year, inhibits growth'. Note the qualification: it is 'high' inflation that damages growth. There is no unambiguous evidence that moderate inflation inhibits growth and it has proved 'extremely difficult to quantify the output gains of moving from, say, 5 per cent inflation to price stability' (Temple, 2001, p.419).

A further qualification must be made to the broad trend of empirical research results. The correlation between high inflation and low growth does not imply that high inflation causes low growth. As noted in Chapter 8, correlation does not establish a causal relationship and certainly does not indicate the direction of causation. Does high inflation cause low growth or does low growth cause high inflation? Or are inflation and (low) growth both the effects of other factors? This interpretation of the evidence is in fact offered by Briault (1995, p.33), who concludes that 'the available evidence supports the view that well-run economies with strong and efficient productive structures tend to exhibit both low inflation and high growth'.

The evidence does not therefore vindicate the choice of price stability as the objective that guides the central banks of the EU and the UK. However, another possible justification for eliminating inflation emerges from statistical work on inflation and growth, one that receives support from some theoretical work. This is that policy makers should aim to keep the inflation rate below about 40 per cent a year, on the grounds that there is a risk that it will accelerate rapidly beyond that rate (Bruno and

Easterly, 1998; Bruno, 1995). The case against 'learning to live with moderate inflation' ultimately rests upon the fear that it might accelerate into high inflation, reducing the rate of economic growth. The policy implication is that the only safe inflation target is price stability, because moderate inflation may accelerate out of control. Section 4 examines the theoretical arguments for this view.

J.M. Keynes on inflation and unemployment

Cartoon by BIF from Peter Pugh and Chris Garratt, *Introducing Keynesian Economics*, Icon Book Limited, 2000

4   INFLATION, UNEMPLOYMENT AND EXPECTATIONS   •••

Some people think we can choose between inflation and unemployment. Let inflation rise a bit they say to get unemployment down. But it doesn't work like that. The two go together. Higher inflation means higher unemployment. It's like an addictive drug, the more you get the more you need and the more damage it does to you.

(Geoffrey Howe, Budget broadcast, 10 March 1981)

Since the late 1970s economic policy in industrial countries has been dominated by the belief that policy intervention based on the assumption of a trade-off between unemployment and inflation will only make things worse – adding to inflation without bringing unemployment down because 'the two go together'.

4.1   THE EXPECTATIONS-AUGMENTED PHILLIPS CURVE

Section 3 showed that the unemployment/inflation trade-off appeared to break down after 1970. This was not in itself fatally wounding to the Phillips curve analysis because it was possible to interpret the combination of rising inflation and unchanged or even rising unemployment as a series of short-run Phillips curves shifting outwards. However, some economists had always been sceptical of the Phillips trade-off on theoretical grounds and they seized upon its empirical difficulties as confirmation of their misgivings.

The theoretical deficiency of the Phillips curve analysis, according to Friedman (1968) and Phelps (1967), concerned its microeconomic foundations, in particular the assumptions it incorporated about the behaviour of economic agents in the labour market. Friedman argued from two main premises. First, he assumed that the demand and supply of labour were functions not of the nominal wage rate but of the real wage rate, that is, nominal wages divided by prices, W/P. Second, he proposed that in bargaining over wage rates, workers use their experience of past inflation to predict future price rises and aim to anticipate these in wage settlements. Friedman's conclusion was that, while there is a trade-off between unemployment and inflation in the short run, a permanently lower level of unemployment cannot be secured by accepting a higher rate of inflation.

Friedman's analysis of the labour market exemplifies the perfectly competitive approach or model (see Chapter 5 and Chapter 7, Section 2). Accordingly, he assumed that workers and unemployed people are rational individual economic agents no less than the profit-maximizing firms they deal with. In other words, the analysis abstracts from considerations of social norms and the psychological pressures of unemployment and from wage bargaining institutions. It presents decisions to accept or reject job offers, to remain in or give up a job, as matters of individually weighing up the disutility of working against its financial rewards. This approach implies that unemployment may occur, not simply because people are actively seeking work but cannot find a job, but also because people are actively seeking work but cannot find a job that provides adequate compensation for giving up leisure or adequate rewards for skills. The concept of frictional unemployment captures the idea that unemployment may occur because of the time it takes to find appropriate work; it underlies the natural rate of unemployment (see below). Friedman believed that government intervention to try to trade off higher inflation for permanently lower unemployment would change agents' expectations and their behaviour in a way that would only make matters worse.

Let us remind ourselves of how a demand expansion works in the absence of inflationary expectations (that is, expectations are for zero inflation and remain unchanged). Policy makers might suppose that a moderate increase in inflation would reduce unemployment. A monetary expansion increases the demand for goods, causing a general rise in prices. Nominal wage rates are slow to respond, so real wage rates fall, persuading employers to move down their labour demand curves and recruit the extra workers they need to increase output. Unemployed people do not incorporate past inflation into their expectations, assuming prices will be stable in the next year. They are willing to work at the unchanged nominal wage rates on offer and unemployment falls. This combination of rising inflation and falling unemployment is shown by a movement north-west from A to B along the short-run Phillips curve PC_1 in Figure 13.4.

Figure 13.4
The expectations-augmented Phillips curve

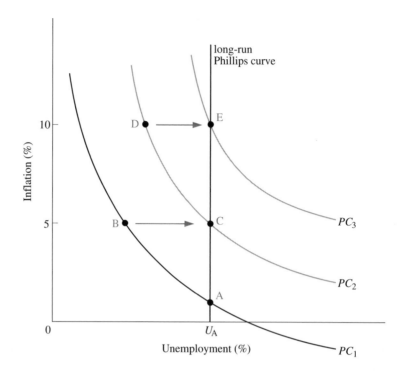

Once we stop and think about this from the perspective of the model of a perfectly competitive labour market, it seems implausible. If people are calculating their prospective rewards from employment – and in the perfectly competitive labour market people are modeled as rational agents who do exactly that – it is commonsense to adjust the money wages on offer for inflation. A rational agent would fail to do so only if there had been so little inflation that the adjustment was not worth the effort. Once we have decided to model people's decisions in the labour market as those of rational agents, we are more or less committed to incorporating expectations of inflation into their behaviour.

That is just what Friedman did. He argued that the process of trading off higher inflation for lower unemployment worked only on the assumption that people did not bother to form expectations about future inflation or that their expectations were mistaken. Once the newly recruited workers incorporate last year's inflation into their expectations of inflation in the next year, they either decide it is not worth working and leave their jobs or negotiate higher nominal wage rates. Either way, unemployment returns to its original level but at the new rate of inflation. This is how the short-run Phillips curve PC_1 shifts outwards to PC_2 as the economy moves from B to C on Figure 13.4.

Policy makers, the story continues, interpret their failure to secure a permanent drop in the unemployment rate as a sign that their choice of expansionary monetary medicine was correct but the dosage was too low. The course of treatment is therefore repeated and the economy moves along PC_2 from C to D while workers are surprised by the new, higher rate of inflation. But once again, as soon as this inflation rate is used as the basis of expectations, the prospect of low real wages reverses the fall in unemployment and the short-run Phillips curve shifts to PC_3 as the economy moves from D to E. The outcome is the original unemployment rate combined with a higher inflation rate, showing that in the long run there is no trade-off between unemployment and inflation. The long-run Phillips curve is vertical, joining the points the economy returns to after each expansionary phase – A, C and E.

Friedman called the rate of unemployment at A, C and E, to which the economy returns after each episode of expansionary monetary policy, THE NATURAL RATE OF UNEMPLOYMENT. The natural rate of unemployment is defined as the rate at which the labour market clears, that is, when labour supply and demand are in equilibrium (Chapter 7). Friedman noted that it reflected some institutional characteristics of the labour market, such as 'the cost of gathering information about job vacancies and labour-availabilities, the costs of mobility and so on' (Friedman, 1968, p.8). Of the other institutional factors mentioned by Friedman, attention has tended to focus on social security benefits. The level of unemployment benefit influences people's individual labour supply curves. If the level of benefit is increased, the urgency of finding work might be diminished, increasing the number of people out of work when the labour market is in equilibrium – that is, the natural rate of unemployment.

THE NATURAL RATE OF UNEMPLOYMENT
The natural rate of unemployment is the rate at which the labour market clears.

In the short run, expansionary monetary or fiscal policies can lower the actual rate of unemployment below this long-run equilibrium, or natural, rate even on competitive assumptions. It follows that the natural rate will prevail only in the absence of expansionary policies. *The natural rate hypothesis*, as this first result of Friedman's analysis is called, states that there is no permanent trade-off between unemployment and inflation because in the long run unemployment returns to its natural rate. The vertical long-run Phillips curve is the diagrammatic representation of the natural rate hypothesis. If expected inflation is the same as last year's inflation, then in the absence of expansionary policies pushing the economy along a short-run Phillips curve actual inflation this year will be the same as last year and hence the same as expected inflation, and the economy is in equilibrium at the natural rate of unemployment. Table 13.1 shows how Figure 13.4 could be interpreted in the light of this model.

Table 13.1 Expected and actual inflation and changes in unemployment

Expected inflation (%)	Actual inflation (%)	Change in unemployment
1	5	falls A to B on PC_1
5	5	rises B to C, PC_1 to PC_2
5	10	falls C to D on PC_2
10	10	rises D to E, PC_2 to PC_3

QUESTION

On this model, how could policy makers maintain unemployment below its natural rate in the long run?

This can be done only by continually expanding aggregate demand, so that the rate of inflation is always accelerating. Workers are therefore constantly surprised by inflation always, if you like, being a year behind in their expectations. This leads to *the accelerationist hypothesis* which is the second of Friedman's results. It states that unemployment can be maintained below its natural rate only by constantly accelerating inflation (Figure 13.5). As people's expectations chase after actual inflation, inflation must accelerate to keep ahead of those expectations. Attempts to peg unemployment below its natural rate will eventually provoke hyperinflation.

Figure 13.5
The accelerationist hypothesis

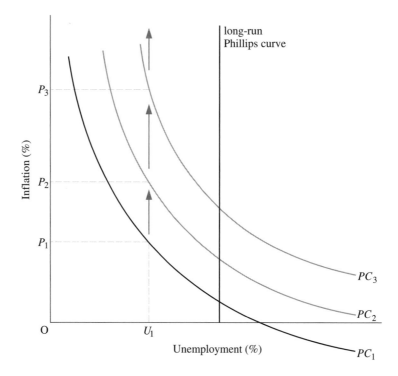

The natural rate and accelerationist hypotheses both depend on Friedman's assumption that expected inflation is precisely equal to last year's inflation. However, while it came to be widely believed in the early 1970s that inflationary expectations were the main cause of the outward shift of the observed Phillips curve, the analysis of those expectations underwent a major revolution.

The main problem with Friedman's assumption about expectations, known as adaptive expectations, was that it committed economic agents to making easily avoidable errors in forecasting inflation. Under adaptive expectations, in forming expectations about the future course of an economic variable, agents rely solely on past values of that variable. They might calculate a weighted average of inflation over the past few years, the greatest weight being attached to last year's inflation and so on.

Or they might learn by their mistakes, incorporating an error-learning mechanism to adjust forecasts by some fraction of the discrepancy between last year's expected inflation and last year's actual inflation – hence the term adaptive expectations. For example, if expected inflation is 6 per cent and the outcome is actually 10 per cent, then the expected inflation rate for next year will be revised upwards.

This procedure works reasonably well if the rate of inflation is stable or changes only slowly but during variable inflation it locks agents into systematic errors, such as constantly being surprised by ever-accelerating inflation. In any case, it is intuitively implausible to suppose that people would focus solely on past inflation to the exclusion of obviously relevant 'background' information, such as the election of a government committed to fighting years of high inflation or the move from national currencies to a single (e.g. European) currency. Surely, it came to be thought, the rational agents who inhabit economic models can do better than adaptive expectations.

4.2   RATIONAL EXPECTATIONS

The rational expectations hypothesis was advanced by Muth (1961), although its significance for macroeconomic theory and modelling was not fully exploited until the 1970s. Muth's basic premise was that 'information is scarce, and the economic system generally does not waste it' (p.316). This probably does not seem particularly remarkable but Muth went on to argue that the information relevant to the formation of inflationary expectations included knowledge of the structure of the model of the economy being used by policy makers. Carter and Maddock explain the significance of this step:

> The innovation introduced by Muth was to consider the expected price as endogenous to the model, and generated by the model itself ... The agents in the market are assumed to know the structure of the model ... and to use this information in order to form their expectations.
>
> (Carter and Maddock, 1984, p.30)

So now 'agents in the market', such as workers negotiating wage claims and unemployed people deciding on job offers, are assumed to know the precise structure – expressible in a series of equations for forecasting the future course of output, inflation and so on – of the economic model used by policy makers. Since economists are notoriously prone to error in making such forecasts, however, it seems implausible to assume that people with no professional interest in them routinely do better.

However, proponents of rational expectations insist that there is no suggestion that all or most individual people in the real world actually form their expectations of inflation in any systematic way. According to Minford and Peel (1983, p.4), all that is being claimed is that the *typical individual* 'utilizes efficiently the information available to him in forming expectations about future outcomes'. Since this is a belief about the 'typical individual', it 'cannot be falsified by examples of behaviour by any actual individual' (p.5). As long as enough real people who 'contribute a dominant proportion of the variability in aggregate behaviour' make the efficient use of all the available information, 'this would be sufficient to generate aggregate behaviour that exhibited rationality' (p.5). What this amounts to is the claim that irrational ways of forming expectations, being randomly distributed across a large sample of the population, cancel out, so that the aggregate outcome is *as if* all agents were rational. The implication is that workers and job-seekers will not make systematic errors, such as those arising from relying solely on past inflation, in forming their expectations of inflation. For example, agents will perceive an expansionary monetary policy aimed at reducing unemployment as a sign of higher inflation, revise their expectations of inflation upwards and act accordingly.

QUESTION

If agents form their price expectations rationally, it seems that they cannot be surprised by a change of macroeconomic policy. Looking back to Figures 13.4 and 13.5 how would this affect the outcome of the strategy of repeated expansions of aggregate demand to peg unemployment below its natural rate?

Under adaptive expectations, the policy reduced unemployment below its natural rate only temporarily, until agents adjusted to the new inflation rate. But, if they form their price expectations rationally, they can never be surprised by policy decisions. So their expectations of inflation will always be accurate and unemployment will not fall below its natural rate even temporarily. The policy will be entirely ineffective. For example, in connection with expansionary monetary policy, Minford and Peel (1983, p.19) argue that if the government changes the money supply rule which they are following, output (and hence unemployment) will not be affected because the new monetary stance is 'incorporated into people's expectations ... and cannot cause any surprises'.

This result requires one more assumption in addition to the rational expectations hypothesis: the further assumption that all markets, including the labour market, clear continuously and immediately in response to shocks, or unexpected changes in the conditions of supply and demand. This is a corollary of the model of perfect competition. The rational expectations hypothesis plus the market-clearing assumption have an important implication for policy: that disinflation, that is, the reduction of the inflation rate, can be achieved without any cost in higher unemployment and lost output.

Rational expectations theory asserts that agents can never be surprised by systematic macroeconomic policy. They incorporate policy rules not only into their forecasts of future inflation but also into their behaviour. So, for example, they react to a contractionary monetary policy by anticipating its downward effect on the rate of inflation, thereby bringing about that effect as they negotiate contracts of various kinds on the assumption of lower inflation. Agents' reactions to policy make the policy work. Price inflation falls but no wage gap opens up and so there is no change in the level of

Agents' expectations

Government policy		do not change	fully anticipate policy
	expansionary	unemployment falls, inflation rises	
	contractionary		

Figure 13.6
Matrix for predicting the effects of inflationary and disinflationary policies on unemployment and inflation

unemployment. If policy makers are convinced that they can rely on agents reacting to policy in this way, they will be much more inclined to tackle inflation without worrying about their policies' effects on unemployment.

EXERCISE 13.2

To check that you have understood the discussion so far, try completing Figure 13.6. The quadrants of the matrix identify the outcomes of the government's inflationary and disinflationary policies, given the reaction of the other economic agents in the economy. The left-hand quadrants show what happens to unemployment and inflation if agents allow themselves to be surprised. The right-hand quadrants show the outcomes if agents rationally anticipate policy effects. The top left-hand quadrant has been completed as an example. Fill in the others.

The implication of the exercise, which you should complete before reading on, is that an expansionary monetary policy to reflate the economy and reduce unemployment is successful if agents fail to react by anticipating upward price level effects, but that under rational expectations (and one further condition explained below) agents anticipate an acceleration in the rate of inflation, thereby bringing it about and leaving the level of unemployment unchanged. A contractionary monetary policy to eliminate inflation works painlessly, without adding to unemployment, provided agents anticipate the downward pressure on prices, but in the absence of this reaction unemployment will rise, at least in the short run.

The effect of introducing adaptive expectations into the analysis of the trade-off between unemployment and inflation was to limit it to the short run. It seems that the impact of introducing rational expectations and market clearing into the analysis is more dramatic: there is no trade-off at all because macroeconomic policy has no effect on output and unemployment.

4.3   THE COSTS OF REDUCING INFLATION

Rising unemployment and the recession have been the price we have had to pay in order to get inflation down – but that is a price well worth paying.

(Norman Lamont, Chancellor of the Exchequer, House of Commons, 16 May 1991)

Section 4.1 discussed the grounds for believing that attempts to exploit the inflation–unemployment trade-off depicted by the short-run Phillips curve will shift the curve outwards, returning unemployment to its natural rate but at ever higher inflation rates. So there is a case for reducing inflation, providing the costs of doing so are acceptable. The view discussed in Section 4.2 and based on rational expectations and market-clearing is that disinflation is 'painless', that is, achievable without any cost in higher unemployment and lost output. However, as the quotation above admits, getting inflation down *has* caused unemployment to rise. This section surveys empirical research on the costs of reducing inflation and discusses some of the theoretical issues it raises.

This account of the costs of reducing inflation draws on Dawson (2002). The costs of reducing inflation are the costs of the higher unemployment brought about by disinflationary policy measures. The standard approach to measuring the costs of reducing inflation, the sacrifice ratio, focuses on the output costs of unemployment, abstracting from the other costs discussed in Section 3.1. The sacrifice ratio is the ratio of the cumulative percentage loss of GDP incurred by the policy for each one percentage point reduction in the inflation rate thereby achieved (Ball, 1994). Considerable uncertainty surrounds empirical estimates of the sacrifice ratio. Reviewing the historical evidence, Ball (1993) estimated average sacrifice ratios for a number of economies; they ranged from 2.92 for Germany and 2.39 for the US to 0.79 for the UK and 0.75 for France. Sacrifice ratios for disinflationary episodes are dispersed around these averages. The different theoretical perspectives on the Phillips curve examined in Sections 2, 4.1 and 4.2 underlie conflicting empirical estimates of the probable magnitude of the output loss. There are five main influences on the sacrifice ratio:

THE INITIAL INFLATION RATE

The standard shape of the short-run Phillips curve shown in Figure 13.1, which is flatter at lower rates of inflation, implies that the output cost of reducing the inflation rate by one percentage point is lower if the inflation rate at the outset is higher. So the cost of each successive percentage point of disinflation increases the more closely price stability is approached.

EXPECTATIONS

Adaptive expectations imply that after a lag economic agents adjust to a new inflation rate, in which case reducing inflation incurs costs only during the lag while unemployment is above the natural rate. The length of this lag and hence the duration of the costs of reducing inflation depends on the speed with which agents' expectations that influence the wage and price-setting process adapt to the new inflation rate.

THE PACE OF ADJUSTMENT

This is the dilemma between gradualism and 'cold turkey'. Policy makers will phase in a disinflationary policy gradually if they believe that people take time to adjust their expectations of inflation, while others believe that a 'shock effect' might precipitate a rapid adjustment of expectations. Cold turkey may be the appropriate policy response to hyperinflation, because the costs associated with a very high inflation rate are likely to be greater than the costs of a sharp disinflation (Briault, 1995).

POLICY CREDIBILITY

Policy makers have credibility to the extent that economic agents believe their announcements of policy rules. In addition to the government's commitment to a systematic disinflationary policy being unequivocal, disinflation can be achieved at low cost to the extent that there is a consensus in favour of the policy (Sargent, 1993).

IMPERFECTLY COMPETITIVE MARKETS

If all markets cleared instantaneously and approximated to the model of perfect competition, there would be a minimum of delay in adjusting to a new policy stance. However labour markets are imperfectly competitive, with wage bargaining between employers and trade unions being informed by assumptions about a 'fair wage' (Chapter 7, Section 4; Chapter 12, Section 2.4). Wage bargaining typically involves annual inflation adjustment. Goods markets are imperfectly competitive, giving firms some discretion in the timing and extent of price changes. Menu costs 'include the time taken to inform customers, the customer annoyance caused by price changes and the effort required even to think about a price change' (Mankiw, 1990, p.1657). While menu costs seem small at the aggregate level (Section 2.2), they may be sufficiently large for individual firms to make them reluctant, in monopolistically competitive markets, to lower their prices when the demand for their goods declines as a consequence of disinflationary policies.

The importance of expectations and credibility is widely appreciated among economists and policy makers but few believe that markets clear rapidly, so the general view is that reducing inflation incurs significant costs at least in the short run. Policy credibility and expectations also influence the scale of those costs. Using a model developed by the IMF, Chadha *et al.* (1992) found that the sacrifice ratio is lower if the policy is phased in gradually, if the policy stance is credible and if expectations of future inflation play a large part in determining wage and price setting. Perfectly informed policy makers would weigh these costs against the costs of inflation and might conclude that 'there are advantages in achieving and maintaining price stability' (Briault, 1995, p.42).

5   UK MACROECONOMIC POLICY

This section will trace the policy implications of the theoretical developments expounded in Section 4, using current UK monetary and growth policies as an illustration. One lesson that policy makers seem to have taken from macroeconomic theory and performance since the 1970s is the importance of keeping inflation low to prevent the damage to output and employment that occurs when it accelerates towards an annual rate of 40 per cent. Another lesson is that if the rate of inflation has to be reduced, costs in terms of lost output and employment will be incurred, mainly because economic agents operate in imperfectly competitive markets. And finally, it is clear that if policy design and implementation take into account the importance of policy credibility and inflationary expectations, the costs of getting inflation down and keeping it low can be reduced. It follows from these considerations that the role of macroeconomic policy is to manage aggregate demand with the objective of maintaining low inflation. This strategy raises two questions, which this section will address. First, what are the implications for the conduct of monetary policy within such a framework? Second, if policy towards aggregate demand is so constrained, what can the government do about unemployment and the growth of output?

5.1   AGGREGATE DEMAND AND INFLATION

In many industrialized economies the central bank has been assigned the task of meeting an inflation objective, and to do so through changes in nominal short-term interest rates. This degree of central bank independence is thought to enhance the credibility of a low-inflation strategy, because central bank officials will not be deflected from pursuing it by considerations of political unpopularity. The central bank seeks to do so by raising interest rates when inflation rises, on the view that such an increase in interest rates will reduce aggregate demand and hence inflation. In acting in this way central banks are following a monetary policy rule (Chapter 12, Section 3.2). The monetary authorities could target a single economic variable, such as inflation, or a combination of variables, such as output, employment and inflation. The simplest monetary policy rule is to change the interest rate in response to variations of inflation. It is the mandatory policy rule of the Bank of England to use the rate of interest to reach a target rate of inflation.

The Bank of England ('the Bank') is the central bank of the United Kingdom. It was founded as a private bank in 1694 but soon became the banker of the government. It was nationalized in 1946 and gained operational independence in 1997. The Bank is responsible for ensuring the effectiveness and the stability of the UK financial system and also for operating monetary policy. If the UK government sets the objective of low inflation (in 2002 this meant inflation in the range 1.5 per cent per annum to 3.5 per cent per annum) the Bank has the duty of staying within these limits through its conduct of monetary policy, that is, through variations in the rate of interest.

> The Bank sets an interest rate for its own dealings with the market and that rate then affects the whole pattern of rates set by the commercial banks for their savers and borrowers. This in turn affects spending and output in the economy, and eventually costs and prices. Broadly speaking, interest rates are set at a level to ensure demand in the economy is in line with the productive capacity of the economy. If interest rates are set too low, [aggregate] demand may exceed [aggregate] supply and lead to the emergence of inflationary pressures so that inflation is accelerating; if they are set too high, output is likely to be unnecessarily low and inflation is likely to be decelerating.
>
> (Bank of England, *Notes on Monetary Policy*, www.bankofengland.co.uk)

Interest rate decisions are taken by the Monetary Policy Committee (MPC) of the Bank. The MPC is made up of the Governor, the two Deputy Governors, two executive directors and four external members appointed directly by the Chancellor of the Exchequer, and meets monthly to make decisions on interest rates. When the inflation rate is forecast to exceed the target range, the Bank of England raises the short-term interest rate in order to reduce the level of aggregate demand. Conversely, if the inflation rate is forecast to fall below the lower limit of the target range, the Bank of England drops the short-term interest rate in order to increase the level of aggregate demand.

The sequence of events through which the central bank affects the level of national income and the inflation rate is known as the transmission mechanism (Chapter 12, Section 3.2). Figure 13.7(a) (overleaf) shows the monetary policy rule line. When the forecast rate of inflation increases from π_0 to π_1, the central bank raises the short-term nominal interest rate from $i(\pi_0)$ to $i(\pi_1)$. As a result of this change, the cost of liquidity for commercial banks is now higher. Banks consider the interest rate i as the direct cost of liquidity over which they mark up their profit margin:

$$r = (1 + m)i$$

where r is the price of loans to firms, that is, the interest rate on loans, and m is the percentage mark-up (i.e. overhead and profit) which the banks apply. It is assumed here that, in general, banks maintain a constant mark-up. Therefore, when central banks change the interest rate i, banks increase their lending rates r by the same proportion. For a given expected return, this means that the investment demand falls. As the investment curve in Figure 13.7(b) illustrates, the increase in lending rates from $r(\pi_0)$ to $r(\pi_1)$ leads to a decrease of the level of investment from I_0 to I_1. Investment demand is a component of the aggregate demand and so, *ceteris paribus*, the level of aggregate demand decreases.

Figure 13.7
The aggregate
demand/inflation
curve

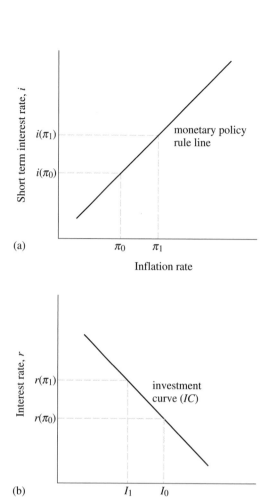

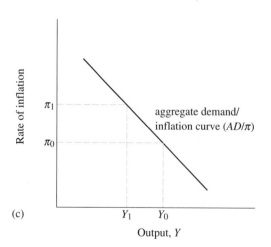

Figure 13.7(c) shows the aggregate demand/inflation curve, which summarizes the relationship between the level of output and the rate of inflation when the monetary policy rule is to change the interest rate in response to changes in the inflation rate: the higher the rate of inflation, the lower the level of output. The monetary policy rule of setting interest rates to maintain low inflation or price stability together with the investment demand explains the negative relationship between the rate of inflation and the level of output.

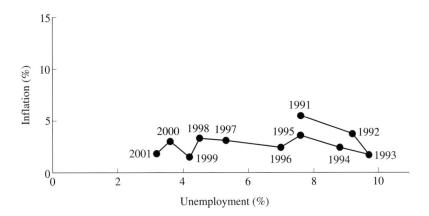

Figure 13.8
The UK Phillips
curve 1991–2001

Source: Office for National
Statistics, 2002

The aggregate demand/inflation curve is a relationship between two economic variables: the level of output Y (equal to the level of income), and the inflation rate π that measures the rate of change of the general level of prices. The rate of inflation is measured on the vertical axis and the level of output on the horizontal axis. The aggregate demand/inflation curve then tells us the total demand of commodities by households, firms, government and foreigners at any given inflation rate, which is translated into a corresponding level of output. The aggregate demand/inflation curve is downward sloping, showing that, *ceteris paribus*, a fall in the inflation rate would raise the demand for goods and services.

The Bank of England's monetary policy rule, and the UK government's anti-inflation stance in the years preceding the Bank's operational independence, have important implications for the shape of the short-run Phillips curve.

QUESTION

> **What does Figure 13.8 tell you about the relationship between unemployment and inflation in the UK in the 1990s?**

The UK Phillips curve in the 1990s resembles the almost flat segment of the original UK Phillips curve (Figure 13.1). Over the period 1991–93 the inflation rate fell while the unemployment rate rose, suggesting a trade-off between unemployment and inflation. Since then the curve has been virtually flat, as unemployment has fallen while inflation has been held steady. This can be explained as the outcome of UK policy makers' recognition that the long-run Phillips curve is vertical and their successful use of a monetary policy rule to maintain low inflation. Why has unemployment fallen in such circumstances? One answer is that rising productivity, in part associated with new information technology, has fuelled output growth and increased employment. Haldane and Quah (1999), for example, argue that current UK policy makers' behaviour 'gives rise to the horizontal Phillips curve, with inflation anchored at target by monetary policy and output driven by productivity shocks'.

Does this mean that policy makers have discovered how to control inflation but have had to acknowledge that output and employment, 'driven by productivity shocks', are beyond their control? Not necessarily, for two reasons. First, the aggregate demand/ inflation curve showed that inflation and output are negatively related, *ceteris paribus*, lower inflation being associated with higher output (Figure 13.7). The explanation is that while inflation is low, the Bank's monetary policy rule implies that interest rates are also low, leading to higher investment and hence higher output. Second, there are other economic policies that governments can deploy to influence productivity and output growth. These can be explained in terms of a shift in the aggregate demand/ inflation curve.

5.2   OUTPUT EXPANSION AND THE SUPPLY SIDE

Policy makers can seek to influence output growth in two ways. Getting inflation down would move the economy along the aggregate demand/inflation curve to a new combination of lower inflation and higher output (Figure 13.7). Increasing the level of output associated with a given inflation rate would shift the aggregate demand/ inflation curve to the right, as shown in Figure 13.9(b). How might this be achieved?

Figure 13.9   A shift in the aggregate demand/inflation curve

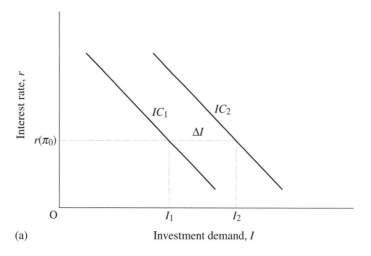

(a)

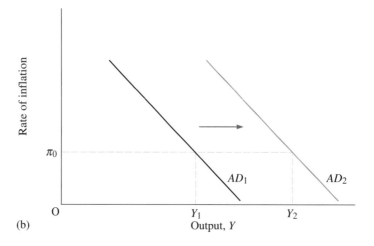

(b)

The interest rate on loans, representing the cost of borrowing money from banks, is one of the main factors affecting investment demand and hence aggregate demand. This relationship explains the slope of the aggregate demand/inflation curve. However, when the expected returns on investment rise (perhaps because firms become more confident about the prospects for future growth), the demand for investment also rises. Figure 13.9 illustrates this situation, in which, for a given interest rate, an increase in the expected returns on investment produces an increase in investment demand and hence in aggregate demand. In Figure 13.9(a), any event that raises the expected returns from investment increases the profitability of investment and so increases investment demand for a given interest rate. The investment demand curve therefore shifts outwards. Figure 13.9(b) shows the positive effect of this change on the aggregate demand/inflation curve. For any rate of inflation, an increase in the expected returns from investment shifts the aggregate demand/inflation curve to the right.

Among the events that might increase the expected returns on investment is a positive 'productivity shock', perhaps caused by the introduction of new technology (Chapters 2 and 3). This would offer the prospect of a greater than proportionate increase in output and hence potentially greater profits from investment in additional inputs of labour and capital. A range of 'supply side' policies can be used to increase the productive capacity of the economy, that is, its potential for supplying goods and services, by increasing productivity. Competition policy seeks to encourage innovation, with potential productivity gains as well as greater efficiency from more intense competition (Chapters 4 and 5). The Chancellor of the Exchequer (UK finance minister) has recognized the possible macroeconomic benefits of competition policy. As one commentator put it, 'Thanks to the Chancellor, we are witnessing a recognition of the fact that competition policy has an important role to play in achieving the macroeconomic goal of sustained non-inflationary economic growth' (Selzer, 2001, p.101). Labour market policy measures to encourage the development of human capital held out the prospect of improved labour productivity (Chapter 7). Governments can reduce frictional unemployment by providing counselling and information services to employees, and recruitment services to employers.

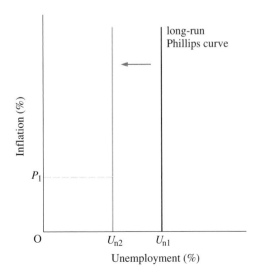

Figure 13.10 The effect of a positive productivity shock on the natural rate of unemployment

The final step in explaining the theoretical foundations of current macroeconomic policy is to relate the increase in output for a given inflation rate, shown by an outwards shift in the aggregate demand/inflation curve, to the long-run Phillips curve. The monetary policy rule has established a nearly horizontal short-run Phillips curve, which represented maintaining low inflation and leaving output to productivity shocks. The implication is that, in the absence of such shocks, unemployment will remain at its natural rate. The falling unemployment rate depicted by the horizontal short-run Phillips curve in Figure 13.8 is therefore likely to be at least in part the result of a series of positive productivity shocks. Technological progress increases the demand for skilled labour and policy measures to improve training and reduce frictional unemployment allow this to be met without increasing inflation through higher wages and hence production costs. Technological innovation and supply side policies may have combined to reduce the natural rate of unemployment, shifting the long-run vertical Phillips curve from U_{n1} to U_{n2} in Figure 13.10. This shows that for a given inflation rate the natural rate of unemployment is lower following a positive productivity shock.

6 CONCLUSION

Unemployment and inflation are the headline issues of macroeconomic policy making, reported by the media month by month and year on year. This chapter has focused on these issues, which used to be thought of as the concerns of short-run macroeconomic policy but which are now much more influenced by considerations of the long-run growth prospects of the economy. In the 1960s and early 1970s macroeconomic theorists generally advised policy makers to tolerate moderate rates of inflation in an effort to achieve full employment. Since then there has been a shift towards the view that price stability is either a necessary condition of long-run growth and high, if not full, employment or at least a sign of a competently, even prudently, managed economy (see Chapters 18 and 20). There is general agreement that an appreciation of the importance of expectations and policy credibility has the potential to improve macroeconomic management, provided that policy is also guided by an understanding of the way in which imperfectly competitive markets work.

WINNERS AND LOSERS FROM GLOBALIZATION: THE INTERNATIONAL ECONOMY

CHAPTER 14 INTERNATIONAL TRADE AND PRODUCTION

Anthony Venables ●

Objectives

After studying this chapter you should be able to:

● understand the role of comparative advantage in determining the pattern of trade
● understand how the terms of trade help to explain the distribution of the gains from trade
● appreciate the importance of market structures in determining the pattern of trade
● discuss the significance of foreign direct investment as an alternative to trade.

Concepts

● globalization
● comparative advantage
● absolute advantage
● terms of trade
● intra-industry trade
● foreign direct investment

1 INTRODUCTION   ●

Globalization is one of the most hotly debated features of today's world economy. Its basis is increased cross-border interaction: primarily in the form of increased flows of trade in goods and services, but also through increased flows of international capital. The UK's international trade in 1999 amounted to around 26 per cent of GDP; that is, imports per head and exports per head both averaged approximately £4300. Nearly one-half of these imports and exports were with partner countries in the European Union (EU), a further third with other high-income countries and the remainder with middle- and low-income countries.

These international flows affect all of us as consumers, and most of us as 'producers'. The prices of the goods we are able to purchase as consumers and the variety available are determined, directly or indirectly, by international trade. Some productive activities are not directly involved in international trade (the standard example is haircuts) – but most of them are. In many sectors of the economy the market conditions faced by firms are determined by competition in world markets. These world market conditions also affect firms' employment levels, and hence wages and incomes throughout an economy.

It is not only individuals in high-income countries who are affected by the flows of trade and investment. Trade creates new opportunities for economic development that have been successfully taken up by some low-income countries. The combined exports of many of the economies of East Asia have increased ten-fold in real terms over the last 25 years. Other low-income countries have been less successful in responding to the opportunities created by trade, and some have even come to see trade as more of a threat than an opportunity.

The objective of this chapter is to lay out the basic economics of international trade and foreign direct investment. In Section 2 I shall outline the facts concerning trade. How large are trade flows, and how and why have they increased? I shall also look briefly at the institutional structures in which trade takes place, in particular at the World Trade Organization (WTO).

International trade poses several questions for the economist.

First, what determines trade flows? Part of the answer to this question can be found in the differences between countries. Some goods are produced more cheaply in some countries than in others, and these differences create profitable opportunities for trade. Differences of this type are referred to as a *comparative advantage* and they will be explored in Sections 3 and 4. But it is not only differences between countries that generate trade. We also observe high volumes of trade between similar countries – within the EU for example. This trade is the natural outcome of competition between firms located in different countries, and it often takes the form of 'intra-industry' trade. I shall examine this phenomenon in Section 6.

Firms also penetrate foreign markets and access foreign sources of supply by becoming multinational – that is, by undertaking production in more than one country. These long-term investments in factories or service operations are referred to as *foreign direct investment* (FDI) and will be the subject matter of Section 7.

The second set of questions looks at the effects of trade on the economy. In particular, they ask about who gains and who loses from trade, and whether trade is beneficial for the economy as a whole. The existence of *gains from trade*, under a wide range of circumstances, is one of the most important conclusions from international trade theory. I shall examine these gains in Section 3. Even if society as a whole gains from trade there may well be individual gainers and losers, so I shall also investigate the way in which trade can redistribute income within an economy.

The third set of questions concerns trade policy. What are the effects of deploying trade policy instruments such as *import tariffs*? Should countries follow a policy of free trade, or should they take a more protectionist stance? If trade restrictions are employed, who gains and who loses from such restrictions? These questions form the subject matter of Section 5.

The method I shall use to answer these questions is the usual one of building models. The topic is potentially enormous, so it is essential that we focus on the key questions and exclude other issues from the analysis. At the outset two such exclusions should be noted. This chapter will not deal with the balance of payments or exchange rate determination (both of which are discussed in Chapter 16). This is not as strange as it may seem. A balance of payments deficit occurs if, collectively, the citizens of a country consume more than they produce. It can be financed only by running down previously held assets or by borrowing from the citizens of other countries, and neither of these activities can continue indefinitely – people will lend only if they expect to be repaid. What this means is that, on average over time, a country's balance of payments must be in balance; a deficit and borrowing today must be associated with a surplus and a paying back at some other date. This chapter is concerned with long-run fundamentals rather than short-run fluctuations, so it is proper for us to concentrate on situations in which the balance of trade is in balance. The same goes for exchange rate determination; we are concerned with the underlying competitiveness of different sectors of the economy, and to investigate this we do not need to study short-run exchange rate movements or inflation rates. Indeed, I shall simply discuss relative prices, without specifying whether they are denominated in dollars or euros.

2 WORLD TRADE

'Globalization' hit the headlines after many years in which world trade increased substantially faster than world income. The ratio of exports to national income over time for countries grouped by per capita income is shown in Figure 14.1. There have been modest increases in the ratio for high- and middle-income countries, and a much larger increase for low-income countries. It has been argued that the picture painted by Figure 14.1 may even understate the importance of the growth of trade, as rich countries devote an ever-higher share of income and expenditure to service activities that are largely non-traded – health care for example. If we exclude this aspect, and simply look at the ratio of trade to merchandise GDP (the value added in the production of physical goods), we see much sharper increases – the ratio for high-income countries jumped from around 40 per cent in the early 1980s to 60 per cent in 2000.

It is interesting to put these changes into historical perspective. The period from the nineteenth century to the start of the First World War also saw a growth in trade to income ratios. The inter-war period saw a collapse in world trade, followed by a steady recovery from 1950 onwards. In the UK, the 1913 level of the trade to income ratio is only now being overtaken.

Figure 14.1
Export to income
ratios

Source: World
Development Indicators,
World Bank, various years

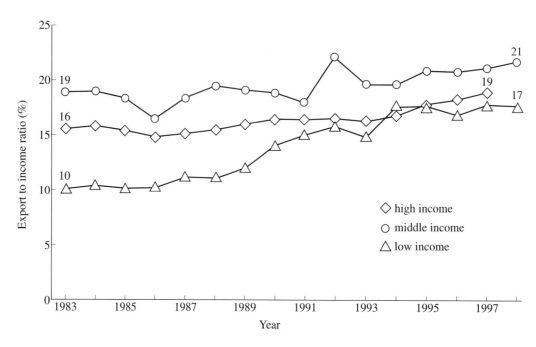

What has driven these dramatic changes in trade volumes? One factor is transport and
communication technologies: estimates of the real costs of ocean shipping show rates
falling by nearly two-thirds between 1830 and 1910, and then halving again by 1960.
Some more recent experience is given in Figure 14.2. Ocean and air freight charges fell
substantially in the post-war period but bottomed out from 1960 for ocean freight and
the early 1980s for air freight. New information and communication technologies have
also had an impact on trade volumes. Furthermore, the combination of better
telecommunications, air freight and faster ocean transport has led to substantial time
savings in international transactions, which have facilitated trade growth.

Figure 14.2
Transport and
communication costs

Source: Baldwin and
Martin, 1999, p.13

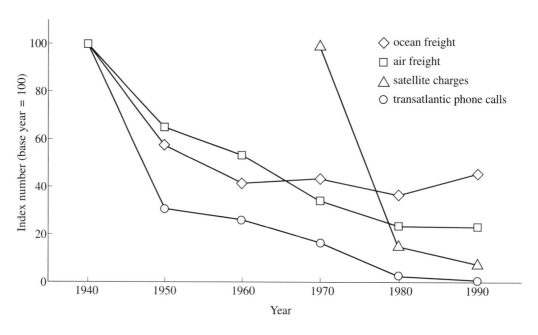

In addition to the steady decline in transport and communication costs, there has been the much less steady pattern of trade policy. The historical record is shown in Figure 14.3. The vertical axis is a measure of import tariffs (that is, the percentage tax rates on imports) for a sample of 35 countries. Nineteenth-century tariff rates were low, and Britain had completely free trade. The average was rising somewhat, however, as the USA and some European countries sought to industrialize behind tariff barriers. The inter-war period saw a dramatic lurch into protectionism by all the major countries. The notorious Smoot–Hawley Act of 1930 raised average US tariff rates to over 60 per cent, and by 1933 the exports of the main industrial nations had fallen to 25 per cent of their 1929 levels.

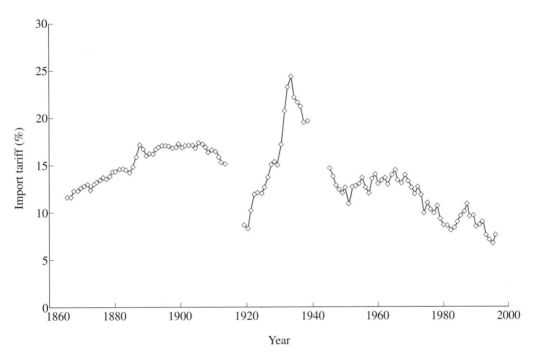

Figure 14.3
World average tariff rates, 35 countries (unweighted percentage)

Note: The gaps mark the dates of the First and Second World Wars. Source: Clemens and Williamson, 2001, p.32

After the Second World War responsibility for liberalizing world trade was taken up by GATT, the General Agreement on Tariffs and Trade. This was set up by the allied powers as part of the post-war settlement, along with the International Monetary Fund (IMF) and the International Bank for Reconstruction and Development (IBRD, more commonly known as the World Bank). GATT initiated negotiations to liberalize trade, and deep tariff cuts were made in the late 1940s and early 1950s. These cuts were followed up by the Kennedy Round of trade negotiations in the 1960s, the Tokyo Round of the 1970s, the Uruguay Round of the 1980s and 1990s, and the recent Doha Round. The success of these negotiations has been impressive and they have brought about a steady decline in tariff rates. In developed countries the import tariffs on manufactures now average less than 4 per cent, although agricultural protection remains high: in 1999 agricultural import tariffs averaged 17 per cent in the EU and 11 per cent in the USA.

Two other developments are noteworthy. The GATT became the World Trade Organization (WTO) in 1995 and extended its role in several ways. One was to start promoting the liberalization of trade in services (under the General Agreement on

Trade in Services or GATS) and the removal of barriers to inwards investment (under the Trade Related Investment Measures or TRIMs agreement). The members also agreed to accept a dispute settlement procedure, under which trade disputes go to a WTO panel with binding powers.

The other development has been the formation of numerous regional integration agreements alongside the 'multilateral' trade liberalizations of the GATT/WTO system, in which countries have agreed to liberalize internal trade between member states. The most successful of these agreements, sometimes known as 'free trade areas' or 'customs unions', has been the EU. Other major agreements include the North American Free Trade Agreement or NAFTA (comprising Canada, the USA and Mexico) and Mercosur (comprising Argentina, Brazil, Uruguay and Paraguay). NAFTA, Mercosur and other countries in the Americas are also currently holding discussions with a view to forming a Free Trade Area of the Americas. In the middle of 2000 some 114 regional integration agreements were in effect and more than one-third of world trade took place within such agreements.

The growth of world trade outlined in this section has occurred only because individual producers and consumers perceived a benefit from trading with foreign countries, despite the inevitable trade and transport costs that international trade incurs. What are the sources of these benefits?

3   COMPARATIVE ADVANTAGE AND THE GAINS FROM TRADE

The basic framework for analysing the determinants of trade flows and the effects of trade on the economy is the idea of comparative advantage. I shall follow tradition by developing the idea in terms that go back to David Ricardo, writing in 1817.

3.1   COMPARATIVE ADVANTAGE

The simplest model is one with only two countries (which I shall call Home and Foreign) and two goods (which I shall call bicycles and coats). Each country can produce both goods, and consumers in each country want to consume both goods. If there is no trade, the consumers must be supplied by local production. What happens when there is trade? The country that is, relatively speaking, more productive in terms of producing bicycles expands the output of bicycles and exports them; the country that is relatively more productive in the coat industry expands the production of coats and exports coats.

This apparently obvious statement has some hidden depths. To bring them out we must first study the productive potential of each economy in more detail. We can do this using the concept of a *production possibility frontier*, which describes how much of the two goods each country can produce. Figure 14.4 illustrates the production possibility frontiers (from now on abbreviated to ppf) for two countries: Home and Foreign. The vertical axis is the number of coats produced and the horizontal axis is the number of bicycles produced. Concentrate for the moment on the bold line H–J on Figure 14.4(a). This is Home's ppf, and the points on the line indicate the output levels that Home can achieve. Thus if Home produces no bicycles it can produce 200 coats; if it produces no coats it can produce 100 bicycles. A number of combinations are possible, so the output mixture 100 coats and 50 bicycles also lies on the ppf line.

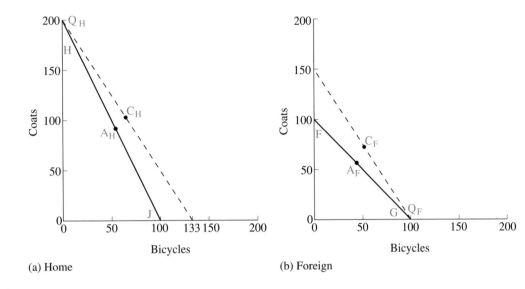

Figure 14.4
Production possibility frontiers and the gains from trade

(a) Home

(b) Foreign

The ppf is a rather general concept. It certainly need not be a *straight* line, as in Figure 14.4, and it can be generalized into more dimensions to handle more than two goods, in which case it can no longer be represented by a line at all. For my purposes here I want to keep the shape of the ppf simple and investigate what underlies the ppf in each country. We can do this by developing a somewhat detailed numerical example. Suppose that Home has 100 workers and that each worker can produce either two coats or one bicycle. The Home ppf is constructed by observing that if all the workers are employed in the coat industry, Home can produce 200 coats; if all the workers are employed in the bicycle industry, Home can produce 100 bicycles. Employing some workers in each industry means that a number of different combinations of bicycles and coats are possible, and these combinations are given by the ppf.

The Foreign ppf is given by the line F–G on Figure 14.4(b). It is constructed in a similar way but using different numbers. Let us assume that Foreign has 200 workers, each of whom can produce either 0.5 coats or 0.5 bicycles. If all workers are employed in the coat industry, the output is 100 coats and zero bicycles, and so on.

If there is no trade between Home and Foreign, a situation known as 'autarky', the level of production in each country is determined by consumer demand at, say, point A_H in Home and A_F in Foreign.

QUESTION

Suppose that the Home economy wants to consume one more bicycle. What is the cost to the Home economy of this extra bicycle?

Although we usually measure the cost of something in terms of money, a more fundamental measure is what has to be given up in order to attain the thing. This is referred to as the *opportunity cost*. Thus, the opportunity cost of a bigger house is the holiday you forego; the opportunity cost of working another hour is the leisure you miss; and so on. In our example, the opportunity cost of one extra bicycle in the Home economy is two coats. This is because one worker has to be reallocated from the coat industry to the bicycle industry to produce the extra bicycle, causing coat production to fall by two units. If we do the same thought experiment in Foreign, we can see that to produce one more bicycle here means reallocating two workers, thereby cutting the output of coats by one unit. The opportunity cost of one bicycle in Foreign is therefore one coat.

Now allow for trade, and suppose that the relative prices on the world market (in which our two countries are the only traders) are such that 1 bicycle costs 1.5 coats. We can think of this in terms of the price of a bicycle being $300 and the price of a coat being $200, although it is not necessary to specify these prices exactly. It is only the ratio that matters – that is, 1.5:1. How does this ratio affect production and consumption in each economy? In Home, the production of each bicycle has an opportunity cost of 2 coats, but importing a bicycle costs 1.5 coats. Home therefore closes its bicycle industry and specializes in the production of coats at point Q_H on Figure 14.4(a). It can purchase bicycles on the world market, and the combinations of bicycles and coats it can attain by producing coats at Q_H and trading are shown by the dashed line.

QUESTION

Why does this dashed line strike the horizontal axis of Home bicycle production at 133 bicycles?

If all Home's coat production were exported it could afford to import 133 units of bicycles (200 coats at a price of $200 can fund the purchase of 133 bicycles at a price of $300). But consumers want to consume both goods, so Home's consumption will not go this far but will stop at a point such as C_H.

In Foreign we have the converse situation. Each bicycle produced has an opportunity cost of 1 coat and exporting a bicycle finances the purchase of 1.5 coats. The bicycle industry expands, and the Foreign economy ends up at point Q_F on Figure 14.4(b), that is, specializing in bicycles (100 bicycles).

QUESTION

If Foreign exports all its bicycle production, how many coats can it buy?

If Foreign exported all of its bicycle production (100 units) it could afford to import 150 coats (100 × $300/$200), but the domestic demand for bicycles will mean that some are consumed at Home. So consumption will end up at a point such as C_F.

Note that the pattern of trade we have outlined is consistent, in so far as each good is exported by one country and imported by the other. It must also be the case that the exact quantity exported by each country equals the quantity imported by the other (that is, supply equals demand in world markets). The world prices of the two goods will adjust so that this is true.

I have spelled out this example in detail as it allows us to draw some important conclusions. First, trade is determined by a comparison of the opportunity costs of producing each good in each country. Bicycles are exported by the economy with the lower opportunity cost of producing bicycles (Foreign) and imported by the economy with the higher opportunity cost of producing bicycles (Home). Because it is cheaper (in terms of opportunity cost) to produce bicycles relative to coats in Foreign than it is in Home, we say that Foreign has a COMPARATIVE ADVANTAGE in bicycles. In the same way, Home has a comparative advantage in coats. It is comparative advantage that determines the pattern of trade.

Note that our example has been constructed with Home having an ABSOLUTE ADVANTAGE in the production of both goods – it is assumed that Home's workers are more productive than Foreign's workers in the production of both bicycles and coats. But this does not mean that Home exports both goods. This is obviously impossible, as Home would be importing nothing in return and Foreign would not have the export revenue to finance its imports. Instead, each country specializes in the good in which it is *relatively* productive (that is, it has comparative advantage) and exports that good. This leads us to a further observation. Every country has a comparative advantage in something. A country may be unproductive in every activity, but compared with other countries it will be relatively less unproductive in some activities than others – and these are the activities in which it has a comparative advantage.

Superficially, there is a paradox here. How can a country that is unproductive in all activities compete in world markets? The paradox is resolved by observing that wages differ from country to country. To apply our example again, recall that the price of a coat is $200. Each worker in Home works in the coat industry and produces two coats; so if the markets are perfectly competitive the worker earns $400. At this wage the cost of producing a unit of output just equals the price it will fetch (assuming for the sake of simplicity that there are no other factors of production that must be paid). In Foreign all the workers are employed in the bicycle industry; each produces 0.5 of a unit of output, which sells for $300, giving the workers a wage of $150. Absolute efficiency differences have therefore created wage differences between the two countries.

Table 14.1 pursues this line of reasoning and summarizes the model. The first block of the table gives the labour inputs required to produce a bicycle and a coat in each country. If the wages are as shown in the second block, the unit costs of production of each good in each country are as described in the third block. If we compare these costs with world prices (which, with free trade, are also the internal prices in each

COMPARATIVE ADVANTAGE

A country has a comparative advantage in the production of good X if the opportunity cost of producing a unit of X, in terms of other goods foregone, is lower in that country than it is abroad.

ABSOLUTE ADVANTAGE

A country has an absolute advantage in the production of good X if it costs less in terms of resources to produce a unit of X in that country than it does abroad.

country) it is clear that the pattern of production and trade must be as predicted by comparative advantage. Home's firms can just break even by producing coats, but any firm attempting to produce bicycles would make a loss. Similarly, Foreign's firms break even producing bicycles, but any Foreign firm producing coats would make a loss.

Table 14.1 Wages, costs and prices in a simple trade model

	Labour units to produce 1 unit		Wages ($)	Unit cost of production ($)		World price ($)	
	bikes	coats		bikes	coats	bikes	coats
Home	1.0	0.5	400	400	200	300	200
Foreign	2.0	2.0	150	300	300	300	200

3.2   AGGREGATE GAINS AND THE TERMS OF TRADE

The argument so far shows why trade will occur and what the pattern of trade will be. Another important conclusion that follows from the principle of comparative advantage is that each country *gains from trade*. Consider Figure 14.4 again. If there is no trade, Home consumption has to lie somewhere along the line H–J, that is, without trade you can consume only what you produce. Similarly, Foreign's consumption has to lie along the line F–G. Trade increases the size of each economy's consumption set, in the sense that each economy can now afford to consume more than it could in the absence of trade. Thus the points C_H and C_F have a higher consumption (of both goods) than do the points A_H and A_F. There are two reasons for this welfare gain. First, trade allows countries to specialize according to comparative advantage, thus bringing about an efficient world allocation of production. Second, countries are no longer constrained to consume what they produce; they can exchange goods through world trade and hence consume along the dashed lines in Figure 14.4.

There may also be individual winners and losers within countries, and trade liberalization often encounters fierce opposition from potential losers. We shall see further examples of this later in the chapter. However, the theory tells us that each country as a whole gains from trade, in the sense that total gains exceed total losses; each country could therefore afford to compensate the losers and still come out with net gains.

Although both countries gain from trade, it does not follow that both countries gain equally. The theory says simply that both countries are better off with trade than they are without trade. To analyse the distribution of the gains between countries we need to look more closely at the prices at which trade takes place. In the example so far, world prices are such that 1 bicycle costs 1.5 coats. What would happen if the price of bicycles fell, so that 1 bicycle could be purchased for 1.25 coats (or, in dollars, if the price of a bicycle falls to $250 while the price of coats stays at $200)? The effect of this would be to flatten the dashed lines on Figure 14.4 (the world price ratio). Home's entire output of 200 coats (point Q_H) now generates enough revenue to purchase 160 bicycles instead of 133 bicycles, but Foreign's entire output of 100 bicycles (point Q_F) will buy only 125 coats not 150 coats. The effect on the consumption points is clear. Home will be made better off by the price change, as C_H can move up and to the right; but Foreign will be made worse off, as the original point C_F can no longer be afforded.

TERMS OF TRADE

A country's terms of trade are the ratio of its export prices to its import prices.

$$\text{Terms of trade} = \frac{\text{index of export prices}}{\text{index of import prices}} \cdot 100$$

The change in the price of bicycles we have just described is referred to as a change in the *terms of trade*. For Home, exporting coats, the fall in the price of bicycles is a terms of trade improvement, and it is made better off as a consequence. For Foreign, exporting bicycles, it is a terms of trade deterioration, and it is made worse off as a consequence.

This shows that it is the terms of trade that determine the distribution of the gains from trade between countries, and that changes in the terms of trade cause one country to gain and the other to lose. Thus falling primary commodity prices in the world economy have caused real income losses for many low-income countries. They are still better off trading than not trading, however. Our analysis of the gains from trade still applies, but a country that has experienced a terms of trade deterioration is getting a smaller share of the gains.

Terms of trade changes can be an important mechanism for spreading the benefits of economic growth in one country to other countries. For example, suppose that rapid technical progress increases labour productivity in the manufacture of computers, and suppose also that the UK has no computer manufacturing industry. The UK has no workers in the computer industry, so it does not gain directly from the productivity increase. But as productivity increases, the price of computers falls. This will show up as a terms of trade improvement for countries importing computers, such as the UK, which are thereby able to share the benefits of the technical progress.

The concepts of comparative advantage and the gains from trade outlined in this section are sometimes regarded as the most important results in the whole of economics. They apply at the national level and at the individual level. It may be that a doctor is better than a farmer both at practising medicine and at growing potatoes. It does not follow that the doctor should both practise medicine and grow potatoes. If each specializes in the activity in which they have a *comparative* advantage, and then engages in trade, they are *both* better off than they would be if each tried to be self-sufficient.

One of economics' first Nobel laureates, Paul Samuelson, was once challenged by a distinguished mathematician to name one proposition in the social sciences that was both true and not trivial. He found it difficult, or so the story goes. But some time afterwards he realized what he should have said – comparative advantage and the gains from trade. To quote from Samuelson (1969): 'that it is logically true need not be argued before a mathematician; that it is not trivial is attested by the thousands of important and intelligent men who have never been able to grasp the doctrine for themselves or believe it after it was explained to them'.

4   SOURCES OF COMPARATIVE ADVANTAGE   • • • • • • • • • •

I have argued that comparative advantage determines the pattern of trade, but I have not examined why a country might have a comparative advantage in a particular product or set of products. In the previous section I took the easy, but unsatisfactory, expedient of simply assuming that some economies were relatively more productive in some goods (as measured by the productivity of the workers in each industry). In this section I shall look a little deeper into the determinants of comparative advantage.

QUESTION

What do you think are the likely determinants of national comparative advantage?

The two main sources of comparative advantage are cross-country differences in technology and in endowments, that is, the stocks of labour, capital and other resources in a country. We saw some of the implications of cross-country differences in technology in Section 3. These differences arise because of different intensities of research and development (R&D) activity, and different speeds of absorption of new technologies in different countries. The study of this takes us well beyond the scope of this chapter, and I shall make just two remarks. First, in so far as technology is itself internationally tradable, this does not provide a basis for comparative advantage. It is only by being able to keep continually ahead that technology gives a country a comparative advantage. Second, to say that technological leadership is a possible source of comparative advantage is not much use unless we know what determines technological leadership. We must therefore push further back, to see what gives a country a comparative advantage in R&D.

This suggests that we should also focus our attention on the second source of comparative advantage referred to above – international differences in endowments. Each economy contains within it quantities of natural resources, land of different types, labour of different skill levels and physical capital of different sorts (machines, roads, houses and so on). We can refer to each of these human and physical resources as a separate *factor of production*. And we can refer to the collective stock of factors of production as the *endowment* of the economy. Endowments may change over time – as saving leads to the accumulation of more capital, or education raises the skill level of the labour force. But at each point in time the endowment determines the productive potential of the economy, the relative productivity of the economy in each good, and hence the comparative advantage of the economy.

The relationship between an economy's endowment and its comparative advantage is the subject matter of the Heckscher–Ohlin theory of trade. (Eli Heckscher and Bertil Ohlin were Swedish economists writing in the first half of the twentieth century.) The theory is based on two observations. The first observation is that economies differ in the relative quantities of their different factors of production. India is relatively abundantly endowed with unskilled labour, the USA with skilled labour, and Germany with physical capital (machinery and so on). The second observation is that the production of different goods requires the usage of factors of production in different proportions: aircraft production is quite skilled labour intensive; the assembly of electronics is rather unskilled labour intensive. Putting these observations together, the theory predicts that countries will have a comparative advantage in goods that are relatively intensive users of the factor of production with which they are relatively well endowed. Thus, the USA has a comparative advantage in aircraft production, for example.

The theory accords well with common sense, although it has not been easy to find empirical support for it. In the first attempt to test the theory (published by Wassily Leontief in 1953) it was found that, contrary to expectations, the imports of the USA were more capital intensive than its exports. This perverse finding was probably due to the fact that Leontief failed to distinguish between skilled and unskilled workers, and hence failed to capture the skilled labour (or human capital) intensity of US exports. More recent studies have disaggregated countries' factor endowments – for example, a study by Bowen *et al.* (1987) looked at seven types of labour, three types of land, and physical capital, but still found only weak support for the theory.

Heckscher–Ohlin theory has more to offer than the observation that countries have a comparative advantage (and hence will export) the goods intensive in factors with which they are relatively well endowed. It also provides a structure within which we can investigate the effects of trade on the prices of different factors of production – that is, on the wages of skilled and unskilled labour, land rents, and the return on capital. Suppose that Foreign is well endowed with unskilled labour and Home is relatively poorly endowed with unskilled labour. One would then expect the wages of unskilled labour to be relatively low in Foreign (there is a lot of it) and high in Home (where it is relatively scarce). Now allow for trade. Foreign will export goods intensive in unskilled labour, and this will have the effect of raising the demand for unskilled labour, and hence will raise the wage. Home will import goods intensive in unskilled labour, so reducing the demand for Home's unskilled labour and reducing the wage. This argument suggests two things. First, that we can identify the gainers and losers within each economy from trade. And second, that trade will tend to bring about the convergence of factor prices across countries.

The identification of gainers, and possible losers, is straightforward. Relatively abundant factors in a country will gain from trade, and relatively scarce factors may lose. For example, consider the enlargement in 1994 of the North American Free Trade Agreement (NAFTA) to include Mexico.

QUESTION

Decide which of the following are likely, in principle, to be in favour of the extension of NAFTA to include Mexico.

- **Skilled labour in the USA.**

- **Unskilled labour in the USA.**

- **Unskilled labour in Mexico.**

- **The owners of capital in the USA.**

It is to be expected that the owners of capital and skilled labour in the USA would have been in favour of the treaty, as capital and skilled labour are the factors that the USA is abundantly endowed with, relative to Mexico. At the same time, it is to be expected that unskilled labour in the USA would have been opposed to the treaty, as their position of relative scarcity would have been removed once there was free trade with Mexico. This was true in the run up to signing the treaty, just as it is now the case that some US labour unions are among the most vocal opponents of globalization. Furthermore, recent decades have seen a large increase in wage inequality in the USA, with the wages of high-skill workers rising much more rapidly than those of unskilled workers. Some of this is probably attributable to trade, although the consensus among people who have researched this issue is that the development of new technologies has been much more important than trade (for example, the replacement of unskilled workers by automated production processes).

The prediction that trade will bring about an international convergence of factor prices has important implications, although it is controversial. Evidently, factor prices are not the same in all countries, and the theory predicts that any barriers to trade or any international differences in technology will limit factor price convergence. (As we saw in Section 3, international differences in technology lead to differences in wages.) Despite these reservations, the idea that trade may lead to an international convergence of factor prices is clearly of great importance in a number of contexts. For example, it suggests that openness to trade is a good policy for a less developed country seeking to raise the wages of unskilled workers. A less developed country is likely to have a comparative advantage in products that require intensive unskilled labour; by exporting these products the country will raise the demand for unskilled labour and bid up their wages.

Another example concerns East–West trade. There are currently enormous differences between wages in Eastern and Western Europe, and the EU is concerned about the possible flows of migrants from Eastern Europe that this might cause. Trade theory suggests that this concern should lead the EU to have a liberal trade policy, permitting Eastern Europe to export labour intensive products to the West. This will raise the demand for labour in the East, and contribute to narrowing the East–West wage gap. This argument can be put in starker terms. Existing East–West wage differentials are probably unsustainable; they can be narrowed either by Eastern workers moving west to take jobs (migration), or by the development of labour-intensive industry in the East that sells its products to the West (trade). The latter is probably politically preferable.

A similar analysis can be applied in other contexts. For example, if NAFTA narrows the gap in wages between unskilled labour in Mexico and unskilled labour in the USA, this may reduce Mexican immigration pressures on the USA in the long run.

Each of these arguments illustrates how trade can change the distribution of income in a country, but we must remember that the gains from trade results still hold. There may be gainers and losers, but the economy gains in aggregate from trade liberalization, so the gainers could afford to compensate the losers (in principle if not in practice).

5 TRADE POLICY ●

So far we have concentrated on two rather extreme situations – no trade and free trade. However, historically at least, free trade has been rather rare. Governments have employed a variety of trade policy measures both to restrict trade volumes and, by taxing trade, to raise government revenue. The main instruments of these interventions have been import tariffs and quotas. A TARIFF is a tax imposed on imported goods, in addition to the usual domestic taxes. A QUOTA is a quantity limit on import volumes, typically administered by making importers obtain a licence and ensuring that a fixed supply of licences is available. Other instruments of trade policy have been used at times – for example, the creation of trade or shipping monopolies. Trade policy can be used on exports as well as on imports. For example, many oil exporters set an export tax on oil.

TARIFF
Tariffs are taxes imposed on imports of goods or services.

QUOTAS
Quotas are quantitative limits placed on the volume of imports of specific goods or services over a specified period.

5.1 THE EFFECTS OF TRADE POLICY

How does trade policy affect the economy? In order to study this problem I shall concentrate on a single good that is both imported and produced domestically, and consider the implications of putting a tariff on the good. I shall conduct the analysis by looking at supply and demand for the single good. However, I must first note a few of the implications of the tariff for the wider economy.

A tariff will cut the volume of imports to the economy. In Section 1 I argued that an economy's trade must be in balance in the long run. If a tariff cuts imports it must, in the long run, also cut exports. The mechanism through which this is brought about is a change in relative prices, which we can think of as a change in the exchange rate. A lower volume of imports will improve the balance of trade, which will lead the exchange rate to be higher than it would have been otherwise, which in turn will reduce exports. This negative effect of import policy on exports is sometimes overlooked, with dire consequences. Many less developed countries have followed policies involving tight import controls, causing their currencies to be 'over valued' and frustrating attempts to develop export industries.

A partial equilibrium analysis of a tariff is given in Figure 14.5. The horizontal axis measures the production and consumption of the good under study; the vertical axis measures the price of the good. The home economy's supply (S) and demand (D) curves are illustrated. If there is no trade the price would have to be P_a, that is, the

Figure 14.5
The welfare effects of
a tariff

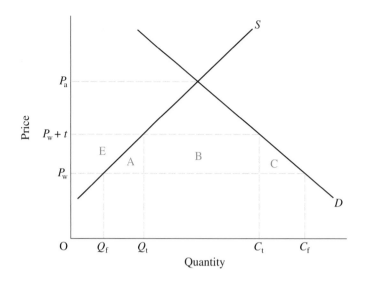

price at which home supply equals home demand. Suppose now that the price of the good on the world markets is P_w (expressed in domestic currency units). If there is free trade this is also the price inside the home economy. At this lower price, consumption is C_f and production is Q_f. The difference between domestic consumption and production, $(C_f - Q_f)$, is met by imports.

EXERCISE 14.1

Explain what would happen if P_w were above P_a in Figure 14.5. Illustrate your answer with a diagram.

Now consider the effects of a tariff at a per unit rate of t. This is added to the world price, giving a price (in the home economy) of $P_w + t$, and a consumption and production of C_t and Q_t respectively. As would be expected, imports fall.

QUESTION

Who are the gainers and losers from the tariff?

Note first that the government collects the tariff revenue; the value of this is the volume of imports $(C_t - Q_t)$ times the tariff rate, t, so it is given by the area B. Consumers lose, as the price they pay for the good has increased by t per unit; the cost is the price increase multiplied by the consumption level C_t, giving the area E + A + B, plus the cost associated with the tariff-induced reduction in consumption (area C), giving a total cost to consumers of area E + A + B + C. Home producers receive a higher price. Their gain is the area E, measuring the higher price on the quantity they produce (E + A), minus the increased marginal cost of supply, A.

Aggregating these items we have a net *loss*; that is:

$$B - (E + A + B + C) + E = -(A + C)$$

The tariff has therefore reduced welfare in the economy as a whole.

In intuitive terms, this loss comes from two sources. Recall that the home supply curve also gives the home marginal cost of production as a function of quantity produced. As production expands from Q_f to Q_t, so the economy is producing at a marginal cost greater than P_w, the price at which the good could be imported. Evidently, this is inefficient, and it costs the economy A. It is similar on the demand side. The demand curve measures the marginal benefit of consuming each quantity. Cutting consumption from C_f to C_t means that consumers forego consuming units of the good for which the marginal benefit (the height of the demand curve) exceeds the cost of supply (P_w), generating a loss C.

A number of remarks need to be made about the observation that a tariff causes a welfare loss. The first is that the result is obviously intimately related to our earlier discussion of the gains from trade. You can see how welfare levels change (how the size of the area A + C changes) as the level of the tariff, t, is varied from zero (free trade) to the prohibitive level at which trade goes to zero ($P_w + t = P_a$).

Second, the analysis makes clear the gainers and losers from a tariff. Government gains revenue from the tariff. In societies with poorly developed tax systems this makes trade an attractive tax base for the government, and goes some way to explain the historical importance of tariffs. Consumers lose from the tariff. Producers in the protected sector are better off. It is worth reflecting for a moment on who these 'producers' are. The beneficiaries will usually be the owners of factors of production used intensively in the protected sector. To take an example, a tariff (or other means of protection) on imports of agricultural produce will usually raise the price of land (a factor used intensively in agricultural production), and thereby benefit landowners. Of course, these landowners are also consumers, but not all consumers are landowners. Thus it is usually the case that consumer losses are widely spread across the population and may be small for each consumer, while producer benefits affect fewer people but are relatively large for each individual affected. It is often argued that this makes it easier to organize effective producer lobbies than it is to organize consumer lobbies, which may result in a protectionist bias to government policy. This is so even though the analysis tells us that the combined gains and losses (to government, consumers and 'producers') are negative, producing a net loss for the society as a whole.

5.2   THE OPTIMAL TARIFF

In the preceding subsection we argued that protection reduced welfare. Are there circumstances in which this result can be overturned? The answer is affirmative in two quite distinct sets of circumstances. These circumstances go under the labels 'the optimal tariff argument' and 'second best tariffs'. I shall explore these circumstances in this and the following section.

In our analysis of tariffs we assumed that the world price of the product under study was constant, and unchanged by the tariff policy. However, this may not be the case, as the effect of a tariff is to reduce demand for the product, and this may be expected to have an effect on the world price. In general, a fall in demand will tend to reduce the world price, and this is a terms of trade improvement from the point of the view of the importing country. It will bring a gain in welfare which could offset the losses identified so far, and it may even bring a net gain to the economy. The optimal tariff is the tariff rate that maximizes this net gain.

EXERCISE 14.2

Explain in your own words how a tariff on imports can reduce the world price for a good.

Figure 14.6
Optimal tariffs and welfare

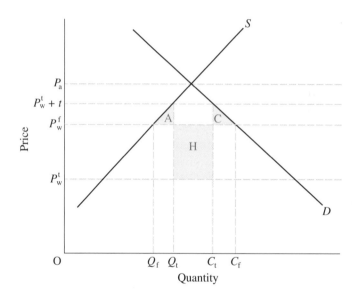

Figure 14.6 illustrates this point. The free trade position is P_w^f with production Q_f and consumption C_f, as before. What happens when a tariff of size t is imposed? The world price now falls. I shall discuss the determinants of how much it falls later on, but for now just suppose that it falls to P_w^t. However, the domestic price, inclusive of the tariff, rises to $P_w^t + t$.

How does this change our welfare assessment? Changes in the welfare of consumers, the welfare of producers and government revenue can be found in the same manner as before. Doing this, the net effect of the tariff is seen to be a loss A + C, as before, plus a new element, a gain H. The interpretation of H is straightforward. The economy is now importing $C_t - Q_t$. The tariff has caused the world price of its imports to go down by an amount equal to $P_w^f - P_w^t$. The value of this reduction in the price of imports (a terms of trade gain) is the quantity imported times the price reduction, that is, the area H. By reducing the world price of imports the tariff has improved the terms of trade of the home economy, and the value of this is the area H. It is certainly possible that the area H is greater than the area A + C, which means that it is possible that welfare can be increased by a tariff. The value of the tariff that maximizes the gain is called the 'optimal tariff'.

Does this provide a practical case for trade policy intervention? Answering this question requires us to consider two points. The first is whether countries can influence their terms of trade. This depends on the elasticity of the supply curve that each country faces for its imports. The foreign supply curve is not shown on Figure 14.6 (which is complicated enough), but we can work through the implications of a number of different cases. If it is infinitely elastic (horizontal) the world price is fixed, the country is unable to improve its terms of trade and the optimal tariff is zero. A less elastic (steeper) supply curve means that reductions in import demand lower the world price and hence support larger optimal tariff rates. The slope of the curve is an empirical matter, which turns on how much of world demand (or supply) of a product a country controls. It is unlikely that Mauritius, for example, can affect the world price of oil by anything it does. But it is likely that if the USA were to raise the domestic price of oil significantly (for example, by a tax or tariff) it would reduce demand by enough to cause a reduction in the world price, thereby improving the terms of trade of oil-importing countries.

The second consideration that must be taken into account is the effect of these policies on other countries. One country's terms of trade improvement is, necessarily, another country's terms of trade loss. A tariff that improves the terms of trade is therefore a 'beggar thy neighbour' policy. If one country employs the tactic it may gain, but only at the expense of others. If all countries employ the tactic, they are all worse off. This is a standard prisoners' dilemma (see Chapter 6). The message is, of course, that international co-ordination of behaviour is needed precisely to avoid mutually damaging trade wars. This is a major function of the World Trade Organization.

So far in this section I have talked about imports, but an exactly analogous argument holds for exports. The optimal import tariff argument is that a country may be able to drive down the price of its imports by importing less. Analogously, a country may be able to drive up the price of its exports by exporting less. This argument is familiar at the firm level from monopoly theory – a firm raises price by restricting sales. At the country level it asserts that a country may be able to exploit monopoly power over the rest of the world by cutting exports, raising price, and thereby improving its terms of trade. At first, it seems a little surprising that a country might want to cut its exports, but the example of OPEC makes the point. By restricting oil exports OPEC was, in the 1970s and early 1980s, able to increase the world price of oil dramatically, and turn the terms of trade in favour of OPEC (and other oil-exporting countries) and against oil-importing countries. Many other groups of primary commodity producing countries have tried to emulate OPEC's initial success by forming export cartels to restrict exports and thereby raise price. However, single countries have not usually had sufficient monopoly power to be able to control world prices effectively, and cartels formed of a number of countries have frequently failed to agree on export limits and so had very limited success.

5.3   SECOND BEST TARIFFS

A perfectly competitive economy leads to an efficient allocation of resources (see Chapter 8). That is, price signals work to equate the marginal social benefits and marginal social costs of different activities in the economy. However, the presence of 'imperfections' in the economy – externalities, monopoly power and so on – mean that price signals are no longer accurate measures of social marginal costs and benefits. When this happens there is a possibility that policy intervention can be employed to bring gains to the economy. The question I shall address in this section is: in the presence of such imperfections in the economy, what is the role of trade policy?

The answer to this question is that trade policy may have a *second best* policy role. The idea is simple. Imperfections call for a policy response, and we define the *first best* policy to be that policy which is targeted directly at the imperfection. For example, if there is domestic monopoly, the first best policy is to regulate so that the firm is forced to set price equal to marginal cost (see Chapters 4 and 5). However, if the first best policy cannot be implemented (for whatever reason) there *may* be a welfare gain from using some less well targeted policy instrument, this being referred to as a 'second best' policy response. Trade policy may be such an instrument. But for imperfections in the home economy, international trade policy is *never* first best.

The idea of policy targeting and the distinction between first best and second best policy are important because trade policy is sometimes advocated as an instrument for just about everything from curing unemployment to preserving national culture. The theory of policy targeting provides a systematic way of appraising these proposals. It says that given a policy proposal, one should first identify the problem and subject it to careful diagnosis. On the basis of this a hierarchy of policies can be formulated, in which the 'first best' is a policy targeted directly at the problem that has been identified, the 'second best' is less well targeted, so may have some undesirable side-effects of its own, the 'third best' is even less focused, and so on.

The general theory of microeconomic policy formulation is well beyond the scope of this chapter. However, I shall endeavour to give a flavour of these arguments using the example of the famous infant industry argument for protection. The infant industry argument is that a new industry – which may be perfectly efficient and profitable in the long run – may need initial assistance to get started, and that this assistance can be provided by offering protection (an import tariff) in the early stages of development. In view of the theory of policy targeting, how should this argument for protection be assessed?

The starting point is the observation that (if there are no imperfections) the economy only wants the industry if it is profitable, in the sense that the present value of future profits are greater than present losses. But in this case, forward-looking entrepreneurs should be able to anticipate the future profits, and investment in the industry would go ahead, even without protection. This just says that in order to make the case for policy intervention, we need to identify the imperfections that might prevent entrepreneurs from undertaking the investment. What might these imperfections be?

Clearly, the particular imperfections depend on the industry and country under study. One sort of problem identified in the literature is associated with 'short termism'. This arises if there is a shortage of entrepreneurs, or if there are problems in the capital market that make it difficult to raise capital to finance current losses on the basis of expected future profits. In this situation there is a case for policy intervention – without it the economy might forego profitable long-run projects. But first best policy is evidently the capital market; markets for 'venture capital' must be established to finance long-term projects. If this is impossible, however, protection could be used to create incentives strong enough to attract even short-term investors. This ensures that the investment is undertaken. But as the policy is not properly targeted, it will have undesirable side-effects. For example, the tariff reduces consumer welfare (the loss of area C in Figure 14.5, Section 5.2). The policy is therefore second best, and there is ambiguity about its overall desirability.

A second sort of imperfection is relevant to the infant industry argument as applied in the context of low-income countries. In many low-income countries urban industrial wages are many times higher than wages in agriculture, which leads to massive urban unemployment and the creation of large 'informal' urban sectors. Relatively high urban wages discourage investment from coming in and soaking up this unemployment. The first best policy response is to subsidize modern sector urban employment, in order to make the wage paid by employers closer to the real supply price of labour in the economy. However, such a policy is probably infeasible – revenue for an employment subsidy is simply not available. An alternative policy is to set an import tariff and protect the industry. Such a policy was widely followed in many low-income countries, and had some initial success in expanding industrial employment. But the policy is certainly second best, and its costs are now widely recognized. Countries that followed these 'import substituting' policies typically ended up with an industrial structure out of line with their comparative advantage. In particular, their industrial structure was relatively capital intensive, and so failed to employ labour to the extent required. Tariffs and import substitution also – as we have seen – damaged export industries, in some countries hitting agriculture in particular. And because the new industries were not in line with comparative advantage, hopes that tariffs could be removed after the industries had 'grown up' proved to be false.

These examples confirm our theoretical expectations about the role of trade policy in acting as 'second best' policy to offset imperfections elsewhere in the economy. Second best tariffs have benefits – for example, they may well enable a country to meet some objective, such as increasing employment in an 'infant' industry. But they also have costs, precisely because they are second best instruments and are not targeted exactly on the distortion in the economy. Some of these costs can be easily anticipated – for example, the consumer welfare loss discussed in Figure 14.5. Other costs (such as the damage that import tariffs cause to export industries) are often not fully anticipated when the policy is introduced. The message is that second best policy will have implications throughout the economy that may be difficult to quantify, which policy makers can overlook, and that the costs of these might outweigh the intended benefits of the policy.

6   TRADE AND MARKET STRUCTURE   • • • • • • • • • • • • • • •

The careful reader will have noted that throughout the discussion so far I have maintained two very strong assumptions. The first is that if a country imports a product, it does not also export products of the same industry; that is, we have assumed that all trade is *inter*-industry. However, in reality a very high proportion of trade, particularly between similar countries, such as trade within Europe, is *intra*-industry trade; that is, trade which involves a country both exporting and importing products of the same industry. The second assumption is that markets are perfectly competitive; we have so far largely ignored issues to do with market structure or firms' market power.

It turns out that these two assumptions are closely related, and in this section I shall relax them both. I shall allow for market structures that are less than perfectly competitive, and investigate the way in which this may generate intra-industry as well as inter-industry trade. As will become apparent, relaxing these two assumptions requires the extension, but not the replacement, of the analytical framework and results discussed thus far.

6.1   THE PATTERN OF TRADE

Why should a country both import and export products of the same industry? There are two very natural explanations. The first is based on variety. Within most industries output consists of the production of differentiated goods; different firms produce different varieties of product, designed to appeal to different sections of the market. If each variety on offer appeals to some consumers in each country we expect to see intra-industry trade, with home varieties being exported and foreign varieties being imported.

The second explanation is based on the behaviour of firms in markets that are less than perfectly competitive. If markets are imperfectly competitive, even putting issues of product differentiation to one side, firms located in the home country will have an incentive to try to export to the foreign market. Foreign firms have the same incentive, so that the natural process of competition between firms will generate intra-industry trade. It is worth exploring this point in slightly greater detail.

Suppose that conditions are such that the price of the product under study is equal in the two countries, home and foreign. If there is perfect competition then each firm chooses the level of output at which marginal cost equals price, and the firms do not care where their output is sold. Under these circumstances we would not observe two-way intra-industry trade in the same product. But if there is imperfect competition the firms will have separate marginal revenue schedules in the two markets. Even though price may be equal in both markets, marginal revenue may not be, and this generates incentives to sell in both markets. Putting the same point differently, firms will form separate sales strategies in each market, and this will generate international trade. The precise form of the sales strategies – and hence the marginal revenue curves and volumes of trade – will depend on the form of the competitive interaction between firms (Chapters 4 and 6).

How does the existence of large volumes of intra-industry trade fit in with our previous discussion (in Sections 3 and 4) of the determinants of the pattern of trade? To combine these ideas we have to distinguish between gross and net trade flows. Gross trade flows are the total volumes of imports and exports in an industry, and net trade flows are the difference between them; so the UK has large gross imports and exports of motor vehicles but is a net importer of vehicles. We now have two complementary theories of international trade. Gross trade flows are determined by product differentiation and the interaction of firms in imperfectly competitive markets. Net trade flows depend on which country has most of the industry's production in relative terms, and this is determined by comparative advantage – the technological and factor endowment differences discussed in Section 4.

6.2 GAINS FROM INTRA-INDUSTRY TRADE

The gains from trade that we have identified so far come from allowing production to locate according to comparative advantage. To this we now add two further potential sources of gain. The first is the product variety effect of trade: trade presents consumers with an increased range of varieties. Although this effect is difficult to quantify, few of us would deny that we would be impoverished if imported varieties of goods ceased to be available.

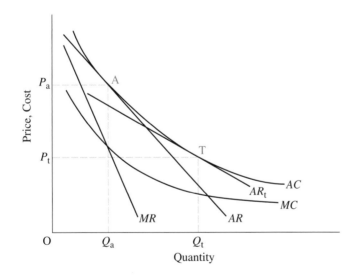

Figure 14.7
Equilibrium of a firm in monopolistic competition before and after trade

The second source of gain is the pro-competitive effect of trade. To see this point, consider a monopolistically competitive industry in an initial position with no international trade. Production in the industry is subject to increasing returns to scale and the number of firms is determined by the condition that there are, in the long run, no abnormal profits. The equilibrium of a single firm in the industry is illustrated in Figure 14.7. Marginal costs are represented by the line, MC, and increasing returns to scale mean that average costs, AC, are falling with output (these can be thought of as long-run average costs). The marginal revenue (MR) and average revenue (AR) curves are downward sloping, and the equilibrium is at point A with output Q_a and price P_a. At this point the firm chooses output to maximize profits (production is where

$MR = MC$), and the number of firms in the industry has adjusted to give zero profits ($AR = AC$). The key point to note about the diagram is that AR is below AC everywhere except at point A, where it is tangential to it; in other words, the best that the firm can do is make zero (abnormal) profits.

What is the effect of trade on such an industry? The simplest thought experiment is to suppose that there are two identical economies, each containing the same number of firms in the industry. Reducing trade barriers between the economies causes intra-industry trade to occur, as each firm now exports as well as supplying its home market. Each market is now supplied by twice as many firms (both home and foreign). This increase in competition in each market will usually squeeze price–cost margins and hence force some firms out of business – through bankruptcy or merger. The remaining firms become larger and, if there are increasing returns to scale, will have lower average costs. This is illustrated in Figure 14.7. Increased competition means that the AR curve facing each firm becomes flatter – if one firm increases price it now leads to a larger loss of sales to rivals. The new AR schedule is illustrated in Figure 14.7 by the line AR_t and equilibrium is at point T, where AC is tangential to AR_t. The number of firms in the industry may have changed, and it must certainly be the case that each remaining firm's scale has increased, from Q_a to Q_t. There are increasing returns to scale, so average cost and price are now lower, with price falling from P_a to P_t. The lower price, lower average cost and increased exploitation of economies of scale provide an additional source of gains from trade. To summarize, the effects of trade are more firms supplying each market, and hence more intense competition, and fewer firms producing in each country, with the remaining firms larger and operating at lower average cost. This reduction in average cost is a source of efficiency gain in addition to the comparative advantage gains and variety effects.

Several further points need to be made about what we have labelled the pro-competitive effects of trade. First, the story above has the gains coming from increased competition driving firms down their average cost curves. It may also be the case that an increased intensity of competition forces firms to improve their internal organization, thus reducing costs further. Such effects have been found by econometric studies of corporate performance (Nickell, 1996, for example).

Second, it is possible that the potential pro-competitive effects of trade can be frustrated by what may appear to be rather small trade barriers. Part of the motivation for the Single Market Programme of the EU in 1992 was the observation that, despite several decades of 'free trade' between member states, national borders were still acting to restrain competition between firms. Obstacles to trade, such as frontier formalities, differing national product standards and a pro-domestic bias in government procurement policies, seemed to be allowing firms to retain dominant positions in their home markets. The European Single Market sought to remove these barriers and thereby increase the intensity of cross-border competition and release the pro-competitive gains of trade outlined above.

The third observation on the pro-competitive gains from trade is the qualification that – unlike gains from comparative advantage – it is not *necessarily* the case that all countries are gainers. This point is best made by modifying the previous example. In Figure 14.7 it was assumed that there were a large number of firms in the industry, so entry and exit reduced abnormal profits to zero. Now consider an industry that has extreme increasing returns to scale – for example, very high product development costs, such as in the aircraft industry. Suppose that these returns to scale are large enough that, when trade barriers are high and there is no trade, each country has just a single firm which acts as a monopolist. This situation is illustrated in Figure 14.8(a) overleaf, in which MC and AC curves are drawn, and the curves AR_a and MR_a are the average and marginal revenue curves faced by the firm. The firm produces at Q_a and charges price P_a. Average cost at this level of output is AC_a. Since P_a exceeds AC_a the firm makes abnormal profits, given by area Π_a. However, these profits are not large enough to encourage the entry of a second firm.

What happens if trade is liberalized? The firms now compete, this squeezing their profit margins. Figure 14.8(b) has the same cost curves as Figure 14.8(a), but the average and marginal revenue curves correspond to those that would be faced by the firm if it were a duopolist, that is, a domestic monopolist competing in world markets with a single foreign firm. These curves are labelled AR_d and MR_d; as discussed previously, increased competition makes the average revenue curve flatter (compare Figure 14.8(b) with Figure 14.8(a)). The example is constructed with AR_d below AC everywhere, illustrating that, with duopoly, the firms are bound to make losses. The minimum attainable loss is area L. This means that one firm must exit the industry.

Figure 14.8(c) is drawn following the exit of one of the firms, so the remaining firm is a monopolist at the world level and has the average and marginal revenue curves AR_t and MR_t. This world monopolist sets price P_m, and makes profits given by area Π_t.

In this example then, trade causes one firm to disappear and the other to become a world monopolist. Who are the gainers and losers from this? As before, increasing returns to scale means that average costs fall, so the world as a whole is getting the product more efficiently. But the country that is now importing the product has to pay the monopoly price, P_m in Figure 14.8(c), whereas before it was paying the average cost of production, AC_a in Figure 14.8(a). This makes the importing economy as a whole worse off – the real cost per unit has gone up from AC_a to P_m. The loss comes from the disappearance of the profits Π_a in Figure 14.8(a) in the importing economy. This is often called the *profit shifting* effects of trade. The remaining firm, of course, now makes larger profits: the area Π_t in Figure 14.8(c) rather than Π_a in Figure 14.8(a).

The points raised here suggest that, if we add some consideration of intra-industry trade and market structure, it is likely that the gains from trade will be many times larger than is suggested by comparative advantage alone. However, once we add these considerations a far richer range of possibilities arises. Large gains are likely, but it is certainly possible to construct examples where one economy loses from opening up to trade.

Figure 14.8
Monopoly and trade:
(a) monopoly before
trade; (b) duopoly
with trade; and
(c) monopoly at a
world level

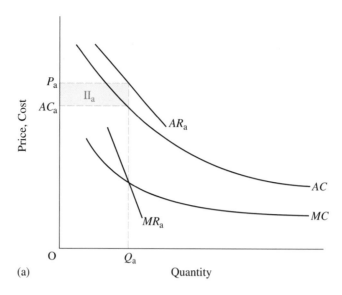

(a)

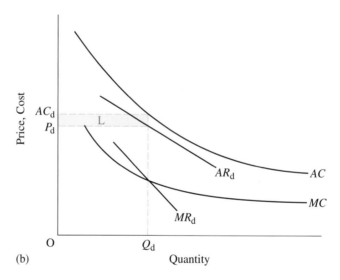

(b)

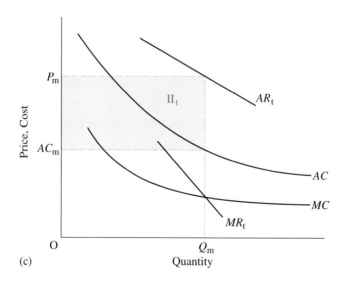

(c)

7   FOREIGN DIRECT INVESTMENT AND THE MULTINATIONAL FIRM   •

Firms' international operations do not take place solely – or even primarily – through international trade. Firms also become multinational by purchasing or constructing production or service facilities in other countries. This activity is known as foreign direct investment (FDI). The word 'direct' refers to the fact that the firms hold a controlling interest in their foreign subsidiaries, and is used to distinguish this sort of investment from foreign portfolio investment. Portfolio investment arises when firms or individuals buy shares in foreign companies (or purchase other financial assets such as foreign government bonds) but do not acquire a controlling interest.

In recent years FDI has increased even more rapidly than has trade. Most FDI takes place between rich countries, particularly within the EU and across the North Atlantic, although there has been an upsurge of firms investing in production facilities in many East Asian countries, especially China. The importance of FDI is perhaps best gauged by looking at the sales of foreign affiliates compared with exports. In manufacturing sectors in the EU, the affiliates of US multinationals have sales that are more than three times larger than the EU's manufacturing imports from the USA. Broadly similar figures hold for the sales of EU-owned firms producing in the USA compared with US imports from the EU. And for services, which generally require local supply rather than international trade, the ratio is many times higher. What these figures suggest is that firms' international activities, at least between high-income countries, take place more through investments than through trade.

The economic analysis of the reasons why FDI occurs has two main elements. One is to explain the advantage obtained by splitting production between countries, and the other is to explain why this should be done inside the firm (or its subsidiaries) rather than simply by trade (for example, by importing component parts made by a foreign firm rather than parts from a subsidiary).

The second of these questions is answered by noting that FDI often involves firms that have a good deal of 'knowledge capital'. This knowledge capital might take the form of particular technical knowledge, or it could be more general skills in the organization of production or marketing, or the reputation of a brand name. These are all assets that are hard to protect, so there is a danger that they may be stolen or abused in a contractual relationship with another firm. For example, a firm may be willing to purchase some of its inputs from other firms, but it may want to keep a particularly specialized component, in which it has invested R&D and which involves high-level production skills, inside the company, rather than license it out to independent suppliers.

Given that the firm wants to keep some of its activities internal to the organization, what is the advantage of producing in many countries, particularly since this is bound to involve co-ordination and management costs? One answer derives from the fact that there may be barriers to importing the product, so gaining access to a market requires local production. This sort of FDI is called 'market oriented' or 'horizontal'; horizontal because it involves duplicating the same stage of production in many plants in different countries. The barriers to importing may arise because of artificial barriers – such as import tariffs – or they may just be due to technical difficulties in importing. Goods that are expensive or slow to ship may be better assembled in the final market place than imported. Of course, this is necessary for services too – Starbucks has to brew its coffee in London, not import it from Seattle.

The other possible advantage from producing in many countries is that different stages of production have different input requirements, and it is thus a cost-saving measure to move the production of each stage to where inputs are cheapest. Thus, the design of a computer chip may take place in Silicon Valley, the fabrication in Taiwan and the assembly in Malaysia, before final sale in the USA. These stages correspond to Silicon Valley's comparative advantage in computer scientists, Taiwan's comparative advantage in production engineers and Malaysia's comparative advantage in low-skilled labour. This sort of FDI is called 'cost oriented' or 'vertical'; vertical because the vertical production process is being broken up between different stages. Unlike horizontal FDI, it does not involve doing the same thing (for example, final assembly) in different places, but involves doing each stage of production in the location with the lowest cost for that stage.

The two sorts of FDI have different motives, and suggest quite different predictions for the sorts of countries in which FDI takes place and the effect of FDI on trade. Horizontal FDI typically goes to where markets are large, and it is a substitute for trade. Thus, most of the FDI within Europe and between Europe and the USA is horizontal; for example, General Motors has car-assembly plants in the USA and in Europe, and the markets are served largely from these plants rather than from trans-Atlantic trade. By contrast, vertical FDI seeks out low-cost locations, and it is a complement to trade. Increased levels of vertical FDI will increase trade flows, as some of the components of the product may cross borders many times – first as components, and then embodied in progressively more advanced stages of the final product.

The fact that vertical FDI is so trade intensive suggests that it will occur as trade barriers and transport costs become very low, and this is consistent with the evidence. Researchers who have sought to distinguish between vertical and horizontal FDI demonstrate that, until recently, most FDI was horizontal in nature (for example, US investments in Europe). However, the recent surge of investments into middle- and low-income countries is increasingly vertical, representing the development of global production networks.

8   CONCLUSION   •

It is likely that international trade will come to play an ever larger role in economic activity. This is partly because of the success of the WTO in reducing trade barriers; partly because of the development of regional trading arrangements such as the EU and NAFTA; partly because many less-developed countries are now pursuing more outward looking economic policies; and partly because technical change continues to reduce the cost of making international transactions. In this chapter I have explored the causes and effects of international trade. Undoubtedly, trade poses many challenges, necessitating adjustment to new economic circumstances and, in the course of this adjustment, creating gainers and losers. However, the main message of the chapter is that there are great gains from participation in the trading system. Trade allows countries to consume at points outside their ppf; it permits the specialization of production according to comparative advantage; it makes new varieties of product available; and it increases the intensity of competition and enables firms to expand and exploit economies of scale.

CHAPTER 15 GLOBALIZATION, INEQUALITY AND ECONOMIC GROWTH

Suma Athreye ●

Objectives

After studying this chapter you should be able to:

- appreciate the extent of the gains from international trade and production
- understand the relationship between globalization and increasing inequality
- understand the relationship between international trade and production and economic growth.

Concept

- the multinational firm

1 INTRODUCTION ●

Your study of the gains from trade in Chapter 14 may have persuaded you that international trade is a good thing and that more of it should make most economies better off. You have also learnt that trade may sometimes be profitably replaced by international production, which brings in efficient global firms and raises investment and possibly productivity and growth in the economies to which it goes. These arguments suggest that greater international trade and production will lead to more prosperity throughout the world. Indeed, the world over, a number of economists have successfully made this case to their governments with the result that the period of the late 1980s and the 1990s saw an unprecedented liberalization of trade and financial flows in the world economy. Tariffs were brought down and domestic markets opened up to international trade in many economies of the world.

The late 1980s and the 1990s were special in other ways as well. You already know that many analysts regard it as the period of the 'new economy', aspects of which were discussed in Chapters 1 and 2. Transportation costs fell generally and the rise and spread of Internet technologies collapsed distance altogether for many products. E-commerce became a reality and many goods and services (books, music, financial services, software) could be bought and sold over the Internet. At the same time the fall of the Berlin Wall meant that new markets opened up in Eastern Europe offering opportunities for trade and foreign investment in those economies. The economic boom of the 1990s also created labour shortages in particular areas, such as software programming, which led to a considerable migration of skilled labour from low income to high income countries. In the popular press all of these happenings were collectively described under the umbrella term 'globalization' and many people expected it to make all the economies of the world better off.

However, the emotive protests against globalization that took place in several nations in 2001 suggest that increased globalization may have produced some bitter 'losers'. Many of these protests have taken place in low income countries with a strong anti-West flavour, but the most vocal of the protests have taken place in the US and Europe (Seattle, Quebec, Geneva, London) – in countries whose peoples we may think have benefited from the whole process of globalization. At the same time multilateral organizations such as the World Trade Organization, the International Monetary Fund, the United Nations and the World Bank are increasingly faced with mediating conflict between the interests of their member states. All of this evidence about strife suggests that the arguments about increased prosperity for all through greater globalization were perhaps misplaced and the actual story of the gains from globalization is more complex.

This chapter will argue that though international trade and production benefit economies by integrating them with each other, such integration in international trade and production has been limited to a few economies, many of which are high income Western economies, with some countries gaining more from integration than others. Even in Western countries where we expect to see gains from specialization and global integration, not all groups or countries have gained uniformly. So, while globalization can increase economic growth, it also creates inequality. Thus, the protests against globalization may actually be protests about its unequal impact across the world economy and sections of society rather than about the phenomenon of globalization itself.

2   WHAT IS GLOBALIZATION?

Dollar and Collier (2001) defined globalization as the growing integration of economies and societies around the world as a result of flows of goods and services, capital, people and ideas. Though the term 'globalization' is of fairly recent origin, a process of integration of the world's economies, which is what is meant by globalization, has been underway for most of human history. In this section we look

Figure 15.1
Anti-globalization protesters
© Sarah Herman, 2002

first at that historical background and then at how the current process of globalization relates to the world economy.

2.1   A HISTORICAL PERSPECTIVE ON GLOBALIZATION

Over many years of human history globalization has been taking place through travel and trade, through the migration of peoples from one part of the world to another, and through the travel of ideas (including scientific, political and religious ideas) from one region to another. Before the Renaissance, the direction of globalization was from East to West, as Arab traders carried important ideas and scarce goods from China and India into Greece and thus to Europe.

In his book, *The Wealth and Poverty of Nations*, the historian David Landes (1998) points out that a thousand years ago China and the Arab world were at the forefront of technological developments just as the Western world is today. The Western world borrowed heavily from these civilizations. This position is reversed today and the reversal happened through a mixture of effective competition, adoption of technologies in the Western world, and the development of institutions of global economic power to perpetuate such growth and development. Since the middle of the nineteenth century globalization has tended to centre more on the West and the movement of goods, services and technology from Western nations to the Eastern and Southern regions of the world.

The current debate about globalization has its intellectual origins in the early nineteenth century. David Ricardo, writing in England in 1817, clearly saw the advantages of free trade and developed the theory of comparative advantage, which we still learn about in our textbooks today (see Chapter 14). Free trade was an important component of the ideology of laissez-faire that dominated British policies from the middle of the nineteenth century. Britain saw a cheapening of food prices in her own economy after liberalizing trade, and this helped to keep wages down in the economy. The economic historians Lindert and Williamson (2001) argue that liberalization of trade by Britain was quite egalitarian in its impact. It saw gains for everyone except the land-owning aristocracy in England, whose main source of income, rent from land, fell as cheaper food imports flooded the country. Food exporters in the New World and some Scandinavian countries prospered, as did English labourers and English factory owners. The historian Eric Hobsbawm (1982) has pointed out that the popularity of laissez-faire policies in Britain occurred at a time when it was the first industrial nation with an unrivalled competitive advantage in manufacturing.

The world looked very different from Germany, which was trying to catch up with Britain who led in the race to industrialize. Not surprisingly the first and most important treatise on the need for protection came from Germany. Soon after David Ricardo wrote about comparative advantage and the gains from trade, Fredric List penned his piece on the benefits of protection for infant industries. He argued that Germany needed to shield its infant industries from foreign competition, in order to give them a chance to learn and grow. In time this protection would allow high-cost domestic industry to learn and thereby lower the costs of production (Chapter 3 and Chapter 14). Many of the industries that Germany wanted to protect, such as steel and chemicals, were in fact increasing-returns industries. Thus, in the nineteenth century, Germany wanted the right to protect its infant industries while Britain wanted free trade.

Lindert and Williamson (2001) tell us that there is at least one other period of history that saw a similar process of globalization to the contemporary one – the period between 1870 and 1914. For about 45 years following 1870, falling transport costs led to sharp increases in world trade relative to world income. The traded commodities were mainly primary products and global integration took place around this trade. The stock of foreign capital in the then low income countries, including in 1870 the US and Australia, rose from 9 per cent of their income in 1870 to 32 per cent in 1914. About 60 million individuals migrated from Europe to the New World. North–South migrations were a small trickle as people from the poorer periphery were kept out of the new labour markets by restrictive immigration policies, much as they are now. Worldwide inequality rose, much of the increase being accounted for by within-country inequality, which was related to the degree of protection afforded to land rents. Then, as now, there were exceptions. In Britain inequality fell, as did the fortunes of much of the aristocracy. There was a limited decrease in between-country inequality as the US, Australia and the rest of Europe caught up with Britain and France. This was also a period of growing divergence between the incomes of colonies and those of the imperial powers.

After the long boom of 1870 to 1914 came a series of retreats from globalization to nationalism that lasted until 1950. The first retreat was on the checks put on emigration that had helped so many poor from Europe flee to better lives in the New World. The second came with the Great Depression, which persuaded some countries, led by the US, to impose protectionist tariffs. The third retreat came in the form of retaliatory tariffs by other countries. It is a sobering thought that the world took so long to recover from the consequences of the end of the rapid globalization of 1870–1914.

Thus, throughout history globalization has divided governments and nations all over the world and today one can hear many modern echoes of this old debate. For example, the recent opposition to the liberalization of trade in services and disagreements concerning the scope of intellectual property laws have divided high income countries, almost crippling the World Trade Organization in the process. Against this background, the question to be explored in this chapter is: why do we find protests against increased globalization when most of what we have learnt so far suggests that more international trade and production is good for all economies? For most of the chapter we consider the recent period of globalization beginning in the late 1980s.

2.2   GLOBALIZATION AND THE CONTEMPORARY WORLD ECONOMY

In this chapter we think about globalization as the increased integration of the world economy through international trade and international flows of capital, which together expand the international production of world output. There are, however, broader aspects of globalization as a process, involving as it does the movement of peoples and of ideas. While the jury is still out on the role and influence of these upon growth, it may well turn out that they are the two most important catalysts in the process of growth and change. Here, we adopt the more restrictive definition that excludes a discussion of the migration of people and ideas for two reasons. First, the study of migration and in particular the migration of ideas and its impact on economic growth is only now being systematically developed. Second and more importantly, the theoretical concepts you learnt in Chapter 14 will help you in understanding the debates about globalization as international trade and production.

The late 1980s and the 1990s saw a remarkable acceleration of international economic flows as measured by increased international trade and flows of capital. This is clear from Tables 15.1(a) and 15.1(b). Table 15.1(a) reports the average annual rate of growth of some indicators of international trade, investment and production for three sub-periods. We look at the annual rates of increase of these indicators to get an idea of the pace at which the world economy is expanding the international content of its production and trade. The rate of growth of these indicators is an indication of the pace of globalization.

QUESTION

What can you conclude about globalization from Table 15.1(a)?

Table 15.1(a) shows, first, that the pace of globalization was fastest in the late 1980s and slowed down somewhat in the early 1990s. Even though all the indicators grew more slowly in the 1990s, their rate of growth was still much higher than that observed between 1980 and 1985. Second, Table 15.1(a) shows that the growth in foreign investment and production was much higher than the growth in international trade. (An exception to this is the growth of trade in technological services; however, the export of technological services is likely to have a big intra-firm component.)

A more useful measure of globalization may be one that measures how *important* international trade, investment and production are in the world economy. This is rather different from measuring how fast they have grown, in that they might have been growing rapidly but from a very small base. One way to assess that importance is to ask how much GDP comes from such international activity. This is what we report in Table 15.1(b).

QUESTION

What conclusions about the importance of globalization can you draw from Table 15.1(b)?

You can see that, whether we look at inward or outward foreign direct investment (FDI) as a proportion of GDP, international investment is equivalent to about 10 per cent of world GDP. Inward international investment is significantly more important for low income countries than it is for high income countries and it is exceptionally important for China.

Table 15.1(a) The pace of globalization (1980–95): annual average rates of growth (%) for selected indicators

	1980–85	1986–90	1991–95
Exports of goods and non-factor services	−0.1	14.6	8.9
Royalties and fee receipts	−0.7	21.9	12.4
Foreign direct investment inflows	–	23.6	20.1
Foreign direct investment outflows	0.8	27.1	15.1
Sales of foreign affiliates	1.3	16.3	13.4
Total assets of foreign affiliates	–	18.3	24.4

Source: UNCTAD, *World Investment Report*, various volumes

Table 15.1(b) Importance of globalization for world production: shares of international investment in world GDP

	1980	1985	1990	1996
Inward FDI stock as a proportion of GDP				
World	4.6	6.5	8.0	10.6
High income economies	3.8	4.9	6.6	7.6
Low income economies, excluding China	4.9	9.1	8.9	14.4
China	–	1.5	4.8	24.7
Outward FDI stock as a proportion of GDP				
World	5.0	5.9	7.8	10.8
High income economies	5.2	5.9	7.8	10.1
Low income economies, excluding China	0.7	1.3	1.9	5.2
China	–	–	0.6	2.6

Source: UNCTAD, 1998

At the heart of the increases reported in Tables 15.1(a) and (b) is the growing economic integration and interdependence of the world's economies through trade and even more through international production. We can see and feel its effect in the production of many everyday goods. We draw upon an article in Abrams and Astill (2001) to illustrate this point.

Consider the example of an ordinary pair of Lee Cooper LC10 jeans, which in 2002 could be bought for under £20 in any one of Cromwell's Madhouse outlets in the UK, and think for a moment about where the different parts of this pair of jeans originated. You may be surprised to learn that the cotton denim used to make the jeans is grown in Benin in Africa while the cotton for the pockets comes from Pakistan. The denim is woven in Italy and stonewashed with pumice in Turkey and dyed indigo blue with dyes made in Germany. The stitching of the jeans is done in Tunisia, where wages are considerably lower than in England, and finally the jeans are shipped to England where they are sold.

Figure 15.2 shows the origin of all the parts of a pair of LC10 jeans, including ones we have not discussed, such as rivets, zips, and the distinctive yellow dyed thread. It also neatly illustrates the high degree of integration among different nations of the world through international trade and international production. A consequence of such integration is that producers in different economies, some of them in very poor areas, become economically interdependent in production. This interdependence has co-operative and competitive consequences.

The co-operative elements are easy to see. All the producers involved in the making of the Lee Cooper jeans gain from the demand for those jeans in England. For each of these individual producers, such as the German dyers, the cotton growers of Benin

Figure 15.2 Global production of Lee Cooper LC10 jeans

© Sarah Herman, 2002

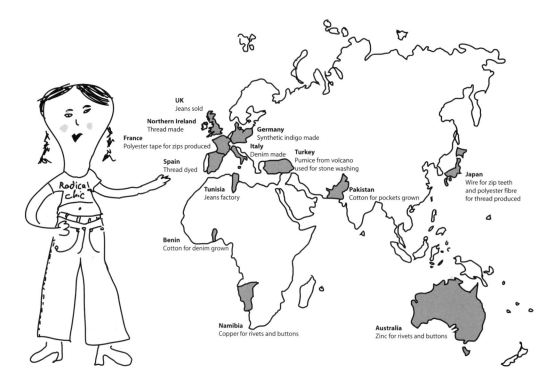

and the women who do the stitching in Tunisia, the existence of a demand from Lee Cooper for their products is a source of sales and revenue. Their interdependence also means that if the demand for Lee Cooper jeans increases, they will all benefit from the increased sales, at least in the short run. Similarly, advances in technology that make threads stronger, zips more easy to use, rivets more elegant etc., will all add to the quality of jeans and maybe eventually to the revenue from the sale of jeans that incorporate these innovations.

Such co-operative interdependence, however, co-exists with increased competition between different manufacturers in any single part of the production chain. Consider for example, the production chain in the making of jeans. While cotton is not grown in England, zips are manufactured in England and so is polyester thread. The English producers of these products compete with each other and the producers of zip teeth in Japan and polyester thread producers from Northern Ireland despite being in different regions. An unemployed worker in England might like to have the chance to operate the machines that do the stitching of the pair of jeans and in an uncharitable moment may even feel that the Tunisian worker stole her job with Lee Cooper.

The increased competition among producers from different regions is also a consequence of increased integration of nations and the fact that with globalization many markets in different countries actually start behaving as if they were one market. This increased competition is of course good for the manufacturers of jeans as they can buy their thread and zips at the best possible prices, but we cannot say the same for the English zip manufacturers and thread manufacturers. Some of these firms probably lose their profits to the increased competition from producers in Japan and Northern Ireland.

Even from this single example of globalization we can see that the sources of gain and loss to the UK economy from the international production of Lee Cooper jeans are different. Furthermore these gains and losses are likely to involve different groups of people. The same is true for the other countries that are involved, such as Benin, Germany, Turkey and Tunisia. In all these countries those parts of the economy that are involved in international production and trade will often gain but other parts of the economy may be worse off. For example, Tunisian producers of wheat may find they have to pay higher wages to their female workers at harvest time as many of them can now work more profitably for Lee Cooper.

Some Sectors Better Off, Other Industries Worse Off. Applies To All Nations

QUESTION

Can you think of other examples of globalization, like that of the Lee Cooper production of jeans?

The making of Lee Cooper jeans is clearly not the only example of globalization. The international production of cars by Ford or Toyota or of computers by IBM or Compaq, are some other examples of globalization, involving both international production and trade. If you were to trace a map of the different countries from which materials and components are sourced by these firms it would show a similar web of integration to the production of Lee Cooper jeans, but involving other countries.

3 HOW MUCH OF A GAIN?

Should all the countries involved in the making of Lee Cooper jeans support increasing international trade and production? We might expect the policy makers of countries involved in the international production of Lee Cooper jeans to evaluate the sources and the extent of gains and losses in order to estimate the net benefits of their participation. In this section we will take a closer look at the extent of gains from international trade and production and argue that both in theory and in fact some economies may gain more than others through globalization.

3.1 THE EXTENT OF GAINS FROM INTERNATIONAL TRADE

Chapter 14 introduced you to the notions of comparative advantage and gains from trade. It also showed that the actual gains from trade between any two countries are indeterminate, because they depend crucially on the terms of trade (that is, the price earned by a country's exports as a ratio of the price paid out for its imports).

There are two principles about the terms of trade that help us to understand the distribution of the gains from trade. The first is that typically the terms of trade will lie between the price ratios that would obtain in the two countries under autarky with no trade. Why? Let us reconsider the example of comparative advantage explained in

Chapter 14, Section 3.1. Initially the ratio of world prices is such that importing a bicycle from Foreign costs Home 1.5 coats rather than the 2 coats that would have to be sacrificed for an extra bicycle in the absence of trade. So Home gains from trade if the ratio of world prices are more favourable than the opportunity costs underlying its domestic production possibility frontier. Second, we also saw that, if the world price of bicycles fell so that 1 bicycle could be purchased for 1.25 coats, Home could buy more bicycles (160 instead of 133) by exporting all of its output of coats (200). Home has experienced a favourable movement in its terms of trade. The most favourable outcome of all for Home would take its terms of trade as close as possible to 1 bicycle for 1 coat, which is the opportunity cost underlying Foreign's domestic production possibility frontier.

QUESTION

Why is the qualification 'as close as possible' necessary? What is stopping Home's terms of trade from actually reaching 1:1, so that it could import 200 bicycles in exchange for its 200 coats?

In the two-country world, Home's terms of trade gain is Foreign's terms of trade loss. If the ratio of world prices of coats and bicycles were ever to reach 1:1, Foreign's terms of trade would be no more favourable than its domestic opportunity costs in the absence of trade and Foreign would therefore have no incentive to trade.

This example illustrates the two principles about the terms of trade that inform our understanding of the distribution of the gains from trade. First, it is clear that the terms of trade must lie between the trading nations' domestic opportunity cost ratios under autarky, because there would otherwise be no incentive for both to trade. Second, the further the terms of trade are from a country's own domestic opportunity cost ratio, the more it gains from trade. This is because it benefits more from the different technology of its trading partner and its own comparative advantage. The trading partner (such as Foreign in our example) benefits more in the opposite situation for the same reasons.

This being the case, it follows that, although both countries gain something from trade when compared to their no-trade positions, they do not gain equally. It also follows that the extent to which any one country (or group of similar countries) gains is dependent upon the extent to which their trading partner(s) do not gain. You also saw in Chapter 14 that several instruments are available to governments to influence the terms of trade they face, among the most common being the use of tariffs and quotas (Chapter 14, Section 5). Institutions like GATT and the WTO exist to mediate international trade conflicts and prevent the misuse of these instruments. These institutions ensure that, in the desire to compete, countries do not engage in mutually destructive retaliatory tariff wars, which would force the world's economies to settle back to their no-trade positions, where everyone is worse off.

QUESTION

Ignoring the presence of such institutions, what economic factors might ultimately determine the prices of exports and imports?

The discussion of markets and prices in Chapters 3, 4 and 5 strongly suggests one factor: the extent of market imperfection. Markets that are more imperfect will have higher prices than competitive markets for the same good. However, market structure is ultimately specific to particular goods. In general, markets for agricultural commodities tend to be more competitive than markets for most manufactured goods and so a country that primarily exports agricultural commodities and primarily imports manufactures may face an adverse terms of trade. In other words, for such a country the price of its exports may rise more slowly than the price of its imports.

Some Markets More Imperfect Than Others.

Affect BoP

Market structure is not the only factor that influences the terms of trade. First, transport costs are important, and a fall in transport costs can cheapen both export and import prices quite dramatically. Second, productivity increases in a particular sector can affect the terms of trade. For example, we saw in Chapter 14, Section 3.2 that productivity increases in computer manufacturing can lead to falling computer prices, which shows up as a terms of trade improvement for computer importing countries such as the UK. Third, a low elasticity of demand for exports can improve the terms of trade for the exporting country if demand rises. In fact, in the period before 1870, primary producers in the New World saw an increase in their terms of trade as food prices increased in the world economy due to a surge in demand for food as urbanization grew in Europe.

Other Reasons
Transport Costs
Productivity
Elasticity of Demand

The modelling of gains from trade in Chapter 14 was based upon a trading model where factors of production such as labour and capital were immobile, while goods could be traded freely across international boundaries. In such a situation only the terms of trade, and the elasticities of demand and supply of exports and imports, determine the extent of gains from trade. The question to ask now is if adding in international production will change any of these conclusions. By including international investment, as firms establish centres of production in other countries, we relax the assumption that capital is immobile, and assume instead that along with goods it too can move across international boundaries seeking the highest rate of return.

MULTINATIONAL FIRMS (also known as multinational corporations or MNCs) are likely to invest in the economies where they believe that their activities will be most profitable. Empirical research on multinational investment suggests that multinational firms largely exploit existing sources of comparative advantage to locate their production activities and thus minimize overall production costs. If this is true, international investment and hence production will reinforce the original comparative advantage of nations in international trade. Growing international production also means that intra-firm trade will account for a larger and larger portion of the trade between nations. Does this affect the gains from trade?

MULTINATIONAL FIRMS
A multinational firm is one that owns and controls centres of production in more than one country.

Intra-firm Trade Accounts for More Nations Trade Because

The answer is yes for three reasons. First, the possibility of having a firm that is headquartered in the US exporting from the UK implies that the gains from trade are not all national gains that accrue to the UK economy alone. Indeed the profits of the firm will be repatriated to the US. (The repatriation of profits is one reason for the divergence between UK GDP and UK GNP (Chapter 8, Section 2)). Governments seek to control the proportion of profits that can be repatriated. However, while the profits of a domestic exporter of goods are likely to be reinvested in the domestic economy, with multinational firms we cannot be sure.

Second, intra-firm trade is subject to different constraints from those on trade between independent firms located in different countries. For example, assuming profit maximization, an independent firm will aim to maximize its own profits. In intra-firm trade, multinational firms will try to maximize the joint profitability of all of their different production arms. If necessary, the profitability – and perhaps the jobs – of one of its overseas factories may be sacrificed to this overall aim.

Third, multinational firms have complete control over the prices that different arms charge each other and it is these prices (also called transfer prices) that determine how much each country gains, rather than the world price for the commodities traded. Transfer prices are often manipulated by multinational firms to transfer pre-tax profits from one country to another with the aim of maximizing post-tax profits for the company. Thus, the MNC subsidiary in the UK may pay out less as dividends but more as royalty payments to the parent firm in the US if they wish to shift profits from the host economy (the UK) to the home economy (the US). Apart from making it difficult to assess the true national gains from trade, transfer pricing also worries governments, who may find their efforts on taxation or on the control of foreign currency expenditures frustrated by multinational firms.

A consideration of the role of multinational firms takes us back to the issue of market structure. Multinational firms mostly operate in imperfect market environments for final goods. There are several signs of imperfect competition – brands, heavy advertising and, in high-tech products, heavy expenditure on research and development (Chapter 4). The effect of market imperfections is to increase price–cost margins and to make supernormal profits for the firms. Thus, Lee Cooper is able to sell its jeans at £19.95 even though the ex-factory price of the pair of jeans in Tunisia is about £5. Even factoring in the 10p per pair price of transportation, the manufacturer of the pair of jeans is able to make a huge profit, especially compared to what the Tunisian economy might gain from the same activity. This is just the price paid by Lee Cooper to the Tunisian women who stitch the jeans – roughly 58p per hour worked (Abrams and Astill, 2001) – multiplied by the total hours required to stitch a pair of jeans.

QUESTION

Should the Tunisian government stop participating in international trade and production because the profits that its firms make are a fraction of the profits made by the multinational firm?

The answer to that question will depend upon two types of factor: what is the opportunity cost of not participating for the Tunisian firms, and what are the macroeconomic impacts of participation in international trade and production for the economy? For many poor countries like Tunisia, with high levels of unemployment and low levels of domestic industrialization, such opportunities for employment as those provided by the Lee Cooper trade are often very welcome. However, if women working for Lee Cooper suddenly found a great demand for their labour in local boutiques, then of course they will not want to work at the less lucrative Lee Cooper wages, and there may be very little the Tunisian government can do to affect this.

From the point of view of the government the more important question may be what proportions of total employment and income come (directly and indirectly) from such exporting activities. Remember that exports add to aggregate demand, which in turn encourages investment and (in turn) the growth of incomes and employment. It also brings in foreign exchange that can be used to buy imports. If the proportion of exports to GDP is not initially very large, the country may be less affected by not participating in such trade. But even then the Tunisian government might want to encourage such production and trade because it brings in foreign currency through exports that can be used to import machinery or medicines. If, however, a large percentage of income and employment does come from such export trade then not participating in international trade could certainly cause a decline in aggregate demand and hence a recession.

Sadiq and Bolbol (2001) report that in 1998 the textile sector in Tunisia that has attracted much international investment accounted for 47 per cent of the country's exports and 6.5 per cent of its GDP and employed over half the workforce of the manufacturing sector. Further, in 1997, exports from foreign affiliates (such as the Lee Cooper jean factory) accounted for 30 per cent of all Tunisian exports. In the UK on the other hand, the textile sector is a fading one, despite the higher profits being made by UK firms relative to Tunisian firms. However, the Tunisian government may still wish to press for more such investment and actively engage in trade in textiles. This is on account of both comparative advantage and the sector being more important in proportionate terms for national income and employment.

EXERCISE 15.1

Use the foreign trade multiplier you learnt about in Chapter 12, Section 2.3 to analyse the relative impact of Tunisian textile exports worth €30 000 to the UK.

1   What would be the impact of this export on Tunisia's national income if the Tunisian consumers have a marginal propensity to consume of 0.6 and there are no imports?

2   If UK consumers reduce their spending on domestically produced goods by the same amount, what would be the impact of imports of textiles worth €30 000 from Tunisia on the UK's national income? Assume that UK consumers have a marginal propensity to consume of 0.6 and a marginal propensity to import of 0.2.

So far we have discussed the gains from trade, while recognizing that in recent years the involvement of multinational firms has meant that a larger proportion of trade is now intra-firm trade. Estimates for the US by Feenstra (1999) suggest that about a third of US exports and 43 per cent of US imports in 1992 consisted of intra-MNC trade, handled between a US or foreign MNC and its affiliates. We have also noted that such trade carried within it the scope for the repatriation of profits through transfer pricing, with adverse implications for the tax revenues of host country governments. In Section 3.2 the focus will shift to a discussion of the gains from international production itself.

3.2   THE EXTENT OF GAINS FROM INTERNATIONAL PRODUCTION

Two aspects of the foreign investment that international production entails have always worried policy makers. The first is the impossibility of completely controlling the activities of multinational firms, precisely because of their spread over two or more nations. The second is that foreign investment and concentration are positively correlated. This has been reported in different studies for the UK economy, but it also seems to be true of other parts of the world, such as France, Germany, Guatemala, Brazil, Mexico, Australia, Canada, and New Zealand. In Table 15.2 we report the results from such a study, conducted by Fishwick (1982), which shows seller concentration in a market and foreign investment in the corresponding industrial sector.

Table 15.2 Seller concentration and foreign shares in sales

Sector	Country (year)	Share of sales (%) obtained by:	
		the 4 largest firms	**foreign-owned firms**
Food	France (1972)	8	16
	Germany (1977)	6	11
	Italy (1977)	25	21
	UK (1972)	39	12
Chemicals	France (1976)	35	27
	Germany (1976)	32	23
	UK (1976)	28	23
Agricultural engineering	France (1976)	65	52
	Germany (1972)	37	23
	UK (1973)	79	83
Electrical appliances	France (1976)	38	18
	Germany (1973)	5	73
	Italy (1973)	15	62
	UK (1975)	41	54
Electronic appliances	France (1976)	34	37
	Germany (1973)	8	51
	UK (1975)	20	77

Sector	Country (year)	Share of sales (%) obtained by:	
		the 4 largest firms	foreign-owned firms
Tyres	France (1974)	88	26
	Germany (1974)	72	50
	Italy (1974)	94	48
	UK (1975)	89	46
Textiles	France (1976)	8	6
	Germany (1976)	5	7
	UK (1976)	31	5

Source: author's compilations based upon Tables 2.3, 2.4, 2.6, 2.7, 2.9 and 2.10 in Fishwick, 1982

EXERCISE 15.2

1   Plot the data on seller concentration and foreign shares in Table 15.2 as a scatterplot.

2   The correlation coefficient is calculated in Tutorial 12. How would you interpret the scatterplot and the correlation coefficient?

Does the positive correlation between seller concentration in a market and the extent of foreign investment in it mean that foreign investment causes the sector to be more monopolistic than it would otherwise have been? The answer to this question is much debated but is still imperfectly understood. On the one hand your study in Chapter 14 of why multinational firms emerge at all should alert you to the fact that they tend to appear in markets that are already imperfectly competitive and often characterized by market failures. So in some sense, imperfect markets attract foreign investment, because profits tend to be higher where market imperfections limit competitive pressures. On the other hand, one can also think of several examples where foreign investment successfully competed against domestic firms to displace the competition from them. Think here about the UK car industry or the UK computer industry. This discussion also underlines an important principle of empirical analysis, which is that correlation between two variables cannot tell us very much about the direction of causation between them.

Despite the hostility and scepticism with which foreign investment has been viewed in the past, we saw that the most recent period of the 1990s has actually seen an acceleration of international foreign investment flows. Many countries, including prominently the UK, have pursued policies of actively attracting foreign investment into their economies. What are the gains that they expect from such investment?

The productivity gains from foreign investment are in fact quite variable across economies. What factors account for this variability? Blomstrom and Kokko (1998) review studies that have attempted to explain the observed variability in the gains from foreign investment and suggest we need to distinguish between demonstration effects of foreign investment and the competitive effects that flow from it. Demonstration effects are one-off effects whereby domestic firms learn to imitate the better organizational practices of the foreign firms. The first reason why many economies want to attract foreign investment is therefore that they expect that it will introduce superior technology, which will then spread in the host countries' economies through imitation and through learning by local firms. Put differently, foreign firms are seen as vehicles through which technology transfer can take place, which in turn can lift long-run rates of growth in the economies into which they flow.

Competitive effects depend upon the ability of domestic firms to compete with foreign firms to win back domestic market shares. In doing so, domestic firms may compete on the basis of pricing strategies or of more innovative and productive technological practices. When this happens the economy as a whole benefits from a virtuous cycle of competition, innovation, increased productivity and more competition. This suggests a second reason for the warm welcome accorded to foreign investment, in that multinational firms are seen to have an important role to play in breaking domestic (often public sector) monopolies. To some extent, and in some countries, they have succeeded. A good example here is the car industry in India, which until the late 1970s manufactured only two models of cars. Foreign investment into the sector began in the form of a joint venture with Toyota of Japan in the 1980s, and after 1991 the sector was fully opened up to foreign investment. The result has been a proliferation of car varieties, domestic and foreign, and a dramatic reduction in car prices. Such stories of the success of foreign firms in catalysing dynamic growth of sectors co-exist with other examples of foreign firms displacing domestic firms, as happened with IBM's entry into the UK computer industry.

However, it is also easy to imagine situations in which domestic firms just surrender their market shares to entering multinationals and are unable to win them back. In such situations governments can come under enormous political pressure to restore the market shares of domestic firms in other ways. Most frequently this happens with some active discrimination against the foreign firm in the form of higher taxes on their goods or inputs, restrictions on their ability to expand production, or strict rules about how much profit they can repatriate. All of these measures effectively reduce the actual profitability of the foreign firm and give the less competitive domestic firms a chance to compete again.

4   GLOBALIZATION AND GROWING INEQUALITY: ARE THEY RELATED?

The integration of economies through globalization has been an extremely uneven process. Some countries and regions have gained much more from it than others, an outcome that has increased inequality *among* economies. At the same time, globalization has increased inequality *within* successfully integrated economies, favouring some groups above others. In this section we will deal with the evidence on each of these issues in turn.

4.1   THE UNEQUAL INTERNATIONAL IMPACT OF GLOBAL INTEGRATION

In Section 2 we drew attention to the increasing shares of international trade and production in the late 1980s and the 1990s as indicative of the growing importance of economic globalization. Tables 15.3(a)–(c) report further data on the distribution of world trade and foreign investment across the economies.

Table 15.3(a) Distribution of world trade: % of total exports

	1970	1980	1991
High income market economies	72.1	63.7	73.2
North America	19.9	15.2	16.3
Europe	45.6	41.7	47.5
Japan	6.5	6.8	9.3
Low income market economies	17.0	29.7	23.7
Oil exporting	5.8	15.6	4.9
Non oil exporting	11.1	14.1	18.8
Eastern Europe and Soviet Union	10.9	6.6	3.1
Eastern Europe	6.6	3.6	1.7
Soviet Union	4.3	3.0	1.4

About The Same

Down Turn

Note: figures may not sum exactly to totals because of rounding.
Source: *Economic Survey of Europe*, 1993, calculated from Appendix Table C.1, p.279

Table 15.3(b) Distribution of foreign investment stocks, 1980–2000

	1980	1985	1990	1995	2000
Total inward stock ($bn)	481.9	734.9	1716.9	2657.9	6314.3
High income economies share (%)	77.5	73.2	80.1	73.9	66.7
Of which, US share (%)	22.2	34.3	28.8	29.2	29.4
Low income economies share (%)	22.5	26.8	19.9	26.1	31.3
Of which, Chinese share (%)	0.0	1.7	4.1	18.6	17.5
Total outward stock ($bn)	513.7	685.6	1684.1	2730.2	5976.2
High income economies share (%)	98.8	96.9	95.9	92.1	87.8
Of which, US share (%)	43.4	37.8	27.0	28.1	23.7
Low income economies share (%)	1.2	3.1	4.1	7.9	11.9
Of which, Chinese share (%)	0.0	0.6	3.6	8.1	3.8

Chinese inward investment 0 → 17.5%

High income economies lose out to ↓ income

Note: percentages may not sum exactly to 100% because of rounding.
Source: Feenstra, 1999, p.333; UNCTAD, 2001, for the 2000 figures

Table 15.3(c) Distribution of FDI flows, 1983–2000

	1983–88	1991	1993	1995	1997	2000
Total inward flows ($bn)	91.6	157.8	207.9	314.9	477.9	1270.8
High income economies share (%)	78.4	73.8	64.8	68.4	56.8	79.1
Of which, US share (%)	47.9	19.3	31.8	29.7	38.1	28.0
Low income economies share (%)	21.6	26.2	35.2	31.6	39.2	18.9
Of which, Chinese share (%)	9.2	10.6	37.6	37.6	23.6	17.0
Total outward flows ($bn)	93.7	210.8	225.5	317.9	466.0	1149.9
High income economies share (%)	94.2	95.8	85.4	85.2	85.2	91.0
Of which, US share (%)	16.1	16.6	35.9	35.3	24.1	13.3
Low income economies share (%)	5.8	4.2	14.6	14.8	14.1	8.7
Of which, Chinese share (%)	8.5	10.3	13.3	7.4	3.9	2.3

Note: percentages may not sum exactly to 100% because of rounding.
Source: Feenstra, 1999, p.334; UNCTAD, 2001, for 1997 and 2000 figures

QUESTION

> **Examine the data in Tables 15.3(a)–(c). Do they suggest that all countries have experienced increases in international trade and investment or have such increases been concentrated in a few economies of the world?**

What is quite remarkable from Tables 15.3(a)–(c) is that only a few countries account for the larger portion of the increases in world trade and international investment. The data suggest that, far from being a general process that has affected economies the world over, economic globalization has in fact been important in integrating only a few countries in the world economy. Consider for example the disproportionate role of China among low income economies in attracting inward investment stocks (Table 15.3(b)) and inward FDI flows (Table 15.3(c)).

Other data support this general point. The World Bank estimates that exports of manufactured goods rose from 25 per cent of poor country exports in 1980 to 80 per cent in 1998. This integration was concentrated in 24 low income countries (including China, India and Mexico) which were home to 3 billion people. These countries doubled the ratio of trade to national income and their per capita incomes rose by 5 per cent per annum. Yet for another 2 billion of population in low income countries, including much of Africa, the ratio of trade to national output fell and income per head shrank in the same period. Similarly more than half of the foreign investment inflows to low income economies are concentrated in just five countries.

Has this uneven distribution of international trade and production contributed to a widening of income differentials between countries in the late 1980s and the 1990s? Table 15.4 reports on some standard measures of inequality, some of which you encountered in Chapter 9.

[handwritten margin notes: OECD Decile = 1/10; organis economic co-op a develop; Poor get Poorer; Rich get Richer]

Table 15.4 More unequal: world income distribution (1988–93)

Inequality measure	1988	1993	% change
Gini coefficient of world incomes	63.10	66.90	6.0
Poorest decile's % of world income	0.88	0.64	–27.3 ✓
Richest decile's % of world income	48.00	52.00	8.3
Median income as % of poorest decile	327	359	9.8
Richest decile as % of median income	728	898	23.4 ✓

Source: Wade, 2001, Table 3

QUESTION

What conclusion can you draw about the changing distribution of world income from the data in Table 15.4?

The data in Table 15.4 point to a widening of world inequalities in income over the 1980s and early 1990s. For example, the Gini coefficient of world incomes increased by 6 per cent from 1988 to 1993. Even more striking is the decline in the percentage of world income available to the poorest decile of the world's population. The richest decile has benefited from a dramatic increase in their incomes expressed as a percentage of median world income.

We may think of global inequality in incomes as being made up of two parts, the inequality of incomes between countries and the inequality of incomes within a country. It has been found that for OECD countries between 1980 and 1985, a greater proportion of the inequality of incomes came from within-country inequality and that within-country inequality increased during this period. Similarly, for the category of more globalized countries (those countries that show a high share of trade to GDP), within-country inequality increased over the period 1980–95.

Rising inequality is always potentially a political issue. But globalization is not the only factor responsible for these widening income differentials. As you will learn in Chapter 18 technological improvements and their diffusion, investment in human capital and the maintenance of a high rate of investment in some economies are also important explanatory factors in explaining growth and divergence of incomes between rich and poor countries.

Nevertheless, globalization is an important factor in that a disproportionate amount of international trade and production originates and integrates economies in the West, and the world is roughly divided between the prosperous West together with a handful of very low income countries and a large group of low to middle income countries. This fact alone goes some way towards explaining why anti-globalization protests often take the form of anti-West protests, despite the fact that many of the low income countries want to emulate the economic achievements of the West.

[handwritten margin notes: Global Inequality can be seen; As Inequality between countries a; Inequality between incomes within a country; OECD: Widening Gap internal; Incomes a between countries]

The evidence on world income inequality in Table 15.4 does not explain why many of the anti-globalization protests have in fact happened in Western countries. Very often they have included vocal sections that were protesting on behalf of the poorer non-Western countries, but this is not true of all the protestors. Could it be possible that in Western countries too there have been large numbers of losers due to increased international integration? It is to this question that we now turn our attention.

4.2   TRADE AND INCOME INEQUALITY WITHIN ECONOMIES

In order to identify the losers from trade we need to look more closely at what happens to economies as they start specializing according to their comparative advantage. In recent decades the UK has discovered that it has a comparative advantage in services and following on this the share of services in UK national income and employment has grown. The other side of the coin however is that UK producers find that manufacturing of many products is best left to the Chinese, or the Taiwanese. These are the UK's sectors of comparative disadvantage, in which production will begin to decrease. At first, people working in a range of manufacturing industries may find that it is harder to find new work and that prices in these industries are higher than elsewhere. As comparative advantage and specialization progress, the share of such manufacturing in national income and employment will fall and the share of services in income and employment will expand. Thus, the structure of production and employment in the economy will have changed.

It is argued that the UK economy went through a period of restructuring in the mid and late 1980s. The UK's comparative disadvantage in manufacturing eroded the manufacturing basis of national production while her comparative advantage in services (financial and business) boosted the share of the services sector in national income. A consequence of this was that several older industries such as steel and coal that depended upon the manufacturing sector for demand had to shut down causing huge unemployment in those sectors. This led to a great contraction of jobs in these industries and arguably contributed to the growing inequality between the south-east UK and the rest of the UK economy.

Such restructuring of the economy is the consequence of trade when there is comparative advantage. While the difference in no-trade price ratios gives the scope for gains from trade, when trade actually takes place each economy ends up facing the same (world) price ratio and producing more of the good in which it has a comparative advantage. In simple models of trade, as one price ratio obtains in both the countries, the wage rates of people working in the sector of comparative disadvantage fall to the levels of the country that has the comparative advantage. This is called factor–price equalization and is an implication of the Hecksher–Ohlin factor endowment model of the sources of comparative advantage (Chapter 14, Section 4). Under some very restrictive assumptions, including the assumptions of the model of perfect competition, the model shows that factor–price equalization is a consequence of free trade. The rather strong result implied by factor–price equalization is this: even if factors of production (labour, capital) were fully immobile across countries, free trade in goods would substitute for the trade in factors and have the same effect on relative wages across trading countries. For example, the implication of factor–price equalization for the UK would be that eventually wages for low-skilled work in manufacturing would fall towards the wages earned for such work in low income economies that are abundantly endowed with low-skilled labour. Low wages give such economies a comparative advantage in manufacturing and specialization and trade will increase their demand for low-skilled labour, causing wages to rise until equality of wages for the same type of labour is achieved across different boundaries.

A lively debate started in the US in the mid-1980s concerning the claim that increased trade was contributing to worsening income inequality in the US economy. Figure 15.3 depicts the main trends in within-country income inequality for selected high income countries for the period 1977–97. It plots the Gini coefficient of incomes (which you learnt about in Chapter 9) for selected OECD countries on the Y-axis, against time on the X-axis.

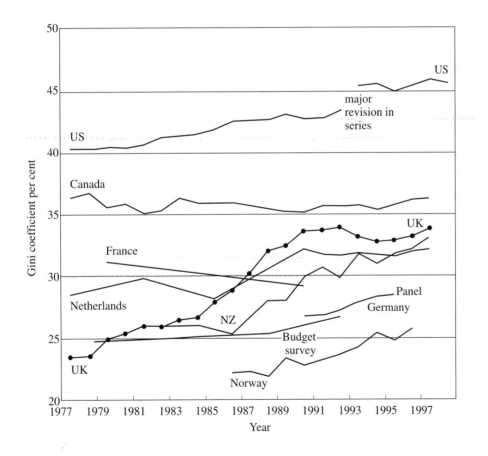

Figure 15.3
Changes in income inequality within selected high income countries 1977–97

Source: Atkinson, 1999, p.4

QUESTION

> **What does Figure 15.3 tell us about within-country income inequality in the high income countries selected over the period 1977–97?**

For many high income economies the 1980s and 1990s were a period of worsening income distribution within their economies. Figure 15.3 shows clearly that in several countries inequality in incomes rose in the late 1980s and the 1990s. The rise was particularly sharp in the UK, but was also observed for New Zealand, Germany, Norway and the US. It is tempting to conclude that the growth in international trade and production was entirely responsible for these trends and that these worsening inequalities merely represent some kind of factor–price equalization. In the same period, however, Canada showed no great change in its income inequality and France showed decreased inequality. There is no evidence at all that they were participating less vigorously in the globalization of their economies. So could this be another example of wrongly inferring causation from observed association?

Some economists such as Atkinson (1999) argue that the growing inequality in the OECD countries cannot be attributed to trade alone. Many more important and significant changes took place in the 1980s and 1990s. In the UK, perhaps the most significant of all the changes of the 1980s was the loss of bargaining power to trade unions after the failure of some famous strikes in the Thatcher era. The same was true in several other countries of Europe as well, and in the US, although there are fewer trade unions there. In contrast, French truckers and farmers still regularly exercise their rights to strike and demand pay increases, as many of us remember from unfortunate ferry crossing experiences. In many cases this change in the strength of unions affected the wages at the lower end, and you may recall that the coal pit workers and miners were not the highest income earners even in the old technology days and neither were their products directly traded. The emergence of new technologies in the 1980s and 1990s also rewarded technological skills and training, widening the wage differential between skilled and unskilled labour. A relative scarcity of such trained workers meant that some of them could earn very high incomes and negotiate very high salaries for their skills.

Both of these different pressures on the higher and lower end of incomes together may have widened income inequality. Indeed there is some evidence suggesting that upward pressure on skilled incomes contributed more to the growth in UK income inequality than downward pressure on the unskilled wage component. Is such a worsening of income distribution inevitable? As you have learnt earlier, governments have many means at their disposal to improve income inequality and the consequences of such inequality. A major tool is redistributive taxation. However, here again the 1980s and 1990s were remarkable in the UK and the US. Tax rates fell drastically in both economies and public investment correspondingly decreased in real terms.

The picture regarding within-country inequality is if anything worse for low income countries, even the so-called globalizers who have benefited from huge increases in per capita incomes over the period 1980–97. Prominent examples in this group are India and China. Even as growth rose and poverty fell, inequality increased. Systematic investigation into the influence of trade on inequality has shown that while on average across all countries there was no relationship between participation in trade and within-country inequality, in low income countries trade was *always* associated with greater within-country inequality.

Foreign investment may also play a role in contributing to income inequalities. While foreign firms are famous for shifting their production to lower cost locations in search of profits and have questionable practices in their treatment of legal and environmental regimes in these countries, foreign firms almost always raise wages in the economies and sectors that they enter. This is a well-established empirical fact, noted by Jenkins (1983) and confirmed in most studies on foreign investment and wage rates.

QUESTION

Why should the entry of foreign firms raise incomes in the sector in which they enter?

It is easy to understand why foreign firms have a favourable impact on wages in the sectors they enter. They simply add to the labour demand for the same supply of labour, raising wages in the sector, and thus increase wage dispersion. Just as an example of how potent that effect can be, it is interesting to note that software engineers working in India earn about 20 times the national average income for manufacturing. Much of this increase happened in the early 1990s when foreign multinationals set up software subsidiaries in India, offering salaries that were 20 per cent higher than those offered by domestic firms.

Foreign investment in low income countries also happens in selected regions, called free trade zones or specialized export zones where better infrastructure conditions prevail and where the investment is often subject to different tax and labour laws from the rest of the country. So the benefits of greater integration are often confined to these regions, increasing the disparity between regions of the entire economy. Thus, in China the inequality between the prosperous south-east coast and the rest of mainland China has increased. In India too, the south and west of the country have prospered with the software boom while the rest of the country has not benefited in this way, contributing to inter-regional inequalities.

5   GLOBALIZATION AND ECONOMIC GROWTH: ARE THEY RELATED? •

In this section we will turn to the macroeconomic impact of globalization and examine the question of whether increased trade and investment raise the growth of national incomes over time.

Do trade and foreign investment affect the rate of growth and, if so, how and why? As you will learn in more detail in Chapter 18, the rate of growth of national income is ultimately determined by three factors: the rate at which the economy as a whole saves and is able to free resources from current consumption for investment in the economy, the rate at which investment is actually undertaken, and the productivity of investment. International trade affects the opportunities that an economy has for profitable investment and so is capable of influencing growth. Foreign investment is in principle capable of affecting all three factors that influence growth. This is true for both inward and outward foreign investment.

Sections 5.1 and 5.2 discuss a variety of evidence on trade, foreign investment and growth. The issue of openness to international trade and production and its effect on growth is a very contentious one on empirical grounds. For one thing, there is the old problem of inferring causation from observed correlations. Can we really tell the difference between growth causing improvements in productivity and therefore greater exports, and exports causing increased productivity and growth? Put differently, is growth a cause or consequence of openness to international trade and production?

There is a second and subtler point. Detailed studies of export-led growth suggest that the success of one country is due in part to policies and failures of all other countries in that time frame. South Korea and Taiwan were the first countries to break out of the mould of growing through expanding domestic production to replace imports by finding some industries where they saw a potential to grow through exporting. They were lucky in being able to seize the opportunity when there was no competition from other countries with similar skills. Mexico also opened up to investment and collaboration with US firms at about the same time. It is useful to think about this as a race between countries for opportunities to better their growth. Some countries are selected as winners. But their victory is as much due to their own abilities as due to what others in the race did not do. In this sense their history is unique and unrealizable in any other way.

5.1   TRADE AND GROWTH

International trade increases the potential market available for the supply of raw materials and demand for products when compared to a less open environment. This has a powerful impact on both investment and the productivity of investment. To understand why this is so, conduct the following thought experiment. If resources were available for investment, how might entrepreneurs go about deciding to invest? First, they may decide how many investments are already there and whether they should step in additionally. Compared to a closed economy an open economy is likely to have many more investment opportunities simply because the demand facing the economy is larger. Second, they might want to rank investment projects according to the return they will get on them. If they were restricted to investment in the domestic economy, the most productive projects may already be taken and they may have to be content with a lower rate of return. But in an open economy there is a greater variety of projects and rates of return. For both these reasons international trade affects investment and the productivity of that investment.

Theoretical possibilities aside, have countries that participated more in international trade grown more? In this subsection we will try to assess the empirical evidence on this issue. As was noted in the introduction to this chapter, several low income countries opened up their economies to trade by adopting a more liberalized policy regime towards trade. Table 15.5 below lists 32 low income economies and when they adopted liberal policies. In the third column of the table we report a figure on the change in growth. This measures the difference between the average rate of growth three years post-liberalization and the average rate of growth observed three years before liberalization. A positive value for this figure means that the average rate of growth of the economy increased after liberalization, a negative value that it decreased.

Table 15.5 Trade liberalization and growth in low income countries (post-1985)

Country	Year of liberalization	Change in rates of growth of national income
Mali	1986	0.1018
Philippines	1986	0.1004
Chile	1985	0.0855
Uganda	1987	0.0807
Malaysia	1988	0.0740
Tanzania	1986	0.0495
Nigeria	1986	0.0364
Malawi	1988	0.0341
Costa Rica	1985	0.0334
Argentina	1989	0.0320
Colombia	1985	0.0314
Venezuela	1989	0.0226
Senegal	1986	0.0226
Madagascar	1987	0.0195
Côte d'Ivoire	1985	0.0184
Vietnam	1986	0.0177
Bangladesh	1991	0.0039
Mexico	1985	0.0018
Indonesia	1986	−0.0006
Korea	1987	−0.0009
Thailand	1989	−0.0014
Sri Lanka	1987	−0.0101
Pakistan	1988	−0.0160
Ghana	1987	−0.0182

Country	Year of liberalization	Change in rates of growth of national income
Kenya	1988	−0.0233
Cameroon	1989	−0.0292
India	1991	−0.0297
South Africa	1990	−0.0370
Peru	1989	−0.0435
China	1988	−0.0531
Brazil	1987	−0.0776
Zaire	1990	−0.0932
Mean change in rate of growth		0.0104
Standard deviation		0.0476

Source: adapted from Greenaway *et al.*, 1997, Tables 1 and 2, pp.1887–8

QUESTION

What can you conclude from Table 15.5 about the effects of liberalization on growth for low income countries?

Surprisingly we cannot draw any very firm conclusions. Of these 32 countries that liberalized, 14 saw negative effects on the rate of growth of national income. Across the group the average increase in GDP growth rates was 1.04 per cent and the dispersion of this increase in both directions was wide, as indicated by the large standard deviation of 4.76 per cent. However, the before-and-after picture of the impact on growth rates of opening up the economy, as illustrated in Table 15.5, can be a misleading one. For one thing, we know that low income countries often liberalized in response to specific balance of payments crises. Second, the benefits associated with increased trade that we have outlined require a long period of integration through trading relations with other economies for their effects to be apparent. So it may be that a better test of the economic impact of liberalization would look for a range of indicators over a long period of time. Dollar and Kray (2001) do just this and their results are reported in Table 15.6.

QUESTION

Do you think that Table 15.6 reveals any significant differences between the globalizing and the non-globalizing low income countries?

Table 15.6 Characteristics of globalizing and non-globalizing low income economies: population-weighted averages

	24 globalizers	49 non-globalizers
Population, 1997	2.9 billion	1.1 billion
Per capita GDP, 1980	$1488	$1947
Per capita GDP, 1997	$2485	$2133
Inflation, 1980	16%	17%
Inflation, 1997	6%	9%
Rule of law index (world average = 0)	−0.04	−0.48
Average years		
Primary schooling, 1980	2.4	2.5
Primary schooling, 1997	3.8	3.1
Average years		
Secondary schooling, 1980	0.8	0.7
Secondary schooling, 1997	1.3	1.9
Average years		
Tertiary schooling, 1980	0.08	0.09
Tertiary schooling, 1997	0.18	0.22

Note: globalizing countries are the top third of the low income countries when ranked according to their trade to GDP ratio. The 24 countries in this group are: Argentina, Bangladesh, Brazil, China, Colombia, Costa Rica, Côte d'Ivoire, the Dominican Republic, Haiti, Hungary, India, Jamaica, Jordan, Malaysia, Mali, Mexico, Nepal, Nicaragua, Paraguay, Philippines, Rwanda, Thailand, Uruguay, and Zimbabwe. China accounts for a third of the total population of this group of countries. The group of non-globalizers includes all the remaining low income countries for which data are available.

Source: Dollar and Kray, 2001, p.15

Table 15.6 classifies economies into 24 globalizers and 49 non-globalizers based upon the trade to GDP ratio. The average import tariff for non-globalizers fell by 11 percentage points while that for the globalizers fell by 34 percentage points. Some interesting differences emerge. The 24 globalizers in Table 15.6 were poorer than the 49 non-globalizers in 1980 yet by the end of 1997 they were richer. They had lower inflation and better educational attainments at primary level compared with their 1980 levels and compared to the non-globalizing countries.

Figure 15.4 plots the rates of growth of national income over the period 1960–90 on the X-axis and the rate of growth of the volume of international trade (exports + imports) between 1960 and 1990 on the Y-axis. Perhaps because of the jeans factories, Tunisia's GDP grew at an annual rate of 5.8 per cent between 1960 and 1990 while its volume of international trade grew at 7 per cent.

Figure 15.4 Growth in trade and GDP 1960–90

Source: Jones, 2001; data provided by Jones, personal communication, 2002

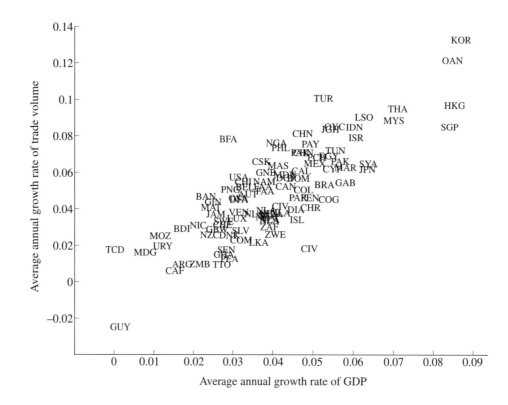

QUESTION

What is the broad relationship between the annual average growth rate of GDP and the average annual growth rate of trade shown by Figure 15.4?

Notice that the scatterplot has a broadly upward drift. This indicates that generally countries that have experienced higher growth in the volume of international trade have also experienced higher rates of growth of GDP. We could try to fit a line to this scatterplot, which would allow us to estimate the effect on the rate of growth of GDP of a 1 per cent increase in the growth of international trade but again, we cannot be sure which is cause and which is effect.

5.2   FOREIGN INVESTMENT AND GROWTH

Over a long period of time, foreign investment contributes to growth in two ways: raising productivity in the host economy and raising the rate of savings because of the higher profitability of foreign firms.

Both of these effects depend however on what foreign investment does to the quantity and productivity of domestic investment. In other words, it depends upon whether the relationship between the level and productivity of foreign investment is complementary or substitutive to the level and productivity of domestic investment. If the relationship between foreign and domestic investment is complementary, so that a rise in foreign investment increases the quantity and productivity of domestic investment, then the long-term impact of foreign investment on growth should be beneficial. If, however, foreign investment largely wipes out domestic investment, then the long-term effect of foreign investment on growth is not beneficial to the host economy. These arguments do not change when we use more sophisticated growth models, or more recent endogenous growth models (Chapter 18).

The impact of foreign investment on growth is not straightforward, because it affects a range of other macroeconomic aggregates such as domestic savings, domestic investment and the balance of payments (see Chapter 16). Casual empiricism too suggests that this is so. China has experienced large foreign capital inflows and high growth in recent years, while South Korea grew rapidly in the 1980s without significant levels of foreign capital inflow. Many Latin American countries have experienced low growth despite openness to foreign capital while much of sub-Saharan Africa has experienced low growth and poor investment flows.

The most careful study of the relationship between FDI, domestic investment and the balance of payments in host countries was undertaken by Fry (1995) for a sample of 16 large low income countries. He found that, in general, inflows of foreign investment seem to have a negative effect on domestic investment, after correcting for a host of other factors. Besides, foreign investment also tends to reduce domestic savings by more than the reduction in domestic investment, so that the impact on the current account (the balance of exports and imports) is often negative. Thus, Fry finds that foreign capital inflows often have a perverse impact on the host economy's balance of payments position. In the longer term, however, foreign capital inflows have a more beneficial impact on investment, savings and growth. Fry finds that, lagged five years, foreign capital inflows are positively related to domestic savings, investment and growth.

Fry also discovers that the impact of foreign investment differs among countries in his sample. Thus, for a sub-sample of Pacific Basin countries, foreign investment raised total investment by the full extent of the FDI inflow, with generally benign effects on growth. Outside the Pacific Basin, foreign investment served as a substitute for other kinds of flows; here lower investment, savings and growth accompanied larger inflows of foreign investment.

6   CONCLUSION   •

The period of the late 1980s and the 1990s saw an acceleration in world flows of international trade and investment, and in international and national debates this began to be referred to as globalization. Participation in international trade and production has the potential for several economic gains. Globalization pulls economies of the world together in production and potentially gives the benefits associated with large single markets. However, the extent of gains from globalization depends on several factors that are likely to vary from country to country. One crucial factor is the terms of trade between countries.

This chapter has shown how the effect of recent globalization has been limited to a few countries, and has on balance been associated with a more unequal world. Even as some countries appear to catch up with the Western world, there is increasing inequality within both high income and low income countries. Whether globalization has been the main factor creating these increases in inequality is a moot point. For the high income countries this link is unclear, while for the low income countries the link between globalization and inequality is stronger.

The current ire about globalization should be understood at least partially in terms of doubtful economic outcomes, which, when they do happen, also appear to be polarizing the world. Inequality always creates the potential for political conflicts.

CHAPTER 16 NATIONAL CURRENCIES AND INTERNATIONAL MONEY MARKETS

Suma Athreye ●

Objectives

After studying this chapter you should be able to:
● understand the main principles of the balance of payments accounts and their macroeconomic significance
● understand a model of exchange rate determination
● discuss the arguments for and against fixed and flexible exchange rate regimes.

Concepts

● the balance of payments
● current and capital accounts of the balance of payments
● bilateral and effective exchange rates
● nominal and real exchange rates
● fixed and flexible exchange rate regimes

1 INTRODUCTION ●

We have seen in Chapters 14 and 15 that the world economy has become increasingly open during the 1980s and 1990s, whether we measure this in terms of increasing trade flows or increasing levels of foreign investment and production. However, this is only half the story. Even more spectacular has been the increasing volume of transactions on international money markets over this period. Thus, in 1991, total world foreign exchange transactions averaged US$880 billion a day, 60 times the volume of world trade.

By international money market transactions, I mean the international purchase and sale of financial assets, usually foreign exchange, foreign bonds and equity. This can be residents of one country buying stocks and shares of a company or of a government of another country. Alternatively, it can be the switching of a bank account from one currency into another. As fewer foreign exchange controls are imposed by individual countries, and with the development of global communications and the associated improvements in financial market information, such transactions can now be effected much more quickly and more cheaply than, say, 30 years ago. Thus, it is getting much easier to be an international creditor or debtor than it was, say, in the 1970s.

Table 16.1 shows that the major economies became much more open to international capital transactions during the 1980s. Note, in particular, the importance of capital movements in the case of the UK economy, where international transactions in bonds and equities amounted to almost seven times the size of UK GDP in 1990. However, with the growth of international trade and production we should expect these developments. So why do these developments concern policy makers (in, for example, the UK Treasury) and policy analysts?

Table 16.1 Cross-border transactions in bonds and equities[1] as a percentage of GDP

	1970	1975	1980	1985	1990
Canada	5.7	3.3	9.6	26.7	63.8
France	–	–	8.4[2]	21.4	53.3
Germany	3.3	5.1	7.5	33.9	57.5
Italy	–	0.9	1.1	4.0	26.7
Japan	–	1.5	7.0	60.5	118.6
UK	–	–	–	367.5	690.1
USA	2.8	4.2	9.3	36.4	92.5

[1]Gross purchases and sales of securities between residents and non-residents.
[2]1982.
– not available.
Source: Bank of International Settlements, 1992, p.193

When you think of international money markets you may recall the spectacular collapse of the Thai baht in 1997, more recently the Argentinean peso in 2002, and you may remember 'Black Wednesday' in 1992 when the pound devalued sharply and the UK left the Exchange Rate Mechanism (ERM). Political fortunes were lost in each of these events. Contrast these strong feelings about national pride in particular currencies with the emergence of the euro; this, too, is a divisive battle with political overtones. Do national currencies have an advantage in Europe or is there an advantage for countries who have voluntarily surrendered their national currencies to join the euro? You may wonder what this debate is all about. Is it more about politics or does economics have something to do with the different political positions?

In this chapter I intend to provide you with an analytical framework for thinking about these questions. In this process you will also learn about the balance of payments, the factors that determine exchange rates and the problems that the international monetary system has faced, albeit from an economic perspective. To start with, however, we need to understand why international money markets exist at all and understand their particular characteristics. For this, your understanding of domestic money markets and the role of domestic finance is a useful starting point.

Just as the buying and selling of goods in domestic markets have to be paid for in money terms, the exports and imports of goods need to be paid for in international currencies. In common usage we call these payments foreign exchange payments. International trade is facilitated by the existence of foreign exchange markets in the same way as domestic exchange is facilitated by the use of national currencies. Put differently, the existence of international transactions gives rise to the need for international liquidity, and international monies and instruments exist to serve this function just as national currencies and monetary instruments for finance create liquidity in the domestic markets of individual countries.

Thus, international money markets resemble domestic money markets in important respects. Both types of markets provide liquidity that facilitates the exchange of goods and services through trade. Both markets have currencies that act as a medium of exchange for such transactions and also function as a store of value.

QUESTION

What is the crucial difference between domestic money markets and international money markets?

The crucial difference between the two markets lies in the fact that domestic money markets have one fiat currency or legal tender. Thus, in the UK, most transactions are conducted in pounds sterling which is the legal tender of the country. In international money markets there is no such legal tender and so a variety of currencies coexist. In open economies, agents in international markets can and do have preferences about which currency they would like to hold. For instance, given the choice, I might like to hold my savings in UK pounds or US dollars rather than Russian roubles or Indian rupees. Not only can I decide which currency I want to hold, my list of possible choices of currency increases as foreign exchange regulations in my country are relaxed. In turn, this gives rise to the possibility that the decisions of people like me, provided there are many more people thinking in this way, can change the price of one currency (pounds, say) vis-à-vis another (such as dollars). In a free market for national currencies this change in demand and supply can give rise to frequent fluctuations in exchange rates, which are the price of one currency in terms of another.

The lack of supremacy of one currency also affects international capital markets in a particular way. International investors can choose between holding money, bonds or equity just like investors on domestic markets. The difference, however, is that they can hold these bonds, money or equity denominated in any national currency that they choose. Consequently, in calculating their returns, international investors compare the relative rates of return in different currencies, assess the relative risk of holding assets in one kind of currency over another, and also factor in the possibility of capital gains or losses on account of exchange rate fluctuations between currencies. This last factor is, of course, absent in domestic stock market calculations about which stocks to invest in, since the price of pounds in terms of pounds is always the same.

These considerations increase the demand for some currencies over others, and thus influence the exchange rate of any one currency. More importantly, the exchange rate of the currency, such as the pound, becomes influenced by the difference in interest rates between the UK and the rest of the world. Policy makers are constrained by this dependence of the demand for pounds on the interest rate earned by deposits in pounds. This is because one of the implications of this dependence is that policy makers cannot tinker with interest rates to stimulate domestic investment without causing changes in exchange rates. It severely constrains the use of monetary policy to meet the needs of full employment in the domestic economy. However, this is not the only headache for governments. The money supply will increase as foreign exchange flows in, with potential inflationary consequences. The treasury has to be very alert about these international capital movements if it is serious about keeping price inflation under control. The value of a national currency is also a political issue, as it is often a symbol of national importance and strength. And to think that all these problems arise because we live in a world where international money and goods move freely!

You now have a flavour of the arguments that will be developed in this chapter. The remainder of the chapter is organized as follows. Section 2 starts with a discussion of the balance of payments, which keeps a record of the economy's transactions with the external sector or the 'rest of the world' as it is sometimes called. The transactions of an economy with the rest of the world are recorded with a particular value given to its currency. In Section 3, I address the question of what factors determine the exchange rate of a currency. In Section 4, I move away from the determination of particular exchange rates and look at the two main exchange rate regimes that have existed in the international monetary system – fixed and flexible exchange rates – and the case for and against them. I also briefly outline the somewhat chaotic history of the international monetary system, which will set the context for an understanding of the debate around the euro. In many respects, opting for something such as the euro amounts to getting rid of the problem of the lack of supremacy of one currency. But does it? Will it stick? Read on and join the debate!

2   INTERNATIONAL MONEY MARKETS AND THE BALANCE OF PAYMENTS

When residents of one country import goods and services from the rest of the world they pay a price for those goods and services usually in a foreign currency. All the transactions of an economy with the rest of the world are recorded in a balance sheet called the balance of payments. A sample balance of payments is shown in Table 16.2. The balance of payments is usually divided into two parts: the current account and the capital account. These two accounts record two different kinds of transactions.

Table 16.2 Balance of payments (£ million)

	1990	2000
Current account		
Inflows		
Exports of goods and services	133 887	265 335
Income (mainly investment)	78 206	133 997
Transfers	9426	13 582
Total inflows	221 519	412 914
Outflows		
Imports of goods and services	148 257	281 024
Income (mainly investment)	81 185	127 880
Transfers	14 358	22 405
Total outflows	243 800	431 309
Current account balance (= inflows minus outflows)	−22 281	−18 425
Capital account		
Net capital transfers	497	1973
Inflows		
Direct investment in UK	19 132	88 652
Portfolio investment in UK	12 880	165 045
Other financial investment	62 709	278 924
Total inflows	94 721	532 621
Outflows		
Direct investment abroad	10 936	165 673
Portfolio investment	15 925	61 493
Other financial investment	52 701	275 165
Reserves	76	3915
Total outflows	79 638	506 246
Capital account balance (= inflows minus outflows)	15 083	26 375
Net errors and omissions	6701	−9923

Source: *United Kingdom Balance of Payments (The Pink Book)*, 2001, Tables 1.2 and 7.1

If I directly import a camera from Japan I may need to pay in yen, if I import a computer from California in dollars, and so on. Similarly, if I provide consultancy services to a firm in Washington, I may bill them in pounds. In order to pay for the imports from Japan, I (or someone on my behalf) will have to buy yen on the international money markets. Since payment for these transactions usually happens at the point of sale, these transactions are sometimes referred to as *current* transactions and payment for them as current payments. The balance of these current payments for goods and services, exported and imported, is also referred to as the balance of trade.

Current payments for exports and imports by residents are not the only kind of transactions that take place on international money markets. Importers and exporters may want to issue short-term bills which are like IOUs for their consignments of imports and exports. Similarly, domestic investors may want to finance, for instance, expansion plans, and may want to borrow foreign exchange that will help them over such a period. These transactions are different from export and import payments.

QUESTION

How is this second set of international money market transactions different from the first type of payments for goods and services imported and exported?

The second set of transactions involves the extending of credit or borrowing: international currency is held for a period of time in the form of some financial instrument which may earn a return. For this reason such transactions are called *capital* transactions and are recorded as credit or debit items on the capital account. They are recorded differently from export and import payments whose payment is current, and not deferred. Capital transactions are concerned with international lending and borrowing, which generally take the form of the international sale and purchase of financial assets. You may also hear newspapers refer to such transactions as international capital transactions.

We can divide the capital account transactions into short- and long-term capital movements. Long-term capital movements include foreign direct investment (most importantly the financing of investment projects by multi-national companies) and portfolio investment (principally the purchase and sale of long-term bonds and equity). These long-term flows are also called autonomous flows since they depend on profitability and real demand conditions in the economies into which they flow, rather than on money market factors such as interest rates.

Short-term capital movements refer to transactions in short-term assets. This can mean simply switching bank accounts from one currency into another as well as the purchase and sale of short-term bills. This is a much more volatile element in capital movements and, generally, it is this kind of short-term borrowing activity which is involved when we refer to highly mobile international capital or 'hot money'.

The short-term flows of capital recorded in the capital account often happen in response to changes in the current account and are therefore called accommodating flows. If there is a shortfall of foreign currency to pay for an excess of imports over exports the economy as a whole will have to borrow from the international capital market or central banks may draw down their reserves of foreign currency to make those payments. Both these transactions will be recorded on the capital account of the balance of payments as credit items because they make currency available.

Undoubtedly, there will be a number of microeconomic transactions that underlie this macroeconomic flow. The importer may borrow from international markets by the issuance of trade bills and be prepared to offer interest on these bills in order to attract foreign currency. Or she may have to apply to the central bank to release some of the reserve foreign exchange. Or the government may sell this foreign exchange at a price to other foreign currency sellers, such as Thomas Cook or American Express. The macroeconomic entities affected by all those individual transactions will be recorded in the capital account of the balance of payments.

Thus, the capital account is like a mirror image of the current account. Items of debit on the current account (e.g. import payments) will be matched by a corresponding item of short-term credit on the capital account. The government can also influence the rate of interest to attract such capital inflows. For both these reasons, the short-term capital (account) flows can be thought of as happening to *accommodate* the balance of trade, thus rendering balance in the balance of payments.

QUESTION

What kind of capital account item is not accommodating?

Foreign investment outflows and inflows are examples of long-term capital flows that are recorded on the capital account but are autonomous of balance of trade considerations.

The current account and the capital account transactions of the balance of payments not only contain different types of transactions, they are also affected by largely different sets of factors. The current account is principally determined by exports and imports, which in turn are determined by domestic aggregate demand and world demand, domestic prices relative to world prices, and the exchange rate. The capital account, on the other hand, is likely to be affected in the short run by interest rate differentials and exchange rate expectations. Thus, an increase in domestic interest rates will tend to attract a capital inflow as international investors take advantage of the improved opportunities in domestic financial markets.

Balance of payments flows also feed back on the money supply and therefore liquidity in an economy. This would happen whenever the authorities are buying foreign exchange and selling domestic currency on the foreign exchange market. You may recall from Chapter 11 that all these transactions affect the amount of base money in the economy. In the case of the UK, if the Bank of England was selling sterling and accumulating foreign exchange, it therefore increases the supply of sterling in circulation. The monetary authorities can take some offsetting action by introducing sterilization policies. For example, the Bank of England could attempt to 'mop up' this increased money supply by open market operations, that is by selling bonds to holders of sterling. If this were successfully achieved, then the financial counterpart of the balance of payments surplus would be increased bond holdings rather than an increase in the domestic money supply.

In fact, the balance of payments is a good index to the health of the underlying macroeconomy and for this reason is scrutinized carefully by international investors and investing agencies. Any macroeconomic imbalance is reflected in the balance of payments. If governments spend too much, or there is excessive borrowing, or the economy is overheated, then all these are reflected in changes in either the capital or the current account.

QUESTION

How would excessive spending by a government be reflected in the balance of payments?

Recall from Chapter 11 that a deficit of taxes over government expenditures can spill over as a balance of trade deficit. Indeed, international investors scrutinize balance of payments figures quite carefully to look for confirmation of fiscal irresponsibility. This is why so much fuss is made of the data that are revealed in it.

EXERCISE 16.1

Would the following transactions appear as a credit or debit item, and on the current or capital account of the UK balance of payments? Explain the reason for your answer in one sentence.

1   Imports of shoes worth £10 000 from Italy by a clothes superstore in the UK.

2   Dividends of £5000 paid to US shareholders by a UK plc.

3   A UK resident buying shares worth US$20 000 in Telecom Inc., USA.

4   A UK student receiving an EU grant worth £6000 for study in England.

3   EXCHANGE RATES AND FACTORS INFLUENCING THEIR DETERMINATION •••••••••••••••••••••••••••••••

All balance of payments transactions are recorded at the prevailing exchange rate of a currency. The exchange rate of a currency is its price in terms of other currencies. In this section we will look into the question of what factors determine exchange rates in the international economy.

3.1 EXCHANGE RATES: DEFINITIONS AND MEASUREMENT

The exchange rate is the rate at which one currency is exchanged for another. It can therefore be regarded as the price of a unit of one currency in terms of another currency. In the UK it is customary to express the exchange rate as the number of units of foreign currency required to buy one unit of domestic currency, for example £1 = US$1.50. A fall in the exchange rate is a depreciation and a rise in the exchange rate is an appreciation of the domestic currency.

A BILATERAL EXCHANGE RATE is the exchange rate between two currencies, and this is the kind of exchange rate that is most frequently cited in the press and the media. Figure 16.1 shows the dollar/pound rate, the euro/pound rate and the Deutschmark/pound rate for the period from 1979 to 2000. Note the depreciation of the pound in the early 1980s, which continued against the Deutschmark and the euro (but not the dollar) until the mid 1990s. This happened just after high interest rates and the confidence of currency speculators in the prospects for the UK economy and, hence, in the future value of the pound had caused a temporary appreciation in the pound in the first years of the Thatcher government. This appreciation of the pound had damaging consequences for those sections of UK manufacturing industry whose performance in world markets depended on being competitive on price.

BILATERAL EXCHANGE RATE

The bilateral exchange rate is the number of units of foreign currency that exchange for one unit of the home currency.

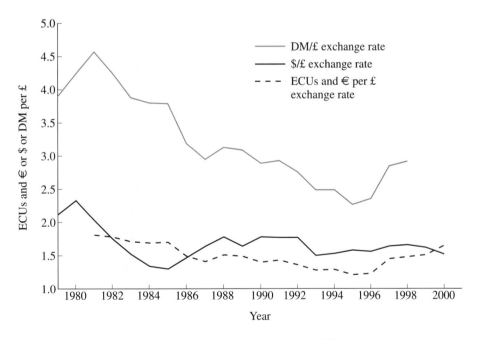

Figure 16.1 UK bilateral exchange rates (DM, US$, ECUs/€), 1979–2000

Source: *Economic Trends*, various years

The international pattern of bilateral exchange rates should always be consistent across financial centres and across currencies. Thus, if the pound is trading at US$1.55 in New York it should also be trading at US$1.55 in Tokyo. If exchange rates are not consistent with each other in this way, then there is scope for arbitrage, which means buying and selling currencies for profit. Arbitrage activities ensure that exchange rates are brought into line with each other.

Bilateral exchange rates show only the relative price of one currency in terms of another. If we are interested in the overall strength or weakness of a given currency,

EFFECTIVE EXCHANGE RATE

The effective exchange rate is the value of the home currency expressed in terms of a basket of foreign currencies, each weighted by its share of trade with the home country.

BILATERAL REAL EXCHANGE RATE

The bilateral real exchange rate is the nominal bilateral exchange rate multiplied by an index of domestic prices and divided by an index of prices in the foreign country.

then we would need to have a measure of a country's exchange rate against the average of all other currencies. In this case, we would require a measure of the EFFECTIVE EXCHANGE RATE. The effective exchange rate expresses the value of the home currency in terms of a basket of foreign currencies, where each currency is weighted by its country's share of trade with the home country. The effective exchange rate is expressed as an index.

Both bilateral and effective exchange rates as defined above are nominal exchange rates. This is to be contrasted with a country's real exchange rate which takes into account relative price levels. The BILATERAL REAL EXCHANGE RATE is the ratio of two countries' price levels, translated into a common currency via the nominal exchange rate. Thus, we have:

$$e = \frac{EP}{P*} \qquad\qquad (1)$$

where e is the bilateral real exchange rate between the two countries, E is the nominal exchange rate, P is the domestic price level, and $P*$ is the price level in the foreign country. The real exchange rate can be taken as a measure of price competitiveness between the two countries. Price competitiveness is determined by the real exchange rate, not the nominal exchange rate. Thus, it is quite possible for a change in the nominal exchange rate to be offset by a change in domestic prices, leaving the real exchange rate (and therefore competitiveness) unchanged. For example, a 5 per cent depreciation of the nominal exchange rate will not affect the real exchange rate if it is accompanied by a 5 per cent faster increase in domestic prices than in world prices.

EFFECTIVE REAL EXCHANGE RATE

The effective real exchange rate is the effective exchange rate multiplied by an index of domestic prices and divided by a weighted average of price indices across foreign countries.

It is also possible to construct an EFFECTIVE REAL EXCHANGE RATE which would provide a measure of the domestic country's price competitiveness vis-à-vis the rest of the world. This would be a trade-weighted average of the relevant bilateral real exchange rates. The construction of such an index is complex since it needs to take into account price level changes in all of the domestic country's trading partners.

If the nominal exchange rate were exactly such as to equalize the purchasing power of a unit of domestic currency in both countries, that is £1 could buy the same basket of goods in both countries, then the real exchange rate would be unity, and the nominal exchange rate would be generating what is known as absolute purchasing power parity. Personal experience suggests that absolute purchasing power parity does not customarily hold, since we know from travelling abroad that some countries are 'cheap' while others are 'expensive'. This is a way of saying that the domestic currency's real exchange rate is relatively high in the former case and low in the latter.

Figure 16.2 sets out the nominal and real effective exchange rate indices for the UK. Note that the real effective exchange rate fluctuates almost as much as the nominal effective exchange rate, and note in particular the period from 1979 to 1981 where both the real and nominal effective exchange rates for the pound appreciated significantly, followed by both rates depreciating significantly through to the mid 1980s.

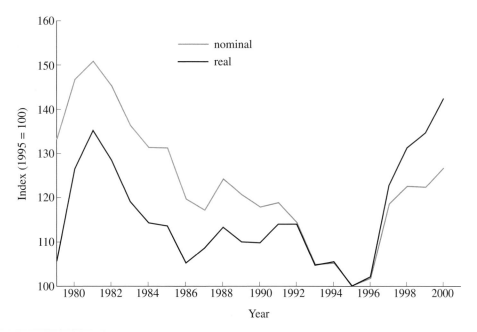

Figure 16.2   UK effective exchange rates, 1979–2000 (1995 = 100)

Source: *Economic Trends*, various years

EXERCISE 16.2

1   You will see on Figure 16.2 that the real exchange rate appreciated by more than the nominal exchange rate in the period from 1979 to 1981. What does this imply about UK inflation as compared with the rest of the world?

2   What would be happening to UK inflation as compared with the rest of the world if the nominal exchange rate appreciated and the real exchange rate depreciated at the same time?

3.2   A SIMPLE MODEL OF EXCHANGE RATE DETERMINATION

Exchange rates are determined in the foreign exchange market which exists, as I explained above, because of the currency needs of individuals and institutions involved in international trade or international capital transactions. In this section, I present a simple model of the exchange rate, based on the limiting assumption that there are no capital account transactions (that is, assuming capital is completely immobile). Everything that is bought is paid for in foreign exchange earned in the same period. This simplifies the discussion in the first instance, but I relax the assumption in the next section.

The demand and supply of foreign exchange in this model is directly related to the transactions needs of importers and exporters. For example, a UK importer buying goods from the USA will have to buy dollars in order to pay the US exporter. Generally, individuals would not buy foreign exchange directly on the foreign exchange market, but rather would work through a bank, which would, in turn, work through a foreign exchange broker.

The key point to note about these transactions is that they must involve the exchange of one currency for another: when selling one currency, an institution must necessarily be buying another currency. Thus, factors affecting the demand for domestic currency in the foreign exchange market are equally factors affecting the supply of foreign currency, and vice versa.

Let me now set out a simple model of the supply and demand for foreign currency in the foreign exchange market with the aid of Figure 16.3.

Figure 16.3   A simple model of exchange rate determination

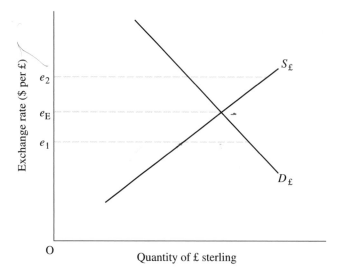

In Figure 16.3 we measure units of the domestic currency along the horizontal axis and the exchange rate (denominated as the number of units of foreign currency per unit of domestic currency, in this case dollars per pound) along the vertical axis. $D_£$ shows the demand for domestic currency in the foreign exchange market to be a downward-sloping function of the exchange rate, while $S_£$ shows the supply of domestic currency on the foreign exchange market to be an upward-sloping function of the exchange rate.

Looking first at the demand for domestic currency, the simplest explanation for the downward-sloping $D_£$ schedule relates to competitiveness and the demand for domestic exports. Recalling equation (1) above, note that for a given P and P^*, a fall in E is both a nominal and a real depreciation. This increases competitiveness and therefore increases the foreign demand for domestic exports. For example, suppose a UK manufacturer was producing a car which sold for £10 000 in the UK when the exchange rate was £1 = US$1.50. This car would then sell for US$15 000 in the USA. Suppose now that the exchange rate depreciates to £1 = US$1.25. With the pound sterling price of the car unchanged, the dollar price would fall to US$12 500, increasing the attractiveness of the car in the US market. We would therefore expect US imports of British cars to increase. US importers would therefore require more sterling to finance these purchases. Thus, a fall in the exchange rate has increased the demand for sterling in the foreign exchange market.

Similarly, the supply of sterling on the foreign exchange market reflects domestic demand for dollars, since in order to buy dollars, sterling holders have to sell sterling. A rise in the exchange rate is an appreciation which, for given dollar prices, must reduce the sterling price of goods imported from the USA. This will increase UK demand for US exports, increasing the demand for dollars and therefore probably increasing the supply of sterling on the foreign exchange market. (I say 'probably' here because it is theoretically possible that a rising demand for dollars does not translate into a falling supply of sterling, since the exchange rate is changing too.)

We now have the ingredients of a simple model of exchange rate determination. At an exchange rate such as e_1 (see Figure 16.3), the demand for pounds is greater than the supply. This can be taken to mean that the value of exports exceeds the value of imports. In the foreign exchange market the price of pound sterling is bid up, that is, the exchange rate begins to appreciate. As this happens, export demand (and therefore the demand for sterling) falls, while import demand (and therefore the demand for dollars and probably the supply of sterling) rises. This continues until the exchange rate reaches its equilibrium value of e_E. An analogous story applies to an exchange rate such as e_2, where the value of imports exceeds the value of exports, and the exchange rate depreciates.

Note that in the above example, the authorities do not intervene at all in the market, and thus the exchange rate is said to be freely floating or flexible. Also note that as the exchange rate rises to its equilibrium, the demand for sterling is falling and the supply of sterling is rising. This reflects falling exports and rising imports as competitiveness is reduced by the appreciating exchange rate. Thus, at the equilibrium exchange rate e_E, exports are equal to imports which, in the absence of capital transactions, implies balance of payments equilibrium.

Of course, there are other factors besides the exchange rate which affect exports and imports. The exchange rate is important because it affects competitiveness, but we have already seen in Section 3.1 that it is the real exchange rate rather than the nominal exchange rate which is the appropriate measure of price competitiveness. Thus, it is possible for competitiveness to increase at a given nominal exchange rate if domestic prices fall relative to world prices (each expressed in their own respective currencies). If, say, foreign prices were to rise and domestic prices remain constant, then exports will rise shifting the demand curve to the right, and imports will fall, probably shifting the supply curve to the left. Under floating exchange rates, the result is an appreciation of the domestic currency. This is an interesting example because it highlights one property which is frequently claimed for flexible exchange rates, namely that flexible exchange rates insulate the domestic economy from the effects of world inflation. Since the appreciation described above will tend to reduce import costs, world inflation is prevented from being 'imported' into the domestic economy.

Competitiveness, however, is not simply a matter of relative prices. Certain non-price aspects of competitiveness (such as styling, marketing, after-sales service, reliability) are also likely to be important. For example, much of Italy's success in promoting export industries in the 1950s and the 1960s was ascribed as much to fashion and style as to price competitiveness. Similarly, perceived reliability may be one of the factors behind the international success of the Japanese car industry. In the 1980s and 1990s technological change and innovation have been the important factors behind the surge in information technology exports from the USA.

Domestic and foreign income levels are also likely to be important in determining trade flows. Increasing incomes abroad will tend to increase demand for the domestic country's exports simply because of market growth. Similarly, increasing domestic income will tend to increase the demand for imports.

Note that changes in any of these factors (other than changes in the nominal exchange rate itself) will affect exports and imports and therefore shift the demand and supply curves in Figure 16.3, with consequences for the nominal exchange rate.

EXERCISE 16.3

1   In the light of the above, what do you think are the likely consequences for a country's exchange rate if its income growth is consistently above that of its trading partners?

2   How do you reconcile your answer with the experience of rapidly growing countries with customarily strong currencies, such as Germany?

Until now, I have assumed that market forces determine the exchange rate. Turning to Figure 16.4, suppose that the authorities, that is the government and the central bank, wish to stabilize or 'fix' the exchange rate at its equilibrium level, e_E. So long as the demand and supply curves remain at $D_{£1}$ and $S_£$ there is no need for the authorities to do anything. However, suppose that world income falls. This means that, other things remaining equal, domestic exports will fall, shifting the demand curve to the left, say to $D_{£2}$. There is now excess supply of sterling (equal to $Q_2 - Q_1$) and under floating rates this would lead to depreciation to e_1. If the authorities wish to prevent this they can intervene in the foreign exchange market by buying sterling (equal to the excess supply $Q_2 - Q_1$). However, if the authorities are buying sterling, they are necessarily selling foreign exchange. The authorities' stock of foreign exchange is called their foreign exchange reserves, and intervention to prevent a depreciation of the currency depletes their stock of reserves. This can only be a short-run measure as such stocks are limited. If the deficit persists, even in the long run, the authorities will need to carry out domestic policies to remove the deficit (e.g. reducing domestic demand and thus shift the supply curve to the left) or let the exchange rate depreciate (which would, in turn, remove the deficit by making exports more competitive).

EXERCISE 16.4

Starting from a balance of payments equilibrium, what form of intervention would be required to peg the exchange rate if:

1   there was a sudden switch in tastes away from domestic exports?

2   world inflation surged ahead of domestic inflation?

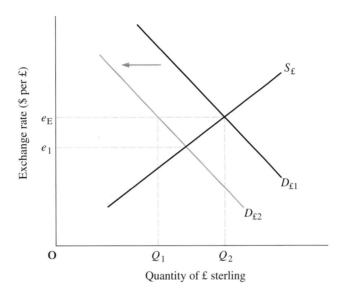

Figure 16.4
Intervention in the
foreign exchange
market

It is worth noting that such intervention policies have implications for the domestic money stock and liquidity. When the authorities buy sterling (that is, when the balance of payments is in deficit), this reduces the amount of sterling in circulation and therefore reduces the domestic money supply. Alternatively, when the balance of payments is in surplus and the authorities sell sterling to peg the exchange rate, then the domestic money supply is increased.

Are the monetary consequences of exchange rate intervention avoidable? To some extent they are if the domestic authorities undertake offsetting action. Such policies are referred to as sterilization policies. One possibility is that a surplus country might sell bonds domestically, to 'mop up' the domestic monetary consequences of exchange rate intervention. A problem, however, is that domestic residents need to be persuaded to buy these bonds, and this will normally require some increase in domestic interest rates. As we shall see, once I introduce capital movements into the picture, such sterilization policies become distinctly problematical.

3.3   EXCHANGE RATES AND THE CAPITAL ACCOUNT

The simple model of exchange rates developed in the last section may provide a relevant explanation of exchange rates in the long run, but it does not provide a convincing account of how the foreign exchange market works in the short run. It is now time to introduce capital movements into our model, since capital transactions now play a dominating role in the foreign exchange market especially in the short run when economic agents needing a particular currency are willing to borrow from others who may have a surplus of that currency. In analysing capital movements, it is useful to think of a world where there is a large number of portfolio holders (such as international fund managers) seeking to maximize the rate of return on their portfolios of financial investments by allocating their funds between assets denominated in different currencies according to expected rates of return of these assets and their perceived risk.

There are two principal factors which taken together measure the relative rate of return of assets denominated in different currencies: relative interest rates and expected exchange rate changes. Interest rates will have a more significant effect on capital flows if domestic and foreign assets are close substitutes. For example, if UK and German assets were very close substitutes and assuming that the exchange rate was not expected to change, then an increase in German interest rates would bid funds away from the UK into Germany. This would bid up UK rates and bid down German rates. The closer are the two sets of assets as substitutes, the nearer will their interest rates be bid to equality.

In the limiting case where assets are perfect substitutes, domestic and foreign interest rates would be equal. This is sometimes referred to as perfect capital mobility. It is certainly the case that the development of international capital markets, associated with financial deregulation and advances in information technology, has increased the degree of capital mobility quite remarkably. However, so long as some assets are regarded as riskier than others, and other factors such as taxation differ between countries, then financial assets will not be perfect substitutes between countries. Under these circumstances, the riskier assets, will have to yield higher interest to compensate portfolio holders, and this is called the risk premium.

Interest rates are not the only factor motivating short-term capital movements. Portfolio holders will also take into account expected future changes in exchange rates in assessing the relative rates of return of alternative assets. As an example, consider a UK investor deciding between holding a UK (sterling denominated) asset bearing 6%, and a US (dollar denominated) asset bearing 8%. If the dollar/pound exchange rate is expected to be unchanged, and if investors are indifferent between the UK and US assets, then the USA can be said to be bearing a risk premium of 2%.

Suppose now that the market forms the expectation that the dollar is going to depreciate with respect to sterling in the coming year by 5%. This affects our investor's calculations in two ways. First, the actual interest payment (assuming it is paid at the end of the year) will be worth 5% less in sterling terms. This is, however, a minor adjustment, on its own reducing the effective rate of interest from 8% to 7.6% (i.e. 95% of 8%). Much more significant is the fact that the capital invested will be worth 5% less in sterling terms if the expected dollar depreciation comes about. It is this expected capital loss which dramatically reduces the rate of return on the dollar asset as compared with the sterling asset, more than offsetting the nominal interest differential between the two countries. In this example, £100 invested in the UK at 6% is worth £106 (£100 × 1.06) at the end of the year. In contrast, the same £100 invested in the US asset, and then converted back into sterling at the end of the year, is worth only £102.60 (£100 × 1.08 × 0.95). In other words, the expected effective rate of return on the dollar asset is reduced by just a little more than the expected depreciation of the dollar over the year, and since this rate of return is now below that of sterling assets, investors would be likely to switch their funds out of dollars and into sterling.

The relationship between exchange rate expectations and interest rates under perfect capital mobility is highlighted in what is known as the 'uncovered interest parity condition', set out in equation (2a). It is important to note that this condition assumes that domestic and foreign assets are perfect substitutes. In that limiting case, in the absence of any expected change in exchange rates, we would expect domestic and foreign interest rates to be equal. That is,

$$r = r_F$$

where r is the domestic (or, in the above example, the UK) interest rate, and r_F is the 'world' (or the US) interest rate.

Now suppose that markets form the view that the sterling exchange rate is going to change in the coming year, where that expected change is denoted by Δe. If Δe is positive, then markets are expecting a sterling appreciation. This would generate a capital inflow, increasing the demand for sterling in the foreign exchange market. This would serve to bring about the uncovered parity condition that

$$r = r_F - \Delta e \tag{2}$$

or alternatively

$$r - r_F = -\Delta e \tag{2a}$$

What this condition states is that if the domestic currency is expected to appreciate ($\Delta e > 0$) then the domestic interest rate should be below the world interest rate by an amount equal to the expected appreciation.

This condition can be amended to take into account less than perfect capital mobility by adding a term to denote the risk premium. Thus, where domestic and foreign assets are imperfect substitutes, we have

$$r - r_F = -\Delta e + x \tag{3}$$

where x is the risk premium on domestic assets over foreign assets. If x is positive, then domestic assets are deemed to be riskier than foreign assets.

Figure 16.5 shows the short-term interest rate differential between the UK and Germany over the period from 1984 to 1998. As this differential has been mostly positive, UK interest rates have been fairly consistently higher than German rates over the period.

QUESTION

Suggest two possible reasons for the UK–German interest rate differential based on your understanding of equation (3).

Equation (3) suggests that one reason for the UK–German interest rate differential is that the assets of the two countries might not be perfect substitutes and that UK assets bear a risk premium over German assets (i.e. the risk premium, x, is positive). The second reason is that markets might consistently have been expecting sterling to depreciate with respect to the Deutschmark over the period, perhaps because of the

Figure 16.5
UK–German interest
rate differentials,
1984–98

Source: *Economic Trends*,
various years

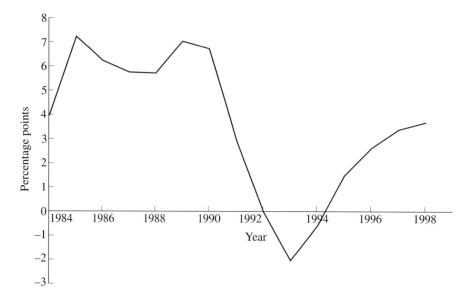

UK's higher inflation rate (i.e. the expected exchange rate, Δ*e*, is negative). Under such expectations, international investors would require higher UK interest rates as a reward for holding a depreciating currency.

QUESTION

Now look again at Figure 16.1. Can you explain the trends in the DM/£ bilateral exchange rate with knowledge of UK–German interest rate differentials?

It can be argued that the appreciation of sterling against both the dollar and the Deutschmark during the period from 1979 to 1981 was the counterpart of Mrs Thatcher's domestic monetary policy. When Mrs Thatcher came to power, she afforded a high priority to reducing inflation through high interest rates. In accordance with this anti-inflationary strategy, sterling appreciated substantially. During the rest of the 1980s, sterling's steady depreciation against the Deutschmark was interrupted only briefly (in 1987) by the strategy, adopted by finance minister Lawson, of pegging the exchange rate to the Deutschmark.

Short-term capital movements can be crucially important in explaining day-to-day changes in exchange rates. Consider once more the behaviour of international asset holders and let us assume that the assets in their portfolios are imperfect substitutes. The demand for any given asset will be a positive function of its expected rate of return, and a negative function of the rate of return on alternative assets. Suppose now that the interest rate on UK assets rises. There is now excess demand for sterling in the foreign exchange market. This will bid up sterling's exchange rate, which increases the relative price of UK assets in international portfolios and should remove the excess demand. The net result of the increase in UK interest rates is a sterling appreciation.

Similarly, an expected change in the exchange rate must affect the current exchange rate. If portfolio holders expect a currency to depreciate in the future, this will reduce demand for that currency, reducing the exchange rate today. Indeed, the current price of any asset must embody all the information currently available which could affect the future price of that asset. Any new information (which we might call 'news') must therefore lead to a change in the current price of that asset. An obvious source of relevant news is credible announcements by the authorities on the future course of policy.

Increased capital mobility has meant that interest rates, exchange rate expectations, and new information have become important determinants of day-to-day fluctuations in the exchange rate. In turn, this implies that it is very difficult for one country's authorities to 'peg' effectively the exchange rate by means of intervention policies alone. First, the potential scale of capital movements is now so large relative to the foreign exchange reserves of most individual countries that they do not have the financial 'muscle' to out-buy or out-sell the market. For example, suppose the authorities attempt to set the exchange rate at a level which the market believes to be too high (or alternatively sets interest rates at a level which is too low for that exchange rate). There will be a large-scale capital outflow. To maintain the exchange rate by means of intervention, the authorities would have to purchase all the sterling being sold as the counterpart of the capital outflow, and it is unlikely that they would have sufficient reserves to do this.

Even if this is not the case, and the authorities do possess enough reserves, those wishing to peg their currency are constrained in other ways. They must implement domestic monetary policies that will deliver an interest rate and price levels that are consistent with their exchange rate target, so that the market accepts the exchange rate as credible. If international investors believe that governments are pursuing inconsistent and therefore unsustainable economic policies they may respond by moving out of the currency before it crashes in value. By doing so, they may cause the currency to actually crash in value. This is what many people believe happened during the East Asian financial crisis of 1997/1998.

3.4   IMPACT OF EXCHANGE RATES ON MACROECONOMIC VARIABLES

An important issue that I have not included in the discussion so far is the influence of the exchange rate on the domestic economy. There are at least two ways in which exchange rates influence macroeconomic variables in the domestic economy. The first is through the exchange rate's influence in contributing to an inflationary or deflationary climate and the second is through its effect on import costs.

In general, exchange rate appreciation has disinflation effects while exchange rate depreciation has inflationary effects on the economy. Appreciation works to cheapen imports and thus reduce aggregate demand in the economy.

By cheapening imports that are used in the production of other goods, it keeps price levels in the economy down. All of this contributes to a disinflationary climate.

A good example of the two sets of disinflationary effects that an exchange rate appreciation can impart is provided by the appreciation of the pound between 1980 and 1992. First, appreciation reduced relative import costs, which in turn reduced inflationary pressures, perhaps through wages as well as costs of inputs. Second, it reduced demand pressures by reducing export demand. Certainly inflation fell very substantially in the UK in the early 1980s, from 18% in 1980 to 4.7% in 1983.

This link between exchange rate policies and the general macroeconomic climate in the economy implies that exchange rate policies can have important consequences on real economic activity. Thus, it is argued that reducing inflation through exchange rate appreciation in the 1980s resulted in increases in output costs, some of which were substantial and long-lasting in the UK. Since the fall in demand hit the export sector, this affected UK manufacturing disproportionately. Between 1979 and 1981, manufacturing output fell by almost 15 per cent and did not recover its 1979 level until 1988. As output growth fell, it affected productivity and therefore the competitiveness and future exports of the manufacturing sector.

Many low income countries have faced a different situation whereby continuous depreciation of their currency has had the same effect on their international trade and the balance of payments as a deterioration in the terms of trade. Falling export prices due to devaluation has not helped the economies import more. Domestic consumption has been forcibly decreased in favour of export production in order to keep inflationary pressures in check. As a consequence, in many of these countries, political leaders argue that there is a net transfer of real resources from their economy to the rest of world through the devaluation of their currencies.

4   EXCHANGE RATE REGIMES: THEORY AND HISTORY •••

We saw in Section 3 that if governments want to keep stable exchange rates they need to have appropriate monetary polices. Among other things there will need to be controls on capital movements and governments must maintain reserves. This guarantee only works as long as governments have the foreign exchange reserves necessary for them to intervene in the foreign exchange market when the demand or supply for their currency changes, whether under the influence of changes to world incomes and price levels or in response to changes in speculative expectations.

If governments go in for flexible exchange rates they will need to be concerned about relative rates of inflation at home and abroad as this will determine the value of the currency. In the shorter term, interest rates are directly related to movements in exchange rates, especially if there are few controls on capital. This constrains governments' fiscal and monetary policy considerably.

Thus, the important policy objectives and the appropriate instruments of domestic policy depend very much on the exchange rate regime the economy subscribes to. In analytical terms, it is convenient to think about two types of exchange rate regimes: flexible exchange rates or fixed exchange rates. Under flexible exchange rates, economies allow forces of market demand and supply to determine the values of their currency, vis-à-vis other currencies. Under fixed exchange rates, governments guarantee a certain value for their currency in terms of other currencies.

Two centuries ago an international monetary system emerged in which national governments experimented with both fixed and flexible exchange rates. Often the international monetary system has operated with hybrid exchange rate regimes that contain some elements of both fixed and flexible exchange rates. However, the absence of an overall governing body has meant that these exercises have been fragile experiments with a strong tendency to break down. In 1999 we had a new experiment, where twelve countries of Europe have come together in a voluntary monetary union under a single supranational currency, the euro. In this section, I will review the analytical arguments for fixed or flexible exchange rate regimes and follow this with a brief history of the international monetary system. Then I will look at the arrangements in the euro zone and how they have evolved over time, culminating in the emergence of the euro.

4.1 FIXED AND FLEXIBLE EXCHANGE RATE REGIMES: ARGUMENTS FOR AND AGAINST

The principal argument in favour of a regime of fixed exchange rates is that it removes an important element of risk from international trade. Import and export deals are frequently struck well in advance of delivery and payment. Thus, given that prices have to be agreed in one currency, a change in the exchange rate between the date of the contract and the date of payment will change the agreed price in the other currency. Under flexible exchange rates there would be no such stability.

Three points are worth noting about this argument. First, the burden of exchange risk is borne by the party in whose currency the price is not fixed. Since importers are generally invoiced in the exporter's currency, this means that importers must bear the exchange risk. Second, importers may win, as well as lose, through exchange rate changes. It is the existence of risk, which is the disincentive, and this will only be important to the extent that traders are risk averse. Finally, at least for short-term contracts, the existence of the forward exchange market enables traders to hedge against exchange risk (at a cost). In these markets importers can buy foreign exchange for delivery in the future at an exchange rate agreed today. However, forward exchange markets generally focus on three- and six-month contracts, and more medium-term exchange risks remain.

A second argument for fixed exchange rates concerns the role of speculators in the foreign exchange market. It is held that flexible rates mean unstable rates. Against this, proponents of floating rates argue that flexibility does not mean volatility, on the grounds that the actions of speculators should ensure that exchange rates are always at, or at least adjusting towards, their equilibrium value. Speculators, on this view, buy when the price is 'too low' and sell when the price is 'too high'. Speculators who consistently make mistakes will go out of business.

But do speculators act in this way? Frequently asset markets are driven by the 'herd' instinct where speculative surges in the market can feed on themselves and market expectations become self-fulfilling. A closely related notion is that of a 'speculative bubble' where even rational speculators know that the exchange rate is, for example, rising progressively away from equilibrium, but the belief that the bubble is not quite ready to burst means that speculators perceive the prospect of a further capital gain which is just enough to compensate them for the risk of the bubble bursting prematurely.

Even when speculators are rational, they may act on false information. The so-called 'finance minister' problem arises when a government leads the market to believe that a particular policy change is about to happen, therefore affecting exchange rate expectations and the current exchange rate, but then proceeds to renege on this policy announcement. The exchange rate then adjusts back. In all these cases the exchange rate is driven, at least in the short run, away from its long-run equilibrium value, distorting both the trading position and the domestic price level of the economy.

What about the case for flexible exchange rates? An important argument is that flexible exchange rates automatically correct balance of payments surpluses and deficits leaving the authorities free to pursue domestic objectives of growth, employment and price stability. This is sometimes described as the retention of economic sovereignty. However, the above argument can be turned on its head. It may be that having to be concerned about the balance of payments acts as a disciplining device on governments. In particular, governments can face the temptation to run fiscal deficits and to finance these by printing money. Such governments are commonly thought of as being fiscally irresponsible. Under fixed exchange rates they would face balance of payments difficulties which would require the government to implement deflationary policies. Under flexible exchange rates, however, this discipline would be removed.

A second argument for a regime of flexible exchange rates is that it serves to insulate the domestic economy from foreign shocks. For example, if there is recession abroad, this can spread to the domestic economy through falling demand for domestic exports. However, under flexible exchange rates, the exchange rate of the domestic economy would tend to depreciate, increasing the competitiveness of domestic exports and offsetting the effects of falling foreign income levels. The domestic economy would therefore, at least to some extent, be insulated from the foreign recession. A similar argument can be put forward regarding world inflation. If domestic inflation is lower than world inflation, then the domestic currency will tend to appreciate, reducing import prices, and therefore insulating the domestic economy from foreign inflation.

It should be clear from this discussion that there are substantial arguments for and against adopting either kind of exchange rate regime. Since the case for any one kind of regime is not clear-cut in economic terms, a mixture of immediate crises and political factors have determined the evolution of the international monetary system. As Section 4.2 will show, it has evolved chaotically, through trial and error, and in response to immediate crises and the political objectives of the dominant trading nations.

EXERCISE 16.5

In Section 4.1 I have outlined two arguments in favour of fixed exchange rates and two arguments in favour of flexible exchange rates.

1   State briefly, in one sentence for each argument, the two arguments in favour of fixed exchange rates.

2   State briefly, in one sentence for each argument, the two arguments in favour of flexible exchange rates.

3   Now for some of the objections to the arguments. State a reason for questioning each of the two arguments in favour of fixed exchange rates.

4   State a reason for questioning each of the two arguments in favour of flexible exchange rates.

4.2   THE INTERNATIONAL MONETARY SYSTEM

An international monetary system based on national currencies emerged with the supremacy of the UK economy in world trade in the eighteenth century. Though international trade and national currencies existed before the eighteenth century, most settlements of trade were made through the transfer of gold bullion between countries.

The Gold Standard emerged gradually from this system of settlement by bullion. In 1821, Britain guaranteed the full convertibility of its currency against gold. America and France soon followed and guaranteed that their currencies were fully convertible into gold. In theory the Gold Standard rested on an automatic adjustment mechanism: a country with a trade surplus would experience a net inflow of gold and so an expanded money supply in the economy. Sooner or later, as the economy hit full capacity, the increase in aggregate spending due to this expanded money supply would result in a rise in prices. This would effectively appreciate the currency, reducing price competitiveness and hence exports until the surplus was wiped out. In practice, however, gold was rarely exchanged. The pound sterling was 'as good as gold' and so the Gold Standard operated with the pound as the centrepiece. This was like a fixed exchange rate regime and imparted stability to the international trading system.

As countries went to war between 1914 and 1918 many de-linked their currencies from gold. Many needed to print more money to finance wartime spending. By the end of the First World War, Britain was no longer the country with the largest export surpluses: France and the USA had caught up. In 1925 Britain returned to the Gold Standard at the pre-war, and by 1925 over-valued, exchange rate. This was followed by the General Strike in 1926 and a huge speculative attack focused on the pound. The central bank in France started cashing in its export surplus in pound sterling for gold between 1926 and 1930. Soon the Bank of England ran out of gold reserves and could no longer maintain convertibility. Notice how much like a run on a bank such a speculative attack is. The Bank of England had to confess it did not have enough reserves of gold. Britain left the Gold Standard in 1931 and international confidence in the currency suffered.

There were two broad effects of Britain leaving the Gold Standard. Countries that had pegged their currencies to the pound sterling, believing it was as good as gold, had to come off the Gold Standard as well, causing wide instability in their exchange rates. This in turn caused large-scale financial failures and bankruptcies as investors in international markets saw their stocks depreciate in value suddenly. A second effect came because some countries remained on the Gold Standard while many others had left. These countries (e.g. France, Italy) had to impose protectionist barriers to protect themselves against the depreciating value of their rivals' currencies. This in turn sparked off a retaliatory tariff war between nations.

After the Second World War, a plan drawn up by Keynes formed the basis of what was to be a new international monetary system. It was to be based on a system of fixed exchange rates with some mechanism for clearing international payments that would be accepted by all nations. Bhaduri (1986) points out that Keynes had suggested this clearing system be based on an international currency called the 'bancor' which would be exchanged against gold. Deficit and surplus states had to agree to accept these 'bancor' units in settlement whatever the actual value of their currencies. In practice, American influence ensured the new monetary system that emerged was based around the US dollar.

For about half of the period since the Second World War the world economy has operated under a system of broadly fixed exchange rates known as the Bretton Woods system, so named because it was established following an international monetary conference held in Bretton Woods, New Hampshire in 1944. Each country's exchange rate was to be fixed (within 1 per cent either way of a central parity) to the US dollar, with the dollar being pegged to the price of gold at US$35 per ounce. The system was not one of completely fixed exchange rates. Individual countries could negotiate an exchange rate change if its balance of payments entered 'fundamental' disequilibrium, devaluing the currency if their rate was too high or revaluing it if it was too low. For example, following a succession of substantial UK balance of payments deficits, sterling was devalued by 14 per cent in 1967 (from US$2.80 to US$2.40). The Bretton Woods system was, therefore, an 'adjustable peg' system, where one-off exchange rate adjustments were within the rules. Multilateral institutions such as the International Monetary Fund were also set up to help member states over temporary balance of payments deficits by allowing them to borrow the required foreign exchange.

The relatively successful operation of the Bretton Woods system was attributable to the imperfect mobility of international capital over most of this period. The continuing existence of foreign exchange controls substantially restricted international capital movements, which made it easier for the authorities of a given country to peg their exchange rate by means of official intervention in the foreign exchange market. Such intervention was more likely to be successful under foreign exchange controls, since these controls restricted the amount of speculative pressure which could be generated against a currency.

However, dollar reserves accumulated in European and American banks located outside of the USA. By the mid 1960s they freely created credit in the form of dollar denominated loans. Soon it was clear that there was more going around as dollar liabilities than the US government could support against its gold reserves. Bhaduri (1986) notes that in 1950 for the USA, the ratio of total international reserves (gold plus foreign currencies) to dollar liabilities held abroad stood at 2.7. This ratio of the reserve backing of the dollar came down to 1.6 by 1956 and was less than 0.5 by 1967. In 1970 this figure had dropped to less than 0.3. Investors became aware of this poor backing of the dollar liabilities to gold. This created a wave of speculative attacks: first against currencies pegged to the dollar, such as the pound which had to depreciate in 1967. Massive conversions of dollar reserves into other strong currencies such as the Deutschmark and the yen also followed. European countries decided to un-peg their currencies from the dollar and have a joint float. Finally, the USA acknowledged that the Bretton Woods system was no longer viable and came out of the system altogether in 1971.

The breakdown of the system in 1971 was followed by a general move to floating exchange rates. Individual countries were no longer committed to keeping their exchange rates fixed by means of official intervention in foreign exchange markets or by interest rate policy. That is not to say that since 1971 all exchange rates have been freely floating. In the first place, even though a given exchange rate may appear to be floating freely, it may not be a 'clean' float. This means that, although an exchange rate changes day to day, the authorities are nevertheless intervening in the market in order to smooth out these changes. While some countries opted for such a 'managed float', others chose to fix their exchange rates either with respect to one key currency, usually the dollar, or to a trade-weighted 'basket' of currencies. No other widely accepted exchange rate regime for the world economy as a whole has emerged since the collapse of Bretton Woods.

Some important lessons can be learnt from these two episodes which revolved around fixed exchange rates based on a dominant currency. Both the pound and then the dollar emerged as the de facto international currency due to the trade supremacy of their nations. While one dominant currency has conferred power and prestige on the dominant nation and given stability to the international economy in the short run, it has been difficult to sustain in the long run without the fixity of the exchange rate breaking down altogether with disruptive consequences for the global economy. There are two principal reasons why the supremacy of one national currency has been difficult to sustain. First, as nationals of other countries started treating the dollar and pound reserves as base money upon which to create more dollar denominated or pound denominated liabilities, the international supply of dollars and pounds increased and the US Federal Reserve and the Bank of England lost control over the reserve to liabilities ratio for their national currencies. This gave rise to speculative attacks. Second, whenever trade positions of the leading currencies declined, some long-term realignment of exchange rates was inevitable and a fixed exchange rate system was bound to break down. Not surprisingly then, the new solutions that emerged after 1971 have sought to impart some flexibility on a fixed exchange rate system. In the next section I narrate the history of one such experiment: the ERM in Europe and its successor the euro.

4.3   THE ERM AND THE EURO

The countries in the European Union have tried several alternative mechanisms to replace the Bretton Woods regime since 1971. All attempts have been guided by a desire to recover some of the benefits of a stable exchange rate for the EU's member states in order to encourage greater trade and integration between them. The first attempt to move towards a more stable exchange rate environment was by means of a joint float against the dollar in the 1970s (an arrangement which became known as the 'snake in the tunnel'). This was the forerunner of the European Monetary System and the Exchange Rate Mechanism. Fundamentally, the EMS, and its successor the ERM, had the ultimate objective of economic and monetary union where all members of the EU share a common currency and exchange rates become immutably fixed. This objective has now been realized for a number of EU countries with the establishment of the European Central Bank and the use of the common currency, the euro, from 1999.

The UK was a reluctant partner in the ERM and its experience with this system has, to some extent, influenced its reluctance to join the euro. In order to understand the current debates about the euro in the UK it is important to understand what happened before, and what some of the economic constraints to a full monetary union are.

In the ERM, exchange rates of the EU currencies were stabilized with respect to each other. The main element was that all bilateral exchange rates had to be stabilized within bands of the agreed central bilateral rates (these bands were fixed at 2.25 per cent until 1993). Once bilateral rates breached those bands, the two central banks concerned agreed to intervene in the international money market with their joint reserves to push the exchange rate back towards its central rate. In practice, these central rates were pegged against the Deutschmark.

The central parities of the bilateral rates were agreed at the outset, but these could be changed by negotiated agreement. Such 'realignments' were quite common in the first half of the 1980s, but became much less frequent as the system 'bedded down'. Thus, between 1979 and 1983 there were seven realignments, while between February 1987 and September 1992 there were none. Realignments were a key element in the system since they rendered the ERM an adjustable peg system, with some elements of flexibility, rather than a system of irrevocably fixed exchange rates.

Thus, the ERM was something of a hybrid system, between fully flexible and fully fixed exchange rates; trying to secure the best of both worlds in the short run, while preparing a path to monetary union and a single European currency in the long run. The benefits of the fixed exchange rate aspect of the system stemmed from the greater stability it was expected to secure. Artis and Taylor (1989) confirmed that nominal and real exchange rates were more stable under the ERM. This had two beneficial effects. First, the more stable exchange rate environment encouraged trade. Second, because exchange rate stability indicates some convergence of inflation rates, the ERM enabled high inflation countries to improve their inflation performance. The argument here was that Germany was the low inflation 'leader' in the system and by fixing exchange rates to the Deutschmark, the high inflation countries gained some increased credibility for their anti-inflation policies. Inflation rates did fall in member countries under the ERM, with France and Italy bringing their rates down quite markedly. However, it should be noted that over the same period inflation rates also fell worldwide, so it is doubtful that the ERM was the only factor to explain low inflation rates.

It was hoped to achieve these benefits without jettisoning the possibility of one-off exchange rate adjustment (realignments) if real exchange rates were getting uncomfortably out of line. For example, a high inflation country could quite quickly become seriously uncompetitive with fixed nominal exchange rates. These tensions explained the regular round of realignments in the system up to 1987.

The UK did not joint the ERM until October 1990, and then only stayed within the ERM until September 1992. During the summer of 1992 some of the weaker currencies within the ERM, particularly sterling and the lira, came under increasing speculative pressure. Then on 12 September the lira was devalued by 7%. This was followed by the dramatic events of 15 September when, in an attempt to defend sterling's position, the authorities raised the nominal short-term interest rate (Chapter 12, Section 3.2) from 8% to 10%. Then a further increase to 15% was 'pre-announced' to create positive exchange rate expectations. This was not sufficient to bolster market confidence in sterling and the UK suspended its membership of the ERM that evening. Sterling depreciated immediately by 16%, and the lira followed the UK in leaving the ERM. At the same time, the peseta was devalued by 5%. In November 1992, the peseta and the escudo were devalued by 6%, and in January 1993 the punt was devalued by 10%. This was followed by further devaluations of the peseta and the escudo in May. Finally, a wave of speculative pressure against the franc in the summer of 1993 led to a widening of all parity bands within the ERM to 15%. Given that member currencies could now fluctuate against each other by as much as 30%, the ERM could no longer be regarded as a form of fixed exchange rate system.

To some extent, the hybrid nature of the system contributed to its virtual collapse in 1993. First, the absence of realignments after 1987, while inflation differentials remained, pushed real rates seriously out of line. Yet one of the reasons why countries did not seek realignments in the face of this was that they did not want to sacrifice their anti-inflation credibility for which they had striven so hard in the 1980s. Second, the whole system was subjected to an asymmetric shock in the form of German reunification. This was essentially an inflationary shock which impinged on Germany but not directly on the rest of Europe. (A symmetric shock would be, for example, a substantial oil price increase, which would hit all the ERM countries in largely the same way.) Germany's preferred response to this shock would have been a Deutschmark revaluation, but other members (particularly France) resisted this, again partly on the grounds of the credibility argument. In the absence of such realignment, Germany increased domestic interest rates. This placed other ERM countries under pressure to follow, in order to keep their exchange rates within the ERM parity bands.

In the case of the UK, this meant that domestic monetary policy was constrained from pursuing domestic objectives. German rates were rising just at the time when the UK authorities were attempting to reduce rates in order to encourage a recovery from domestic recession. These tensions damaged the credibility of the whole system and specific currencies now came under speculative attack. Financial investors could see the inconsistency of the two objectives and speculated that the UK would eventually reduce its interest rates. It is interesting to note that the currencies of those economies most closely integrated with the German economy (e.g. the Dutch guilder) did not come under such attack.

At this point, two particular features of the system become important. First, in a system of narrow bands, when a currency comes under speculative pressure, speculators are essentially taking a one-way bet. When a currency reaches the floor of its band, the only question is whether the floor is going to be adjusted downwards. There is no risk of the ceiling being adjusted upwards. If the realignment occurs, speculators win, if it does not, they are not significantly worse off. Moreover, it is difficult for countries to use interest rates in order to defend a currency when there are expectations of a realignment. This is because the expectation of, say, a 5 per cent capital gain in the next month translates into a very high annual rate of return. Thus, it requires quite unrealistically high interest rates to compensate portfolio holders for this expected one-off devaluation.

The second feature of the system worth noting is the pattern of intervention by the central banks of the member countries when currencies come under pressure. The central bank of the weak currency is constrained by its finite stock of foreign exchange reserves, but this does not apply to the strong currency. Thus, intervention by the Bundesbank usually implied purchases of the weak currency and sales of Deutschmarks. If this intervention was not sterilized then this results in an increasing German money supply, with the threat that carries for domestic inflation if the economy is already close to full capacity.

This was a central issue in the operation of the ERM. I have already mentioned the anti-inflation benefits of fixed exchange rates for other members of the ERM. The counterpart of this for the German economy was less comfortable. If the Bundesbank supported other currencies (and therefore kept non-German inflation rates lower) this is at the risk of that intervention increasing the German money supply and generating domestic inflation. When the German economy was strong, and when interventions could be sterilized, this was not necessarily a problem. However, a larger scale of intervention at a time when German inflation was increasing due to reunification, as was the case in 1992, put the system under much greater strain.

It should be clear from the above that at least some of the reasons for the effective collapse of the ERM in the autumn of 1992 can be traced back to the fact that the ERM was essentially a half-way house between fully flexible and fully fixed exchange rates. In that sense there are a number of similarities between the ERM and the Bretton Woods system. Moreover, in the same way that increasing capital mobility was weakening the operation of the Bretton Woods system in its later years, so it has become apparent that in today's world of highly mobile capital, such a half-way house is difficult to sustain. Flexibility within narrow bands with the escape clause of possible realignments presents speculators with a one-way bet, while wider bands seriously weaken the credibility and therefore the anti-inflationary benefits of the system. The choice facing the EU was whether to opt for fully flexible rates or move towards a single currency.

In the event, the EU member states signed the Treaty of Maastricht in 1992, committing them, with the exceptions of the UK and Denmark which negotiated opt-outs, to the adoption of a single currency. The euro was introduced in 1999 and national currencies abolished in 2002. In order to minimize the risks of failure, conditions were set for membership of the euro project which were designed to ensure that participating member states converged on similar inflation rates and interest rates. The inflation rate had to be not more than 1.5 percentage points above the average of the three lowest inflation rates among participating economies. Interest rates had to be not more than 2 percentage points above the average of the three lowest interest rates in participating economies. Other criteria limited the budget deficit to 3 per cent of GDP and the national debt to 60 per cent of GDP. The aim was to ensure that 'excessive' government borrowing did not exert upward pressure on interest rates. An independent central bank was the other main feature of monetary union. The European Central Bank (ECB) was set up with the primary objective of maintaining price stability and operational independence in setting a single short-term interest rate for all of the participating member states.

While the ECB was widely expected to tend towards high interest rates to maintain the value of the euro and keep inflation very low, as a practical approximation to price stability, this strategy was 'applied rather pragmatically' for the first year (OECD, 2000, p.4). This is probably explained by the circumstances of the euro's introduction. First, the 'euro zone' economies had experienced a decline in export demand and hence in aggregate demand as a consequence of the South-East Asian crisis, which saw large falls in GDP and currency depreciations among the 'tiger' economies of the region. Second, inflation rates in the euro zone economies were already low, following sustained efforts throughout the 1990s to meet the Maastricht convergence criteria. However, by 2002, growth rates in the euro zone economies were low relative to those in the UK and the USA, yet the ECB has shown little inclination to respond by cutting interest rates.

A single currency such as the euro may be a more attractive proposition for those countries with fully established low inflation credentials, and whose economies may already be closely integrated. For other economies, such as the UK, the single currency option could involve an extremely painful adjustment. A more palatable alternative is that of exchange rate flexibility in the immediate future, with a credible anti-inflation strategy that does not need the aid of a fixed nominal exchange rate. This is, in fact, what the UK opted for initially. In 1997, the incoming Labour government established the independence of the central bank – whose task is to keep the rate of inflation in check – and adopted a flexible exchange rate strategy for the pound.

A tension that remains unresolved is the harmonization of monetary and fiscal policies if the euro is not to break down as a currency. One of the conditions of being a euro member is that each government must sign up to keeping the deficit on its budget below 3 per cent of its GDP, and also agree to maintaining balanced budgets in 'normal times'. This is the 'stability and growth pact' signed by the euro nations. By now, you should understand this condition: if any member countries run large government deficits, then the euro zone as a whole would suffer a depreciation of its currency vis-à-vis the dollar and other currencies. If in normal times, when economies are working at nearly full capacity, budgets are not balanced, then inflation would occur in the euro countries again depreciating their currencies vis-à-vis other currencies.

This pact imposes strong fiscal policy constraints on the euro countries which may leave them unable to react to the needs of their domestic economies. The first instances of a failure to comply had already emerged by the summer of 2002. At the time of writing, Portugal is likely to sustain a deficit on its budget equivalent to about 9 per cent of GDP. More worrying, however, is the behaviour of France, Italy and Germany, who account for about 70 per cent of the euro area's GDP. These countries have not been balancing their budgets.

At the time of writing in late 2002, the UK is not in the euro zone but is committed to low deficits and balanced budgets in normal times. It has very low levels of public debt, but some would argue that this is not without adverse consequences. The UK economy needs to invest in public services, but has desisted from doing so for fear of fiscal imbalance. This investment would come out of public borrowing and taxation. Sceptics point out that joining the euro would tie up this area of policy even more than it is now. Euro enthusiasts, particularly big businesses, see the stability and trade advantages of the single currency which would undoubtedly confer long-term increases in the level of national incomes. Both are powerful economic arguments and not surprisingly political parties in the UK are divided on the question.

5   CONCLUSION   ·

The chapter began by explaining the need for international liquidity and drawing analogies between the domestic and international money markets. As trade expands, such markets become more important in the international economy. I noted a key difference with domestic money markets in that international money markets do not have the hegemony of any one currency. I ended the chapter by showing how this fight for the status of a hegemonic currency, between competing national currencies, has given rise to unstable regimes in the international monetary system and rendered it somewhat chaotic and prone to disruption in its operation. One way to reduce the chaos would be to move towards a new supranational currency, which is what the euro represents.

A great deal of this chapter has been about understanding foreign exchange markets and the implications of trading currencies for determining exchange rates in the short and in the long run. I also discussed the macroeconomic variables that could be affected by the exchange rate, such as the price level, interest rates and ultimately aggregate demand in the economy. The nature of the exchange rate regime emerged as a decisive factor in the ability of governments to control these macroeconomic variables.

Under fixed exchange rates the authorities lose control over domestic liquidity. They must therefore choose between a monetary target and an exchange rate target. This result depends crucially on the assumption that capital is internationally mobile; in fact, the world economy has moved in this direction. The consequence is not only that monetary and exchange rate targets are incompatible but also that fixed exchange rate systems, however appealing their perceived benefits, are hard to sustain. Under flexible exchange rates, the inflation of the domestic economy relative to those of its international competitors and the interest rate differential between domestic and foreign currencies become the most important determinants of the exchange rate. Unless a new worldwide exchange rate system emerges to replace Bretton Woods the choice facing European policy makers (including those in the UK) is, therefore, between a single currency, such as the euro, or floating exchange rates.

LOOKING INTO THE LONG TERM: INVESTMENT, GROWTH AND SUSTAINABILITY

CHAPTER 17 INVESTMENT AND CAPITAL ACCUMULATION

David A. Spencer ●

Objectives

After studying this chapter you should be able to:
- appreciate the importance of investment and capital accumulation for output growth
- understand the determinants of investment
- understand the short-run and the long-run implications of investment for business cycles
- understand government policy towards investment.

Concepts

- fixed capital investment
- gross and net investment
- human capital
- variable productivity
- discounting
- capital–output ratio
- 'animal spirits'
- the warranted rate of growth

1 INTRODUCTION ●

> Who can seriously doubt that Britain has been chronically under-invested in for 20 years or that it harms not just our quality of life but our future prosperity. Every school we invest in helps our children earn more. Every extra nurse we employ in the NHS is a guarantee people won't be forced to go private to be treated when ill. Every penny spent on new track and trains ... is a step towards the transport system that this country ... needs. Yes, it takes time. It takes patience. But it takes, above all, investment. That is the choice we must make.
>
> (Tony Blair, Speech, 22 November 2000)

> We want to see a world class British industry created through effective and targeted investment to tackle our productivity gap … We need 'smart support' to give us a high wage, hi-tech manufacturing sector that will trail blaze 'made in Britain' across the globe.
>
> (John Monks, TUC General Secretary, Budget submission)

These statements illustrate the importance often given to investment in economic policy. You may wonder, however, why there should be such a fuss about a component of aggregate demand that accounts for less than one fifth of GDP.

Chapter 12 focused on the short-run implications of investment. It assumed that economic capacity and technology were unchanged, and so investment mainly played the role of creating demand. An important difference in the treatment of investment in this chapter is that it considers both the short-run and the long-run implications of investment. In the long term, investment enhances output creation and income growth in the economy by adding to the productive capacity of the economy. However, investment is quite volatile, being dependent on expectations and uncertainty, so it often takes place in fits and starts, giving rise to output cycles in the economy. Above all, it is this dual nature of investment, as capacity-creating in the long run as well as demand-enhancing in the short run, that makes it such a key variable in economic policy. On the one hand, fluctuations in investment provide a major source of instability in national incomes. On the other hand, investment, whether in the form of the acquisition of productive assets, the creation of new productive capacity or the development of human resources, is a catalyst for economic growth.

Not surprisingly, then, investment is the subject of keen interest at the policy level. Policy makers in the UK and elsewhere have seen the rate of investment and its stability as crucial to economic success, and the problem of under-investment has been singled out as a key reason for economic decline in the UK.

In this chapter I will explain why investment is important, what factors determine it and how it influences the tempo and rate of economic activity. The chapter begins by considering the nature of investment. Section 3 then examines the decision to invest and the various factors that influence that decision, ranging from the cost and availability of finance to profit expectations and the degree of uncertainty. Section 4 considers the short-term and, very briefly, the long-term aspects of investment: its impact on output stability and output growth. Section 5 looks at policy issues and explores the different options available to governments for raising investment levels in the economy.

2   INVESTMENT

We start by considering what we mean by investment and note the different measures of investment. We then look at the different forms that it can take, its links with productivity and how it is financed.

2.1   WHAT IS INVESTMENT?

When economists use the word investment, they refer to the acquisition of additional capital, that is, to the process of capital accumulation. The general notion of capital is that it is something that yields benefits now and into the future. The capital stock of the economy is built up period upon period through investment flows. Some of this investment merely replaces worn-out capital stock and some of it adds to the capital stock in the economy. In terms of the circular flow of income (Chapters 8 and 11), some income from the current period is kept aside as savings by households and made available to firms to expand production in successive periods. Investment is thus that part of current income that is not consumed but used to expand the productive capacity of the economy.

How is investment measured? The total expenditure on capital goods is a broad measure of GROSS INVESTMENT in the economy. However, plant and machinery do not last indefinitely and are liable to be less productive as time goes on. The contribution of physical assets to total output is diminished through the effects of 'wear and tear', and the term 'depreciation' is used to measure the extent of the deterioration of the contribution of existing capital over time. Capital-replacing investment denotes the purchase of new physical capital to replace worn-out physical capital. Such investment ensures that the stock of capital available to firms remains at a constant level. With the ongoing development of superior physical capital and technology, existing capital and technology will become obsolete. So firms will need to update their stock of capital to maintain output and productivity levels in relation to industry 'best practice'. Such replacement investment will also normally involve the upgrading of existing capital stock to enable increases in output and productivity (capital-enhancing investment). Gross investment consists of both replacement investment and capital-enhancing investment, and is undertaken to expand production capabilities through increasing the capital stock.

GROSS INVESTMENT
Gross investment measures total expenditure on capital goods during a given period of time.

A useful concept is therefore that of NET INVESTMENT. Net investment refers to capital-enhancing investment alone and is calculated as gross investment less replacement investment (depreciation). Most analytical discussion of investment is based around the accounting concept of net investment. When net investment in the economy is zero the economy just maintains its capital stock. The effect of positive net investment is to increase the amount of capital available to firms. Net additions to the quantity of total capital may give rise to increases in productivity.

NET INVESTMENT
Net investment is gross investment less replacement investment, and measures the net increase in the amount of capital available to firms.

QUESTION

Recall the discussion of the production process in Chapter 3. Why would increases in net investment give rise to increased labour productivity?

There are three possible routes by which net investment can increase labour productivity. First, net investment may give rise to an increase in the scale of production and a consequent rise in productivity due to economies of scale. Second, there may be an increase in the capital intensity of production – that is, more capital is used for each worker. This should make each worker more productive. Third, net investment is new investment, which may be technologically superior to the existing capital stock, thus giving rise to an overall increase in productivity. Increased productivity in production is important because it allows the economy to realize a higher level of output with the same resources. It is this association of investment with higher productivity that explains why investment is given such a high priority at a policy level.

FIXED INVESTMENT
Fixed investment is the purchase of fixed capital assets by firms for the purpose of creating additional output.

It is also useful to draw a distinction between FIXED INVESTMENT, which is also called 'fixed capital formation', and investment in stocks that results in increased 'inventories'. Investment in stocks is the accumulation of work-in-progress, raw materials, and finished output (these are what are referred to as 'inventories'). Firms will choose to hold surpluses of raw materials in case of unforeseen contingencies, which might otherwise disrupt the flow of production. Finished output will also be held in stock in case of sudden increases in future demand. Stocks play an important role in granting firms flexibility in dealing with the unexpected. In circumstances where production takes time to be completed, at any one moment in time there will be output that is incomplete and thus some fraction of stocks will be held as work-in-progress. Accounting data usually classify changes in stocks separately, although they are included in total investment expenditure by firms (Chapter 11).

Table 17.1 provides data on the composition of gross fixed investment across different sectors of the UK economy. Investment is measured by total expenditure on fixed (capital) assets and the cost of these assets is calculated at current prices. It can be seen from the data that gross fixed capital formation (GFCF) totalled £165 247 million in 2000; this represented roughly 18 per cent of total expenditure. In 2000, private non-financial corporations accounted for 60 per cent of total GFCF, by far the largest contribution of any of the individual sectors listed. This share rose since 1992 reflecting the relatively strong economic growth of the latter half of the 1990s. Government accounted for a relatively small proportion of total gross investment; for example, expenditure on fixed capital by central and local government combined only accounted for 7 per cent of total fixed investment in 2000. The data show that spending by central government on fixed capital assets actually fell through the 1990s. Investment expenditure by households on fixed assets includes the purchase of new dwellings and the data show that investment of this kind increased through the 1990s. Gross fixed capital investment as a whole was some 65 per cent higher in 2000 than in 1992, with the rate of growth being stronger between 1996 and 2000 than between 1992 and 1996.

Table 17.1 Gross fixed capital formation (GFCF) at current producer prices by sector and by type of asset (£ million)

	1992	1996	2000
GFCF by sector			
Public non-financial corporations	5669	5256	4831
Private non-financial corporations	54 277	72 413	99 845
Financial corporations	5683	6696	11 737
Central government	7840	5293	4557
Local government	6205	5913	6792
Households and NPISH[1]	20 909	30 191	37 485
Total GFCF	100 583	125 762	165 247
GFCF by type of asset			
Tangible fixed assets			
New dwellings, excluding land	18 825	22 448	27 823
Other buildings, and structures	31 539	32 842	45 312
Transport equipment	8420	12 213	16 746
Other machinery and equipment and cultivated assets	35 071	49 727	61 827
Total tangible fixed assets	93 855	117 230	151 708
Intangible fixed assets	3782	4136	4839
Costs associated with the transfer of ownership of non-produced assets	2946	4396	8700

Components may not sum to totals due to rounding
[1] NPISH stands for 'Non-profit institutions serving households' (for example, housing associations)
Source: *United Kingdom National Accounts (The Blue Book)*, 2001, Tables 9.1 and 9.3

Table 17.1 also gives figures on gross investment by type of asset purchased. In terms of tangible fixed assets, most gross investment falls into the category of 'other machinery and equipment and cultivated assets' ('cultivated assets' includes livestock and forestry). Total expenditure on tangible fixed assets has increased by some 62 per cent from 1992 to 2000, again with a more rapid rise in the latter half of the 1990s. Investment in intangible fixed assets incorporates expenditure on such things as mineral exploration, computer software, entertainment, and literary or artistic originals; the purchase by a firm of computer software would be classified under this definition as investment in intangible fixed assets. These assets remain a very small fraction of total gross investment, and total expenditure on intangible fixed assets has shown only a modest rise over the course of the 1990s.

2.2   FORMS OF INVESTMENT

The dominant image that springs to mind in the discussion of investment so far is that of huge factories and expenditures on machinery but this is by no means the only form that investment takes. Many different forms of expenditure constitute investment.

QUESTION

Can you think of other examples that satisfy the attributes of investment that we have identified?

The chief attribute of investment is that it is expenditure undertaken at the present time that is capable of yielding a flow of benefits in the future. Expenditures on the building of roads and the construction of new railway lines, and on education and the training of labour, are all examples of investment. This investment in building roads and railroads has to be financed through loans or through taxation, both of which entail a sacrifice in current consumption for the economy as a whole. Similarly, training of labour enhances the productivity of labour and, where financed by individuals, usually requires a sacrifice in current consumption by their households.

It is instructive to think about three broad forms of investment: investment in physical capital, investment in infrastructure and investment in human capital and training.

'Physical investment' is the purchase of productive assets (namely plant, machinery, buildings and vehicles) by producers in the economy and is by far the largest category of measured investment. These producers may be private firms or public sector corporations, but as we have seen in Table 17.1, private firms make much the largest contribution to physical investment. The important feature of investment in physical capital is that firms expect to more than cover the current costs of purchasing capital goods with enhanced future returns derived from the use of those goods in production. These returns will accrue from being able to cut costs and/or produce a higher output, or from enhanced revenues through the production and sale of new products. These potential gains from investment motivate firms to increase their expenditure on capital goods, that is, to invest.

Another form of investment is 'infrastructure investment'. This takes the form of investment in public goods, such as roads, railway lines, satellite lines, or fibre optic cables. Infrastructure investment has some peculiar features as an investment good. First, it usually requires large 'lumpy' investments, which take a long time to yield a return. This makes it somewhat unsuitable for private sector investment which is perceived to be more short-term in its outlook than the public sector and therefore less willing to undertake investment that generates full returns only over many decades into the future. Second, it has a public good nature, which means that private sector firms are likely to under-invest in it because they will not reap the full rewards from that investment. (Look back to Chapter 9 if you need to remind yourself of why public goods are likely to be under-provided by private firms.)

Governments provide an important source of such investment. In the UK, however, privatization of much of the former public sector has meant that the responsibility for investment in key parts of the infrastructure of the economy (for example, railways, communication networks) has now shifted from government to the private sector. You can see this in Table 17.1 where the government sector share of investment declined between 1992 and 2000. However, there remains a strong rationale for public investment in infrastructure. It is not always possible, nor indeed desirable, for the government to levy universal charges on the provision of certain basic goods and services like roads, and we have seen that investment in such public goods is unlikely to be undertaken by the private sector.

We look at the third form of investment – investment in human capital and training – in the next section.

2.3 INVESTMENT AND HUMAN CAPITAL

Firms are not just concerned with amassing fixed assets (whether tangible or intangible) but also retain an interest in improving intangible human assets. The development of human resources can be viewed as at least as important as the accumulation of physical capital in terms of improving output and productivity. The enhancement of education, skills and training is likely to aid the process of economic growth. Starting from the work of Gary Becker (Becker, 1962), considerable attention has been given to the effects of skill and knowledge on the productiveness of workers (see Chapter 7, Section 2.4). Becker shifted the focus away from physical investment and towards investment in what he terms 'human capital'. We refer to workers being endowed with HUMAN CAPITAL, with the latter acting as a proxy for the 'skilfulness' or 'knowledgeableness' of labour. Human capital impacts upon the quality of labour as measured by the output of each worker. Those workers who have accumulated more qualifications through schooling or attendance on relevant training courses may be expected to be better able to contribute to productive activity than those workers with fewer years of schooling and no formal training.

HUMAN CAPITAL
Human capital denotes the knowledge and skills embodied in workers.

Human capital will vary among workers according to family background, educational attainment and skill acquisition. Becker claims that in view of this variation workers will have unequal access to well paid jobs, which will manifest itself in an uneven distribution of earnings. Workers will be motivated to make an investment in education and training to improve their human capital by the prospect of higher pay in high-productivity and high-skilled jobs. Higher monetary rewards in this case will cause workers to invest resources in acquiring qualifications via extended years of schooling and/or through participation on training courses. A student on an Open University course is investing in human capital to the extent that the objective of study is to enhance his or her work-related skills, productivity and hence future earnings.

Becker (1962) argued that individual workers will act like 'mini firms' in gaining human capital. That is, individual workers are assumed to undertake investment (in this case, investment of time and perhaps also money) in education and training to accumulate superior human capital (here reflected in the acquisition of new skills and knowledge). Just as the individual firm undertakes investment in physical capital to enhance the opportunities for higher future profit, so the individual worker will invest in human capital in anticipation of higher future earnings. While there are obvious financial benefits from education, there are also costs. The most obvious cost is that of forgone income during the period of time workers spend in education. Thus, someone deciding to enter college will forgo some finite level of income by not taking up paid work on a full-time basis. According to the theory of human capital, she will do this only if the loss of current income is more than offset by the potential for higher earnings in the future (see Figure 7.4 in Chapter 7). Investment in human capital in this case will be a matter of weighing up the current costs and future benefits of time spent in education or on training courses.

Firms will benefit from the investment made by workers in human capital. Firms will not only gain access to a larger pool of qualified applicants to fill outstanding vacancies, they also stand to benefit from higher productivity once workers begin work. Workers gain job-specific human capital through 'on-the-job' training, acquiring tacit skills through the experience of working on the same or similar tasks. These skills provide an additional source of productivity gain beyond the level of formal education and training. Workers may invest time in acquiring 'on-the-job' training with a view to raising their bargaining power when it comes to negotiating for higher pay. Whether or not firms accede to demands for higher pay will depend, in part, on the extent to which workers' investment in human capital feeds through into higher productivity. In this case, there is the possibility for mutual gains from the investment made in human capital if not all the productivity gains have to be paid out in higher wages.

The discussion has so far been cast in terms of the investment in human capital being undertaken by workers themselves. While this is the norm in the case of education (for example, a school leaver entering college), many firms are active in the development of human capital. They may seek to administer training courses with the aim of raising the individual and collective productivity of their workforce. The enhancement of human capital enables firms to get more output from their workforce, and in turn provides a source of productivity gain beyond the physical limits imposed by the amount of available capital or the scale of production (where the latter is measured by available productive capacity).

There may well be a trade-off between investment in physical capital and investment in human capital. Faced with finite funds for investment, firms must prioritize their investment plans, and compromises may well have to be made in terms of pursuing investment in one direction rather than another. If firms opt to spend more on training their workforce, this expenditure may come at the expense of investment in physical capital.

Investment in certain capital inputs may require a particular type of skilled labour in order to be carried through successfully and the effectiveness of these capital inputs in yielding productivity gains may be held back by the skill levels of incumbent workers. If a firm is planning to invest in capital with a high-technology content, then it may be anticipated that the firm will need to undertake additional investment in equipping workers with the technical know-how required to use this capital in the most productive way possible. Investment in labour and capital are likely to be complementary aspects of production and hence firms undertake these forms of investment side by side. Indeed, the effective use of new capital equipment can require that existing workers be retrained.

QUESTION

Until now we have treated investment in human capital and investment in physical capital as similar. In what ways do you think these forms of investment differ for a firm?

One crucial difference between investment in physical capital and investment in human capital is that the former involves the purchase of fixed assets, which may be sold off at a price once purchased, while the latter involves the development of knowledge and skills that are non-tradable (at least outside of a society ruled by slavery!). A decision to purchase fixed assets is often reversible, but a decision to acquire 'human capital' cannot be reversed. The decision by a firm to invest in physical capital is reversible in the sense that, if the profits achieved through the use of purchased capital goods turn out to be below expectations, firms can liquidate (that is, sell) some or all of those goods to others at a price. Once capital goods have been produced, they cannot (usually) be reconverted into other capital goods, and thus it would be inappropriate to refer to the reversibility of physical investment other than in terms of the resale value of purchased capital goods. Assuming the existence of a second-hand market for capital goods (a realistic assumption for vehicles, say, but not for a nuclear power station!), firms will be able to recuperate some of the potential losses incurred through the pursuit of physical investment. The potential reversibility of physical investment means that firms will be willing to accept a lower chance of success (in the form of lower expected profits) from buying capital goods than might otherwise be expected if capital goods were non-tradable.

However, in the case of investment in human capital, the decision to invest is irreversible. The costs of training include not only the direct costs of training provision but also the indirect costs of lost output whilst workers are trained – where the latter represents the opportunity cost of the time workers spend being trained. These costs cannot be simply recuperated by firms through the sale of trained workers on the open market. If firms endow their workforce with 'transferable skills', which could be used in other firms if there exists some degree of labour mobility, there will be a risk that the offer of higher wages will entice workers away from their present jobs once their training is completed. In this case, while the firm undertaking the training incurs the full cost of training, it will receive none of the benefits. This need not be the case where firms equip their workers with job-specific skills that limit the options for workers to exit their jobs and which therefore offer firms greater scope to capture the productivity gains from training. In general, firms will have an incentive to pay for training only if they expect their present workforce to remain with them in the future. One way round the problem of firms covering the cost of equipping workers with transferable skills is to share these costs with the workers themselves. In this situation, firms can offer workers lower wages whilst the training is administered, with the inducement of higher wages in the future if the workers successfully complete their training and remain in their present jobs.

One criticism of the human capital approach is that it neglects to consider the non-economic benefits of undertaking education. In the human capital approach, the return to education has as its main motivation for investment the prospect of higher future earnings. It may well be the case that firms have economic motives in training their workforce but this same logic need not always apply to individual workers when they come to make the decision to enrol on a college course or to attend a training course. Learning involves important non-economic considerations, which may override the expected increases in labour productivity and future earnings that may result from education. Thus, for example, one may be motivated to pursue education by the pleasure derived from studying. In this case, the pursuit of economic interest will be of secondary importance in the decision to undertake education.

2.4   VARIABLE PRODUCTIVITY AND INVESTMENT

VARIABLE PRODUCTIVITY
Variable productivity is the potential for output to vary for the same input of labour (where labour is measured either by total hours worked or by total employment).

One important point to take from the above discussion is the VARIABLE PRODUCTIVITY of workers. Skills, in particular, will influence the quality and hence productivity of labour. However, there is also a wider issue here of the status of labour and its relation to investment. Labour does not just involve hours worked, as a quantitative measure of total labour input used. It also encompasses the dimensions of effort and work intensity, which relate to the actual work done by workers. Economists have usually defined labour in 'extensive' terms alone, that is, by the number of hours worked – given by the number of workers employed and the duration of work time. This is to be distinguished from the actual contribution made by labour to total output, which is defined in 'intensive' terms by the total effort expended by workers.

This raises the question of how work hours are converted into work effort. This depends on the organization of work and the use of technology. Investment in this case is not simply about adding more physical (capital) inputs to the production process via the acquisition of greater numbers of machines and additional plant. There is also an issue of getting more from existing labour inputs. Employers will seek to alter the organization of work and the use of technology in order to extract more effort from workers. The technical division of labour is a case in point in that the specialization of work tasks enables firms to gain greater bargaining leverage over workers. Employers' enhanced control over workers can then be put to use in intensifying the pace of work. Technology that makes it easier for employers to monitor their workforce may be used to achieve the same outcome. The operation of an assembly line, for example, circumscribes workers' behaviour and reduces their ability to resist increases in the intensity of work. Firms can exploit this situation with a view to gaining more output from their workforce. One could also envisage the positive effects of an increase in the number of supervisors on work intensity. Under circumstances of tight supervision, there will be fewer opportunities for workers to evade the discipline of work, and the outcome is an intensification of work.

Employers' investment strategies for raising work intensity do not necessarily enhance skills. Some radical commentators have argued that employers will look to *reduce* the skill content of labour as part of a so-called 'divide and rule' strategy (Bowles, 1985). Firms may invest in training to enhance human capital by reaping the technical benefits of improved skills, where these benefits arise from workers' increased knowledge of ways of improving the flow of output. Yet, just as workers can learn how to enhance production, so they can learn how to impede production. Workers can draw individual and collective strength from the possession of specific skills. Employers may therefore pursue a policy of deskilling in order to enhance their control over production. Through this route, employers aim to reduce the potential for opposition from workers to any moves to increase the intensity of work.

QUESTION

What does this discussion suggest to you about the influences on firms' decisions to invest?

The above discussion highlights the scope for investment decisions to be influenced by non-technical and social considerations. Firms will not be concerned just with the contribution made by physical assets and workers' skills to total output. They will also be interested in how physical capital and human capital affect the extraction of effort from their workers. Investment in capital may also be used to improve the amount of work done per hour. Employers may opt to invest in certain types of capital with the intention of reducing the amount of control exercised by workers over production, and investment of this sort may well come at the expense of investment in human capital.

Conventional measures of investment are in practice biased in favour of fixed investment and some types of infrastructure investment such as those undertaken by the government. The large category of expenditure on training is not usually included in measures of investment. We should however be mindful that increasingly economists consider these forms of investment as extremely important in explaining the long-term growth of incomes.

EXERCISE 17.1

Explain whether the following expenditures should be regarded as investment, and give reasons for your answers.

1   Research and development expenditures by firms.

2   Government spending on education.

3   Government spending on the NHS.

4   Payments into pension funds by employers.

2.5   THE FINANCING OF INVESTMENT

We have seen that firms are the main agents undertaking physical investment plans in the economy. The question then arises of how firms finance their investment plans. Any source of finance involves costs so far as the firm is concerned. In this section we look at the principal internal and external sources of finance available to firms to carry out their investment plans. The source of finance a firm uses depends on its availability as well as the costs of using it.

INTERNAL FINANCE

Firms may rely on internal sources of finance to raise the funds required to finance investment. Internal finance takes the form of retained profits. The owner of a firm faces a choice about whether to use profit for consumption or investment. So there is an opportunity cost to be borne in devoting more profit to one type of expenditure as opposed to the other. The opportunity cost to the owner of a firm in using retained profits to fund investment is measured by the level of present consumption forgone.

Firms may prefer to rely on retained profits to fund their investment programme, since that involves no interest payment (although as indicated below it still involves an opportunity cost to the firm in terms of alternative revenues forgone). The use of external finance means a commitment to make future interest payments, which may create difficulties for the firm in the event of an economic downturn. Further, internal finance gives firms a degree of independence over the direction of investment, whereas external finance requires a lender (such as a bank) to be persuaded of the merits of the proposed investment.

QUESTION

Why might firms be limited in their access to internal finance?

Internal finance depends on a firm having retained profits, that is profits that have been retained by the firm rather than paid out as dividends. Access to retained profits will vary with the size and age of the firm. Internal finance will not be an option for newly formed firms. Smaller firms, which may face tight profit margins, may also face problems raising internal finance. Thus it may be expected that larger (profitable) firms will have greater scope to finance investment using retained profits. The level of retained profit will also fluctuate with the level of economic activity and there will be no guarantee that firms will have sufficient internal finance to fund investment at any particular point in time. In periods of economic slowdown, existing investment levels may come under severe pressure as profit levels are eroded. If recovery is gradual after a recession, then it may take time for profits to be replenished to the levels required to support previous levels of investment. This is a potentially serious problem given that recessions lead to erosions in the capital stock and losses in productive capacity.

However, it remains an open question as to whether investment is the cause or effect of retained profits. On the one hand, increases in retained profits provide the necessary stimulus for firms to undertake additional planned investment. Yet, on the other, it is possible that the desire for higher investment motivates firms to retain additional profits: in this case, the motive for investment precedes the growth in retained profit. While retained profits and investment may be observed to move in the same direction, it is not always clear what the direction of causation is between these two variables.

EXTERNAL FINANCE

Faced with insufficient internal finance, firms will have to seek external finance to realize their investment plans. Two sources of external finance may be distinguished, namely the issue of securities and bank borrowing.

Securities take two forms: shares and debentures. Firms may issue shares or equities and use the funds raised in this way to finance planned investment. The sale of shares by a firm may appear at first sight to provide a way of raising finance at no cost (other than the transaction costs involved in the selling of the shares). However those buying shares expect that there will be some future dividends payable on the shares, in addition to the prospect of a capital gain on their eventual sale. Dividends are payments made to shareholders out of profits. When a firm issues additional shares, future dividends will be shared among more people (that is, both the new and the old shareholders). The dividends payable to existing shareholders will fall unless the increase in the number of shares is matched by an expansion in the firm's profits and hence in total dividends. There is also a question here of the relation between dividends and profitability. Profits can be used to pay dividends but if they are retained they are a source of internal finance for investment. It can be argued that in the UK problems have arisen from the unresponsiveness of dividends to profits, so that high dividends have been maintained on occasions at the expense of higher investment, in spite of falling profits (Hutton, 1995). The trade-off between shareholder returns and investment in new capital (both physical and human) raises broader issues concerning the power of shareholder interests.

Firms may also seek to raise finance through the issue of securities in the form of debentures or loan stock. These entitle the purchaser to a fixed sum paid at some future date (usually referred to as the 'redemption date'), plus a fixed interest payment up until the debenture becomes redeemable. Debentures therefore create a liability for the firm, which needs to be weighed against the expected proceeds gained from the investment. The advantage of debentures is that they offer firms a medium- to long-term source of finance at a guaranteed and predictable cost, so that firms are able to plan ahead their investment levels. Debentures are secured against the issuing firm's assets so that in the event of the firm going bankrupt debenture holders will be compensated with the revenue gained from selling those assets. Shareholders will only receive what, if anything, is left after paying all other parties with a claim on the firm. The scope for a firm to issue debentures may therefore be limited by the value of the fixed assets owned by the firm.

Bank borrowing is the second main source of external finance. This entails a firm entering into a loan agreement with a bank, which raises a number of issues. First, firms will be concerned with the cost of bank finance. The interest paid on bank borrowing will be a major influence on the decision to invest, with lower (higher) interest rates providing a positive (negative) stimulus to planned investment. Second, firms may be concerned with the length of time over which a loan is to be repaid, if the length of the loan, in this case, might not match with the length of time during which the investment project yields profits. For example, a loan to be repaid over three years would mean that the firm not only has to make sufficient profits (on the project financed by the loan) to cover the interest charges, but also to repay the full amount of the loan at the end of the three year period. However, the project being financed may be one which yields steady profits but over a longer period of time.

Third, firms may be concerned with the availability of finance as much as its cost. From the banks' perspective, there is always some risk that a loan will not be repaid if the investment project being financed turns out to be unprofitable (as well as the risk that the borrower may default on the loan). Small firms, in particular, may be deemed as high risk owing to the greater probability of their demise and thus there may be greater reluctance on the part of banks to lend to small firms as compared with medium-sized and large firms. This greater reluctance may result in banks charging higher interest rates to those perceived to be at greater risk of defaulting on the debt. It may also come through in banks refusing loans altogether to those with poor credit ratings.

There is also the question of the flexibility of finance and whether firms have sufficient scope to adapt to changing economic circumstances in repaying outstanding debt. These issues are important for a firm's ability to continue investing on an ongoing basis. Where loans give firms little flexibility to cope with economic downturns by delaying repayment, investment plans (at least those with a medium- to long-term time horizon) may be severely circumscribed, perhaps to the point of being ruled out altogether. Think, for example, of loan finance taking the form of bank overdrafts secured against assets held by the owner(s) of a firm (in the case of a small business, security against debt default may take the form of the owner's house). In this case, it is highly doubtful whether planned investment will be able to survive downturns in economic activity. As pressure mounts on firms' finances owing to falling revenues, costs will need to be reduced in order to make repayments on the existing debt and stay within the limits of available overdraft facilities. The prospect of breaching these limits will cause firms to be more cautious in their investment behaviour and make them more reluctant to undertake investment on a long-term basis.

Under circumstances where the nature of loan finance is inflexible in relation to changes in the level of economic activity, 'risky' investment projects may not be undertaken by firms to limit the possibilities for debt default. This may be a potentially serious problem with regard to raising productivity levels. High-risk investment projects are more likely to fail, but promise high returns in the form of increased productivity if successful. No one would undertake high-risk investment projects if the high risk was not compensated for by high potential returns. So the limits imposed by inflexible forms of loan finance on risk-taking behaviour may have adverse effects on the rate of investment. In many advanced economies, specialized venture capital funding has now emerged as an alternative to banks for such finance.

3   INFLUENCES ON INVESTMENT   •

In this section we look at some of the factors that can influence a firm's decision to invest, including the cost and availability of finance, the rate of interest, the level of uncertainty, and future expectations.

3.1   DISCOUNTING AND THE PRESENT VALUE CRITERION

Investment is undertaken at some cost now in the hope of benefits in the future. A firm building a new factory incurs the costs of construction and so on in the present and hopes that the output to be produced in the new factory will be sold at a profit in the future. An individual may undertake training and acquire skills, which cost time and money in the present but offer the hope of enhanced earning power later on. In all these examples, there is an income flow in the future about which a decision has to be made today.

QUESTION

Would a pound earned today have more or less value to you than a pound earned tomorrow?

For most individuals a pound earned today would be worth more than a pound earned tomorrow. This is because we are uncertain about what might happen tomorrow, and so we prefer to be able to consume out of the pound now than postpone this consumption to an uncertain tomorrow. Put differently, I will need to be paid something more to be persuaded to postpone my consumption to tomorrow. This is sometimes termed *positive time preference*, and is cited as the rationale for having a rate of interest on any saving.

In the presence of such positive time preference how might we measure the value of an income flow in the future? This is an important question for an investor who has to decide whether or not to invest today for returns in the future. The technique of DISCOUNTING allows future benefits to be compared with money spent today. This section spends some time explaining the technique and its use in decisions to invest.

DISCOUNTING
Discounting offers a technique for converting future returns into an equivalent value in the present – the present value of that future benefit.

Let us consider a simple example. Suppose you have £100 and you are undecided about whether to buy yourself a camera. Someone comes along and says that if you would postpone your purchase until the next year and instead lend them the money for this year, then they would pay you interest in return for borrowing the money for a year. The rate of interest you would be willing to accept for making such a loan is the rate at which you are willing to discount benefits (in this case the use of a camera) when they are postponed for one year. You perceive consumption now as more valuable to you than consumption in a year's time. However, maybe £110 to spend in a year's time is the equivalent (in worth to you) of £100 to spend today. In that case you will agree to lend your £100 at 10 per cent interest and therefore get £100 + £10 = £110 back in a year's time.

More generally, if £100(1 + r) in a year's time has the same worth to you as £100 today, then we say that you 'discount the future' at a rate r. Another way to put this is that £100(1 + r) in a year's time has a present value of £100. In the example above, if you agreed to make the loan at 10 per cent interest it would be because the £110 you would get back in a year's time would have a present value of at least £100 – the £100 that you would forgo today to make the loan. With a 10 per cent interest rate, £100(1 + 0.1) = £110 has a present value of £100. Here, the discount rate r is expressed as a decimal rather than a percentage – in this numerical example, 0.1 for 10 per cent.

QUESTION

1 **If you discount the future at a rate of 10 per cent, what is the present value of £100 in a year's time?**

2 **If you discount the future at a rate r, what is the present value of £100 in a year's time?**

Let us return to the example. The present value of £100 to be received in one year's time is:

$$PV = \frac{£100}{1.1} = £90.91$$

What is the present value of £100 to be received in two years' time? It is:

$$PV = \frac{£90.91}{1.1} = \frac{£100}{(1.1)^2} = £82.64$$

PRESENT VALUE (PV)

The present value, PV, of a future benefit, FB, in t years' time is given by the formula:

$$PV = \frac{FB}{(1+r)^t}$$

In general, the PRESENT VALUE (PV), of a future benefit, FB, is given by the formula:

$$PV = \frac{FB}{(1+r)^t}$$

where r is the discount rate and t stands for the number of years which elapse before the benefit becomes available.

Let us apply the discounting formula to an investment decision made by a firm. Take as an example a firm deciding on whether to purchase a new machine, which is expected to produce £3000 per annum. The machine is to be scrapped after five years. The machine costs £10 000, so the firm can either invest £10 000 in this machine or keep the £10 000 in a bank and earn a rate of interest on it.

In order to decide whether or not to invest in the machine, the firm needs to compare the present value of the future benefits (in this case, £3000 each year for five years) with the cost of the machine. If the present value of the future benefits is greater than the cost of the machine, then the firm is better off making the investment in the cost of the machine rather than holding the money in a bank. If the present value is less than the cost of the machine, then obviously the firm is better off holding its profits in a bank.

QUESTION

What is the rate of discount the firm should use in working out the present value of the future benefits?

The rate of discount the firm should use is the rate of return on holding money as a bank deposit, because this is the alternative use of its money.

The present value of £3000 a year for 5 years, assuming banks pay an interest rate of 10 per cent on deposits, is calculated as follows (rounded to the nearest pound):

The present value of the return in the first year ($t = 1$) is given by:

$$PV = \frac{£3000}{1+0.1} = \frac{£3000}{1.1} = £2727$$

This implies that £3000 in a year's time is worth £2727 today. Another way to put this is that £2727 deposited in the bank today at an interest rate of 10 per cent would realize £3000 in a year's time.

Following the same procedure as above, the return in the second year (£3000 in two years' time) has a present value given by:

$$PV = \frac{£3000}{(1+0.1)^2} = \frac{£3000}{(1.1)^2} = £2479$$

The total present value of the investment to the firm is the sum of the present values of its returns in each of the next five years:

$$PV = \frac{£3000}{1.1} + \frac{£3000}{(1.1)^2} + \frac{£3000}{(1.1)^3} + \frac{£3000}{(1.1)^4} + \frac{£3000}{(1.1)^5}$$

$$PV = £2727 + £2479 + £2254 + £2049 + £1863 = £11372$$

This figure of £11 372 is an estimate of the present value of all future returns arising from this investment. It is not as much as the total returns of $5 \times £3000 = £15\,000$, because these are not all available today and so have to be discounted in calculating their present value. In this case, the firm will invest in the new machine because the present value of future benefits (£11 372) exceeds the cost of the new machine (£10 000). The NET PRESENT VALUE (NPV) of an investment is the present value of its returns net of (minus) the cost of the investment. In this case, the net present value of the investment is £11 372 – £10 000 = £1372. Because the investment's net present value is positive, using a 10 per cent rate of discount, the firm should make the investment.

NET PRESENT VALUE (NPV)
The net present value of an investment is the present value of its returns net of (minus) the cost of the investment.

Deciding on this basis is called using the net present value criterion. If the cost of the machine exceeded the present value of the expected returns from the investment, then its net present value would be negative. In this case, the firm will gain more by depositing the money it would have spent on the machine in the bank and earning interest on it.

3.2   THE RATE OF INTEREST AND THE RATE OF DISCOUNTING

We can use discounting and the net present value criterion to illustrate more clearly the impact of changes in the rate of interest and the rate of discounting upon investment decisions. You have already seen this intuitively in Chapter 12, but discounting shows clearly how and why lowering the rate of interest can work to increase the volume of investment.

Consider the example of Section 3.1 again. Suppose a firm does not have £10 000 to spend but would have to borrow from a bank to finance that investment project. The firm would need to apply the rate of interest that the bank charges on loans as its rate of discount in evaluating its investment projects. The rate of interest that the bank charges on borrowing is 10 per cent. We saw that at this rate of discount, the net present value of the investment would be £1372.

QUESTION

How would the net present value of the investment change if the bank were to charge a higher rate of interest of 20 per cent on its loan?

The present value of returns to the investment in the first year would now be:

$$PV = \frac{£3000}{1.2} = £2500$$

and the present value of the investment over all five years would be:

$$PV = \frac{£3000}{1.2} + \frac{£3000}{(1.2)^2} + \frac{£3000}{(1.2)^3} + \frac{£3000}{(1.2)^4} + \frac{£3000}{(1.2)^5} = £8972$$

This means that the net present value of the investment is £8972 – £10 000 = – £1028, which is negative. So at this higher rate of interest, the investment is no longer profitable as the present value of the returns it will yield to the firm will be less than it costs the firm to pay for the machine. Note that this conclusion would hold even if the firm were not borrowing the money. Why? Because the firm could earn more by lending out its money than it would by investing in this project (assuming it would receive the same rate of interest). Since all producers in the economy are likely to behave in this way, we can conclude that the higher the cost of borrowing (i.e. the higher the rate of interest), the lower will be the volume of investment, since fewer investment projects will be undertaken.

EXERCISE 17.2

Use a calculator to work out the net present value of this investment if the interest rate is 15 per cent. Would the project be undertaken in this case?

Thus far, we have been using the rate of interest charged for loans as the rate of discount. This is reasonable when we think of a firm deciding whether to hold money in the bank or to invest in plant and machinery, if it feels quite secure about the returns it would get in either case. The financial asset (leaving the money as a bank deposit) and the investment project are 'substitutes' (using the term in the sense explained in Chapter 3). But this may not always be the case; one or other option may be perceived as particularly risky. Sometimes bank deposits may not inspire confidence and people may not want to hold them. Alternatively, people may believe that investment is the riskier option. In times of market instability, for example, firms may not be sure they will be able to sell their products in the future and reap the planned returns on their investment. How would firms then evaluate their investment projects? In these cases the rate of discount applied would include a subjective element that depends on perceptions as to relative risks. In risky times people are likely to see present income as more secure than promises of future income; they may therefore apply a rate of discount that is higher than the rate of interest charged for loans.

Again, the higher the rate at which the future is discounted, the lower is the present value of future income. So, the higher the rate of discount, the smaller would be the number of projects whose anticipated present value exceeds the initial costs, that is, have a positive net present value. There is always a negative relationship between the volume of investment and the rate of discount.

The central bank of a country may have some control over the rate of interest, but in so far as producers use subjective rates of discount to value their investment projects, then it is their expectations with respect to risk that matters. These expectations may be influenced by any manner of guesses about the future and they usually come into play in circumstances of financial instability. These expectations are also out of the control of any policy-making body.

3.3   EXPECTATIONS AND UNCERTAINTY

We saw in the last section how expectations could affect the valuation of a future stream of investment through influencing the rate of discount. Following Keynes, economists have stressed the importance of expectations about the future (especially of demand and profitability) on the decision to invest. Firms will hold vague expectations about the future course of economic activity and there will be a tendency for firms to revise their expectations in a sporadic and sometimes volatile manner. Keynes (1936) referred to the 'animal spirits' of investors, which sums up the volatile and precarious nature of business confidence. This section briefly explores the role of expectations and uncertainty, using once again the technique of discounting.

First let us consider the case when expectations change dramatically. Imagine you are an airline company, thinking about buying a new aeroplane for £7000 in the expectation of selling summer holidays with water sports activities in the Hawaiian Islands. Lending rates are 6 per cent and market surveys lead you to have buoyant expectations. You expect to earn revenues of £2000 in the first year, followed by £4000 in the next two years and £6000 in the following year. Should you make the investment? You calculate the present value:

$$PV = \frac{£2000}{1.06} + \frac{£4000}{(1.06)^2} + \frac{£4000}{(1.06)^3} + \frac{£6000}{(1.06)^4} = £13\,557.82$$

You find that this is well over the cost of the new aeroplane and so you decide to invest in it. While you are in the midst of negotiating a deal on the new plane, the events of 11 September 2001 happen. Market surveys now tell you that airline travel to the US is at an all time low. You have to revise your demand expectations. Now the revenues predicted are £700 in the first year, £900 in the next two years and £1000 in the fourth year. Would you still go ahead with your purchase? No, because your present value calculations now tell you that the investment is only worth £3009.125, less than half of what you would spend on the plane. Notice that interest rates have not changed at all, but pessimistic expectations of market demand have made your valuation of the same investment different within the space of a few months.

EXERCISE 17.3

The government senses a fall in investor expectations and lowers the interest rate to 4 per cent. Would you now invest in the additional aeroplane?

3.4   A CHANGE IN INCOME LEVELS

If growth is strong in the present period, firms will be able to use the higher profits gained from increased sales to finance a higher level of investment. However, strong current growth in sales may also cause firms to increase investment for another (indirect) reason. Firms may choose to take the current growth of output as a guide to future demand and profitability. Firms may form the expectation that the growth of output is going to continue into the future, and their optimistic expectations about the future will motivate them to pursue a higher level of investment. In this case, firms' optimism about the future may lead to investment that goes beyond the limits of retained profit and requires borrowing. Sudden rapid increases in demand also put pressure on firms' existing capital and force revisions in investment plans. In these circumstances, firms are encouraged not only to replace existing capital as it wears out but also to invest in new physical capital to meet the increase in demand. The idea that there exists a relationship between (demand-induced) changes in output and net investment forms the basis of the accelerator model.

The need for net investment arises from the fact that firms need more capital to be able to produce more output. Firms have some idea of what capital stock they want in light of what they expect to produce and sell, and make decisions on investment in order to reach this desired capital stock. A theory of investment must then include a model of the planned level of capital stock and how firms realize these plans through their investment activities. Remember the capital stock at the end of period t is simply the capital stock at the end of period $t-1$ plus the net investment in period t. Investment is simply the means by which the actual capital stock K is adjusted towards the desired stock K^*. When $K = K^*$, net investment will cease and the only gross investment will be replacement investment to keep the capital stock at K^*. So the rate of growth of K will be zero, since firms would have fully realized all their investment plans.

A very simple model of investment, known as the 'accelerator model', assumes that there is a fixed CAPITAL–OUTPUT RATIO, that is, that the amount of capital used per unit of output does not vary. If firms then use the level of demand (output) in the economy to form their views of the desired capital stock:

$$K^* = vY$$

Where v is the capital–output ratio.

CAPITAL–OUTPUT RATIO
The capital–output ratio is a measure of the amount of capital required for production.

The second assumption of the accelerator model is that firms take just a single period to make whatever investment is necessary to realize their desired capital stock. So, at any point in time, actual capital stock K equals desired capital stock K^*. This means that net investment in each period is simply a result of changes in output:

$$I_t = K_t - K_{t-1} = K^*_t - K^*_{t-1} = v(Y_t - Y_{t-1})$$

This model is known as the 'accelerator' because an increase in output leads to greater investment, augmenting the capital stock and thus accelerating the growth in output.

4   INVESTMENT AND OUTPUT CYCLES   •••••••••••••

A disputed question in the theory of investment and capital accumulation is whether the adjustment to K^* happens instantaneously or over time. This question pertains only to the medium or long term as in the short term capacity is fixed. In the medium term additions to capacity are realized slowly and desired capital stock may be quite different from the actual capital stock. This might mean that in some circumstances the investment plans are out of step with aggregate demand and short-term equilibrium (Chapter 12). Section 4.1 will show that this can give rise to output cycles.

In the medium term, the accelerator operates in conjunction with the 'multiplier', which you met in Chapter 12. The notion of the multiplier expresses the idea that an increase in aggregate demand will bring about a more than proportionate increase in output and income. This is because the initial increase in aggregate demand will have important knock-on effects on the employment, income and consumption of workers throughout the economy. If a firm decides to increase investment in new plant and machinery, this will lead to employment gains in the sector producing capital goods.

The additional workers employed in this sector will spend their new income on goods and services. Extra workers will then be employed to produce these goods and services. These workers will, in turn, spend their new income on goods and services and so on. In this case, the initial increase in expenditure on investment will have a multiplied effect on total output and income. The initial increase in aggregate demand expands the total income of an economy via the multiplier by more than the initial increase in demand.

This expansion of total income in turn gives rise to greater investment via the accelerator. With increases in aggregate demand, firms' desired capital stock will be higher. This requires new investment spending above that needed for replacement purposes. This additional investment spending also has a multiplier effect as above and thus generates a further increase in aggregate demand. So the desired capital stock that firms would like also rises and further new investment is required. And so the process continues.

In the boom phase of the cycle, these two mechanisms, the accelerator and the multiplier, reinforce each other to generate increases in output and investment. The boom will persist so long as output continues to grow. However without any increase in output, investment would fall to the level consistent with the replacement of existing capital and this fall will feed through via the multiplier to lower aggregate demand and lower output – a downturn in economic activity. In the downturn phase of the investment cycle, reductions in output and investment reinforce each other in the opposite direction. Each reduction in output generates a reduction in investment (via the accelerator) that, in turn, generates a reduction in output (via the multiplier).

Unless some external limit is reached, booms and recessions would continue in this manner unabated. From the interaction between the accelerator and the multiplier, we also gain some insight into the cyclical pattern of economic activity as captured by the notion of the business cycle. To produce a cycle some exogenous factor(s) must stop booms and recessions. In an upturn such an exogenous factor could be reaching full employment or a bottleneck in some part of the economy. The movement out of recession could be caused by a surge in export demand or in government spending, or by more favourable business expectations increasing investment spending.

EXERCISE 17.4

In Table 17.2 below, an economy that has a capital–output ratio of 2 begins in period 1 with a constant output (= income) of 100 units and a capital stock of 200. In the absence of an external shock, the economy will reproduce itself indefinitely as in period 1. There is now a shock to the economy and output rises to 110 in period 2.

Table 17.2 The multiplier and the accelerator

Period	Output	Change in output	Total capital	Net investment	Change in investment
1	100	0	200	0	—
2	110	10			
3					
4					
5					
6					
7					

1   If we assume the multiplier is 1.5, what will be the effects on net investment of an increase of 10 units of output in period 2? Fill in the rest of the table for period 2

2   Complete the table for the remaining periods. What will happen to output in period 8?

3   What does the above table tell you about the operation of the accelerator?

The interaction of the accelerator and multiplier provides one view of the causes of fluctuations in the level of economic activity over the course of the business cycle. But some have argued that the accelerator does not operate for all of the business cycle: 'It is well known that large reserve capacities exist, at least throughout a considerable part of the cycle, and that output may therefore increase without an actual increase in existing capacities' (Kalecki, 1954, p.285). That is, firms will tend to retain large reserves of capacity because this gives them the flexibility to respond to sudden changes in demand. The accelerator will be much more relevant in periods where economic activity is growing rapidly and firms encounter capital shortages in meeting the demand for their output.

5   INVESTMENT AND POLICY •••••••••••••••••••••••

Given the centrality of investment to economic growth and the different influences upon investment, what can governments do to encourage investment? Governments confront many different policy options for raising investment levels. The policy chosen will depend in part on the government's views on the barriers to higher investment.

One approach, which has been applied in the UK and elsewhere, is to offer various tax incentives. For example, lower taxes on profits may be pursued as a positive spur to investment. The problem with this approach, however, is that there is no guarantee that the higher after-tax profits gained by firms will feed through into higher investment. Higher after-tax profits may simply go to pay shareholders higher dividends or the tax reductions may be appropriated in the form of higher salaries.

Measures to reduce taxes on profits may therefore have a negligible impact on investment. A more targeted strategy at the fiscal level is to introduce capital allowances, either for all investment or for particular types of investment (e.g. investment in new technology). These allowances offer firms tax exemptions if they increase the capital-intensity of production. However, even these may not work: 'Academic consensus is that tax and subsidy measures generally only affect the timing of investment, rather than its quantity' (Driver, 1998, p.195). From this perspective, there would seem to be more important obstacles to raising investment levels.

Governments could also manipulate interest rates in order to stimulate investment. Changes in interest rates alter the cost of investment and can provide both a positive and negative stimulus to investment. However, aside from the question of how responsive investment is to changes in interest rates, governments may no longer have the power to manipulate interest rates to target investment. Over recent years, most governments have handed over responsibility for the setting of interest rates to independent central banks, and the priority of interest rate policy is usually the achievement of low and stable inflation. The manipulation of investment, in this case, comes about only as a by-product of moves to control inflation, and raising the level of investment is never the direct focus of interest rate policy.

The present (2002) New Labour government in the UK has sought to increase investment by creating a more stable environment for businesses to make investment decisions. It argues that past macroeconomic instability, particularly a high and volatile inflation rate, depressed investment levels in the UK. In part, this explains the investment gap between the UK and other countries. Historically, UK businesses have tended to invest less in new and replacement capital than most competitor nations: 'The capital stock per worker in the UK business sector is estimated to be around 20 per cent lower than in the US and Germany. This is a reflection of past low levels of business investment and is a major factor in the UK's relatively low level of labour productivity' (Budget Report, 2000). Though there are some signs that this gap closed during the late 1990s, there remains a significant capital deficit in the UK. The New Labour government has sought to close this gap by setting clear rules for the conduct of fiscal and monetary policy. The creation of a more predictable policy environment, one which allows firms to plan ahead with greater certainty, is seen as desirable in underpinning moves to raise investment levels in the economy. 'In a global marketplace with its increased insecurities and indeed often volatility and instability', the chancellor Gordon Brown argued, 'national economic stability is at a premium ... and no nation can secure the high levels of sustainable investment it needs without both monetary and fiscal stability together' (Brown, 2000).

Whether or not stability alone is sufficient to reverse the problem of under-investment in the UK remains an open question. Firms invest in order to make profits, but there may be other less expensive routes to higher profitability. One such route involves labour intensification by which firms extract greater effort from their existing workforce – in the extreme case, workers may be expected to work harder for no extra pay. Unlike a policy of higher investment, this route cannot lead to sustained increases in output in the longer run. Where incentives exist for firms to increase profitability that can be fulfilled through increases in the intensity of work, firms may well forgo increased investment in preference to gaining more output from their existing labour input. The labour intensification option, the 'low route' to greater profitability, may offer greater short-term gains and also involves less immediate financial expense than the investment option, the 'high route' to greater profitability. Firms will face least resistance in terms of pursuing the 'low route' where the workers' bargaining position is weak.

So, we cannot just expect firms to respond to lower interest rates or lower taxes by raising investment; we also need to consider the incentives created for non-investment routes to higher profitability. Where firms can exploit the vulnerable position of workers (e.g. because of low trade union power), there may well exist significant obstacles to increased investment even with favourable changes in interest rates and taxes. Certainly, evidence for the UK economy indicates that productivity gains were achieved through higher work intensity during the 1980s – a period in which the strength of unionized labour was greatly diminished (Chapter 7, Section 4.1; Green, 2001). This indicates the need for a broader discussion on the barriers to investment and on the policies needed to overcome these barriers.

6   CONCLUSION   •

This chapter has focused on the nature and determinants of investment. It has been established that investment is vital for achieving and sustaining economic growth. Investment adds to the productive potential of the economy by creating new physical and human assets. The use of these assets within production in turn provides the basis for growth in output and productivity. However, investment requires finance and firms will be reluctant to undertake much investment if they expect only moderate growth in future sales. The problem for firms is to balance the costs of investment against the potential gains as measured by higher revenues. Governments can create incentives for firms to invest though, as suggested above, policy towards investment is far from straightforward. The volatile and precarious nature of investment behaviour means that the problem of sustaining a high level of investment remains a key concern for policy makers in the UK and elsewhere.

CHAPTER 18 GROWTH

Gavin Cameron ●

Objectives

After studying this chapter you should be able to:
- understand the long-run determinants of the growth of national income
- distinguish between factors that can create a higher level of income and factors that increase the rate of growth of income
- understand how per capita consumption can be maximized
- understand the impact of technical change on the growth of national income
- understand growth accounting
- understand how permanent growth can be created in economies
- understand why levels of national income between countries converge or diverge.

Concepts

- steady state
- growth effect
- levels effect
- rate of growth of total factor productivity
- absolute income convergence
- conditional income convergence

1 INTRODUCTION ●

Economic growth and persistently rising standards of living constitute a surprisingly recent phenomenon. For most of human history, improvements in the level of technology have either been small or have led to population increases rather than improved living standards. In 1803, this observation prompted Thomas Robert Malthus, a clergyman of the Church of England, to publish his *Essay on the Principle of Population*, which argued that there was a natural tendency for population growth to outstrip growth in resources. Between the discovery of agriculture about 10 000 years ago and the start of the Industrial Revolution in the middle of the eighteenth century, the population of the world rose from around 5 to 10 million to some 700 to 800 million, but living standards for most of the world's population remained at a subsistence level. For good reasons, this period is often called the 'Malthusian era'.

In contrast, in the two and a half centuries since 1750, average living standards have doubled every generation. The change in the growth rates in these two periods is staggering, and the change has been accompanied by equally staggering revolutions in mortality rates, birth rates and population growth rates, such that the population of the world had risen to over 6 billion by the year 2000. The importance of thinking about economic growth is also underlined by many growth 'miracles' and growth 'disasters', especially since the Second World War. Table 18.1 shows the growth rates of GDP per worker, an index of labour productivity, between 1960 and 1990 for ten countries considered to have had growth miracles and ten countries that represented growth disasters.

As Lucas (1993) has pointed out, one only has to compare the experience of South Korea (a growth miracle) with that of the Philippines (not shown as a disaster or a miracle in Table 18.1). In 1960 these countries had quite similar living standards, industrial structures and expectations. But by 1985 South Korean living standards had more than quadrupled, while living standards in the Philippines had risen by only about a half. To take another example, Japan had a lower standard of living than Brazil, Malaysia and Chile after the Second World War, but it then experienced such a dramatic growth that, by the late 1980s, many Americans were worried that Japan was about to overtake the USA as the biggest industrial economy in the world.

Table 18.1 Growth miracles and disasters: annual average growth rate of GDP per worker, 1960–90

Miracles	Growth	Disasters	Growth
South Korea	6.1	Ghana	–0.3
Botswana*	5.9	Venezuela	–0.5
Hong Kong	5.8	Mozambique	–0.7
Taiwan	5.8	Nicaragua	–0.7
Singapore	5.4	Mauritania	–0.8
Japan	5.2	Zambia	–0.8
Malta*	4.8	Mali	–1.0
Cyprus	4.4	Madagascar	–1.3
Seychelles	4.4	Chad	–1.7
Lesotho	4.4	Guyana	–2.1

* Figures for Botswana and Malta based on 1960–89.

Source: Temple, 1999

Many people ask why economists are interested in, if not obsessed by, economic growth. After all, since the publication of *Small is Beautiful* by E.F. Schumacher in 1973, it has been almost respectable to suggest that economic growth is a bad thing, leading to all sorts of vices, environmental harms and inequalities. Amartya Sen (1999) reminds us of the benefits of economic growth. He argues that development can be seen as a process that expands the freedoms enjoyed by people (whether those are political freedoms, economic freedoms, social freedoms, open government or protective security). Improvements in living standards go hand in hand with improvements in these freedoms.

This chapter will provide a theoretical framework for thinking about modern economic growth. Underpinning this theoretical framework is the assumption that unemployment and business cycles are important in explaining short- and medium-run growth, but play almost no role in the analysis of long-run economic growth. Thus, in the long run, national output is determined by supply-side factors. The main source of rising living standards is increasing labour productivity, which is itself due to the accumulation of physical capital and technological progress.

Section 2 examines some of the stylised facts that characterize modern economic growth. The Solow growth model is discussed in Section 3. In Section 4 the Solow model is extended by including the influence of technological change on economic growth. Section 5 discusses the economic factors that can influence technological progress, focusing on profit-seeking research, human capital formation and openness to foreign ideas. Armed with these different ways of thinking about economic growth, I shall look at the evidence on the growth of nations in Section 6. In particular, I shall look at why the economies of some countries have grown while the economies of others have not.

2   THE 'CLASSICS'

In 1958, the economist Nicholas Kaldor suggested that modern economic growth could be characterized by the following stylised facts.

- Output and labour productivity grow at a broadly stable rate, typically around 2 per cent per year, despite short-term fluctuations.

- The amount of capital employed per worker rises over time, at approximately the same rate as the growth of output and labour productivity.

- The rate of profit (return on capital) is roughly constant, despite short-term fluctuations.

- The share of profits and wages in output is roughly constant, at around one-third and two-thirds respectively.

Some of these stylised facts would have surprised classical economists such as Malthus and Ricardo. They predicted that because natural resources, such as land, were fixed factors of production, there would be diminishing returns to other factors of production, and thus the rate of profit and the share of profits in output would steadily fall. They would certainly not have expected the growth of output to keep going at a steady rate, although they would have expected the amount of capital goods per worker to rise to offset falling labour productivity.

Thus these stylised facts paint a picture of growth that is less constrained than that of the classical economists. Why? The simple answer is technological progress and factor substitution (that is, the ability of firms and the economy to substitute away from more expensive to less expensive factors of production). Today, some people argue that these stylised facts will not continue to hold unless growth takes place in a sustainable way, otherwise the limits posed by natural resources will come into play. You will meet these arguments again in Chapter 19. This chapter will explore a variety of different growth models and examine how well they explain these stylised facts.

3   THE BASIC SOLOW MODEL   • • • • • • • • • • • • • • • • • •

3.1   INTRODUCING THE SOLOW MODEL

In 1956, Robert Solow published a path-breaking paper on economic growth, in which he developed a model of growth in the economy as a whole, where total output Y is produced using total labour L and a stock of total physical capital K. By physical capital, we mean things such as plant, machinery, buildings and office equipment. It may seem strange, but it is actually not too unreasonable to lump together a whole bunch of disparate items of capital of the sort mentioned above and just call the result K. Indeed, we have of necessity already used aggregates, such as Y, L and K, in our stylised facts to talk about growth at the level of the economy as a whole.

In the basic Solow model, in which there is no technological change, both labour and physical capital are subject to diminishing returns individually but yield constant returns to scale when taken together. Diminishing returns to capital mean that increasing the amount of capital, while holding the number of workers constant, yields a smaller and smaller additional amount of output per unit of additional capital. So, labour productivity rises as the capital stock increases, but at a diminishing rate. Eventually, each worker has so much capital equipment that giving her some more doesn't affect her output at all. In much the same way, increasing the number of workers, while holding the capital stock constant, yields smaller and smaller additional amounts of output per additional worker. However, the assumption of constant returns to scale means that doubling the number of workers *at the same time* as doubling the amount of capital leads to a doubling of output. Put differently, the output per worker depends only upon the ratio of capital to labour employed.

This situation is represented in Figure 18.1, where capital per worker, k (= K/L), is measured along the horizontal axis and output per worker, y (= Y/L), is measured along the vertical axis. The curve denoted by $y = f(k)$ is the production function for the economy as a whole. It shows that output per worker, y, increases as the amount of capital per worker, k, increases. However, the production function gets less steep as output rises because of diminishing returns to capital per worker. Functions that bend over in this way are known as 'concave' functions.

An economy is in a STEADY STATE if capital per worker and output per worker do not change. To keep the economy in such a steady state, exactly the right amount of investment is needed to replace worn-out capital goods and to equip any new workers that enter the labour force with the current level of capital per worker, k. A steady state also requires equilibrium in all markets, that is, all participants must be able to realise

STEADY STATE
The steady state represents the long-run equilibrium path of the economy such that there are no economic forces exerting pressure on either capital per worker or output per worker to change; that is, they are constant over time.

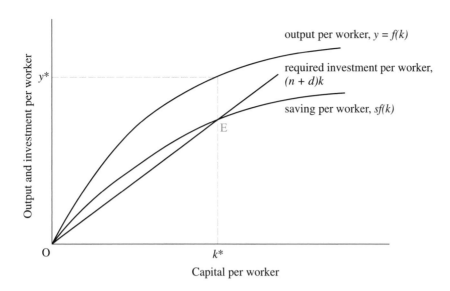

Figure 18.1
The Solow model

their plans, so that output equals income, all savings are invested and there is no unemployment. If we take account of the fact that some people cannot or do not want to have jobs, this last assumption is equivalent to having a constant proportion of the population employed.

If there is no investment, the stock of capital per worker will fall at the rate of physical depreciation d plus the rate of workforce growth n, which is assumed to be equal to the rate of population growth. So, maintaining the level of capital stock *per worker* in the face of depreciation and an increasing labour force requires an investment of $(n + d)k$ per worker. This is known as 'capital widening', and it is represented in Figure 18.1 by the required investment line. More investment than this will lead to the creation of new capital goods and hence a rise in the stock of capital per worker, in which case 'capital deepening' takes place.

To investigate the conditions under which this would happen, Solow assumed that a constant fraction, s, of income is saved (the rest is consumed) and that these savings are all invested. So, total gross investment, I, is given by $I = S = sY$. So gross investment per worker is equal to sy – which is equal to $sf(k)$ – and is represented by the saving per worker curve on Figure 18.1. The saving per worker curve has the same shape as the output per worker curve, because saving per worker is simply output per worker multiplied by the propensity to save (s).

An economy is in steady-state equilibrium when the amount of new capital being created through saving is equal to the amount of investment required to offset physical depreciation and workforce growth. In short, in steady-state equilibrium, gross investment (savings) must equal required investment, leaving a net investment of zero. On Figure 18.1 this happens where the required investment and the saving per worker curves cross, at point E. Accordingly, k^* and y^* represent the steady-state levels of capital and output per head respectively. At this steady state, output *per worker* and capital *per worker* are constant, and hence both total output and capital, and thus the economy as a whole, must be growing at the rate of population growth, n.

3.2 EXPLORING THE SOLOW MODEL: THE EFFECT OF ONE-OFF CHANGES

The basic Solow model assumes that the saving rate, the rate of depreciation of capital and the rate of population growth are all fixed and that there is no technological change. In this section I shall explore each of these assumptions by considering the impact of a one-off change on the resulting steady state. The effect of such a change could be on k^* and y^*, the steady-state levels of capital and output per worker, or on the growth rate of the economy, g.

A CHANGE IN THE SAVING RATE

Suppose an economy begins in a steady state with a saving rate of s_1, giving capital per worker k_1^* and output per worker y_1^*. Now suppose this saving rate is permanently increased to s' (for example, because of a tax change that encourages saving – remember the assumption that all saving is invested). In Figure 18.2 this shift in the saving rate is shown as an upward shift of the saving per worker line.

Now saving and hence investment at k_1^* exceeds the amount needed to keep the capital stock per worker constant, so it begins to rise and so does output per worker. They both keep rising until a new steady state is reached with a higher level of capital per worker k_2^* and output per worker y_2^*. The increase in saving temporarily raised the growth rate of output and capital above the rate of population growth, n, as the economy moved to a new steady state (otherwise it would not have been possible for capital per worker and output per worker to have increased). But once the new steady state was reached, the growth rate of the economy returned to its previous level, n.

Figure 18.2
Exploring the Solow model: the effect of higher saving

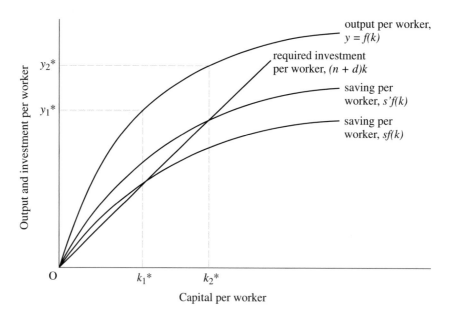

This situation is shown in Figure 18.3, where before $t = 0$ the saving rate of the economy is s and the economy is growing at the rate of population growth, n. A one-off permanent increase in the saving rate at $t = 0$ increases the rate of growth of output temporarily, but the effect on the rate of growth will eventually tail off. After some time, the rate of growth returns to its original level, n, despite the increased saving rate. However, the level of capital and output per worker is now permanently higher as a result of the period of increased growth brought about by the permanent rise in the saving rate.

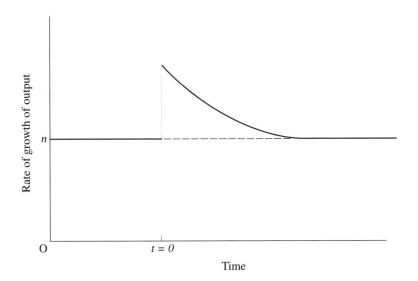

Figure 18.3
The temporary growth effect of a change in the saving rate

In the Solow model, a permanent rise in the saving rate leads to a higher level of income per capita, but not higher growth in the long run.

A CHANGE IN THE RATE OF POPULATION GROWTH OR THE RATE OF CAPITAL DEPRECIATION

A higher rate of population growth will increase capital-widening requirements, because the new workers being added to the workforce will need to be equipped with capital goods. Remember that the model assumes equilibrium in all markets, including the labour market, so an increase in the population will lead to a corresponding increase in the numbers of workers employed. Similarly, if capital begins to wear out faster than before, capital-widening requirements will increase. This is shown in Figure 18.4. A rise in both the rate of growth of the workforce and the depreciation rate (from n_1 and d_1 respectively to n_2 and d_2) rotates the required investment function upwards.

The existing amount of saving from current output does not produce enough gross investment to maintain capital per worker at its existing level, k_1^*. So k will fall, that is, there will be negative capital deepening until the economy reaches a new steady state with a lower level of capital per worker, k_2^*, and lower level of output per worker, y_2^*. To reach this point both output and capital grow at a slower rate than the workforce during the period of transition. When the steady state is reached, output and capital will again grow at the same rate as population.

Thus changes in both the rate of depreciation and the rate of population growth affect the steady-state level of income per capita, but do not affect the steady-state rate of growth of income per capita, since the rate of growth of the economy remains the same as that of the population.

Figure 18.4
Exploring the Solow
model: the effect of
higher population
growth and/or a
higher depreciation
rate

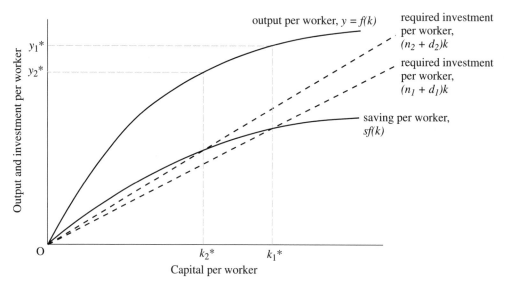

A ONE-OFF IMPROVEMENT IN TECHNOLOGY

QUESTION

What happens in the Solow model when there is a one-off improvement in technology?

A one-off improvement in technology can occur because of some invention (for example, the compass, which helped ships to navigate) that leads to an increase in the marginal productivity of capital for every unit of labour input. This will rotate the production function upwards and, if the saving rate remains unchanged, will lead to a rise in gross investment for any given level of capital per worker. This will enable a rise in the capital stock per worker, capital deepening, until required investment is once again equal to saving per worker (gross investment). Hence, a one-off rise in the level of technology will raise the amount of capital per worker and raise the steady-state level of output per worker, but not affect the long-run growth rate. This is similar to an increase in the saving rate, except that the output per worker will rise faster. It will rise not only because the capital per worker has risen, but also because the improvement in technology has increased the amount each worker can produce with a given level of capital.

EXERCISE 18.1

Suppose there were a world war, which caused the death of many scientists and the destruction of manufacturing factories all over the world. Use the Solow framework to explain the effect of the resulting one-off fall in the level of technology, drawing figures like Figure 18.2 and Figure 18.4.

In the Solow model, policy changes to increase savings, reduce population growth or decrease the rate of depreciation can increase growth rates in income per capita, but only temporarily as part of the transition to a new steady state. Such a policy change can have no long-term GROWTH EFFECT, but may have a LEVELS EFFECT. A permanent change in the saving rate, the population growth rate or the rate of depreciation can permanently change the level of per capita income. Note that these effects are defined as 'per capita', meaning per head of the population, because we are interested in the standard of living of the whole population. However, the production function and the diagrams that we have been using so far are all expressed 'per worker'. Because of the assumption that there is equilibrium in all markets, including the labour market, this does not matter, because we can assume that output equals income and there is no unemployment. This means that output per worker translates directly into income per capita (via a constant that gives the proportion of workers in the population), and we can use the terms 'income' and 'output', and 'per worker' and 'per capita', interchangeably.

GROWTH EFFECT

There is a growth effect when a change leads to a permanently higher growth rate of income per capita.

LEVELS EFFECT

There is a levels effect when a change leads to a permanently higher level of income per capita.

This is shown in Figure 18.5, which is similar to Figure 18.3 except that it is the growth rate of income per capita that is measured on the vertical axis. Consider the effect of a change at $t = 0$ in a policy variable that has levels but not growth effects (all the changes considered in this section). Before the change, income per capita is steady; it has a zero growth rate. The change in the policy variable increases the rate of growth of income per capita temporarily, but the effect will eventually tail off. After some time, the rate of growth returns to zero. However, the level of output per worker is now permanently higher as a result of the period of increased growth brought about by the change in the policy variable.

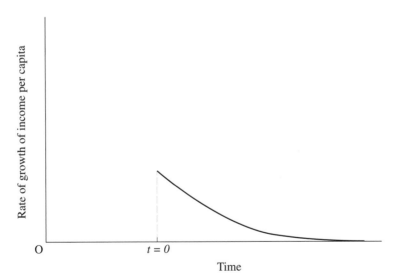

Figure 18.5
The temporary growth effect of a change in technology

In the next two sections I shall begin to explore the role of technological change, first within the framework of the Solow model, and later within a number of more recent 'new growth theory' models.

4   TECHNOLOGICAL CHANGE   •

In the absence of technological change, the Solow model predicts that output per worker will be constant in the long run and that total output will rise at the same rate as the exogenously determined population growth rate. Solow clearly did not believe that this was in fact what had happened in the US economy. Indeed, he wrote a paper in 1957 that examined the empirical data on economic growth. His data suggested that gross output per hour worked in US manufacturing doubled between 1909 and 1949, with only 12.5 per cent of this increase attributable to increases in capital per worker. What accounted for the other 87.5 per cent? Solow's answer was that it was technological change, that is, improvements in the level of technology, which he labelled A.

To measure technological progress by a single variable A may seem strange, as so many of the products that we consume today, and the processes by which they are made, were unknown a hundred years ago. In 1901, at the end of the Victorian era, Guglielmo Marconi was just about to send the first radio signal across the Atlantic; the Wright Brothers had not yet flown; the transistor and the laser were not yet invented; and Raymond Kroc, the salesman responsible for creating the McDonald's restaurant chain, was yet to be born. Nevertheless, we can get quite far thinking of technological progress as something that can be measured by a single variable, A. In the next two sub-sections, I shall examine first what adding such a notion of technological progress does to the Solow model, and then examine its use in another contribution of Solow's to the understanding of growth, his method of growth accounting.

4.1   THE SOLOW MODEL WITH EXOGENOUS TECHNOLOGICAL CHANGE

In the growth model examined so far, there has been no possibility of sustained growth in output per capita. Output itself grows, but only at the rate of population growth. There might be temporary adjustments in output per worker, but none of the one-off changes considered in the last section could lead to permanent, steady-state growth in output per worker.

A model in which output per worker grows in the steady state must include continuous technological change. Solow adapted his model to consider labour-augmenting technological change, that is, technology that makes labour more productive by a factor of A, where A is a variable measuring the level of technology. Intuitively, we can think of labour as becoming A times more efficient, so that each worker makes the contribution of A previous, or non 'technology-adjusted', workers. A workforce of L workers now contributes the same as AL non technology-adjusted workers. If such technical progress proceeds at a constant exogenously given rate g_A, and the rate of growth of population is n, then the rate of growth of the workforce measured in terms of technology-adjusted workers is $n + g_A$.

The main conclusions of the Solow model remain the same, but we now have to write them in terms of capital per technology-adjusted worker and output per technology-adjusted worker. This is shown in Figure 18.6, which is similar to Figure 18.1. Capital per technology-adjusted worker $\tilde{k}$ ($= k/A = K/AL$) is measured along the horizontal axis, and output per technology-adjusted worker is measured up the vertical axis. To keep $\tilde{k}$ (pronounced 'k tilda') constant, the capital stock must grow at the same rate as the number of technology-adjusted workers, that is, at a rate of $n + g_A$. So, allowing for depreciation, maintaining the level of capital stock per technology-adjusted worker requires investment of $(n + d + g_A)\tilde{k}$ per technology-adjusted worker.

In a steady-state equilibrium, there is no growth in output per technology-adjusted worker, but output per worker grows at the rate of technological change, g_A, so total output rises at the rate of technological change plus the rate of workforce growth, $n + g_A$.

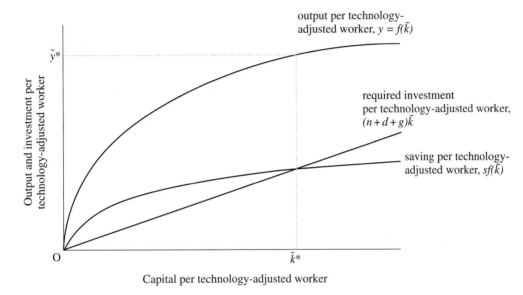

Figure 18.6
The Solow model with labour-augmenting technological change

With labour-augmenting technological change, the growth rate of output in the long run depends upon the rate of workforce growth and the rate at which technological change occurs.

4.2   GROWTH ACCOUNTING

In his 1957 empirical paper, Solow demonstrated the possibility of decomposing growth into contributions from the growth rates of factor inputs of labour and capital weighted by their factor shares plus a 'residual' term interpreted as exogenous technological progress. Calling exogenous technological progress 'a residual' means that it is there to account for any change in the level of output that is not explained by changes in the levels of inputs, labour and capital. Because the production function takes account of changes due to changes in the level of inputs, Robert Solow thought of any kind of upward shift in the production function as representing technological progress. If technological change is neutral (that is, if it does not affect the relative use of labour and capital), it becomes relatively straightforward to decompose output growth into the contributions of technological progress and increased factor inputs. Then we can write the growth rate of output as:

rate of growth of output = rate of growth of technology + rate of growth of inputs

Which means that:

rate of growth of technology = rate of growth of output − rate of growth of inputs

Here the rate of growth of inputs means the weighted average growth rate of labour and capital, with each input being weighted by its factor share (the share of payments to that factor in national output). This is the classic *growth-accounting* equation, which shows clearly what is meant by talking about technological progress as a residual.

The rate of growth of technology is also known as the rate of growth of total factor productivity (TFP), because it tells one how much more productive the factors of production, capital and labour, have become in total. TFP is another version of *A*, the single variable that measures technological progress. However, unlike the previous model, where technological progress was solely labour augmenting, the growth-accounting model assumes technological progress that is 'neutral' and augments the productivity of both labour and capital equally. In this case, the RATE OF GROWTH OF TFP is equal to the growth rate of output minus the weighted growth rates of labour and capital inputs, where the weights are the shares of national income that accrue to each factor. As we saw earlier, initial estimates of the contribution of TFP growth to output growth were impressive.

RATE OF GROWTH OF TFP

The rate of growth of total factor productivity is the increase in output resulting from technological progress, with all inputs unchanged.

QUESTION

How can we calculate the growth rate of TFP?

Suppose that the growth rate of output is 10 per cent per year, while capital and labour inputs grow at an annual rate of 4 per cent and 2 per cent respectively. Furthermore, suppose we have an economy where the payments to labour account for 60 per cent of national income and payments to capital account for 40 per cent. The production function, we assume, is characterized by constant returns to scale and both factor and product markets are perfectly competitive.

The growth accounting equation is:

rate of growth of output = rate of growth of technology (TFP) + rate of growth of inputs

Now the rate of growth of inputs means the weighted average growth rate of labour and capital, with each input weighted by its factor share (the share of payments to that factor in national income). If we assume that the shares of labour and capital in national income do not change, then:

rate of growth of inputs = α(rate of growth of capital) + $(1 - \alpha)$(rate of growth of labour)

Here α is the share of capital in national income and so $(1 - \alpha)$ is the share of labour in national income. The rest of the calculation now becomes straightforward: substituting the rates of growth of capital and labour inputs (4 per cent and 2 per cent respectively) and the shares of payments to capital (40 per cent = 0.4) and labour (60 per cent = 0.6) gives:

rate of growth of inputs = (0.4) 4% + (0.6) 2% = 2.8%

So, the rate of growth of TFP (technology) growth can be calculated as the residual.

rate of growth of technology = rate of growth of output – rate of growth of inputs

= 10% – 2.8%

= 7.2%

So the rate of growth of total factor productivity is 7.2 per cent

The growth rate of output per capita and capital per worker can be obtained as follows.

rate of growth of output per worker = rate of growth of output – rate of growth of population

= 10% – 2%

= 8%

rate of growth of capital per worker = rate of growth of capital – rate of growth of population

= 4% – 2%

= 2%

EXERCISE 18.2

Suppose that, in the above example, with the same factor shares in national income, the annual rates of growth of labour and capital inputs are 6 per cent and 8 per cent respectively. Also assume that total factor productivity grows at the rate of 3 per cent per annum. Compute:

1   The rate of growth of outputs in the economy.

2   The rate of growth of output per worker.

3   The rate of growth of capital per worker.

The growth-accounting approach was the dominant methodology for empirical studies of productivity from Solow's ground-breaking 1957 paper until the early 1970s. Solow's original conclusion, that technological progress accounted for almost all of economic growth, was gradually watered down as national accounts statistics and statistical methodology improved.

Nonetheless, even recent studies suggest that the 'growth residual' accounts for a significant part of economic growth, usually around one-third. Table 18.2 compares growth rates of TFP and labour productivity for the OECD between 1960 and 1997.

A sharp slow-down in both is apparent in the 1970s, following the first oil shock and the final collapse of the Bretton-Woods fixed exchange rate system in 1973. Note that Japan experienced a huge decline in its TFP growth in the 1970s and then only marginally picked up post-1979, while both Italy and Germany continued to experience a slowdown in their rate of growth of TFP for the next two decades as well. This trend was also reflected in the growth rates of labour productivity for all three countries. Both the UK and the US experienced a similar decline, but managed to raise their productivity growth rates (of both TFP and labour) by significant amounts in the period 1979 to 1997.

Table 18.2 Recent estimates of TFP growth in the business sector of OECD economies (percentage per annum), 1960–97

Country	TFP growth			Labour productivity growth		
	1960–73	1973–79	1979–97	1960–73	1973–79	1979–97
OECD	2.9	0.6	0.9	4.6	1.7	1.7
EU	3.4	1.2	1.1	5.4	2.5	1.8
USA	1.9	0.1	0.7	2.6	0.3	2.2
Japan	4.9	0.7	0.9	8.4	2.8	2.3
Germany	2.6	1.8	1.2	4.5	3.1	2.2
France	3.7	1.6	1.3	5.3	2.9	2.2
Italy	4.4	2.0	1.1	6.4	2.8	2.0
UK	2.6	0.5	1.1	4.1	1.6	2.0

Source: OECD data, various years

These studies in the Solow tradition produce estimates of the rate of technological progress, but they do not shed any light on the causes of technological progress or economic growth. Is it likely that economic growth would continue without increased workforce skill levels, investment in R&D and public infrastructure, the installation of capital equipment embodying new technologies, or changes in the types and varieties of goods? More importantly, which of these, and many other factors, is the most significant cause of growth? These are the kinds of questions on which new growth theory may be able to shed some light.

5   NEW GROWTH THEORY   •

Economists have been interested in explaining technological progress for a long time and much effort has been devoted to the subject since Solow's work in the 1950s. However, it was not until the 1980s that interest in the area really took off with the development of endogenous growth models. In contrast to the Solow model, where technological progress is exogenous (like 'manna from heaven'), new growth theory attempts to explain the sources of technological progress. Three important candidates for the source of such progress are profit-seeking research, openness to foreign ideas, and human capital.

In the Solow model, technology is exogenous and there are diminishing returns to labour and capital individually, but constant returns to scale. A model with increasing returns to scale would produce very different results. In particular, constant or increasing returns to scale determine whether policy changes have a levels or a growth effect. To see this, we can look first at a simple model in which there are constant returns to capital (but increasing returns to scale).

5.1   THE AK MODEL OF BROAD CAPITAL

In the Solow model, firms are able to capture all the returns to their own investments. In reality, however, the social return to new investment may be higher than the private rate of return. This will happen if there are externalities on capital formation, so that others benefit from a firm's investment in new capital goods through an enhancement of the productivity of their existing capital stock (for discussions of externalities, see Chapter 3, Section 4.2; Chapter 9, Section 2.1; and Chapter 10, Section 2.2). These externalities could arise, for example, because of some form of learning by doing, with workers moving between firms and taking their knowledge of using the new capital goods with them. In an extreme case, this might lead to there being constant returns to capital at the level of the economy as whole, even if there are diminishing returns to capital for individual firms.

In the AK model there are constant returns to capital, so output is a linear function of the 'broad' capital stock. It is called the AK model because the aggregate production function can be written as $Y = AK$, and output per worker is therefore $y = Ak$. The diagram for this model looks rather different from the diagram for the Solow model. Figure 18.7 shows that the linearity has the effect of making the output function into a straight line rather than a curved (concave) function. The saving function, $sy = sAk$, is therefore also a straight line, as is required investment, since that is a fixed proportion, $(n + d)$, of k. Provided savings are greater than required investment, these two lines never meet (except when $k = 0$). This means that there is no point at which gross investment is equal to required investment, and hence there is no steady-state level of output or capital per worker.

If savings are greater than required investment, investment is available to generate growth through capital deepening. This is given by the distance between these two lines, that is, the difference between gross investment and required investment. Such capital deepening gives an AK economy a positive growth rate whose level depends on the saving rate. Government policy to raise the saving rate will raise the growth rate if it is successful.

This is an example of an endogenous growth model. It is called that because it explains growth not by exogenous factors, such as exogenous technological change, but by the accumulation of capital, which happens inside the model. In endogenous growth models, unlike the Solow model, policies can have permanent effects on the rate of growth, not just levels effects. The next three subsections examine three potential influences on the level of technology, A: profit-seeking research, openness to foreign ideas, and human capital.

Figure 18.7
The AK model

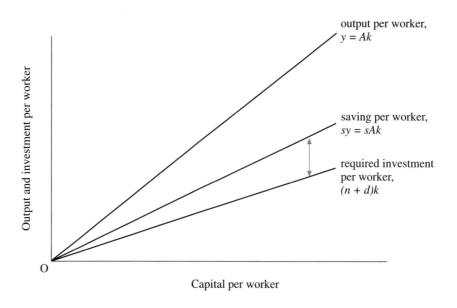

5.2   THE CREATION OF NEW IDEAS THROUGH RESEARCH

In this section I shall focus on research-based growth models. In these models, research leads to growth through the development of new goods and better goods, as well as new and better production processes.

One of the most influential new growth models is that of Paul Romer, which stresses the importance to the growth process of research that produces new ideas for technological progress. In his model, the economy's production function is similar to that of the Solow model with respect to labour and capital. Capital is accumulated through saving and the population grows at the rate n. The main difference from the Solow model is that technological progress is no longer exogenous, but depends on the stock of ideas. At any point in time, this stock of ideas is increasing because of the new ideas thought up by current researchers. How many new ideas there are depends on the number of researchers.

The productivity of these researchers in producing new ideas may depend on the stock of existing ideas. (You can think of the stock of ideas as the 'capital stock' that researchers use to produce new ideas.) But unlike physical capital, this sort of stock may reduce productivity. This would be the case if ideas were subject to 'over-fishing', so that the more ideas that are discovered the harder it is to find new ones. Or it could work the other way, with a 'standing on the shoulders' effect, in which accumulated ideas from the past make current researchers more productive.

If the 'over-fishing' effect and the 'standing on the shoulders' effect exactly cancel each other out, the stock of ideas has no effect on the productivity of existing researchers. In this case, the number of ideas discovered will depend simply on the number of researchers. A constant number of researchers will discover a constant number of ideas each year. Although the stock of ideas will grow, and there will therefore be technological progress, the growth rate of the stock of ideas will eventually fall to zero (that is what happens if an increasing stock is increased by only the same amount each year). So, for growth to persist, we need the number of researchers to grow over time.

This scenario is illustrated in Figure 18.8, where before $t = 0$ a constant proportion of the population is employed in research. Because the population is growing, the number of researchers is growing at a rate sufficient to ensure a steady rate of technological progress, g_A. A one-off permanent increase in the proportion of the population engaged in research at $t = 0$ initially increases the rate of growth of new ideas, but the effect on the rate of technological progress will eventually tail-off as shown in Figure 18.8. After some time the rate of growth of technology returns back to its original level, despite the increased number of researchers. However, the level of technology is now permanently higher than it would have been otherwise, and there has been a similarly positive effect on the level of output.

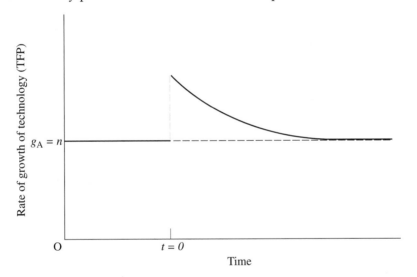

Figure 18.8
A temporary increase in the rate of growth of technology

It follows that, among countries that are otherwise similar, a country with a higher number of researchers will have a higher income than a country with few researchers, because the level of technology will be relatively higher. (For further discussion of these issues, see the excellent book by Charles Jones, 2002.)

Romer's original model (1990) made a different assumption about the effect of the stock of ideas on the productivity of existing researchers. He assumed that the productivity of research was simply proportional to the stock of existing ideas. In this case, an increase in the current stock of ideas has a 'standing on the shoulders' effect that leads to a proportionate increase in the productivity of research. This means that a constant number of researchers can keep the rate of production of new ideas constant, because their productivity increases as they increase the stock of ideas. So, the growth rate of ideas will depend just on the number of researchers. That number does not need to keep growing in order to produce increases in the growth of technology. This has the implication that countries with more researchers should have faster growth rates.

These two models have different implications for the effect of research on productivity and an economy's growth rate. Does the number of researchers in an economy affect the rate of technological progress or does it affect only the level of technology used, but not its rate of growth? Romer's (1990) formulation that the stock of ideas has a proportionate impact on the productivity of researchers implied that more researchers should lead to faster growth. The empirical evidence, however, contradicts this. As Charles Jones (1995) has pointed out, the number of researchers in the USA increased five-fold between 1950 and 1990, but the long-run growth rate continued to hover at about 2 per cent.

If the number of researchers in a country depends on its population, these two models shed light on an important issue in the new growth literature: whether a larger population in a country will lead to a faster rate of growth or a higher level of income. This distinction can be thought of as the difference between a growth effect of scale and a levels effect of scale (the scale of the population and hence the number of researchers employed). The balance of evidence suggests that the latter is more likely.

5.3   OPENNESS

QUESTION

Why should open economies grow faster than closed ones?

Of course, no one country can hope to be the source of every idea and innovation that it needs. In practice, there are large and significant flows of ideas between countries, such as the adoption of Japanese-style production techniques in Europe and the USA during the 1980s. This then suggests that growth too can be derived either from domestic innovation or from technological transfer from abroad.

Cameron *et al.* (1999) discuss a model in which there are three influences on the rate of growth of a country's TFP. First, there is the rate at which technology can be adopted from abroad. Second, there is the proportion of foreign technologies that can be adopted. Third, there is the domestic rate of growth in the absence of technology transfer. The idea is that a technological follower grows at its domestic growth rate, plus some extra 'catch-up' that is generated by the gap between its own TFP level and the TFP level of the leader. Meanwhile, a technological leader grows at its own domestic growth rate.

This model implies that all countries will grow at the same rate (the domestic growth rate of the technological leader) in equilibrium, but will differ in their productivity and thus in their level of income per capita. A follower country can maintain a growth rate equal to that of the leader because it derives 'catch-up' growth from the productivity gap between itself and the leader, which makes up the difference between their domestic growth rates.

This suggests that the steady-state gap between the follower and the leader is dependent upon their domestic growth rates, the speed of catch-up, and the proportion of technological knowledge that can be copied. Although the model implies that a bigger gap between the follower and leader leads to faster catch-up, it is also possible that countries that are further behind the technological frontier can copy only a small proportion of the leader's knowledge (this is often called an *appropriate technology* problem). Griffith *et al.* (2000) examined OECD economic performance after 1970 and concluded that countries with large technology gaps with the USA tended to grow faster, and that countries with more skilled workforces and higher R&D spending caught up faster yet.

There are a number of additional ways in which international openness (typically defined as openness to international trade) could affect growth. You will have met some of these in Chapter 14, on international trade. First, there is the static effect through specialization by comparative advantage. Second, there are dynamic effects through increased market size, and increased product market competition. In this section we have shown that access to foreign ideas and capital, and possibly the elimination of duplication in innovation, are also important benefits of openness.

5.4   HUMAN CAPITAL

Another influential kind of new growth theory model examines human capital. If we think of human capital, H, as being an index of the quality of the workforce in the same way that we thought about the level of technology, A, affecting worker productivity in the Solow model, it is clear that the incentive to accumulate human capital could be an important determinant of growth. How can human capital be accumulated? One way is for workers to be given incentives to spend time learning new skills in return for higher rewards in the workplace.

The simplest model treats human capital as just another form of capital (that is, it is produced using the same production function as physical capital and output). This kind of model will typically yield results similar to that of the AK model. This is what we would expect if physical and human capital are produced in the same way, with a production function that has constant returns to this form of broad capital and hence increasing returns to scale overall. Growth is endogenous in this model, as the more time that people spend learning, the faster the growth rate.

Evidence on the effect of human capital on growth and incomes can be obtained from a variety of sources. For example, the field of labour economics contains many studies that look at the effect of extra schooling on earnings. However, it is never clear whether people choose extra schooling because it will earn them more, or whether people with high abilities choose extra schooling in order to signal their abilities to prospective employers. Nonetheless, labour economists tend to think that there are significant social benefits to increased schooling.

QUESTION

How can we measure human capital?

It is important to note that there are many difficulties associated with measuring human capital, that is, what it constitutes – schooling, training or experience, or all three – and how we are to measure it (usually school enrolment rates or years of secondary education). Other questions relate to issues such as the health of the workforce, and so on.

Further, a high level of human capital may not be a sufficient condition for growth. There are many examples of low-income countries that have invested heavily in education programmes only to see the returns to education fall and unemployment rates rise. Korea before 1960 is a good example, as are modern day Zimbabwe and Sri Lanka. Zimbabwe and Sri Lanka both have high adult literacy rates compared with their peers in Africa and Asia (that is, 87.2 per cent and 91.1 per cent respectively).

It is also possible to conduct *growth-accounting* studies that relate the level of TFP in a country to the level of schooling. One such study, by Angus Maddison in 1987, suggests that improvements in the quality of the workforce typically added between 0.1 and 0.5 percentage points to annual growth rates between 1950 and 1984 in France, Germany, Japan, the Netherlands, the UK and the USA.

5.5   SUMMARY

There is a number of different ways that models can generate endogenous growth. This section has examined profit-seeking research, openness to ideas, and human capital. The Solow model does not generate permanent growth in the absence of technological change because there are diminishing returns to capital and hence the production function is curved (concave). In contrast, new growth models do generate permanent growth because they contain a linearity, that is, the production function is a straight line (due to some sort of constant returns to a particular factor, such as physical capital, human capital or ideas, which leads to increasing returns to scale overall). In the AK model, this occurs in the production function, and in the endogenous growth models we considered different ways in which A could be increased.

There are many endogenous growth models; most of them look at either technology creation or human capital formation as the source of long-run growth. They suggest that, in the long run, government policies should be able to affect either the level of income per capita or its growth rate. In practice, the exact linearity required for a growth effect is unlikely to be found in the real world and the best we can hope for is that government policies have permanent effects on income levels.

In order to generate permanent growth in the absence of population growth, endogenous growth models require constant returns to scale to some factor such as physical capital, human capital or ideas.

6   GROWTH PERFORMANCE

This section examines two questions about the growth performance of economies. First, do economies with different initial levels of output tend to converge towards the same standard of living? Second, are there political, social and cultural factors that help to explain why some countries are rich and other countries are poor?

6.1 INCOME CONVERGENCE

In the Solow model, for countries with the same steady state, poor countries should grow faster on average than rich countries. This is an optimistic result, in that it implies that all countries will eventually converge on the standard of living initially enjoyed only by the rich, provided it is sustainable (that is, not greater than the steady state). How does this convergence come about?

Suppose that one economy starts with a lower initial level of capital per worker than another but has the same steady-state level of capital per worker (for example, because the two countries have the same levels of technology, saving rates, depreciation rates and population growth rates). The country with the lower initial level of capital per worker will be able to accumulate capital faster. The reason for this is that the marginal productivity of capital, that is, the increase in output from using one more unit of capital, with labour held constant, is higher. Remember that the production function in Figure 18.1 becomes less steep as output rises because of diminishing returns to capital per worker. So the production function is steeper for the country with the lower initial capital per worker. As that country's savings per worker curve is also steeper, it will see a bigger increase in its capital stock. The country with the lower initial capital per worker will also have lower capital-widening requirements. Hence the output per worker gap between the two countries will narrow over time as both economies approach the same steady state. This is known as ABSOLUTE INCOME CONVERGENCE.

A less optimistic scenario implied by the Solow model concerns economies with different steady-state incomes. In this case, the countries' growth rates converge while their steady-state incomes remain different. This is known as CONDITIONAL INCOME CONVERGENCE. If two countries have different levels of technology, saving rates, depreciation rates or workforce growth rates, their steady-state incomes will differ but their growth rates will eventually become the same. So an initially poor country will eventually grow as fast as a rich country, but it will remain relatively poor and will fail to match the rich country's standard of living.

The predictions of endogenous growth models are ambiguous. To the extent that growth effects occur, little convergence can be expected; in the extreme case, a country that benefits uniquely from a permanently higher growth rate cannot be caught up by other countries. In the Solow model, where there are only levels effects, convergence is possible to the extent that poor countries are the beneficiaries of changes that lead to permanently higher levels of income per capita. In the AK model, the growth rate does not depend upon the economy's initial capital stock, so there is no convergence between economies with different initial capital stocks.

So there are broadly two interpretations of the empirical evidence on convergence. The first is pessimistic, seeing the evidence as indicating polarization rather than convergence. The Solow model provides a simple way of thinking about the polarization of incomes across countries. Figure 18.9 shows a situation where the shape of the production function leads to there being two stable equilibrium income levels and one unstable equilibrium. In other words, it shows the effect of abandoning the assumption that the production function can be represented by a curve showing diminishing returns to capital along its entire length.

ABSOLUTE INCOME CONVERGENCE
Absolute income convergence is the tendency for poor countries to grow faster than rich ones at the same steady state.

CONDITIONAL INCOME CONVERGENCE
Conditional income convergence is the tendency of poor countries to grow as fast as rich ones, albeit with differences in their steady states.

Figure 18.9
The Solow model: explaining income polarization

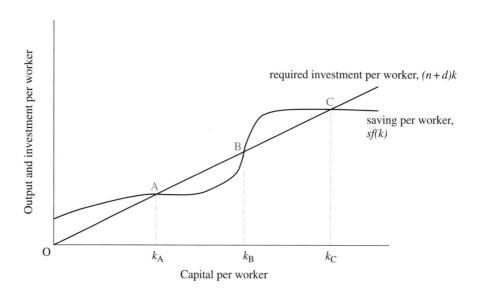

QUESTION

Why is the middle equilibrium unstable (point B in Figure 18.9)?

The middle equilibrium is not stable because there is a tendency for the economy to converge towards either point A or point C (which are both steady states), depending on whether it lies to the left or to the right of point B. Consider a point slightly to the left of point B, such that the capital stock per worker is slightly below k_B. At such a level, required investment is greater than gross investment (shown by the saving per worker line). Hence negative capital deepening takes place, and the economy starts converging to point A. At any point above k_B, the required investment function lies below the gross investment line: the stock of capital per worker will increase and the economy will converge to point C.

There are, however, reasons for a degree of optimism, as there are signs of conditional convergence in many parts of the world. Easterlin (2000) points out that during the epoch of modern economic growth, real per capita incomes across the world doubled every generation. In the half century after the Second World War, average living standards as measured by real GDP per capita grew by a factor somewhere between 2 and 3, with sub-Saharan Africa being the main exception. This increase in living standards has been matched by a huge rise in life expectancy. The less developed areas (that is, 80 per cent of the world's population) saw their life expectancy at birth rise from 40.9 years in 1950–55 to 61.9 years in 1990–95, with even sub-Saharan Africa seeing a rise from 35.5 years to 47.0 years.

Table 18.3 provides further evidence that conditional income convergence is taking place. The growth rates of the more developed and the less developed world were surprisingly similar between 1950 and 1995. Although the mean income per capita in the world was about US$5000 in 1999, the median was much lower at US$1000. This is because the world distribution of incomes is very skewed. In 1999, the 891 million people of the high-income economies (15 per cent of the world population) produced

Table 18.3 Annual average growth rate of GDP per capita across the world, 1950–95

	Growth	Ratio of GDP per capita at end to beginning	Share of world population, 1998
More developed	2.7	3.1	20
Less developed	2.5	2.9	80
China	3.8	5.0	21
India	2.2	2.5	17
Rest of Asia	3.7	4.6	21
Latin America	1.6	1.9	9
Northern Africa	2.1	2.4	2
Sub-Saharan Africa	0.5	1.2	11

Source: Easterlin, 2000

23 trillion US dollars of output (79 per cent of world output). A recent study examining the overall trends in world inequality reveals that a US citizen who is in the bottom 10 per cent of the US population is better off than two-thirds of the world population. Moreover, the ratio between average income of the world's top 5 per cent and the world's bottom 5 per cent increased from 78 to 1 in 1988 to 114 to 1 in 1993 (Milanovic, 2002).

6.2   EXPLAINING ECONOMIC SUCCESS AND FAILURE

QUESTION

Why are some countries rich and others poor?

This is one of the most important questions in economics and many papers have been published on the subject. A good starting point is the work of Xavier Sala-i-Martin (1997), which reviews the importance of a number of different factors in explaining international growth rates between 1960 and 1990. His conclusion is that countries that grew quickly tended to have high levels of equipment investment; to have been open to trade for some time; to have a well-established rule of law; and to be located a reasonable distance from the equator. In contrast, countries with low levels of growth tended to have had reduced political rights and civil liberties; to have had a coup; to be in Latin America or Sub-Saharan Africa; or to have had large exchange rate distortion.

The problem with studies of this kind is that there is a large degree of interaction between the various factors. To take but one example, a number of researchers have found that political rights and democracy are good for growth, but others have argued that causation flows in the opposite direction: the more 'well-to-do' a country is, the more likely it is to sustain democracy. Essentially, many of the suggested variables are possibly endogenous (for example, openness to trade, social capital, the presence or otherwise of conflict-management institutions). In other words, the direction of causation between these variables and economic growth is not clear.

In general, it certainly appears to be the case that economically successful countries tend to be politically stable. There is also evidence that indicates that effective government institutions are good for economic growth. As Rodrik (1999) suggests in the context of the East-Asian economies, there are at least four dimensions to these institutions: the quality of bureaucracy; the rule of law and smooth and orderly transitions of power; an independent judiciary and the protection of private property; and a low risk of the repudiation of government contracts. What is less obvious is how these dimensions can be translated into practical advice. He also notes that democracies have the following economic properties: first, democracies have less volatile growth rates; second, democracies handle adverse shocks better; and third, democracies pay higher wages.

Rodrik also suggested that domestic social conflicts are important in understanding why growth rates can change so dramatically and why so many countries have experienced a growth collapse since the mid-1970s. The countries that experienced the sharpest drops in growth after 1975 were those with divided societies (as measured by indicators of inequality, ethnic fragmentation and the like) and those with weak institutions for conflict management (as measured by indicators of the quality of governmental institutions, rule of law, democratic rights and social safety nets).

There has also been some interesting work on the concept of 'social capital', much of it by Robert Puttnam (2001), who suggests that features of social organization, such as trust, norms and networks, can improve the efficiency of society by facilitating co-ordinated action. The World Values Survey collects data from different countries on the extent to which people trust one another (that is, the percentage of people replying 'Yes' to questions such as 'Can most people be trusted?'). Although it is difficult to draw solid conclusions, trust does appear to be correlated with variables such as national income, and there is some evidence that trust is more important in countries with low income levels. Of course, it could be that trust is correlated with other, unmeasured yet important, factors that help to explain income levels, or even that a rise in income causes a rise in trust. At this stage, the evidence is unclear.

This discussion of trust leads naturally on to the issue of corruption. Corruption is notoriously hard to measure, and there has not been a huge amount of economic research into the subject. Such research as has been done has usually looked at public corruption (that is, corruption within governments), rather than at private corruption (that is, the corruption of individuals and corruption within private enterprises).

There are three main ways of thinking about how to reduce corruption. A lawyer would typically say that tougher sentences for corrupt government officials will do the trick. A businessman might say that officials are corrupt because government salaries are low, and that if they were raised there would be less corruption. In contrast, an economist might suggest that it is possible to ask for bribes only where there is little competition. Consider a situation in which a company needs to export some goods by air. If there is only one airport, corrupt officials at that airport might be able to demand a large bribe. However, as the number of potential airports increases, the likelihood of finding an honest official (or an official willing to accept a lower bribe) will increase.

Therefore an economist would argue that monopoly power is an important source of corruption. Research has found that there tends to be more corruption where there is less competition. Corruption is especially high in countries where domestic firms are protected from foreign competition; where only a few domestic firms dominate the economy; where there are large government subsidies; where there are several different exchange rates (say, one for tourists and one for investors); and where the laws against monopolies are not well enforced. The main consequence of corruption is that relative prices in the domestic economy are distorted. Activities where there is a lot of corruption become more expensive than other activities. Corruption often affects investment and trade, as they require licensing. As this means that it is more costly to invest and more costly to trade, there will be too little investment and trade.

Lastly, there is the importance of openness to international trade for economic growth. As mentioned earlier, openness has a number of effects that may raise either the income level or the growth rate of an economy. There is some good evidence that open economies tend to grow faster than closed ones, and that open economies converge to one level of income, while closed economies converge to another lower level of income. This suggests that openness is important because it allows poor countries to catch up with rich ones. Being closed to trade suggests stagnation at the lower income level. It has also been noted that the return to liberal policies in international trade in the 1950s and 1960s coincided with the most rapid period of growth ever experienced by the developed world.

7   CONLUSION •

Understanding the 'engines' of economic growth provides an insight into why some countries have 'developed' while others have struggled (often without success) to break free from the poverty trap. One of the most important attempts to explain growth, and to account for the sources of growth, has been the neo-classical Solow growth model and the growth accounting studies that followed it.

Although flawed in many respects, the Solow model was important in that it served as a benchmark for further research. A central issue in growth literature is the effect of policy changes, that is, whether there is a growth effect of scale, such that the growth rate of output permanently increases, or a levels effect of scale, in which the level of output is permanently higher. The Solow model highlighted the importance of technological growth and suggested that higher savings rates would leave the growth rate unaffected. On the other hand, it showed that the savings rate *can* affect the level of income per capita by raising the capital stock. This suggests that a prudent government might wish to encourage the population to consume less of their income and save more of it in order to raise the steady-state level of income per capita.

The model showed that the long-run, steady-state growth rate of a country was equal to its population growth rate in the absence of technological progress. It also provided an important insight into why some countries with relatively low population growth rates were characterized by high standards of living: high population growth rates increased the capital-widening requirements of a country and thus reduced the steady-state output per worker.

Furthermore, one significant prediction (and also a major criticism) of the neo-classical approach concerned the convergence of countries over time. Solow suggested that countries characterized by identical steady states but different initial levels of capital per worker would experience a narrowing of the gap in their output per worker. The reasoning behind this was simple: countries with lower stocks of capital per worker would grow much faster than those with higher initial levels.

AK models dispensed with a concave production function in favour of a linear one, and showed that it was possible for an economy to achieve permanent growth in output per worker. Further, in these models the growth rate of output was not dependent upon the initial capital stock. This meant that there would be no convergence between economies with different initial capital stocks, even if they were characterized by identical saving rates, levels of technology and depreciation rates. Moreover, unlike the Solow model, where growth did not occur in the absence of technological progress, it was possible to have permanent growth in the AK model without technological change, as long as the return on investment was greater than the depreciation rate.

On the other hand, new growth theories have successfully identified three broad sources of growth: profit-seeking research, human capital formation and openness to ideas. No wonder early studies showed the 'residual' to be so large in magnitude! The term contained so much more than just exogenously determined technical progress.

One of the most influential models in this area was produced by Paul Romer. Technological progress was no longer exogenous – instead it became a function of the number of researchers in a country and the number of ideas that they generate in a given period. Research is instrumental in the development of new and better products, as well as new and more efficient production processes, in addition to generating significant positive externalities.

Another issue is the sort of convergence that could take place among countries. There is little support for the prediction of absolute income convergence, that is, for poor countries growing faster than rich ones. Indeed, there is some evidence for income polarization rather than income convergence. However, there is a substantial body of evidence to support a middle position of conditional income convergence. Growth rates converge, rather than steady-state incomes per capita.

Over the past few decades economists have also explored different factors/variables that interact with and impact upon the economic growth of a country. These include the levels of 'trust' (social capital) in a society, the indicators of corruption, and the quality of governance, law enforcement and democracy. As with human capital, the direction of causality between these variables and growth is often questionable. The empirical evidence also remains mixed.

What is not in doubt is that the world is a very unequal place; a typical worker in the USA or Switzerland is 20 to 30 times more productive than a worker in India or Kenya. The Solow model suggests that the first place to look for an explanation of differences in living standards is factor endowments, but even after adjusting for the fact that Kenyans have much less capital per worker than the Swiss there are still substantial differences. These differences can be explained only by substantial obstacles to the diffusion and implementation of best-practice technologies across the world.

CHAPTER 19 ENVIRONMENTAL SUSTAINABILITY

Graham Dawson ● ● ● ● ● ● ● ● ● ● ● ● ● ● ● ● ● ● ●

Objectives

After studying this chapter you should be able to:

- discuss some of the ethical arguments about the environmental impact of economic growth
- understand the argument from ecological economics that there are physical limits to growth
- appreciate the strength and weaknesses of carbon trading as a policy response to climate change.

Concepts

- ecological economics
- sustainable development
- intergenerational justice
- the land ethic
- emissions trading

1 INTRODUCTION ●

On 23 March 2001 debris from the Mir space station, most of which had burnt up on re-entry to the Earth's atmosphere, crashed into the South Pacific (Figure 19.1). To those watching from the island of Fiji, it looked like a shower of shooting stars, beautiful but potentially dangerous if it had come much closer. To the Russian technicians at mission control outside Moscow, the splashdown, at the right time and place, was the final success in a triumphant era of space exploration. To one economist it evoked thoughts of comets and shooting stars as portents of hard times or even disaster. Was this man-made comet a metaphor for environmental catastrophe?

Shortly before the Industrial Revolution, the English philosopher John Locke propounded a theory of property that reflected the emerging capitalist system. This theory has often been interpreted as supposing that we, the human race, live on a frontier with the natural world, looking across to plentiful resources and untameable wilderness. In the 1960s, Kenneth Boulding, an economist from Liverpool who worked mainly in the USA, caught the mood of environmental anxiety by labelling this approach 'the cowboy economy'. He contrasted it with the idea of Spaceship Earth, its

Figure 19.1   The end of an era: the remains of the Mir space station light up the sky over the Pacific Ocean

astronauts, the human race, depending for our lives on the fragile atmosphere and depleted resources of a tiny planet spinning through an indifferent universe. Will Spaceship Earth land on a new frontier or crash burning into the ocean? There are those who predict disaster, seeing the human race as Icarus, the young man in Classical Greek mythology whose ambition outstripped the technology available to him. He flew using wings made for him by his father, Daedalus, but the wax holding the wings together melted when he approached too close to the sun. (In Figure 19.2, Bruegel's *Landscape with the Fall of Icarus*, you can just see Icarus's legs sticking out of the water in the bottom right-hand corner of the painting.)

The aim of this chapter is to explore some of the ways in which economists think about environmental sustainability, using as a case study potentially the most serious environmental problem of all: climate change or global warming. The first question is whether there are physical limits to economic growth (Section 2). According to ecological economists, much economic activity and theory overlooks the brute fact of physical limits to growth, forever frustrating technological attempts to overcome them. They believe that it is important to locate the economy in the physical world, in ecology. For example, one of the things that are illustrated by global warming is the concept of 'carrying capacity'. The Earth's atmosphere can absorb only so much carbon dioxide without climatic stress, and economic activity should be informed by an appreciation of these physical limits to growth.

Figure 19.2
Landscape with the Fall of Icarus, by Pieter Bruegel the Elder (c.1558)

What are the prospects for a consensus? Are enough people ever going to share a belief in putting environmental concerns first? This raises the question of values (Section 3). As markets are the institutions that define market or capitalist economies, we must consider how values are treated in markets and in the economic analysis of markets. Can markets reflect a social consensus that may evolve, or are they irretrievably dominated by the forces of self-interest and hedonism to the detriment of ethical principles? Are there ethical or social limits to economic growth?

Policy interventions to try to achieve an environmentally sustainable economy see markets both as the cause of the problem and as part of the solution. The state regulates the markets that cause environmental damage and uses market-based instruments, such as pollution taxes, to modify market incentives (Chapter 9, Section 2). The state may even create markets where they did not previously exist, setting objectives and then using markets as a means of achieving them efficiently (Section 4). Climate change negotiations, which try to reduce global warming by reducing greenhouse gas emissions, often envisage the use of markets in this way. At Kyoto in 1997 the negotiating states agreed to try to reduce greenhouse gas emissions and decided to set up a market in emissions permits as one way of achieving their aims. And a 'carbon market' already exists, despite the collapse of the Kyoto negotiations.

2   PHYSICAL LIMITS TO GROWTH   • • • • • • • • • • • • • • • • •

Climate change negotiations in a series of international summits, from Rio to Kyoto via Montreal and Berlin, have put the prospect of global warming, its consequences and the question of how to reduce vehicle and industrial emissions firmly onto the political agenda. It is widely known that many scientists believe that greenhouse gas emissions must be reduced and that many politicians of different political persuasions accept their claims. The aim of this section is to place the problem of climate change in the context of the physical limits to economic growth, and to examine the idea of sustainable development as a response to the identification of such limits.

2.1   CLIMATE CHANGE

The term 'global warming' refers to an increase in the mean global temperature as a result of the 'greenhouse effect'. The greenhouse effect is a natural process. Energy from the sun passes through the atmosphere. Some of the heat that is radiated back from the Earth is blocked by atmospheric gases, usually called 'greenhouse gases' (GHGs) because they cause the atmosphere to warm. These gases include carbon dioxide, ozone, water vapour, chlorofluorocarbons (CFCs), methane and nitrous oxide. Carbon dioxide (CO_2), the most important GHG, is mainly the result of the burning of fossil fuels such as oil and coal to meet our energy needs. At the moment these emissions occur predominately in the industrialized North. The atmosphere can assimilate (absorb and process) some but not all of the GHGs, and some human activities 'use up' the Earth's capacity to absorb CO_2 and other GHGs. Deforestation intensifies the 'greenhouse effect' by contributing some 15 to 20 per cent of the GHGs in the atmosphere. At a meeting in Shanghai in February 2001, the Intergovernmental Panel on Climate Change (IPCC) estimated that the global mean temperature would rise by 2.5 °C to 10.4 °C over the next 100 years.

Three main effects of the resulting climate change are expected. First, sea levels will rise as global warming causes the water in the oceans to expand (Houghton, 1997, p.109). Sea levels may rise by 3 to 10 centimetres a decade if no action is taken to prevent climate change, and low-lying land by the sea may be inundated. Second, agriculture in many areas will be more vulnerable to disruption by drought. A reduction in the levels of soil moisture and the risk of summer drought may be accompanied by changes in regional rainfall, which could make arid zones even more arid. Third, there may be an increased risk of extreme weather events, such as floods, heat waves, storms, cyclones and typhoons. All of these effects will tend to have a bigger impact on low-income countries than on the industrial world that caused the climate change. For example, coastal defences against a rise in sea levels are feasible for the Netherlands but well beyond the financial reach of most low-income countries. Also, agriculture constitutes a greater percentage of the economic activity in low-income countries, which tend to have a large subsistence sector with poor farmers who are unable to afford insurance.

There are, however, many scientific uncertainties in this field. There is evidence that the climate has changed since the Industrial Revolution, but this slight warming is consistent with natural variations in the climate. The uncertainty surrounding the predicted rate of warming leaves plenty of scope for fierce debate concerning the gravity of the effects that may (or may not) take place. In fact, some scientists have reasoned that global warming is a myth, or at least is so uncertain that we are under no obligation to take remedial action. Nevertheless, it is clear that in the last 200 years human activity has increased the amount of CO_2 in the atmosphere by 30 per cent. It is difficult to see how this increase could fail to have some impact on the world's climate. Moreover, there is already some evidence, from the insurance industry for example, that extreme weather events have become more frequent over the last 30 years. It may be too late to avert entirely the adverse consequences of global warming, including the possible creation of millions of environmental refugees.

2.2 ECOLOGICAL ECONOMICS AND PHYSICAL LIMITS TO GROWTH

Climate change can probably best be understood in economic terms as an example of the physical limits to economic growth that ecological economists, and others, have warned of since the 1970s.

Until the 1970s economists had generally assumed that the physical world did not impose any limits on growth. This was not an oversight, but an implication of the way in which most economists had traditionally looked at the economy. The intuition behind this approach was that, if one natural resource ran out, it would always be possible to replace it with another that would maintain the rate of economic growth. It is important to recall here the definition of economic growth that these economists relied upon.

All goods or services that are exchanged for money count towards the value of the national income (Chapter 8). This assumes that there is nothing unique and irreplaceable about any particular component of economic growth, or about any particular resource used in producing goods and services. Using the concepts of capital and the production function, this section seeks to clarify the assumption that economic growth is free from physical limits.

Capital – defined broadly – provides a stream of benefits over time. Thus capital provides a return, and current and future generations are believed to derive well-being from this return. Chapter 3 set out the production function, which specifies the way in which inputs such as manufactured capital are transformed into outputs through production processes:

$$Q = f(F_1, F_2, ..., F_n)$$

This time Q is human well-being and the Fs are forms of environmental and manufactured capital. The basic idea is that if we have less of one particular capital component then, other things being equal, we would expect to be able to generate less well-being. A simple rule for economic growth to continue is that capital should be left intact, that is, productive capacity should not be eroded. This might be achieved via capital bequests; the current generation must pass on a capital stock that is at least as large as the one it inherited in terms of its productive capacity.

Does this mean that the composition of the capital stock must remain unchanged? Must we have as much of each F, or can the Fs be substituted for each other? The example in Chapter 3 suggested that, in general, each of the inputs can be combined in many different ways with each of the other inputs. For example, consider the way in which a restaurant combines inputs to produce meals: it is clear that employing skilled chefs would make it possible to use fewer raw materials because of the reduction in waste. Let us turn this example around and suppose that there is a long-term shortage of raw materials. It would be possible, in principle, to maintain the output of meals by recruiting skilled chefs to make the reduced quantity of raw materials 'go further'. What has happened here is that the restaurant has substituted one input, the skill and knowledge of chefs, for another, raw materials. Economists tend to assume that inputs or productive resources – the Fs – can be substituted easily one for another. It is not unusual for a firm to substitute new technology for unskilled or low-skilled labour.

However, it may in practice be very hard to replace the loss of environmental capital (raw materials) with human capital (skill and knowledge) and manufactured capital (machinery). The extent to which human and manufactured capital can be substituted for environmental capital over time is a highly contentious issue.

For ecological economists, the economy must be situated in or be seen as embedded in the physical world (Lutz, 1999, pp.226–35). In Figure 19.3 energy is drawn from the environment, from the physical world, to be used in production and consumption and returned to the environment as waste.

Figure 19.3
A model of the economy embedded in the environment

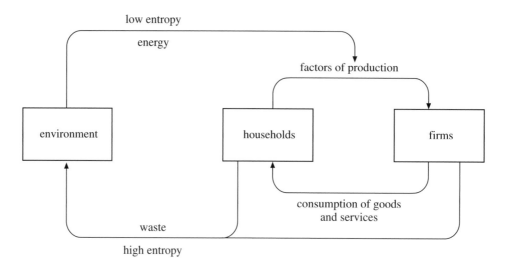

The significance of this way of thinking about the economy is its demonstration that the foundation of ecological economics lies in the natural sciences, and ultimately in physics. In this view, economics is based on the second law of thermodynamics and the concept of entropy.

Physics tells us that matter and energy are governed by the laws of thermodynamics, or the 'science of energy'. The first law of thermodynamics states that matter and energy can neither be created nor destroyed. The second law of thermodynamics, which is also known as the 'law of entropy', goes on to state that entropy always increases. In a thermodynamic system the unchanging quantity of energy undergoes a qualitative change from available, concentrated or low-entropy energy to unavailable, dissipated or high-entropy energy. For example, oil is found in the Earth's crust in a state of low entropy, it is turned into fuel and emits CO_2, which is dissipated throughout the atmosphere in a state of high entropy. It is beyond the scope of this chapter to explore the epistemological status of the entropy law, so I shall simply note that it stands on solid experimental ground; that is, it has withstood experiments designed to falsify it.

The application of the entropy law to economics is contentious. Georgescu-Roegen (1971) introduced the concept of entropy into economics, claiming that economic processes are entropic; that is, they transform low-entropy energy into high-entropy energy, or available energy into unavailable or waste energy. Since low entropy is a necessary condition of usefulness, the entropy law is essential to understanding the concept of scarcity. This line of thought is therefore the theoretical foundation for the central principles of ECOLOGICAL ECONOMICS, which are that economic processes must be understood as part of the physical world and that there are physical limits to economic growth. It is possible to draw out the implications of these principles by considering the irreversibility of time.

The theoretical basis of irreversibility as a source of environmental problems is that energy flows in one direction and cannot be recycled. When the energy from the raw materials that the environment provides has been used up, economic activity comes to an end. Natural resources are used in the manufacture of goods and eventually transformed into pollution, thus depleting the available energy. So, for the ecological economist, the terrestrial stock of these natural resources represents a physical limit to economic activity. Climate change is another example of the effects of resource depletion. The atmosphere's capacity for absorbing waste GHGs is a natural resource, and it is the exhaustion of this capacity that is the main cause of climate change. In the longest of long runs, the only sustainable economy is one that leaves the stock of energy-bearing natural resources undepleted. This is a stringent condition to impose on economic activity, and Georgescu-Roegen (1971) concluded that the future for humanity is reversion to a 'berry-picking species'. The more that energy use can be curtailed, and the more efficient energy use can be made, the longer it will take us to reach this situation.

ECOLOGICAL ECONOMICS
Ecological economics holds that there are physical limits to growth because economic processes are part of the physical world and hence subject to the law of entropy.

QUESTION

Please read the following extract from James Greyson's (1996) article for *Renew*. Greyson uses the term 'quality' to mean the opposite of 'entropy', and the shift from low to high entropy is described here as a movement from high to low quality. Can you detect any grounds for a less pessimistic forecast for the future of humanity than Georgescu-Roegen's?

Quality

The scientists described our dependence on nature in terms of quality, defined as the concentration and structuring of matter. Quality is the material value of a resource; higher quality means it's more useful. Pure water is more useful than polluted water. Concentrated iron is more valuable than ore, whilst iron structured into, say, a girder is yet more valuable. Nature structures concentrated materials using genetic information whilst we do it using human designs. The important thing about quality is that there's no free lunch. Absolutely the only way to produce quality is to consume more quality from somewhere else. In material terms, the real price of production in any economy is the inevitable consumption of quality elsewhere. This loss of quality is evident as waste; dispersed matter with lost concentration and structure. Fortunately nature continuously produces quality by reconcentrating and restructuring waste into valuable resources. This production is done by the green cells in plants which can use energy arriving free-of-charge from the sun. This quality cycle has run smoothly throughout history, until our recent linear economy started consuming quality faster than it could be reproduced in nature. The resulting loss of quality is our debt to nature, evident as mounting wastes and diminishing resources.

> Throughout evolution the Earth has experienced a continual increase in quality. The surface
> has become steadily cleaner and capable of supporting more complex forms of life.
> Humanity is now experiencing evolution-in-reverse. Each day this goes on diminishes
> everyone's prospects for prosperity, health and, sooner or later, survival. We know we must
> urgently re-establish a global economy which pays its debts as it goes. We will know when
> we are successful because wastes of all kinds will no longer accumulate.
>
> (Greyson, 1996)

There seem to be grounds for a moderate optimism in the processes by which 'nature continuously produces quality by reconcentrating and restructuring waste into valuable resources'. The implication is that the physical limits to growth are not so much a buffer at the end of the line as more of a speed limit. The problem is that 'our recent linear economy started consuming quality faster than it could be reproduced in nature'.

What then are the implications for the question of economic growth of taking an ecological approach to economics? Ecological economics insists on placing the economic system in the context of physical limits to growth. This is particularly relevant to the question of the 'new economy' (Chapter 2). An early statement of the ecological point of view put it in these words.

> But we can be fairly certain that no new technology will abolish absolute Scarcity because
> the laws of thermodynamics apply to all possible technologies.
>
> (Daly, 1973)

Some proponents of the absolute newness of the new economy have contradicted this claim, however, arguing that overthrowing the physical limits to growth is exactly what it does.

> Gone is the view of a thermodynamic world economy, dominated by 'natural resources'
> being turned to waste and entropy by human extraction and use ... The key fact of
> knowledge is that it is anti-entropic: it accumulates and compounds as it is used ...
> Conquering the microcosm, mind transcends every entropic trap and overthrows matter
> itself.
>
> (Gilder, 1989)

The ecological economist would reply that it is still necessary to use materials in making PCs and other physical manifestations of the new economy and to use energy in manufacturing them and shipping them all over the world (Lutz, 1999, p.231).

What light does this understanding of the physical limits to growth shed on the specific issue of climate change? Global warming is likely to be irreversible in practice, because of the pressures of growing populations and economic growth. Population growth increases the pressure on natural resources, while economic growth may increase resource requirements per head of the population. Both result in increased energy use and, as more fossil fuels are burnt, an increase in the emissions of GHGs. Even if countries were to commit themselves to reducing emissions of GHGs, the concentrations of these gases in the atmosphere would still increase for some time to come (although this will vary with the extent of the reduction). So future warming of global temperatures is already inevitable, even if action were to be taken now. Global warming might also be irreversible in practice simply because current generations find the adjustments required unpalatable. Given the uncertainty associated with alleged environmental change, they may well prefer to carry on 'business as usual'.

This issue will be taken up in Section 3, but part of the groundwork for thinking about it is the idea of environmental sustainability. The feasibility of sustainable development depends in part upon the view that is taken of the physical limits to growth.

2.3   THE IDEA OF SUSTAINABLE DEVELOPMENT

The most commonly cited public definition of SUSTAINABLE DEVELOPMENT came from the 1987 World Commission on Environment and Development (WCED, or the 'Brundtland Commission'). Sustainable development is development that 'meets the needs of the present without compromising the ability of future generations to meet their own needs' (WCED, 1987, p.8). So, sustainable development is development that generates current human well-being without imposing extra costs on the future. For the Brundtland Commission, significant costs mean the inability to meet future development needs. For Pearce and Warford (1992), sustainable development is development that secures an increase in the well-being of the current generation without decreasing the well-being of future generations. This effectively takes the same form as the Brundtland definition but substitutes 'welfare' for 'needs'. What it implies is that we should not acquire well-being now at the expense of well-being in the future.

SUSTAINABLE DEVELOPMENT
Sustainable development can be defined as an increase in human well-being for the current generation without compromising the well-being of future generations.

If it is accepted as a worthwhile social goal, sustainable development implies that development should be distributed evenly across the generations. This does not mean that economic progress is sacrificed so that each generation is guaranteed equal levels of well-being. What it means is that progress today must not be reversed at a future date. The way in which the current generation is using the environment may entail large costs being passed on to the future. In this sense, we may be buying our development at the expense of our descendants. The suggestion that this is not an acceptable trade-off raises philosophical issues concerning fairness or justice which are not easy to resolve.

Sustainable development is therefore based on a concept of 'intergenerational' justice that refers to its distribution across generations. This is distinct from distribution within a generation, or 'intragenerational' justice (Chapter 9). It is worth noting that environmental problems also impose significant costs on the present generation, and raise their own questions of intragenerational justice. For example, pollutants emitted from power stations, such as sulphur dioxide (SO_2), generate significant current costs in terms of their adverse effects on human health.

How could the current generation secure sustainable development, assuming for the moment that it wants to do so? The current generation holds a stock of capital that can be used to derive well-being now and into the future. Sustainable development is connected to the notion that the current generation should aim to bequeath to the future at least as much capital as it inherited. However, using up this capital by degrading the environment erodes the opportunities of future generations. Is it feasible to compensate them for this loss?

Two schools of thought can be identified, which are related to the rival viewpoints on the physical limits to growth. One school believes that it does not matter what form this bequest takes, while the other believes that particular components of environmental capital must form part of the bequest. The first school is that of the 'technological optimists', who believe that improved technology will always look after the interests of future generations. They regard the concept of sustainable development as irrelevant, because technological progress ensures that it is always the current generation that is the poorest. The assumption behind the second school, which is associated with ecological economics (Section 2.2), is that these resources are unique and their contribution to development cannot be equalled by substitutes. I propose to explore this debate a little further by examining the possibility of technological progress.

Technological progress expands the opportunities open to the future, enhancing the production and consumption possibilities of an economy by raising the productivity of capital. One way to think of this is that greater output can be obtained for the same level of inputs. This reduces the onus on the current generation to pass on to the future as much capital as it inherited. It also raises another possibility. Environmental capital, which ecological economists and others suggest is a unique provider of certain benefits, may not be seen in this way in the future because of the development of substitute goods or substitute processes made possible by technological breakthroughs. The technological optimists would argue that history is full of such instances.

Technological optimists are convinced of the pervasiveness of improved technologies in overcoming constraints on development, but surprisingly little is known about how such change actually comes about. According to the 'theory of induced innovation', the development of new technologies represents a response to pressing problems. For example, a number of technical solutions to global warming have been put forward. One suggestion is the emission of dust particles into the atmosphere, which would have a cooling effect on the climate by reflecting the sun's rays. Similarly, sulphur dioxide from the burning of fossil fuels may help to mitigate the global warming process by reflecting radiation from the sun. Sulphur dioxide is transformed in the atmosphere by chemical reactions to form sulphate aerosols, which reflect radiation in the same way as dust particles but are probably more powerful coolants. However, sulphur dioxide is a pollutant, both in its own right and as a precursor of acid rain, which is a significant source of damage to human health, buildings, materials and ecosystems. In addition, sulphate aerosols contribute to visibility loss. Many scientists regard attempts to control the global climate with suspicion. Induced innovation is more likely to contribute to the gradual abatement of climate change through, say, the development of fuel cells.

QUESTION

Please read the following extract. What do you think is the significance of fuel cell technology for the debate between technological optimists such as George Gilder and ecological economists such as Herman Daly?

Get ready, because life is about to change forever. In the next 20 years global warming will subside, the Los Angeles smog will disappear, people will head for downtown Tokyo in search of a breath of fresh air and who knows, nightingales may yet sing in Berkeley Square.

Sounds crazy, perhaps. But life could be like that if fuel cell technology takes off, as many people expect it to. While car makers focus on powering future cars and other vehicles, fuel cells are already being tested to generate electricity for houses and factories all over the world.

Fuel cells may well prove to be the energy source for the 21st century, but they have actually been around for some time. Welsh judge and amateur scientist, Sir William Grove, first had the idea in 1839 when he reckoned it should be possible to reverse the process of electrolysis, where hydrogen is extracted from water using electricity.

He was right, and fuel cells now consume hydrogen and oxygen to produce electricity, with only water as a waste product. They are shaping up to be a vital source of power to mankind because unlike fossil fuels – petroleum, oil, gas and coal – hydrogen is not only a renewable form of energy but also the most abundant element in the universe. ...

Vauxhall's parent company, General Motors, is at the forefront of fuel cell development and has just demonstrated its fuel cell car for the first time. Based on a Vauxhall-Opel Zafira, the fuel cell car is called HydroGen1 ... [and it] has a stack containing 200 cells. ...

Manufacturers will face new challenges: Were GM to produce one million cars a year, it would need to produce over half a million individual fuel cells per day. ... Think about it. No fossil fuels burnt by cars, power stations or heating systems would ... reduce emissions of the greenhouse gas CO_2 enormously.

By using pure hydrogen, they would eradicate it altogether, providing a solution to one of the biggest problems yet faced by mankind.

(adapted from Crosse, 2000, pp.22–4)

There is no doubt that fuel cell technology could reduce significantly CO_2 emissions and make a major contribution to the abatement of climate change. To that extent it provides a way of alleviating a physical limit to growth. But there are grounds for doubting whether fuel cell technology vindicates the technological optimists' claims that knowledge, such as that embodied in fuel cells, can overcome entropy. The manufacture of cars and fuel cells – perhaps half a million a day from one car

Figure 19.4   HydroGen1, a fuel-cell car

manufacturer – clearly entails a continuing drain on environmental resources. What matters is the rate at which the environment is degraded. Fuel cell technology will help to bring GHG emissions below the rate at which the atmosphere can absorb them without climate change. But that amounts to changing economic activity in the light of knowledge about the physical limits to growth, rather than surmounting those limits.

Can the distinction between technological optimists and pessimists be applied more generally to climate change? The main difference seems to be between engaging in less carbon-emitting activity, which is implicit in the pessimistic view, and reducing the carbon emissions associated with an unchanged level of such activity, as the optimists suggest. In practice, it is likely that a workable and effective response to climate change must draw on both approaches. Box 19.1 indicates how much carbon emission can be saved by scaling down various everyday activities and turning to more carbon-efficient methods of engaging in others. The problem is devising a structure of incentives or constraints that would be adequate to the task of achieving such changes in behaviour.

QUESTION

Examine the list of carbon-saving measures in Box 19.1. In what ways are you a carbon-saver? The list is not complete, and you may be saving carbon in ways that are not mentioned here. What do you think would be the most effective way of persuading you to save more carbon? Think, for example, of fuel taxes and utility prices, of laws and regulations, and of campaigns to raise awareness of the importance of saving carbon.

BOX 19.1   CUTTING DOWN ON CARBON

Low flow showerheads reduce hot water use by 10 to 15 per cent and can save up to 300 lb of CO_2 emissions per year.

Lowering your thermostat by $2°$ Fahrenheit can eliminate 500 lb of CO_2 emissions per year.

Insulating your water tank can save 1000 lb of CO_2 emissions per year.

Replacing three regular light bulbs with compact fluorescent bulbs can eliminate 750 lb of CO_2 emissions per year.

Insulating your home can save 1000 lb of CO_2 emissions per year.

The average car in the USA emits approximately 1 lb of carbon per mile, which can be halved by switching to a more fuel-efficient vehicle.

Every mile you ride on a train is responsible for 0.5 lb of CO_2 emissions.

Recycling all your newspapers every week can reduce CO_2 emissions by 250 lb per year.

Recycling six glass bottles every week can reduce CO_2 emissions by 250 lb per year.

What, if anything, would make the consumers and voters of industrial countries – past, present and future – change their behaviour in these ways? If political resistance by voters in some countries has obstructed measures to alleviate climate change, political pressure from environmentally concerned voters has pushed governments elsewhere towards an early implementation. Moreover, markets in renewable energy and energy saving technology have evolved alongside increasing public awareness of environmental degradation. What have economists had to say about the ethical values, principles and beliefs that inform the choices of voters and consumers? How can economists address the role of the ethical and social norms that constitute part of the institutional structure of the societies in which markets are embedded?

3   ETHICS AND THE SOCIAL LIMITS TO GROWTH   ● ● ● ● ● ●

Chapters 4 and 5 highlighted the advantages of competition: perfect competition reduces costs and the competitive process speeds innovation. There is, however, another perspective on competition, put forward by Fred Hirsch in *The Social Limits to Growth* (1976), which draws attention to its disadvantages. Hirsch argued that competition can be socially destructive. In clarifying this argument, he introduced the concept of positional competition to denote competition among consumers for finite resources when the acquisition of those resources involves denying them to others. For example, people moving out of the city to be closer to the tranquillity of nature cause more houses and roads to be built, thereby denying that finite and fragile resource to others. For Hirsch, the root of the problem was self-interest, which economists generally assume to be the most powerful motive driving competition among producers and consumers alike. The solution Hirsch recommended was 'moral re-entry', so that economic agents believe themselves to be obliged to co-operate, on the basis of traditional social norms, religious beliefs and a sense of civic duty. In order to appreciate Hirsch's position, it is necessary to consider some aspects of ethics and, in particular, the role of reason in ethical decision making.

3.1   SUBJECTIVE PREFERENCES AND ETHICAL PRINCIPLES

In economics, values are generally treated as subjective tastes or preferences. In explaining shifts in the demand curve, Chapter 3 mentioned changes in tastes or in fashion as a possible cause. If the demand in question is for, say, ice cream, then it seems reasonable to think of the value consumers place on different flavours in this way. Perhaps consumers become bored with vanilla and strawberry, and so ice-cream parlours try to renew their enthusiasm for the product by introducing pistachio, caramel fudge and tequila sunrise. But something seems to be left out if the same approach is taken to the demand for solar panels, electricity from renewable sources or low-emission vehicles.

What seems to be left out of the standard economic approach to values is reason. The distinction between positive statements and normative judgements is characteristic of a certain interpretation of reason and the scope for rational thought. Positive statements are objective or scientific explanations of the way the economy works. Normative judgements are recommendations, reflecting subjective or personal feelings or preferences. This distinction underlies the 'instrumental' conception of reason, according to which subjective or personal feelings provide us with wants, needs or desires, while reason gives us the means to achieve those wants, needs or desires. The eighteenth-century Scottish philosopher David Hume, a friend of Adam Smith's, put it rather memorably: 'Reason is, and ought only to be, the slave of the passions, and can never pretend to any other office than to serve and obey them' (Hume, 1906, pp.414–5).

The passions dictate to us what we want, and reason tells us how to get it. For example, your 'passions', inflamed no doubt by advertising, might tell you that you must have the new fragrance from Karl Lagerfeld or a grooming product for men from

Aramis. Reason, according to Hume, does not come into wanting such things. What rational thinking does is to show you how to get what you want in the world as it is. Reason, in the shape of scientific investigation, helps us to understand how things really or objectively are – the way the economy works, for example – whether we like them that way or not. If economists remain within the bounds of the positive, their advice deserves to be treated as expert knowledge – and the conduct of monetary policy will be no less scientific an endeavour than the generation and control of electricity. But if their judgements are wholly personal or subjective, as positive economics insists that all value judgements are, economic debate will be constructed upon highly subjective foundations, which are not themselves amenable to rational debate.

This interpretation of reason does not, I suggest, do justice to the situations of moral conflict, reflection and uncertainty familiar to most people. It fails to distinguish between subjective tastes, such as a liking for toffee fudge ice cream, and moral principles, such as loyalty, responsibility, sympathy or a sense of duty. Every motive or desire, every spring of action, is regarded as a 'passion', a subjective feeling. This seems to me to be an excessive restriction of the role of reasoned argument and critical reflection in human affairs, for we *do* revise our normative judgements, and even our feelings about moral matters, in the light of experience.

An interpretation of our moral experience that can accommodate reflection and affords a more positive role for reason is provided in a tradition of moral philosophy that goes back to the Ancient Greek philosopher Aristotle. The philosophy and economics of Karl Marx have their roots in an Aristotelian account of human nature and human flourishing, and the medieval philosopher and theologian St Thomas Aquinas developed a system of thought from Aristotelian foundations which continues to be influential today in Catholic social teaching. This very brief statement of broadly Aristotelian views draws on Yuengert (2001).

For Aristotle, human happiness or flourishing comes only through virtue. A virtuous person is one who is disposed to perform good actions, which requires three conditions to be met. First, she must have a worthy goal in mind, rather than a merely subjective preference. Second, she must be able to identify the best action in a particular set of circumstances. This second capacity Aristotle thought of as 'practical wisdom', and it is clearly very close to the instrumental rationality of the typical economic account. Third, the virtuous person must perform the action identified as good. This means that 'he must not be ruled by his passions, which often militate against reasoned deliberation and moral action' (Yuengert, 2001, p.6). It is an approach that offers some scope for a more active role for reason than that found in Hume and in the instrumental rationality of much economics. This more active role is mainly concerned with rational reflection on the goals of action, which are understood to include upholding principles and embodying virtues as well as expressing preferences. The wisdom of following a particular principle or being guided by a particular virtue is a matter for rational reflection on experience. The implication is that, as economists, we should not be satisfied with an account of environmental values that presents them as just another set of subjective preferences.

As the Aristotelian approach suggests, it seems that ethical principles have something in common with economic theories: both are susceptible to revision after we confront them with data, evidence or experience. In other words, the passions are subject to guidance and direction by reason. I am not saying that we put our economic theories to the test of experience in the same way that we revise our moral principles in the light of experience. All I am suggesting is that the relation between economic theories and values is too subtle and complicated to be captured by a simple dichotomy between subservient reason and the active passions. Our ethical principles, and even our feelings about moral issues, are subject to critical reflection as a kind of 'testing' – unlike our subjective tastes, which we tend to take as 'given'.

Amartya Sen has argued for the importance of a 'careful assessment of aims, objectives, allegiances, etc., and of the conception of the good' (Sen, 1987, p.42). In order to illustrate the 'careful assessment' characteristic of moral reasoning, I want to consider a hypothetical example based on Sen (1976). Suppose that you are a geologist and that you have spent your career exploring for oil reserves. Soon after you arrive in an area that is vulnerable to sea level rise for your latest assignment, you decide that you must confront the growing disquiet you have felt for some time about the role of fossil fuels in causing climate change. You consider the options that seem to be open to you: these consist of returning home to early (and financially comfortable) retirement, continuing to direct the oil exploration project, joining an environmental pressure group to campaign for a GHG emissions reduction programme, and setting up your own renewable energy supply firm.

You might try to calculate what is in your own self-interest and rank the options as shown in column A of Table 19.1. But should self-interest be your guiding principle? You might try another ranking, based on your conception of what would be the 'most moral' thing to do (column B). But can you live up to such a rigorous moral code? Do you have the personal qualities required of an environmental campaigner or an entrepreneur? A careful assessment of your past behaviour, the likely consequences of the different courses of action and your capacity for political lobbying and business leadership, leaves you in little doubt that your actual decision will reflect the ranking shown in column C. Nevertheless, you are aware that a person of greater moral courage would take the risks involved in campaigning or in business enterprise. This suggests that moral choices prompt us into a process of critical reasoning and self-examination. You might also rank the rankings themselves, perhaps in the order B, C, A.

Table 19.1 Ranking moral choices

A 'Self-interest'	B 'Most moral'	C 'Actual'
Drill for oil	Environmental campaign	Early retirement
Early retirement	Renewable energy entrepreneur	Drill for oil
Environmental campaign	Early retirement	Environmental campaign
Renewable energy entrepreneur	Drill for oil	Renewable energy entrepreneur

QUESTION

Try constructing a table ranking the moral choices for the ethical investment opportunities in Box 19.2. You may choose your own descriptions of the preferences for the top of the columns. One possible set of descriptions might be something like this: profit maximizing investment free of ethical constraints; environmentally sensitive investment; investment avoiding gambling, tobacco and alcohol; investment avoiding armaments; and 'across the board' ethical investment avoiding all the other categories.

BOX 19.2   OPPORTUNITIES FOR ETHICAL INVESTMENT

Consider a list of investment opportunities that you can avoid on ethical grounds: say, environmental degradation, armaments, tobacco, alcohol and gambling. Is there something more than a chance set of tastes or feelings linking the list of ethically blocked investments, or some of the items in it?

Are the different prohibitions applications of, or derivations from, a general moral principle or set of core values?

What role in selecting ethical investment options might be played by a consideration of the consequences of the prohibited activities?

Suppose that you came to the list with a disapproval of one item on it but no strong views on the other investment categories. Would seeing the activities listed together put you under an obligation to try to take a consistent or coherent line on all of them?

What difference would it make to your deliberations if you were informed that some categories of ethical investment are substantially less profitable than investment unconstrained by ethical considerations? Should it make any difference at all?

This approach does not confine reason to the discovery of reliable means to ends determined solely by subjective feelings. It argues that reason is also concerned with bringing our beliefs, experiences, feelings and values into some sort of harmony or coherence. In that case, we can begin to work out a role for values or normative judgements in economics without compromising its claim to be a systematic and rational form of inquiry. The next section applies this approach to ethics by considering Hirsch's ideal of 'moral re-entry' in the context of climate change.

3.2   MARKETS, SELF-INTEREST AND ENVIRONMENTAL VALUES

Hirsch's ideal of moral re-entry can be illustrated using two ethical principles of particular relevance to the issue of climate change. If political resistance to a GHG emissions reduction programme is to be overcome, many environmentalists and ecologists advocate two departures from the self-interest that Hirsch deplores. These altruistic principles are a sense of justice for future generations and a perception of the intrinsic worth of the non-human environment.

A SENSE OF JUSTICE FOR FUTURE GENERATIONS

Chapter 8 explained the concept of Pareto efficiency or the Pareto principle. The Pareto principle states that society is better off if a change in the allocation of the inputs or outputs of economic activity leaves at least one person better off without making anyone else worse off. This gain is known as a Pareto improvement, and when all such gains have been exhausted, Pareto efficiency is achieved. When the Pareto principle is used to analyse the efficiency with which resources are allocated between current and future generations, it can generate implications that are somewhat similar to those of sustainable development. If environmental resources are being used up, such as the capacity of the atmosphere to absorb CO_2 without climate change, this particular environmental endowment will decrease. Consequently, there is less to be passed on to future generations, which decreases the economic opportunities open to future generations to meet their development goals. This violates the requirement for sustainability laid out in the Brundtland Report. It also contradicts the Pareto principle if it is extended to consider future generations. A gain in current well-being at the expense of future well-being is not an improvement by the Pareto criterion.

INTERGENERATIONAL JUSTICE

Intergenerational justice is the obligation to ensure a fair distribution of resources between the current generation and future generations.

The concept of INTERGENERATIONAL JUSTICE underpins the argument for sustainable development, and hence the arguments for climate change abatement policies. This concept has been debated at length by philosophers, political scientists, economists and environmentalists. The basic problem, as the economist and philosopher John Broome (1992) points out, is how to weigh up goods and bads that occur at different times. This is particularly relevant to global warming, as global climate change would continue for 70 years, as a consequence of past emissions, even if CO_2 emission ceased today. Climate change abatement is therefore inescapably altruistic, and intended to benefit people who do not yet exist.

Some commentators have raised the issue of uncertainty and set it against the equal consideration of future welfare. We, the current generation, do not know what future generations will want, so discounting future benefits may be a reasonable response to this uncertainty. Discounting is a technique for comparing the worth of goods and bads that occur at different times by expressing future benefits and costs in terms of an estimate of their present value (Chapter 17, Section 3). Uncertainty about what future generations will want could be a reason for preferring current benefits over future benefits that are, at the time they occur, of the same magnitude.

The problem is that such discounting favours the present generation over future generations and therefore seems to involve an unacceptable concession to self-interest. We may feel instead that, morally, the well-being of future generations should be given equal consideration to that of the current generation. We might derive such a principle from a concept of fairness, perhaps understood as impartiality between individuals. We could extend this impartiality across time, in arguing that the well-being of each generation should be equally valued.

THE LAND ETHIC

A sense of the intrinsic value or moral worth of non-human nature expresses a very different attitude to nature from the perception of it as a repository of resources for production. The idea of 'use value' captures the economic attitude to nature as something to be appropriated and exploited. By contrast, the concept of 'existence value' captures the valuing of something in and of itself rather than for its uses. People clearly value the existence of species such as elephants, mountain gorillas or humpback whales, and they value whole ecosystems such as rain forests. Donations to environmental groups represent one mechanism by which existence values are revealed in people's behaviour.

A classic statement of one aspect of existence values is THE LAND ETHIC propounded by the American environmentalist, Aldo Leopold, in his *A Sand County Almanac* (Leopold, 1970). Much of the book is devoted to celebrating the virtues of the non-human world: the grace of a plover, the valour of a chickadee, the harmony of a river eco-system, the 'accumulated wisdom of a stand of pine trees – a natural wisdom which silences the people who walk below' (Leopold, 1970, pp.37). The main principle of the land ethic is the aspiration towards 'a more positive, sustainable position of respectful dwelling in nature'. This entails a rejection of the assumption that use values are the only way of valuing nature: 'We abuse land because we regard it as a commodity belonging to us' (Leopold, 1970, p.94). The alternative view hopes that when 'we see land as a community to which we belong, we may begin to use it with love and respect' (Leopold, 1970, p.92). The implication for economic activity is that the 'destruction, overuse or excessive appropriation of nature is morally wrong' (Cafaro, 2001). In Leopold's own words, 'A thing is right when it tends to preserve the integrity, stability, and beauty of the biotic community. It is wrong when it tends otherwise' (Leopold, 1970, pp.158–9).

> **THE LAND ETHIC**
> The land ethic expresses a sense of the intrinsic value of non-human nature.

Climate change threatens to disturb, and arguably has already disturbed, the integrity and stability of many biotic communities across the world. This aspect of the effects of climate change did not figure prominently in the negotiations leading up to the Kyoto Protocol.

MORAL RE-ENTRY AND MARKETS

A concern for the well-being of future generations and a sense of the intrinsic value of the non-human world are both excluded from consideration in the market process, where the competitive process operates to induce innovations that in many cases cause environmental degradation. Clearly, future generations cannot themselves be market agents because they do not yet exist. Any part of the non-human environment that is not someone's property – for example, the atmosphere – is vulnerable to environmental damage. If it is not owned by anyone, using it does not entail having to pay, and so it may easily become an apparently free receptor of waste products or pollution. Can values such as a concern for future generations and a sense of the intrinsic worth of non-human nature be accommodated by markets along with everyday consumer preferences? Can they be found a place in economic analysis among the norms and values that surround and shape market activity? The following discussion may help to clarify some of the issues involved.

Read the following brief extract from the transcript of the BBC Radio 4 programme 'What austerity does for you', first broadcast on 11 January 2001 as part of the series *Analysis*. Those taking part are:

- Frances Cairncross, BBC presenter and economics journalist and writer
- George Monbiot, environmentalist
- Daniel Bell, Emeritus Professor of Sociology, Harvard University
- Dr Zaki Badawi, President of the Muslim College and Chairman of the Islam Mosque Council.

Cairncross: What might persuade the spoilt and wealthy children of the early 21st century to make communal sacrifices? The environment perhaps?

Monbiot: There are certain activities which are so environmentally costly that we should not be pursuing them or not pursuing them in the way we do today.

Cairncross: Do you think that people care enough about the environment to impose the necessary restraint upon themselves?

Monbiot: It's not simply going to happen through people's free will. We need regulation to say there are certain environmental toxins that we should not be pouring into the environment. Regulation creates the commercial environment in which companies operate and in which consumption operates. With the right kind of regulation you can ensure that people's quality of life remains just as high – or hopefully very much higher – while preventing the most damaging environmental effects.

Cairncross: But the austerity that environmentalists seek would need to be lasting with the benefits fairly distributed not just within a nation but across the globe. Daniel Bell, do you think that capitalist society is capable of such a response?

Bell: To the extent that capitalism depends upon the stimulation of demand and this is a response to various forms of display and hedonism, intrinsically no. But at the same time there's still an awareness of the excesses of the market or the fact that markets often fail. So there's a need for certain kinds of redress and certain kinds of restraint.

Cairncross: So capitalism, with its intrinsic hedonism, is quite incapable of inspiring austerity in a society for any length of time. The intervention of government is needed. What about the clerics? How does Zaki Badawi think he can hold at bay the forces of consumerism?

Badawi: By preaching. There's very little else, I'm afraid. But we are helpless really because the people who are producing the consumer goods are the people who control the media and they want people to consume more because they make more profit.

Monbiot: The only way to persuade of the virtues of austerity is to show
that in some respects it leads to an enrichment of the quality of life, perhaps to
a slowing down of life, which allows you to ponder, to wonder what it's all
about.

Source: http://news.bbc.co.uk/hi/english/s...analysis/transcript/austerity.txt

QUESTION

Now answer the following questions.

1 **What do you think are the main implications of the views expressed in
the extract for Hirsch's idea that there is a need for moral re-entry in
contemporary society?**

2 **Drawing on your own values, as well as on the economic understanding
you have gained from the course, comment on the views expressed in
the extract. With which of the points made do find yourself most
strongly in agreement, and which do you find least convincing?**

In response to Question 1, the discussants seem to be in agreement with Hirsch's
critique of the centrality of self-interest in contemporary society. They believe that
markets are imbued with the prevailing values of capitalist society, which are
hedonistic and self-interested. Bell refers to a hedonism on which capitalism depends
and to the excesses of markets, while Badawi believes that the prevailing values of
society are those that increase profits. For both discussants it seems that capitalist
values arise from complicity between consumers and producers, with each group
pursuing its own self-interest. However there seems to be a general pessimism about
the prospects for change in the direction of Hirsch's moral re-entry. In their different
ways both Badawi and Monbiot believe that preaching is the only source of alternative
values, with Badawi advocating it in a specifically religious context and Monbiot
urging the attractions of a more austere and hence less pressured way of life. Neither,
however, holds out much prospect of a shift towards the values they seek to promote.
For Monbiot, action from consumers or private citizens for a more environmentally
sustainable economy seems to be out of the question, and Badawi believes that the
power of commercial interests is overwhelming.

There is no single 'right' answer to Question 2 because it asks for personal judgements.
You might have thought of some of the following points. Monbiot's claim that
government regulation 'creates the commercial environment' within which firms and
consumers operate in markets accords with a view in which markets are shaped by the
institutional frameworks in which they are embedded. In view of the political
resistance to climate change regulation, not only in the USA, it is important that
government intervention should reflect a consensus. Perhaps Monbiot's suggestion
that the virtues of austerity enrich the quality of life expresses an awareness of this
point. Building a consensus involves preaching, by political as well as religious
leaders, and by environmentalists, entrepreneurs and scientists, too.

Second, I am not convinced by the pessimistic view of values in markets that seems to be shared by the discussants. It seems to me to be true that economic activity in contemporary market economies is overwhelmingly driven by values that it is reasonable to think of as self-interested, hedonistic and concerned with display, as Bell claims. I also share the discussants' view that this is a cause for concern rather than celebration. However, I do not agree with their dismissal of the markets as beyond redemption or retrieval.

QUESTION

Please read the following extract from Greyson's (1996) article for *Renew*. Do you think that it offers support for a less pessimistic view of markets and environmentally sensitive values than that expressed by the discussants in the radio programme?

Dr Robèrt started The Natural Step organization so the consensus process could include everyone who was willing to participate. These days 19 networks of ten thousand professionals (scientists, engineers, doctors, business executives, etc.) are working with The Natural Step. Some of these people have extended the initial consensus towards 'what can be agreed' in their fields. Others put the concepts into practice, leading the market-place and providing examples of what can be achieved. The largest companies working with The Natural Step have formed a 'Challenge' group to co-ordinate their planning and investments. The Swedish Rail company, SJ, is collaborating with Bilspedition (one of Europe's largest freight companies), IKEA and Electrolux to drastically reduce road haulage. One of the country's largest oil companies, OK Petroleum, is investing in bio-fuels and lobbying for increased taxes on fossil fuels. The Challenge group's chief executives met with the Prime Minister of Sweden in March 1995 to tell him the goal of economic growth was illusory and that the time is ripe for the shift to a cyclic economy. He agreed.

These examples are important for The Natural Step since it only works with consensus information. It doesn't prescribe to people what changes they should make since everyone knows their own business best. Instead The Natural Step asks people's advice about how this consensus might apply in their area and then supports exemplary practice.

(Greyson, 1996)

It seems to me that the significance of this extract is that markets can, in principle, reflect values other than hedonistic and self-interested ones. It is possible for economic agents in markets to co-operate as well as compete, on the basis of traditional social norms, religious beliefs and a sense of civic duty, aspects to which Hirsch (1977) drew attention.

One reason it is not always easy to see this is that economics tends to explain the motivation of consumers and producers, of buyers and sellers in markets, in ways that lend credence to the depiction of them as hedonistic and irretrievably self-interested.

From the standpoint taken by most economists it is difficult to understand how ethical principles, environmental values, a sense of civic duty and so on can get a foothold in market transactions. They must do so if economic activity is to be redirected towards less environmentally damaging products and, in particular, towards low-carbon or no-carbon technologies.

What policies might be used to guide economic behaviour in a more environmentally sustainable direction? One way of redirecting economic activity is for the state to intervene in markets where there is market failure, shaping market incentives through taxes and regulation (Chapter 9, Section 2). The next section examines a rather different market-based policy instrument: emissions trading.

4   BEYOND KYOTO: MAKING A CARBON MARKET?   •••••

In Chapter 9, Maureen Mackintosh introduced the idea of 'smart government' – for example, designing regulations that both encourage competitiveness in markets and tackle social exclusion. It seems reasonable to develop the idea of smart government to encompass the use of markets as instruments for achieving objectives set outside the markets through the political process. The climate change negotiations that culminated in the Kyoto Protocol envisaged a major role for market mechanisms, notably emissions trading, in reducing GHG emissions in accordance with agreed targets or aspirations. Once permits to emit agreed quantities of CO_2 and other GHGs have been issued, they can be traded. Participants able to emit less than their permits allow can sell the surplus permits to participants who find it costly to bring their emissions down to the agreed level. In principle, the market in permits to emit GHGs could both enhance competitiveness and innovation and help to avert the adverse consequences of climate change. However, the fact that markets are inevitably embedded in society opens them up to other social and political pressures and constraints. These might or might not be conducive to the sort of technological progress that is required in response to climate change.

4.1   THE CLIMATE CHANGE NEGOTIATIONS

The UN Framework Convention on Climate Change (UNFCCC) set the overall objective of stabilising the concentration of GHGs to prevent dangerous climate change, while ensuring that food production was not threatened and sustainable economic development could proceed. The story of the Kyoto negotiations is that collective agreements to that end were modified to add 'flexibility', through international transfer mechanisms such as emissions trading. This reflects the key clash between the desire of the European Union (EU) for a co-ordinated approach based on flat-rate emission reductions and the anti-interventionist stance of the USA, which was sensitive to its citizens' and industries' attachment to cheap fuel. The EU sought a flat-rate GHG emissions reduction target for all Annex I countries (the industrial polluters) of 10 to 15 per cent, while the USA and Japan aimed for an average 0 to 5 per cent decrease with differentials and flexibility.

The outcome of the Kyoto negotiations was a set of reduction targets averaging out as a 5.2 per cent cut on 1990 levels of GHG emissions by 2008–12. There are different national targets around this average, ranging from the EU's 8 per cent reduction on 1990 levels of GHG emissions by 2008–12, through 7 per cent for the USA, 6 per cent for Japan and 0 per cent for Russia and Ukraine, to increases of 8 per cent for Australia and 10 per cent for Iceland. It was not possible to sustain the commitment to flat-rate targets proposed by the EU after the EU departed from its own principle, arguing for differential targets across EU countries, averaging to 8 per cent. The 5.2 per cent GHG emissions reduction programme agreed for the period 2008–12 should be assessed in the light of the IPCC judgement that a 60 per cent cut in GHG emissions is needed in order to stabilize atmospheric concentrations by 2050. Friends of the Earth described the outcome of the negotiations as 'pitifully inadequate'. Furthermore, there is little prospect that even these reductions will be achieved.

Most industrial countries are falling short of their Kyoto aspirations. Japan's weak economic performance during the 1990s has slowed the rise in emissions there, but not enough to put Japan on track to meet its 6 per cent Kyoto target. In the EU only Germany, because of economic collapse in the former East Germany, and the UK, after the 'dash for gas' (the fossil fuel with the lightest GHG emissions) associated with utility privatization, are likely to comply with their targets under Kyoto. In the USA, emissions had risen 12 per cent above 1990 levels by 1999 and were predicted to rise another 10 per cent by 2008. Achieving the Kyoto target for the USA of a 7 per cent reduction from 1990 levels would now require a 25 per cent decline from 'business as usual'. According to Victor (2001, p.2), US citizens are unlikely to accept the high costs of compliance with Kyoto. For example, half of US electricity is supplied by coal, the fossil fuel that emits most GHGs. The US Congress refused 95–0 to ratify the Kyoto Protocol, and in March 2001 President Bush abandoned it. Other countries, notably the EU member states, remain committed to the objectives of the climate change negotiations.

The significance of creating markets as a policy response to climate change is associated with the role of competition in reducing costs, and hence making compliance with Kyoto more politically acceptable. In the USA, for example, 'full-blown trading could lower the annual costs [of compliance with the Kyoto target] by a factor of ten – to a more palatable $100 per American household' (Victor, 2001, p.3). By 'full-blown trading', Victor means the combination of three international transfer mechanisms that were negotiated at Kyoto: joint implementation agreements, the clean development mechanism and emissions trading. Under the joint implementation (JI) agreements, two industrial countries can each earn credits towards their emission reduction targets by jointly investing in a project that cuts emissions. The clean development mechanism (CDM) allows an industrial country to earn credits towards its emission reduction target by investing in an emission-reducing project in a low-income country. The idea behind EMISSIONS TRADING is that an industrial country can increase the maximum level of GHG emissions it is allowed during a set period by buying unused allowances from another industrial country.

EMISSIONS TRADING
An emissions trading regime applies when countries are given permits to produce maximum levels of GHG emissions that they are then allowed to trade.

4.2 EMISSIONS TRADING

The governments of the countries participating in the Kyoto negotiations stipulated a quantitative target for the reduction of GHG emissions, and decided to make use of market processes to achieve that target. Permits to emit GHGs were issued up to an agreed maximum for each country. Countries could then buy and sell their permits. A country that needed to reduce emissions might choose to buy other countries' permits if it was cheaper than reducing their own emissions. A country facing relatively low costs for investment in energy-efficient technologies to reduce GHG emissions would sell the permits it no longer required to one facing higher costs. In this way, the costs of reducing GHG emissions could be minimized.

In the case of climate change, the world's biggest polluter, the USA, is reluctant to incur the costs of reducing its GHG emissions in accordance with the Kyoto Protocol. It is not only that those costs could be as high as $1000 per US household (without emissions trading); there is also the fear that the sacrifice will be futile if emissions from low-income countries, in particular China and India, increase on a 'business as usual' basis. This is where economists can help. You will recall that markets can reduce costs and speed innovation. In applying this general insight to the case of carbon emissions, the following extract explains the potential benefits of emissions trading, or carbon trading.

What are the key benefits of carbon trading?

The key benefit is flexibility and, therefore, cost-effectiveness. Because the cost of reducing greenhouse gasses varies enormously from company to company and from country to country and because the global environment benefits regardless of where emissions are reduced, it makes sense for reductions to take place initially where it is least costly. For example, rather than investing in costly emission reduction technologies within its own plant, a company can decide to make a less costly investment in reductions elsewhere and obtain credits which can then be applied towards its own net greenhouse reductions.

Trading also encourages the development of new environmentally advanced plants and processes. It allows flexibility to innovate and experiment and encourages the adaptation and financing of new technologies in developing countries. Inevitably, it will mobilize large amounts of resources towards poorer nations leading to greater engagement by the developing world in global efforts to reduce emissions.

Source: http://www.carbonmarket.com/FAQs.htm#top.Anchor

Emissions trading might therefore make a post-Kyoto GHG emissions reduction programme more politically acceptable to US voters and facilitate a much less carbon-intensive development trajectory for China and India.

A serious problem with carbon trading is that government intervention is required to define property rights, that is, to set the targets for GHG emission reductions for each country and hence the number of permits that can be issued. Without property rights there is nothing to be exchanged. You cannot be a seller unless you actually own what you want to sell. There is also the need for an authority to monitor and enforce the contracts that are made, explicitly or implicitly, whenever goods change hands in a market. These preconditions of market processes are particularly important in the case of climate change. Since it is a global problem being addressed through intergovernmental negotiations, a 'world government' seems to be required. In the absence of such an organization, the difficulties of defining property rights in CO_2 emissions have so far proved insuperable. As Victor (2001, p.14) puts it, 'international law has no central authority that can compel countries to remain part of a treaty'.

EMISSIONS TRADING IN THE KYOTO PROTOCOL ...

The difficulties of creating a system of emissions trading – a market in emissions permits – under the Kyoto Protocol demonstrate the importance of clearly assigned property rights and adequate monitoring and enforcement procedures to the functioning of markets. The history of the Kyoto negotiations also shows that the effectiveness of a market in emissions permits depends crucially upon the political and social pressures in which market processes, including the creation of the new market itself, are embedded. The capacity of an emerging market in emissions permits to reduce costs and induce innovation may therefore be compromised by the political pressures that have shaped it. To understand emissions trading in the Kyoto Protocol, we must look at its origins. Who proposed it? What might they have stood to gain from it? To what extent has this presumed pursuit of self-interest impeded the functioning of the market in emissions trading?

It was representatives of the fossil fuel industries who lobbied most strenuously in favour of a flexible approach to emissions reduction targets, including emissions trading. The fossil fuel lobby includes the coal, oil and automotive industries, states whose economies are energy intensive and countries that are dependent on the export of fossil fuels or on their use. The Global Climate Coalition (GCC) is a pressure group for predominantly US fossil fuel interests, that is, the coal and oil industries, but also the chemical and car industries. GCC ran mass-media campaigns seeking to discredit the scientific evidence for climate change, lobbied energetically at Kyoto and formed an alliance with the OPEC countries. It is estimated that US industry 'threw probably up to $100 million into fighting the whole process' of climate change regulation (Grubb *et al.*, 1999, p.112).

It is clear that the appeal of emissions trading to the fossil fuel lobby was that it held out the prospect of allowing leading emitters to avoid taking serious domestic action. The USA faced high costs for reducing GHG emissions, in the form of political resistance from the powerful fossil fuel lobby and from voters. The USA 'got virtually everything it wanted in terms of flexibility for Annex I (industrial countries) commitments' (Grubb *et al.*, 1999, p.93). Russia and Ukraine were in the best position to sell surplus permits as they have zero abatement costs (the costs of reducing GHG emissions). In Russia and Ukraine, emissions fell as a consequence of economic collapse, and 'over successive months teams of US officials went to the East to explain the windfall that could be waiting' (Grubb *et al.*, 1999, p.93). As Victor (2001, p.10) concludes, the accidental nature of the surplus means that the US scheme 'buys paper compliance but no reduction in global warming'. The emissions reductions in Russia and Ukraine were 'free', in that they came about as the unintended side-effects of economic collapse. Rather than 'ring fence' this zero cost contribution to climate change abatement, the US proposal would have allowed it to be dissipated in higher US emissions.

As the negotiations at Kyoto continued it became clear that Japan and other industrial countries wanted to take part in emissions trading with Russia and Ukraine. However, the difficulties of establishing property rights in emissions permits, and in devising workable monitoring and enforcement procedures, proved to be insuperable. Negotiations over emissions trading among participating countries were therefore deadlocked when President Bush announced the US abandonment of the Kyoto Protocol. Is this the end of the road for attempts to create a 'carbon market' as a way of curbing GHG emissions? Or are the potential advantages of such a market sufficient to make a resumption of attempts to create it probable or even inevitable?

The justification of the original US plan to buy all, or almost all, of the surplus emissions permits from Russia and Ukraine appealed to the standard arguments concerning the advantages of markets. Markets not only reduce costs and allocate resources efficiently, but they also encourage innovation.

QUESTION

1   **Can you think of any reasons for doubting whether the case for the advantages of markets applies to a market in emissions permits?**

2   **If so, is there anything that Russia and Ukraine could do with the proceeds of the sale of emissions permits that might lead you revise that judgement?**

    You might find it helpful to consult the discussion of perfect competition in Chapter 5 in connection with the first question, and the account of monopoly in Chapter 4 with respect to the second.

It seems to me that there are two reasons for being sceptical about the benefits of markets. First, the argument for markets reducing costs and achieving allocative efficiency is based on the model of a perfectly competitive market. Among the conditions a market must satisfy, if it is properly to be described as perfectly competitive, is the presence of large numbers of buyers and sellers. Only if there are many transactions among numerous buyers and sellers can a prevailing market price emerge to convey the information they need to make the decisions that yield cost reductions and hence an efficient allocation of resources (Rosenbaum, 2000, pp.477–8). The possibility of useful price signals in a market consisting of one buyer and two sellers seems remote. Second, there is the nature of the costs to be reduced. You might have felt that the political rather than the economic nature of the US's costs of abatement undermines its case. I agree. Japan, for example, has high abatement costs because it is already highly energy efficient. Reducing its GHG emissions would therefore require a difficult choice between engaging in substantially less carbon-emitting activity and improving still further the efficiency of an unchanged level of such activity (Section 2.3). In the USA there is still considerable scope for relatively low-cost improvements in energy efficiency.

On the other hand, it could be argued that political resistance in the USA to a GHG emissions reduction programme is the most serious obstacle to climate change abatement. The economic case for emissions trading rests in part on the reduction of the costs of abatement, precisely because lower costs would make an agreement on a GHG emissions reduction programme more politically acceptable.

Turning to the second question, you might have wondered whether Russia and Ukraine could use the money from the sale of surplus emission permits to modernize and restructure their industries, with the aim of making them more energy efficient. Indeed, the US delegation to Kyoto argued that emissions trading would enable the USA to finance investment in carbon-saving technology in Russia and Ukraine. The US position is that it does not matter *where* GHG emissions reductions are achieved, as long as they are achieved. In this way, emissions trading could, in principle, exemplify the capacity of the competitive process in monopolistic markets to encourage innovation.

Two comments seem appropriate here. First, Russia and Ukraine could use the proceeds of surplus emissions permits in many other ways, and their investment in carbon-saving technology would need to be monitored and, if necessary, enforced. This is an example of the dependency of markets on state institutions. Second, the US case applies to the purchase of surplus emissions permits by any country, not just the USA.

... AND AFTERWARDS

An extraordinary thing is happening across the world today. Firms and other organizations are buying and selling CO_2 emissions permits, they are trading in the carbon market, even though the governments of the world have not yet set the rules for such a market. There is no international agreement governing property rights in CO_2 emissions or procedures for monitoring and enforcing contracts. Yet a carbon market exists.

How is it possible to set up a carbon market in advance of internationally agreed rules for trading carbon? There are a number of specific trades taking place, not only in CO_2 but also in other GHGs (see *Environmental Finance*, 2001). Consider the UK Government's Emissions Trading Scheme (ETS) (see Rosewell, 2001). The UK government believes that, sooner or later, there will be an internationally ratified agreement to reduce GHG emissions, and it has policies in place, such as the Climate Change Levy – a tax on energy use by businesses. So it is worth establishing the ETS if it promises lower abatement costs and more advantages than other measures. The first step in setting up a market is to establish property rights, so that economic agents, firms in this case, have something they can sell. Firms can enter the ETS through an auction, bidding for permits to emit no more than a specified quantity of particular GHGs, perhaps at specified sites, for a year. If they meet their targets, that is, emit less than the specified amount of GHGs, they can collect an incentive payment from the government or they can sell the surplus permits to any firm that is willing to buy them. The government has set aside £215 million to fund the incentive payments over the first five years of the ETS. By the end of that period, emissions trading should be working sufficiently well to make further incentive payments unnecessary.

QUESTION

Please read the following extract from a carbon trading website and answer the following questions. You might find it helpful to consult the account of 'high-tech' industries in Chapter 2.

1 **Why are firms trading in the carbon market in the absence of the normal and apparently indispensable legal framework?**

2 **What makes it worth incurring the risk of trading partners reneging on contracts or being unable to enforce their putative property rights?**

Specific carbon trades

Suncor, the Canadian energy company, has purchased 100,000 metric tonnes of CO_2 from U.S.-based Niagara Mohawk Power Corp. This deal was one of the world's first international emission trades. Carbon emissions reductions will occur as Niagara Mohawk switches from coal to natural gas, undertakes renewable energy projects and promotes the efficient use of energy by customers. Reductions will be measured and verified by the Environmental Resources Trust, an independent third-party organisation, to ensure they have a true net benefit to the atmosphere. Suncor also has an option to purchase an additional 10 million tonnes of greenhouse gas reductions from Niagara Mohawk after the year 2000.

Tesco, the UK supermarket chain, is buying carbon from the Carbon Storage Trust to absorb the CO_2 emissions caused by a particular fuel's consumption. This fuel is then being marketed as having no net carbon emissions.

Toyota has created an $800,000 model forest which is being monitored with emissions measuring equipment to calculate CO_2 absorbed. They are also working with botanists to develop genetically engineered trees that absorb CO_2 faster.

BP has initiated an internal carbon trading system, involving 10 business units around the world. The scheme will see trading amongst the business units as well as trading between the units and outside parties. One of the first external trades has been between BP's Kwinana refinery in Western Australia, and the state forestry organisation.

Pacific Power, one of Australia's largest electricity generators, has purchased the carbon credits from a newly planted 1,000 hectare forest plantation on the north coast of New South Wales (NSW) from the NSW State Forests organisation. The trade covers a ten year period during which the plantation is expected to sequester 250,000 tonnes of CO_2.

Source: http://www.carbonmarket.com/FAQs.htm#top.Anchor

The answers to both questions are based on the idea of 'first-mover advantage' (Chapter 6). Firms believe that despite the failure of the Kyoto negotiations to establish the rules for carbon trading, a carbon market is inevitable in the near future. There are advantages in being among the first participants in such a market. These include 'learning by doing', that is, learning about the successful tactics and pitfalls of the process of trading carbon by actually doing it and so preparing the culture and systems of the firm for the day when the carbon market is fully established. There may also be public relations advantages to a firm gaining a high profile in efforts to control climate change. Firms engaged in carbon trading before the establishment of property rights and arrangements for monitoring and enforcing contracts will be consulted by governments drawing up the legal framework that will eventually regulate such matters. The opportunity will be there to influence the design of these institutions to the firms' advantage.

There seem to be three conclusions to be drawn from this review of the scope and limits of emissions trading in reducing GHG emissions. First, the emerging carbon market has considerable potential to enhance the political acceptability of a GHG emissions reduction programme by reducing the costs of compliance and accelerating innovations in carbon-saving technology. Second, there is a risk that the industrial countries responsible for most of the GHG emissions to date will find ways of using the carbon market to secure 'paper compliance', avoiding the need to take serious domestic action. Third, if this risk is to be minimized, a central legal authority with powers to establish property rights and to monitor and enforce contracts may need to be created by international agreement.

5   CONCLUSION ••••••••••••••••••••••••••••••••••••••

This chapter has discussed some of the ways in which economists think about environmental sustainability, with particular reference to climate change. Ecological economists argue that there are physical limits to growth, one of which is the carrying capacity of the Earth. A sustainable economy would be one in which economic activity is organized in recognition of these limits. It is unlikely that such an economy could be constructed on the foundations of contemporary market norms and behaviour. First, an ethical dimension needs to inform economic understanding, establishing a critical distance from which reason and reflection can comment upon existing tastes and preferences. Second, markets can contribute most effectively to climate change policy by being used to achieve objectives set through the political process.

CHAPTER 20 MACROECONOMIC PERFORMANCE AND STABILIZATION

Nicholas Crafts ●

Objectives

After studying this chapter you should be able to:
- appreciate the importance of historical data in assessing macroeconomic performance and the limitations of standard measures of macroeconomic performance
- understand the perennial problems faced by macroeconomic stabilization policy makers
- understand the interactions between the forces influencing long-run economic growth and the effects of short-run stabilization policies.

Concepts

- GDP per head
- inflation
- unemployment
- real GDP
- NAIRU (non-accelerating inflation rate of unemployment)
- shadow economy
- Taylor Rules
- hyperinflation
- economic growth

1 INTRODUCTION ●

The approach taken in this chapter is relatively uncommon in macroeconomic textbooks. It provides you with the opportunity to: (a) explore a wide range of historical experience using basic macroeconomic concepts without needing lots of prior knowledge, (b) consider the long-run consequences of policy decisions aimed at dealing with short-run problems, and (c) examine the difficulties for short-run policy making of changes in long-run economic trends.

The first question to answer is, of course, 'what happened?' Economic history offers a wide range of outcomes, including mass unemployment, hyperinflation, full employment, severe deflation and strong growth with price stability. Awareness of this diversity of experience is one key ingredient in addressing a second question, 'how good is a country's present performance?', although this knowledge clearly needs to be supplemented by an assessment of the conditions under which it would be feasible to emulate the best results from the past.

Probably the most common reason for (generally spurious) comparisons of economic performance is to score party political points about the effectiveness of economic policy – as in the rough and tumble of Prime Minister's Question Time in the British House of Commons. This prompts two further closely related issues worth exploring in some detail and with some care, namely, 'how far is economic policy responsible for short- or long-term outcomes such as recessions or differences in growth rates?' and 'what explains failures in the design of economic policy for stabilization?'

1.1 MACROECONOMIC PERFORMANCE: AN HISTORICAL OVERVIEW

Research by economic historians has produced a wealth of data from which this section draws some edited highlights. Inevitably we must consider a good deal of quantitative information. In doing so, the objective will be to extract key points rather than to drown in a sea of minute detail. The account that follows concentrates on the standard measures of macroeconomic performance, namely, growth, inflation, unemployment and volatility. In Section 1.2 the value and reliability of these indicators are considered, but our first task is to see what the data say.

QUESTION

> Consider Tables 20.1 and 20.2 which contain a summary description of levels of real GDP per head and of economic growth in industrial countries since 1870. What surprises you most in the tables? How would you describe the relative performance of the UK?

Assessment of relative growth performance is a topic which is fully developed in Section 4. For the moment, however, it seems appropriate to notice that the long-run experience of the UK has been one of continuing relative economic decline, although in absolute terms incomes have risen steadily. Table 20.1 shows that the UK has fallen from second highest GDP per head in 1870 to seventeenth in 1999. This implies that over the long term UK economic growth has been less rapid than in other countries, which is confirmed in Table 20.2. The UK is below the median growth rate in each period. As to the biggest surprise, there could well be many different answers, but I suspect the most popular might be to pick out the exceptionally rapid growth of the 'Golden Age' (1950–73). Explanations for that unusual episode and the marked slow down that followed it in the last quarter of the twentieth century will be reviewed in Section 4.

In a typical year OECD countries experience economic growth, but these long-period averages conceal substantial short-run fluctuations. Table 20.3, which is divided into periods that will be convenient for subsequent discussion, reports a sizeable standard deviation of the growth rate especially prior to the Second World War. Put differently, all economies go through years of recession when real output contracts rather than

Table 20.1 Levels of real GDP per head for benchmark years, 1870–1999 ($, 1990 international)

	1870		1913		1950		1973		1999	
1	Australia	3645	Australia	5715	USA	9561	Switzerland	18 204	USA	27 975
2	UK	3191	USA	5301	Switzerland	9064	USA	16 689	Norway	23 717
3	Netherlands	2753	New Zealand	5152	New Zealand	8453	Canada	13 838	Singapore	23 582
4	New Zealand	2704	UK	4921	Australia	7493	Denmark	13 945	Denmark	22 389
5	Belgium	2697	Canada	4447	Canada	7437	Sweden	13 493	Switzerland	21 609
6	USA	2445	Switzerland	4266	Denmark	6946	Germany	11 966	Canada	21 331
7	Switzerland	2202	Belgium	4220	UK	6907	France	13 123	Australia	21 045
8	Denmark	2003	Netherlands	4049	Sweden	6738	Netherlands	13 082	Netherlands	20 805
9	Germany	1913	Denmark	3912	Netherlands	5996	Australia	12 759	Japan	20 431
10	France	1876	Germany	3833	Norway	5463	New Zealand	12 513	Germany	20 415
11	Austria	1863	France	3485	Belgium	5462	Belgium	12 170	Hong Kong	20 352
12	Ireland	1775	Austria	3465	France	5270	UK	12 022	France	20 054
13	Canada	1695	Sweden	3096	Germany	4281	Japan	11 439	Belgium	19 892
14	Sweden	1664	Ireland	2736	Finland	4253	Norway	11 246	Ireland	19 756
15	Italy	1499	Italy	2564	Austria	3706	Austria	11 235	Sweden	19 380
16	Norway	1432	Norway	2501	Italy	3502	Finland	11 085	Austria	19 264
17	Spain	1376	Spain	2255	Ireland	3446	Italy	10 643	UK	19 030
18	Finland	1140	Finland	2111	Spain	2397	Spain	8739	Finland	19 012
19	Portugal	997	Greece	1592	Singapore	2219	Greece	7655	Italy	17 994
20	Greece	913	Japan	1385	Hong Kong	2218	Portugal	7343	Taiwan	15 720
21	Japan	737	Singapore	1279	Portugal	2069	Hong Kong	7104	New Zealand	15 355
22			Portugal	1244	Japan	1926	Ireland	6867	Spain	14 746
23			South Korea	893	Greece	1915	Singapore	5977	South Korea	13 317
24			Taiwan	747	Taiwan	936	Taiwan	4117	Portugal	13 289
25					South Korea	770	South Korea	2841	Greece	11 620

Source: derived from Maddison, 2001, updated to 1999 using World Bank, 2001. Estimates for Germany refer to the area of West Germany prior to unification throughout from Maddison, 1995; the 1999 figure is extrapolated from 1994 using growth rate of unified Germany

increases; for example, in the post-war period the UK has experienced decreases in real GDP per head in eight years (1952, 1958, 1974, 1975, 1980, 1981, 1991 and 1992). In fact, in most of these cases the declines were small (2 per cent or less). In really bad times, falls in GDP have been much more severe. The worst experiences in the West came in the Depression of the early 1930s when for the advanced countries the average decline in real GDP between 1929 and 1933 was 17 per cent and in the USA it was 25 per cent (Maddison, 1983). By comparison, the turbulence of the recent past pales into

Table 20.2 Rates of growth of real GDP per head for selected periods, 1870–1999 (% per year)

1870–1913		1913–50		1950–73		1973–99	
Australia	1.0	Australia	0.7	USA	2.4	Switzerland	0.7
UK	1.0	USA	1.6	Switzerland	3.1	USA	2.0
Netherlands	0.9	New Zealand	1.4	New Zealand	1.7	Canada	1.7
New Zealand	1.5	UK	0.9	Australia	2.3	Denmark	1.8
Belgium	1.0	Canada	1.4	Canada	2.7	Sweden	1.4
USA	1.8	Switzerland	2.1	Denmark	3.1	Germany	1.7
Switzerland	1.6	Belgium	0.7	UK	2.4	France	1.7
Denmark	1.6	Netherlands	1.1	Sweden	3.1	Netherlands	1.8
Germany	1.6	Denmark	1.6	Netherlands	3.4	Australia	1.9
France	1.4	Germany	0.3	Norway	3.2	New Zealand	0.8
Austria	1.4	France	1.1	Belgium	3.6	Belgium	1.9
Ireland	1.0	Austria	0.2	France	4.0	UK	1.8
Canada	2.3	Sweden	2.1	Germany	5.0	Japan	2.3
Sweden	1.5	Ireland	0.7	Finland	4.2	Norway	2.9
Italy	1.3	Italy	0.8	Austria	4.9	Austria	2.1
Norway	1.3	Norway	2.1	Italy	5.0	Finland	2.1
Spain	1.2	Spain	0.2	Ireland	3.0	Italy	2.0
Finland	1.4	Finland	1.9	Spain	5.8	Spain	2.0
Portugal	0.5	Greece	0.5	Singapore	4.4	Greece	1.6
Greece	1.3	Japan	0.9	Hong Kong	5.2	Portugal	2.3
Japan	1.5	Singapore	1.5	Portugal	5.7	Hong Kong	4.1
		Portugal	1.4	Japan	8.0	Ireland	4.1
		South Korea	−0.4	Greece	6.2	Singapore	5.4
		Taiwan	0.6	Taiwan	6.6	Taiwan	5.3
				South Korea	5.8	South Korea	6.1

Source: derived from Table 20.1

insignificance, although the oil shocks of the 1970s marked the end of a long post-war boom characterized by exceptional stability.

Table 20.3 also introduces a summary of inflation performance. Here it is apparent that average inflation in the G7 countries has varied substantially over time – much more so than the rate of economic growth. Prior to the Second World War, peacetime inflation rates were generally close to zero. Indeed, prices were generally falling between the mid 1870s and mid 1890s and in the inter-war period policy makers

Table 20.3 G7 macroeconomic indicators (% per year)

	Inflation		Real GDP growth	
	Mean	Standard deviation	Mean	Standard deviation
Gold Standard (1880–1913)	1.0	3.4	1.5	3.7
Inter-war (1919–39)	–1.1	7.7	1.2	6.8
Bretton Woods (1945–71)	3.6	4.6	4.2	2.7
The OPEC years (1974–89)	7.2	3.3	2.2	2.3
1990–99	2.2	1.1	1.8	0.8

Source: Bordo, 1993; IMF, 2000

worried about price deflation rather than inflation. The period after the breakdown of the Bretton Woods international monetary system stands out as one of high inflation.

In Table 20.4's more detailed account of inflation in the UK, the 1970s stand out as an aberration. In 1975, the peak year, inflation reached the record level of 27.2 per cent, over four times the rate experienced in West Germany. By contrast, in the early 1920s when prices fell by over 30 per cent in three years in the UK, Germany experienced hyperinflation. This highlights the point that, while there can be common inflationary threats such as oil price shocks, domestic policy and circumstances tend to matter much more, at least in episodes of very rapid inflation.

Table 20.4 also displays information on estimates of the rate of UK unemployment over time, based on the OECD definition, namely, 'persons without work, available for work and seeking employment for pay or profit'. The number of people unemployed

Table 20.4 UK inflation and unemployment rates (%)

	Inflation	Unemployment
1870s	–1.0	4.3
1880s	–0.6	5.9
1890s	0.6	5.2
1900s	0.6	6.6
1920s	–3.1	7.7
1930s	0.3	11.1
1950s	4.2	2.0
1960s	3.6	2.7
1970s	14.1	4.4
1980s	6.1	10.6
1990s	3.3	8.8

Source: inflation is measured by the GDP deflator, Feinstein, 1972; *Economic Trends*, 2001; unemployment relative to civilian work force pre-First World War, Boyer and Hatton, 2002; inter-war, Feinstein, 1972; post-war, Layard *et al.*, 1994; OECD, 2001

is estimated from a survey of a sample of the population, unlike the official UK figures which are derived from counting the number of people claiming unemployment benefit (Chapter 13). These estimates are constructed so as to be broadly comparable, which is in fact quite difficult given the varying sources of information that have to be used. The difference between periods is pronounced. Whereas the inter-war years and the late twentieth century were times when many of those looking for work were unsuccessful, the 1950s and 1960s stand out as an age of exceptionally low unemployment. Moreover, in the 1980s, even with over 10 per cent unemployed, inflation averaged about 6 per cent. This compares with inflation around 4 per cent while unemployment was under 3 per cent in the early post-war decades.

Table 20.5 reports unemployment rates on the standardized (OECD) definition which sometimes differs from the headline rate most commonly reported in individual countries. The OECD definition can be applied consistently across countries and so enables international comparisons to be made. The inter-war data are not as accurate as those for the recent past but the broad picture is informative. There are clearly some common features across countries. Thus, 1933, at the worst of the Great Depression, was a year of relatively high unemployment in every country, while the universal

Table 20.5 Standardized unemployment rates (%)

	1929	1933	1937	1973	1983	2000
Australia	8.2	17.4	8.1	2.3	9.9	6.6
Austria	5.5	16.3	13.7	0.9	3.7	3.7
Belgium	0.8	10.6	7.2	2.7	12.1	7.0
Canada	2.9	19.3	9.4	5.5	11.8	6.8
Denmark	8.0	14.5	11.0	1.0	10.4	4.7
Finland	2.8	6.2	2.6	2.3	5.4	9.8
France	n/a	n/a	n/a	2.7	8.3	9.5
Germany	5.9	14.8	2.7	0.8	8.0	8.1
Ireland	n/a	n/a	n/a	5.7	14.0	4.2
Italy	1.7	5.9	5.0	4.4	7.0	10.7
Japan	n/a	n/a	n/a	1.3	2.6	4.7
Netherlands	1.7	9.7	10.5	2.9	12.0	2.8
Norway	5.4	9.7	6.0	1.5	3.4	3.5
Spain	n/a	n/a	n/a	2.5	17.2	14.1
Sweden	2.4	7.3	5.1	2.0	2.9	5.9
Switzerland	0.4	3.5	3.6	0.0	2.4	2.6
UK	7.2	13.9	7.7	3.1	12.5	5.5
USA	3.1	24.7	14.2	4.8	9.5	4.0

Source: inter-war from Maddison, 1991; post-war from Layard *et al.*, 1994, updated using OECD, 2001

experience in 1973, at the end of the post-war Golden Age, was the opposite. The late twentieth century, however, saw some interesting differences in unemployment trends; it is instructive to compare France and Italy with Ireland and the Netherlands.

QUESTION

Compare Tables 20.1 and 20.5. What relation across countries is there between the level of unemployment and of GDP per person at the end of the twentieth century?

The answer is that unemployment tends to be lower in countries with relatively high income and productivity levels (the rank correlation coefficient is –0.61). This is an interesting observation because it goes against a widely held belief that adopting better technology and improving labour productivity inevitably leads to higher unemployment. The same inference can be drawn by looking at what has happened to unemployment over time. Clearly, by 1973, labour productivity was much higher than in the inter-war years, yet unemployment rates were much lower. Similarly, the USA, which experienced a late twentieth century boom based on massive investment in information and communication technology (ICT), had lower unemployment in 2000 than in either 1973 or 1983.

The message is that a theory of unemployment based on job losses caused by new technology would not be valid. Unemployment depends on economic and social factors. Broadly speaking, there are two aspects to bear in mind. The first deals with institutional arrangements in the labour market with regard to industrial relations, training and the terms on which unemployment benefits are made available (see Chapters 7 and 9). These are fundamental to the true 'tightness' of the labour market associated with any recorded level of unemployment and thus to the unemployment rate that is consistent with stable prices – the NAIRU or NON-ACCELERATING INFLATION RATE OF UNEMPLOYMENT. These arrangements affect how quickly unemployed people can find appropriate work and hence the rate of frictional unemployment, which underlies the natural rate of unemployment (NRU) (Chapter 13, Section 4.1). The NRU is the rate of unemployment to which the economy returns after each episode of expansionary monetary policy and accelerating inflation, for example after the movement from B to C in Figure 13.4. So the NRU is reached after a period of rising unemployment at a stable, or non-accelerating, inflation rate and is therefore related to the NAIRU. The term 'NAIRU' does not imply that unemployment is the outcome of voluntary choices by unemployed people waiting for a more appropriate job offer. Instead, it reflects the mutual consistency between wages and prices for both firms and workers. For firms, the prices they are setting for their products give an adequate mark-up over the wages they pay. For workers, the wages agreed are satisfactory, given the prices they face. This mutual consistency prevents any upward or downward pressure on prices and hence underlies a stable, non-accelerating inflation rate.

Institutional arrangements in the labour market influence both the NRU and the NAIRU. Industrial relations, training provision and the level and eligibility conditions of unemployment benefit affect the NRU. Social norms concerning the adequacy of

NON-ACCELERATING INFLATION RATE OF UNEMPLOYMENT
The non-accelerating inflation rate of unemployment (NAIRU) is the level of unemployment at which the inflation rate is constant.

mark-ups (and hence profits) for firms and real wages for workers influence the NAIRU. Since both sets of institutional arrangements have varied over time and across countries so have the NRU and the NAIRU.

The second factor to consider is demand. In order to sustain employment at the NAIRU, the output which is produced must be purchased: demand and supply must balance. In fact, demand fluctuates unpredictably from year to year, sometimes by large amounts as in times of adverse macroeconomic shocks such as in the Great Depression of the early 1930s or the OPEC oil price rises of the 1970s. Keynesian theories of unemployment claim that depressed demand is a key factor (Chapter 12). This is perhaps most plausible as an explanation of short-term fluctuations in the labour market but these can leave long-term 'echoes' if they lead to changes in the skill base of the labour force. Persistently high unemployment brings long-term unemployment with attrition of the skills and morale of unemployed people, which permanently reduces sustainable output.

1.2 HOW GOOD ARE STANDARD MEASURES OF MACROECONOMIC PERFORMANCE?

This question can be broken down into three parts:

1   Are the statistics that are commonly used measured accurately?

2   Are the right aspects of performance being measured?

3   What relative importance should be given to different aspects of performance?

Each of these deserves serious consideration.

From time to time there are debates about the accuracy of economic statistics. One reason for this is that politicians devise new ways of presenting data which are more favourable to the assessment of their policies, for example, the many changes to the official claimant count of UK unemployment in the 1980s. This is not, however, the central issue and in any case the scope for such activity is heavily constrained by international agreements to collect statistics, such as GDP and labour market measures, on a common definition. The data presented in Tables 20.1–20.5 have not been contaminated by political manipulation.

On the other hand, conventional methods of compiling the statistics may sometimes lead to misleading results. The best-known, and perhaps the most important, recent example of this kind of problem was highlighted by the report of the Boskin Commission in the USA (Boskin et al., 1996). The report examined the procedures used to calculate changes in the cost of living and concluded that in the mid 1990s inflation was being overestimated by about 1.1 percentage points per year. Some of the commission's concerns related simply to the sampling procedures in the collection of prices against a background of rapid changes in retailing. Other problems concerned the methods used to aggregate price changes for individual items into an overall index. Finally, and most importantly, the commission found that there was a failure to allow adequately for improvements in quality and to introduce new products into the index quickly enough (see Chapter 2).

The problems to which the Boskin Commission drew attention are not, of course, unique to the USA nor do they affect only the measurement of inflation. In fact, when inflation is wrongly measured so too is the growth of real GDP. The output of the economy is measured in terms of the sum of value added in the economy each year measured in current prices. To work out how much of the increase since the previous year is accounted for by greater volume of production and how much by higher prices, the figure in current prices is deflated by a price index and the result expressed as GDP in the prices of the base year (Chapter 8). A tendency to overestimate the rate of inflation therefore implies that the rate of economic growth will be underestimated by a similar amount.

Why should we measure macroeconomic performance at all? Presumably we care because it says something about economic welfare or well-being, and a very common use of the national income accounts is to compare standards of living either over time or across countries (Chapter 8). If this is the case, then there are genuine reasons for concern as to the accuracy of GDP measurement. The concept of GDP was originally devised as a way to measure changes in production, which would be useful for attempts to stabilize the level of economic activity and to assess the pressure of demand on productive resources in the market economy.

Even as a measure of production, GDP is inadequate in important respects. First, there is the existence of the 'shadow economy', that is, production of goods and services which could be bought and sold quite legally but which are hidden from the statistical agencies typically to avoid either taxation or regulation. Some estimates of this component of economic activity are shown in Table 20.6. By its very nature, the shadow economy is, of course, very difficult to quantify. The estimates in Table 20.6 are derived from the proposition that in general such transactions rely disproportionately on the use of cash and are based on inferences from changes in the demand for currency. They should be used with caution, as their authors frankly admit.

QUESTION

What are the implications of the estimates in Table 20.6 for the use of Tables 20.1 and 20.2?

The main feature of Table 20.6 is the general increase in the relative importance of the shadow economy in the last decades of the twentieth century. This implies that growth rates of real GDP are underestimated by conventional national income accounting and that the slow down after the European Golden Age was not quite as bad as official estimates suggest. However, since most countries are affected to a similar extent (about 0.4 to 0.5 percentage points per year), relative growth performance across countries is not seriously distorted by failing to take the shadow economy into account. Discrepancies in the relative size of the shadow economy between countries do change the rank order of the level of GDP per head; in 1999, for example, Belgium moves above Switzerland if these adjustments are applied. This underlines a general point: economic statistics are typically measured with error, but how much this matters depends on the question that is to be answered.

Table 20.6 Shadow economy as a percentage of GDP

	1960	1970	1980	1998
Australia				14.1
Austria	0.4	1.8	3.0	9.1
Belgium		10.4	16.4	22.6
Canada			10.6	15.0
Denmark	4.3	6.4	8.6	18.4
France		3.9	6.9	14.9
Germany	2.0	2.8	10.8	14.7
Greece				29.0
Hong Kong				13.0
Ireland		4.3	8.0	16.3
Italy		10.7	16.7	27.8
Japan				11.3
Netherlands		4.8	9.1	13.5
Norway	1.5	6.5	10.6	19.7
Singapore				13.0
South Korea				38.0
Spain		10.3	17.2	23.4
Sweden	1.6	7.3	12.2	20.0
Switzerland	1.2	4.1	6.5	8.0
Taiwan				16.5
UK		2.0	8.4	13.0
USA	3.1	3.6	5.0	8.9

Source: Schneider, 2000; for Hong Kong, Singapore, South Korea and
Taiwan (estimates for 1990), and Japan (estimate for 1997) from
Schneider and Enste, 2000; in some cases estimates are mid-point of
a range

Further, GDP does not include production such as housework and care of relatives
that would contribute to value added if it were performed in the context of a market
transaction (Chapter 8, Section 2). These activities are substantial relative to GDP; for
example, valued at industrial equivalent pay rates in a pioneering attempt at
measurement, in 1995 they comprised output equivalent to 56 per cent of the national
accounts total (Murgatroyd and Neuburger, 1997). If, as more married women have
participated in market work, household production activities have declined over time,
then growth as estimated by the national accounts concept is overstated.

National income, as famously defined by Hicks (1939), is the maximum amount that
can be consumed while leaving the capital stock intact. This essentially sees matters in

terms of sustainability and raises a series of issues taken up elsewhere in this book. Nevertheless, it reminds us that it is consumption rather than production that contributes to well-being and that GDP overstates potential consumption because it includes investment expenditures to make good depreciation.

This suggests that, in principle, it would be preferable to measure national income in terms of utility (that is, its value to consumers) rather than production, and just such an approach has been suggested by Nordhaus (2000) (see Chapter 8). This would have several important implications. First, it would imply that some aspects of GDP are 'bads' rather than 'goods', for example, reflecting the costs of commuting or making good environmental damage, as explained in Chapter 8, Section 2. Second, it would imply that we should explicitly recognize that the same GDP per head produced with less hours worked or with lower mortality risks represent superior outcomes. It would then be natural in looking at changes of living standards over time to ask how much extra consumption of final goods included in GDP would be needed to compensate people for giving up gains in leisure and/or life expectancy. Given that in the UK hours worked per year in full-time employment have nearly halved and life expectancy at birth has nearly doubled since 1870, it is plausible that growth of real GDP per person significantly understates gains in living standards over that period (Crafts, 1997).

QUESTION

Which is better: a fast growth economy with high unemployment or a low growth economy with low unemployment?

Presumably everyone would agree that a fast growth economy with low unemployment is to be preferred to either of these eventualities but the options on offer are each better on one indicator but worse on the other. The answer that people give to the question will depend on how big the differences are in each aspect of performance and how much they value each outcome, in other words, what trade-off they would make between unemployment and growth if that is the choice with which they are confronted. Politicians are likely to view such a trade-off in terms of votes won and lost and at least in Britain their implied assessment seems to have varied over time; for example, in the Thatcher period growth was accorded relatively more weight compared with unemployment than had been the case previously (Crafts, 2002).

Is it possible to devise a weighting scheme based on empirical grounds as opposed to value judgements or political considerations? Probably not, but there is some evidence to hand in the form of responses to opinion polls which ask questions about happiness. Analysis of these data by Blanchflower and Oswald (2001) results in an estimate that to compensate an unemployed American man for lack of work would require on average a payment of US$60 000 per year. This suggests that, when there is a trade-off at the margin, policies designed to make labour markets work better should be a higher priority for policy makers than those aimed at improving productivity growth of those already in work.

One further important point to note is that over the long run economic growth has not been associated with increasing happiness in OECD countries; on the contrary, levels of happiness reported to the opinion pollsters have tended to decline slightly since the 1970s. The best interpretation of this seems to be that aspirations tend to increase with income (Easterlin, 2001). This means that threatened with a reduction to past income levels people would see that as making them worse off and regard the prospect of future growth as making them better off. But it is better to travel hopefully than to arrive.

2   MACROECONOMIC MANAGEMENT: SOME PERENNIAL PROBLEMS •

In an ideal world what would macroeconomic management achieve? The answer might be to maintain price stability at the NAIRU with the level of output consistent with these objectives. The requirement for this would be to smooth out fluctuations in demand that push economic activity away from this equilibrium level. In the short run, excessive demand causes output to rise above and unemployment to fall below the optimum and is associated with rising inflation, while the opposite is true for inadequate demand. In the long run, if demand growth, fuelled perhaps by excessive creation of money, is persistently above the growth of production there will be persistent inflation which becomes generally anticipated and the economy will return to the NAIRU. Thus the long-run macroeconomic management task would be to ensure that the growth of purchasing power matches the growth of productive potential in the economy.

2.1   TAYLOR RULES

The government can influence the pressure of demand in the economy through a number of policy instruments including both monetary and fiscal policy. In situations where demand needs to be restrained, the options are to raise interest rates and/or tax rates and/or reduce government expenditure. If demand needs to be raised, the menu of policy options comprises the reverse of these actions. In the so-called Keynesian era of the 1950s and 1960s, there was widespread belief in governments' ability to undertake 'fine-tuning' of demand and achieve good outcomes both in terms of low inflation and low unemployment. The experience of the 1970s and 1980s made this earlier faith seem illusory. In the 1990s, however, when, across the OECD, monetary policy was increasingly delegated to central banks with 'constrained discretion', successful macroeconomic management once again seemed within the realms of possibility.

The 'constrained discretion' that central banks exercise in conducting monetary policy usually means in practice that they follow a monetary policy rule linking interest rates to macroeconomic variables such as the inflation rate and the level of aggregate demand (Chapter 13, Section 5.1). These are sometimes known as Taylor Rules, after the US economist John B. Taylor who proposed a rule for the US central bank (Taylor, 1994).

QUESTION

Recalling the discussions of monetary policy in Chapters 12 (Section 4.2) and 13 (Section 5.1), when do you think the central bank is likely to raise interest rates and when is it likely to reduce them?

The central bank is likely to raise interest rates if the inflation rate is forecast to rise above an upper limit usually set by the government, because higher interest rates will reduce investment, aggregate demand and inflation. The central bank is likely to reduce interest rates if the level of aggregate demand is forecast to fall below that which is required to keep the economy operating reasonably close to full employment (or the NAIRU), because lower interest rates will increase investment, aggregate demand and reduce unemployment. A Taylor Rule for the nominal interest rate on loans, r, that embodied these two principles might look like this:

$$r = \pi + 1.5(\pi - \pi^*) + 0.5(Y - Y^*)$$

Since it is the real interest rate that influences investment decisions, the nominal interest rate, r, must first respond to the inflation rate, π. It must also respond to any deviation of inflation, π, above its target rate, π^*, the coefficient on that deviation is greater than 1 to ensure that, if inflation picks up, real interest rates increase. The final part of the equation can be read as saying that for each percentage point that output Y falls below the level associated with the NAIRU, Y^*, interest rates fall by half a percentage point.

Although demand management can play a key role in stabilization of prices and in reducing the severity of economic fluctuations, these days supply-side policy instruments are rightly regarded as the key to achieving a lower NAIRU and a higher rate of long-term economic growth. With regard to the former, microeconomic labour market policies relating to training, welfare programmes and industrial relations are at the heart of the matter; while with regard to the latter, policies that influence the incentives to invest and/or to innovate, such as competition policy and addressing market failures in research and development, are central. Having said that, it does seem to be the case that macroeconomic instability in the form of pronounced business-cycle fluctuations does have an adverse effect on long-term growth through adverse effects on the rate of investment (Oulton, 1995) and severe recessions can provoke policy responses which are damaging to the supply-side so that good macroeconomic management may have a bonus in terms of raising medium-term productive potential.

QUESTION

Why has demand management not delivered better results (see Tables 20.3 and 20.4)?

Successful demand management depends on a great deal of accurate information and the ability to act quickly if need be. The latter tends to be much more possible if interest rates are the main policy instrument rather than adjustments to tax and government spending. The most obvious reason is that the policy makers are blown off course by unpredictable macroeconomic shocks.

If these are big and unpleasant enough, there may be no way to achieve a satisfactory outcome quickly. Broadly speaking, this is true of the exceptional situation facing OECD countries in the 1970s when oil prices quadrupled in the first and then doubled in the second OPEC shock. The impacts of these events were 'stagflationary' in that they pushed inflation up while also reducing domestic demand. In the short term, the choice was how much extra inflation and/or unemployment to accept; attempting to stop prices rising through reducing demand would push unemployment up still further.

Referring to the Taylor Rule as set out above, a more pervasive problem is to know how big the output gap is, given that the underlying rate of productivity growth may vary over time and the NAIRU itself will respond to changes in labour market arrangements. In retrospect, this was a major aspect of the 1970s inflation both in the UK and the USA. Towards the end of the Golden Age in the UK, productivity growth slowed down, wage bargaining became less centralized and benefits more generous. At the time, economic policy makers failed to appreciate the implications of these developments and so allowed excessive demand growth; econometric analysis suggests that this may have been responsible for as much as half of UK inflation in the 1970s (Nelson and Nikolov, 2001). But the pleasant surprises of the 1990s have also posed problems with regard to the output gap, especially in the USA in the context of the so-called new economy in which the ICT revolution stimulated productivity growth but also created great uncertainty about how big its medium-term impact would be. This is discussed further in Section 5.2.

2.2 INFLATIONARY BIAS

If there are 'cock-up' reasons for poor macroeconomic management, are there also 'conspiracy' aspects? There is indeed a serious problem in that encouraging policy makers to use discretionary intervention creates the opportunity for misuse of policy for short-term political ends. In general, the problem is one of 'inflationary bias'. This is the conclusion of the influential Barro–Gordon model (Barro and Gordon, 1983). The Barro–Gordon argument is captured in simplified form in the pay-off matrix of Figure 20.1. (You might want to refer to the discussion of the pay-off matrix in Chapter 6.) The public is assumed to be worse off if inflation deviates from its expected rate. The government gains by raising demand to create surprise inflation which lowers unemployment as workers temporarily believe that real wages have risen. Conversely, creating lower than expected inflation hurts the government because it raises

Figure 20.1
The Barro–Gordon model

		Public	
		zero expected inflation	high expected inflation
Government	zero actual inflation	0, 0	–2, –1
	high actual inflation	1, –1	–1, 0

unemployment. The government loses from higher anticipated inflation which annoys voters with no compensating output gain because real wages are predicted correctly.

EXERCISE 20.1

With reference to the Barro–Gordon model and Figure 20.1 answer the following questions.

1   Given the pay-offs, explain why it is better for the government to have inflation.

2   Would you believe a promise by the government not to create inflation?

3   Which cell of the matrix shows the outcome if the public have rational expectations?

The example is of a situation where the government has a dominant strategy: high inflation is better for it whatever the public expects (compare the government pay-offs under either zero or high expected inflation). The implication of the example is that governments will break promises not to create inflation. We should expect that the government's optimal strategy will be anticipated by the public and will thus lead to inflation without raising output – ending up in the bottom right-hand cell. If the government can make binding commitments about inflation through a rule that cannot be broken, the problem would be avoided. This is because there would be no possibility of imagining that surprise inflation could benefit the government; hence rules are better than discretionary demand management according to this line of argument (see Chapter 17).

What are the downside risks of committing yourself to a policy rule? The most obvious is that it is no longer possible to respond to adverse demand shocks. In other words, there may be a trade-off between the welfare losses from inflation if discretion exists for the government and from possible unemployment if there are rules that bind the government. Even more worrying is the possibility that, if the 'wrong sort of shock' occurs, the policy rule may exacerbate its effects. A graphic example of these problems, discussed in Section 3.2 and in Chapter 16, can be found in the consequences of remaining on the Gold Standard in the Great Depression.

Fixed exchange rates are one way to eliminate discretion and thus to address the issue of inflationary bias (Chapter 16). In a world of capital mobility, maintaining a fixed exchange rate implies that independent monetary policy is not possible since arbitrage will force interest rates at home and abroad to be the same. Since the end of the Bretton Woods era in 1971, a world of generally floating exchange rates has permitted independent monetary policy to coexist with international capital mobility. The conduct of that monetary policy has increasingly been delegated to central banks, who are given an inflation target rather than strict instructions as to how to achieve it, and are not seeking votes for re-election. Their lack of immediate democratic accountability is an antidote to inflationary bias and constitutes a form of pre-commitment by the government.

Such arrangements are still vulnerable to adverse external shocks such as those of the 1970s, however. Given a serious oil price increase, an attempt to stick rigidly to a pre-existing inflation target would imply an episode of high unemployment. This might lead to calls for the return of discretionary policy since delegation to the central bank is not an irrevocable act. Alternatively, there has to be some mechanism for temporarily adjusting or suspending the inflation target.

2.3   COMMON PROBLEMS

In sum, macroeconomic policy is formulated by economists whose understanding is limited by an inability to perform controlled laboratory experiments and by governments who wish to get re-elected. All this makes policy errors only too likely. More specifically, the key problem areas which lead to departures from the equilibrium position are:

- the exercise of discretion by short-termist politicians
- unwelcome shocks from abroad
- relying on an *ex post* unfortunate policy rule
- incomplete information and forecasting errors.

Damaging consequences ensue because the economy has rigidities that prevent markets clearing immediately (Chapter 17).

3   CASE STUDIES OF STABILIZATION FAILURE   • • • • • • • • •

This section reviews some episodes of macroeconomic crisis. The historical notes provided are, of course, no more than thumbnail sketches and are written so as to illuminate and extend key ideas introduced above. References are given to more comprehensive accounts.

3.1   GERMAN HYPERINFLATION, 1918–23

The inflation in early 1920s Germany is deservedly famous. By the end of November 1923 a one-kilo loaf of rye bread cost 428 billion marks. At the end of the war in 1918, currency in circulation was 33 billion marks; this had grown to 608 million trillion marks by December 1923. (The most useful academic study for macroeconomists remains that of Webb, 1989.) Table 20.7 displays some details of the inflationary experience.

Several features of Table 20.7 should be noted:

- the inflation stopped, restarted and then accelerated spectacularly
- during the inflation the government ran huge budget deficits, yet the real value of its outstanding debt was almost completely wiped out
- although we know the nominal money supply had soared, prices had risen much more so that the real money supply fell dramatically.

Table 20.7 Hyperinflation in Weimar Germany

	Wholesale prices (1913 = 1)	Real M0 (1913 = 1)	Real government debt (1913 billion marks)	Real budget deficit (1913 billion marks)
1919I	2.74	2.63	54.1	1.50
1919II	3.08	2.49	50.0	3.39
1919III	4.93	1.59	32.1	1.98
1919IV	8.03	1.18	17.3	0.78
1920I	17.09	0.65	10.9	0.35
1920II	13.82	0.93	14.2	1.19
1920III	14.98	0.91	14.8	1.65
1920IV	14.40	1.03	16.0	0.74
1921I	13.38	1.07	17.5	0.20
1921II	13.66	1.12	18.4	1.82
1921III	20.67	0.82	12.4	1.23
1921IV	34.87	0.65	8.70	0.92
1922I	54.33	0.47	5.62	0.50
1922II	70.20	0.45	4.15	0.30
1922III	287	0.22	1.20	0.58
1922IV	1475	0.17	0.95	0.83
1923I	4888	0.23	1.30	1.05
1923II	19 385	0.22	0.68	1.09
1923III	23 900 000	0.26	0.47	2.64
1923IV	1 261 600 000 000	0.09	0.21	1.93

Source: Holtfrerich, 1983; Webb, 1986, 1989

In a proximate sense the inflation resulted from the massive rise in the money supply and the excess demand for goods that this provoked. As inflationary expectations took hold, people tried to avoid holding money. This added further to the inflationary pressure and is reflected in the falling value of M0 (the narrowest form of money consisting of notes and coins and reserves held by the banks with the central bank) as the price level rose even faster than the money supply (Chapter 11, Section 3.3). Webb rightly points to more deep-seated causes:

> The inflation did not happen because the Reichsbank's printing press had a faulty tachometer. It happened because the German government faced irreconcilable demands from labour, industry, and the Allies. The German government chose the policies that led to inflation because they appeared to offer lesser evils in the short run.

> (Webb, 1989, p.v)

As might be expected, the policy regime in place during the hyperinflation did not contain rules to discipline politicians. There was a floating exchange rate and, unlike the post-Second World War Bundesbank, the Reichsbank was not independent and freely purchased government debt, thereby translating the government deficit into the monetary base of the economy. The public recognized that this created inflation and rational expectations of inflation increased when additional public expenditure unmatched by new taxes was announced.

Early Weimar governments were coalitions of centrist parties threatened by extremists on both the left and the right. Raising additional taxation was extremely difficult politically. Nevertheless, by 1920, sufficient had been done to persuade the financial markets that the public finances and thus monetary growth were basically under control. In May 1921 the Allies demanded reparations (compensation for the costs of the First World War) amounting to an initial flow of about 10 per cent of national income. When it became clear that taxes were not to be further increased, monetary growth and inflationary expectations were revived. Stabilization was delayed because there was something akin to the war of attrition now familiar to the political economy literature (Rodrik, 1996) over who should bear the costs. Failure fully to meet reparations payments then provoked, in 1923, the French invasion of the Ruhr and the final acceleration of inflation with excess demand now exacerbated by falling production.

QUESTION

Stabilization was achieved and hyperinflation ceased at the end of 1923. Reviewing the above and the ideas of Section 2, what would have been required to bring this about?

The basic ingredient had to be a credible commitment by government to curtail its borrowing and the monetization of its debt. In turn, this had to seem less painful politically than the alternative of continuing to slide further into economic collapse. The stabilization was achieved by a return to the fixed exchange rate Gold Standard system, by the introduction of strict limits on purchases of government debt by the Reichsbank, and, conditional on this, by the 1924 Dawes Plan which reduced reparations and provided a large international loan.

3.2   THE GREAT DEPRESSION OF THE EARLY 1930s

The Wall Street Crash of October 1929 and the slump which followed it are legendary. Naturally such momentous events raise a huge range of issues in the historical literature. Here the focus is narrowed to three related questions which illuminate the abstract arguments of Section 2. These are:

1   Why did output decline so dramatically in the USA?

2   What were the implications of the US slump for other countries?

3   Why did Britain escape so lightly by comparison?

Table 20.8 The UK and the USA in the Great Depression

	GDP	Exports	Consumption	Investment	Price level	M0	M3	Equity prices
UK								
1929	4216	986	3765	461	100	558	2542	113
1930	4210	849	3822	463	99.6	565	2549	91
1931	3980	684	3863	454	97.2	555	2523	71
1932	4008	669	3839	396	93.7	560	2571	68
1933	4046	678	3937	409	92.5	613	2782	84
1934	4334	704	4051	498	91.7	627	2721	102
1935	4496	794	4163	518	92.6	626	2874	113
1936	4633	771	4285	565	93.1	658	3080	131
1937	4834	810	4357	584	96.6	699	3205	122
USA								
1929	104.4	5.2	79.0	16.2	100	7.1	46.2	260.2
1930	95.1	4.0	74.7	10.5	96	6.9	45.2	210.3
1931	89.5	2.9	72.2	6.8	85	7.3	41.7	136.6
1932	76.4	2.1	66.0	0.8	77	7.8	34.8	69.3
1933	74.2	2.2	64.6	0.3	75	8.2	30.8	89.6
1934	80.8	2.7	68.0	1.8	80	9.1	33.3	98.4
1935	91.4	2.8	72.3	8.8	79	10.7	38.4	106.0
1936	100.9	3.0	79.7	9.3	82	12.2	42.9	154.7
1937	109.1	4.0	82.6	14.6	83	13.4	45.0	154.1

Note: components of aggregate demand in £, 1938 million (UK) and in $, 1929 billion (USA); money supply measures in £ million (UK) and $ billion (USA); equity prices 1938 = 100 (UK) and 1941/43 = 100 (USA)

Source: Mitchell, 1988; US Bureau of the Census, 1960; Capie and Collins, 1983; Temin, 1976

Among major countries, the slump in the USA was the most and that in the UK the least severe of the 1930s. Table 20.8 shows that US prices and output both fell abruptly during 1929–33. The contraction in the money supply and investment were both pronounced and most famous of all was the collapse of stock market prices. (A useful textbook treatment can be found in Hall and Ferguson, 1998.)

It is generally accepted that the American Great Depression resulted primarily from demand shocks and that errors in monetary policy played a major role in precipitating the crisis. It is clear, however, that output fell by more than can be explained simply by a money supply shock by itself (Bernanke, 1983). Precise attribution of the relative importance of the various components of the demand shock is still highly controversial. Factors which undoubtedly mattered included uncertainty linked with the volatile behaviour of stock prices which, together with rising real debts, hit consumer spending, and in addition house-building investment was drastically curtailed as earlier overbuilding was corrected.

The USA also experienced a major financial crisis culminating in 1933 when over 3000 banks failed. This engendered a 'scramble for liquidity' as the public sought to convert bank deposits into cash and further contracted the money supply. M3 (a broad measure of money defined in Chapter 11, Section 3.3) fell rather than M0. The supply of loans was curtailed as banks were forced to hold higher reserves and collateral dried up (Calomiris and Wilson, 1998). The problems of a fragile banking system were a strong testimony to the weakness of bank regulation in the USA as the Roosevelt Administration's subsequent legislation underlined.

Initially, very restrictive monetary policy sought to restrain the stock market boom of the late 1920s. When recession set in policy was slow to respond but in any event was effectively precluded by membership of the Gold Standard, especially from autumn 1931 to spring 1933. Recovery came after leaving gold and was stimulated by the subsequent vigorous monetary expansion (Romer, 1992) which stands out in Table 20.8.

What stood in the way of better policy making? To an extent problems resulted from lack of appropriate data and experience. More fundamentally, the decentralized decision-making structure of the Federal Reserve System (central bank) made decisive and rapid counter-cyclical monetary policy very difficult and commitment to a strict policy rule in the form of the fixed exchange rate severely limited freedom of action (Eichengreen, 1992).

How did all this affect other countries? Most obviously it cut back demand for other countries exports and curtailed US foreign lending, thus undermining balance of payments positions abroad. More subtly, but more importantly, impacts came through the Gold Standard system of fixed exchange rates based on convertibility of currencies into gold, as the excellent introductory analysis by Newell and Symons (1988) reveals.

Deflation in the large US economy led to the prices of internationally traded goods falling generally by about 25 per cent between 1929 and 1932. Restrictive US monetary policy had to be matched by other countries to protect convertibility and the fixed exchange rate and exposed other fragile banking systems to bank failures (Grossman, 1994). Unilateral expansionary initiatives, whether monetary or fiscal, threatened the exchange rate via their implications for the balance of payments and were thus precluded by the Gold Standard. Restoration of internal balance and international competitiveness needed large falls in both prices and wages but wage adjustments were far too sluggish to play this role (Bernanke and Carey, 1996).

In these circumstances, in the absence of co-ordinated international monetary expansion, leaving the Gold Standard and allowing the currency to depreciate made a lot of sense. This restored policy makers' discretion to use stabilization policy, permitted unilateral monetary expansion and interest rate cuts, and removed the need for further falls in prices and wages. Figure 20.2 shows clearly the different outcomes for countries that left the Gold Standard, such as Sweden, whose exchange rate fell and whose economy recovered, and for countries that persevered with the Gold Standard, such as France, who remained mired in depression with an unchanged exchange rate. In 1925, returning to the Gold Standard had looked highly desirable as a rule that would prevent inflation; thinking of the German experience of hyperinflation, the Governor of the Bank of England called it 'knave proof'. By 1931, adherence to this policy rule in the face of the shock of the world depression inflicted deep wounds, and discretion in economic policy seemed much more desirable.

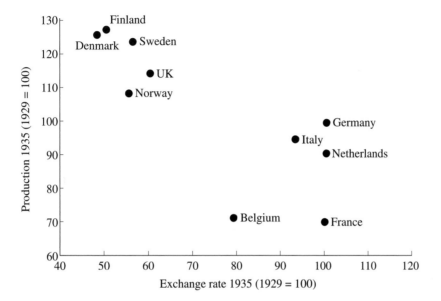

Figure 20.2
Changes in exchange rates and industrial production, 1929–35

Source: Eichengreen and Sachs, 1985

The UK experienced a relatively early recovery. This is despite the apparent downward inflexibility of money wages much remarked by contemporaries. Moreover, Keynesian demand stimulus through fiscal policy was not pursued in the early 1930s. Compared with the USA, the favourable circumstances were rather to be found in being forced out of the Gold Standard in September 1931, in the absence of bank failures and in much more buoyant investment opportunities in house building. Accordingly, Table 20.8 shows that M3 fell only very slightly in 1930–31 and rose appreciably in 1932–33, while prices fell much less than in the USA.

Changes in economic policy included imposition of a general tariff on manufactures and encouragement to firms to collude to raise prices and restore profitability. After 1935, rearmament provided a significant fiscal stimulus. Unfortunately, the general implication of these policy moves was to reduce the competitive pressures on British firms to make productivity improvements (Broadberry and Crafts, 1992). This is quite a good example of how recessionary shocks can impact via induced policy responses on future trend growth (Section 4).

QUESTION

> **Why was the aftermath of the 1987 stock market crash so different from that in 1929?**

The Wall Street Crash is often talked of as the reason for the Great Depression. Clearly, this is too simplistic given the different experience 60 years later when there was no subsequent decline in economic activity. This section suggests some reasons why the late 1980s did not see a repeat of the early 1930s. Most obviously, the policy response was very different. Mindful of the lessons of the earlier experience, monetary authorities around the world co-ordinated an immediate easing of monetary policy in response. Equally important, the world was not locked into the Gold Standard. Finally, it is very doubtful that in the absence of restrictive monetary policy the 1929 Crash would have had devastating consequences for the US economy.

3.3   THE ASIAN CRISIS OF 1997–98

The so-called Asian tigers were the most spectacular growth success stories of the last quarter of the twentieth century (see Tables 20.1 and 20.2). The 'developmental state' approach taken by countries such as South Korea, Singapore and Taiwan was much praised for its blend of market economics supplemented by government intervention to address capital market failures and to mobilize high levels of investment; it was heralded by the World Bank (1993) as *The East Asian Miracle*. Against this background, the crisis of 1997–98, which was marked both by large falls in real GDP and massive currency depreciations, was a tremendous shock to most observers. The shock was compounded by the absence of the usual warning signs of macroeconomic distress in the form of fiscal deficits, soaring inflation or balance of payments problems. Yet, as we shall see, the crisis was not an aberration or an indicator of the capriciousness of financial markets but had its roots in badly designed economic policies.

The policy mix that had prevailed in the region during the early 1990s was based on exchange rates pegged to the dollar together with financial liberalization that saw large foreign capital inflows and the build up of a great deal of short-term foreign debt denominated in dollars. The period was one of investment boom which, at least in retrospect, was characterized by excessive risk taking and in which tendencies to overheating could not easily be dealt with by macroeconomic stabilization measures, since the fixed exchange rate removed the option to use monetary policy and a big fiscal squeeze was out of the question. A clear description of this episode and its implications is in Corbett and Vines (1999). Why did output decline so much in 1998? The proximate reasons were a very sharp outflow of foreign capital, a severe contraction of credit availability and with it investment, and a large fall in wealth combined with a loss of consumer confidence that deterred consumer spending (Berg, 1999).

QUESTION

Consider the data presented in Table 20.9. What macroeconomic or financial variables seem to be most closely correlated with slump of output and collapse of the exchange rate?

The answer is that signs of fragility of the banking system in the form of loans that could not be serviced and weak regulation are the key to vulnerability in East Asian countries in 1997/98. This problem was not by any means universal – it did not apply to Hong Kong, Singapore or Taiwan – but it was of huge significance in South Korea

Table 20.9 Aspects of the Asian crisis

(a) Growth rates (% per year)

	1996	1997	1998	1999	1997/98 exchange rate fall (%)
Hong Kong	4.5	5.0	−5.3	3.0	0
Indonesia	8.0	4.5	−13.1	0.8	77
Malaysia	10.0	7.3	−7.4	6.1	35
Philippines	5.8	5.2	−0.6	3.4	32
Singapore	7.7	8.5	0.1	5.9	12
South Korea	6.8	5.0	−6.7	10.9	34
Taiwan	6.1	6.7	4.6	5.4	13
Thailand	5.9	−1.4	−10.8	4.2	36

(b) Pre-crisis danger signs

	Fiscal surplus (% GDP)	Current account (% GDP)	Real exchange rate (1990 = 100)	Non-performing loans (%)	Banking regulation rank
Hong Kong	1.9	−1.2	145	4	2
Indonesia	1.4	−2.8	108	17	6
Malaysia	3.6	−7.6	112	16	3=
Philippines	−0.9	−4.6	122	14	3=
Singapore	2.4	16.3	122	4	1
South Korea	0.1	−2.7	98	16	5
Taiwan	0.3	3.2	95	4	n/a
Thailand	1.0	−7.2	112	19	7

Source: Burnside *et al.*, 1999; Caprio, 1998; IMF, 2000

and Thailand. The implication for these countries was that financial liberalization entailed substantial risks and this should not be particularly surprising given that, across the world, financial liberalization is frequently a leading indicator of financial crisis (Goldstein *et al.*, 2000).

The impetus to financial liberalization and, in particular, a prominent role for foreign capital came from a shift away from a heavy state involvement in industrial finance towards greater reliance on the market as development moved beyond the early stages. Handled well, this promised a better allocation of resources and access to more funds without having to sacrifice domestic consumption. But the banking system is notoriously prone to market failure from problems of incomplete and asymmetric information which can give rise to excessive risk-taking because no one has sufficient incentive to monitor bank lending behaviour, especially if deposits are guaranteed (implicitly or explicitly) by the government. To address such problems typically requires strict regulation that insists on capital adequacy, transparent accounting and risk management. This was noticeably absent in the countries which experienced financial crises (Mishkin, 1999).

What precipitated the events of 1997–98? The answer seems to be an increasing realization that the balance sheets of the financial institutions were becoming stretched, combined with a fear that governments either might not be able to honour the guarantees that underpinned the banking system or were facing massive fiscal deficits if they did. Either was sufficient to trigger capital flight and a currency crisis (Burnside *et al.*, 1999). A big devaluation would, however, only make matters worse in the financial system since it raised the value of all the foreign claims in terms of home currency.

In some ways this story is reminiscent of the experience of the USA in the early 1930s. Badly designed macroeconomic policy combined with a poorly regulated financial system was in each case a lethal mixture in economies which had a strong growth potential. There are differences, however. In the US case there were no guarantees to depositors and the country was a net exporter of capital and devaluation was an unmitigated blessing.

3.4   A PERSPECTIVE ON THE CASE STUDIES

The three examples above comprise a set of examples of desperate failure of macroeconomic stabilization policies. They are, of course, exceptional episodes and do not represent anything like the average experience. A marked contrast will be found in the happy experience of the 'Golden Age' (1950–73) which is reviewed in Section 5.1. These examples do, however, illustrate the scope for things to go very badly wrong. As such, they put in perspective the much smaller failings that have damaged the reputation of British governments, for example, in the mid 1970s or early 1990s.

In sum, two themes stand out in the case studies:

- there is a crucial recurrent question of the choice of an appropriate policy framework to limit policy-makers' freedom of action; both complete discretion and badly chosen rules can do great damage

- adverse shocks can reveal the flaws in financial systems with devastating consequences for macroeconomic stability as they overwhelm the ability of policy makers to respond; a high standard of financial regulation is crucial to complement conventional monetary and fiscal policy instruments.

4   INTERACTIONS BETWEEN TREND GROWTH AND STABILIZATION POLICY

Long-run growth in output per worker results from capital accumulation and technological progress. Decisions to invest and/or to innovate depend on expected rates of return and are thus influenced by the economic environment. Important aspects of this include the supply of complementary factor inputs, such as human capital and infrastructure, and the stability of the economy as well as more immediate business concerns such as taxes and subsidies, the structure of industrial relations and the availability of finance. In firms where managers are not well-controlled by their shareholders, pressure of competition is likely to be important in keeping management on its toes in terms of rapid implementation of cost reducing innovations.

At the same time, understanding how fast growth in labour productivity will be over the medium term is central to assessing the output gap and thus to implementing Taylor Rules for demand management (Section 2). Labour productivity growth also determines how much wages can increase without leading to price inflation and/or reduced profits for employers. In periods when labour productivity growth is low relative to real wage aspirations, the level of unemployment required to keep wages consistent with normal profits, that is, the NAIRU, is increased. Conversely, when labour productivity growth is high relative to real wage aspirations, the level of unemployment required to keep wages consistent with normal profits is reduced.

Accordingly, there are several important potential interactions between stabilization policy and trend growth. For example, a badly designed policy that creates uncertainty and volatility is likely to reduce investment and growth (Ramey and Ramey, 1995). Severe recessions and financial crises have in the past led to protectionist and regulationist policy responses that have reduced the degree of competition and supply of finance. Conversely, the achievement of a credible agreement between workers and employers that delivers wage moderation in return for high investment might be expected to promote both a low NAIRU and faster growth (Eichengreen, 1996). As was noted earlier, the surprise of the productivity slow down in the 1970s was important in derailing stabilization policy at that time.

This section looks at the historical record in the light of these points. In order to do so, it is necessary first to build up some basic ideas about both the proximate sources and also the underlying determinants of long-run economic growth. This will also enable us to consider comparative growth performance both over time and across countries. This will prepare the way for case studies of the Golden Age of European growth and the new economy of the 1990s in the following section.

4.1   THE PROXIMATE SOURCES OF GROWTH

Growth in real income and output per person requires increases in labour productivity. In turn, these result from the use of extra capital per person and from additions to total factor productivity (TFP) which accrues from greater efficiency in the use of factors of production (obtained via better technology, improved organization of production and so on). Increases in the amount of capital available come from net investment which should be thought of in a broad sense to include investment not only in plant, equipment, etc. but also in the skills and expertise of the labour force, that is, in human capital.

Technological progress is the main driving force for long-run growth in labour productivity. This has both an embodied and a disembodied component. The former arrives in new varieties of capital goods (such as steam engines in the eighteenth century and computers in the twentieth century) while the latter can be thought of as making possible additional output from existing factors of production (such as occurred with the reorganization of factories that electrification made possible) which lead to growth of TFP.

These proximate sources of growth explain how growth comes about but not why. More fundamental reasons for why growth rates differ relate to the determinants of international differences in capital accumulation strategies and in real cost reduction. These are to be found in incentive structures, institutions and political decision making which are discussed in Section 4.2.

Growth accounting techniques provide a systematic framework to quantify the proximate sources of growth and some results are displayed in Table 20.10. Growth accounting seeks to assess the contributions of capital and labour to output growth, and then it attributes the remaining growth to TFP growth. TFP growth comes from greater efficiency of factor use. The theory behind growth accounting is set out formally below.

The increase in output due to increased capital equals the change in the amount of capital employed, ΔK, multiplied by its marginal product, $\dfrac{\Delta Y}{\Delta K}$, and the increase in output due to using more labour equals the change in the amount of labour employed, ΔL, multiplied by its marginal product, $\dfrac{\Delta Y}{\Delta L}$. So the total increase in output due to changes of both kinds is:

$$\Delta Y = \left(\frac{\Delta Y}{\Delta K}\right)\Delta K + \left(\frac{\Delta Y}{\Delta L}\right)\Delta L \tag{1}$$

Dividing through by the level of output, the rate of growth of output, $\dfrac{\Delta Y}{Y}$, is given by:

$$\frac{\Delta Y}{Y} = \left(\frac{\Delta Y}{\Delta K}\right)\left(\frac{K}{Y}\right)\left(\frac{\Delta K}{K}\right) + \left(\frac{\Delta Y}{\Delta L}\right)\left(\frac{L}{Y}\right)\left(\frac{\Delta L}{L}\right) \tag{2}$$

where the first term on the right-hand side has been multiplied top and bottom by K (leaving it unchanged) and the second term top and bottom by L (leaving it unchanged). If factors receive their marginal products as they would if all markets conformed to the model of perfect competition, then

$$\frac{\Delta Y}{\Delta K} = \text{the rate of return on capital}$$

So

$$\left(\frac{\Delta Y}{\Delta K}\right)\left(\frac{K}{Y}\right) = \text{the share of profits in national income}$$

Similarly

$$\left(\frac{\Delta Y}{\Delta L}\right)\left(\frac{L}{Y}\right) = \text{the share of wages in national income}$$

Equation (2) shows that the rate of growth of output, $\frac{\Delta Y}{Y}$, is a weighted sum of $\frac{\Delta K}{K}$, the rate of growth of capital, and $\frac{\Delta L}{L}$, the rate of growth of labour, where the weights or 'coefficients' are given by the respective shares of capital and labour in national income. So the share of profits in national income, $\left(\frac{\Delta Y}{\Delta K}\right)\left(\frac{K}{Y}\right)$, gives the coefficient on the growth rate of capital, and the share of wages in national income, $\left(\frac{\Delta Y}{\Delta L}\right)\left(\frac{L}{Y}\right)$, gives the coefficient on the growth rate of labour. These coefficients can be interpreted as the percentage growth in national income that a 1 per cent growth in capital (or labour) would produce. That these coefficients equal the respective shares of capital and labour in national income has been found to be a reasonable approximation in empirical work which for the recent past has found a coefficient of 0.3 on $\frac{\Delta K}{K}$ and of 0.7 on $\frac{\Delta L}{L}$. The TFP growth is then calculated as a residual, the excess of actual growth over that predicted by filling in the values of the right-hand side of equation (2).

The formula to account for growth of labour productivity is:

$$\Delta y = \alpha \Delta k + \text{TFP growth}$$

where the lower case symbols represent output per labour input (y) and capital per labour input (k) and α is the share of profits in national income. The first term on the right-hand side is known as the contribution of capital-deepening.

A number of problems with this approach have been much discussed. The most serious is the treatment of human capital. In principle, this can be incorporated into growth of the labour input and when this is done the usual method is to adjust for years of schooling and the extra wages that workers gain from education. Any improvements in labour quality not measured by adjustments to the quantity of the labour input will end up in residual TFP growth, as in the estimates of Table 20.10.

QUESTION

Consider the estimates reported in Table 20.10. How do the growth accounts for 1950–73 compare with those for other periods?

The period 1950–73 is commonly referred to as the 'Golden Age' of European growth and this is reflected in West Germany's productivity growth in these years. This resulted from a relatively strong contribution from capital accumulation but especially from extraordinary TFP growth. More detailed investigation suggests that this owed a good deal to reconstruction which put the capital stock (most of which survived the Second World War intact) back to work as, for example, the transport system was rehabilitated. On top of this, Germany gained from improved efficiency as the economy was opened up to freer trade and agriculture contracted, and from the emulation of US technology. The key feature of these years was the reduction of a large US productivity lead that had built up in the first half of the twentieth century. The

Table 20.10 Accounting for labour productivity growth (% per year)

	UK	Germany	USA
1871–1911			
Labour productivity growth	0.80	1.40	1.60
Capital deepening	*0.45*	*0.55*	*1.35*
Total factor productivity	*0.35*	*0.85*	*0.25*
1911–37			
Labour productivity growth	0.90	1.10	1.10
Capital deepening	*0.20*	*0.10*	*0.30*
Total factor productivity	*0.70*	*1.00*	*0.80*
1950–73			
Labour productivity growth	2.99	5.18	2.34
Capital deepening	*1.69*	*1.20*	*0.68*
Total factor productivity	*1.30*	*3.98*	*1.66*
1973–99			
Labour productivity growth	2.13	2.29	1.08
Capital deepening	*0.90*	*0.65*	*0.65*
Total factor productivity	*1.23*	*1.64*	*0.43*

Source: 1871–1937 derived worksheets underlying Broadberry, 1998; 1950–99 from Crafts and O'Mahony, 2001. Note for 1871–1937 analysis is based on output per worker but for 1950–99 on output per hour worked. Changes in the quality of labour from human capital formation are not explicitly accounted for and will contribute to residual TFP growth. Estimates pre-1937 rounded to nearest 0.05

post-war period saw a much more rapid and complete transfer of US technology to Europe than had been achieved before as unique US advantages from a large market and cheap natural resources diminished, multinationals flourished and Europe raised its technological capabilities (Nelson and Wright, 1992).

QUESTION

What does Figure 20.3 suggest about the importance of catch-up in the periods 1950–73 and 1973–99?

Figure 20.3 shows a strong inverse relationship between initial GDP level and subsequent growth for 1950–73 but not for the later period, at least among the more developed economies. (Note the difference in the scale along the horizontal axis in the two parts of the figure.) The earlier period is indeed one where growth performance was dominated by catch-up. This suggests that some of Germany's superiority in TFP growth relative to the UK in those years is explained by its initially larger productivity gap and greater scope for catch-up. It is very important to normalize for these differences in evaluating growth performance. Having said that, there also seems to be

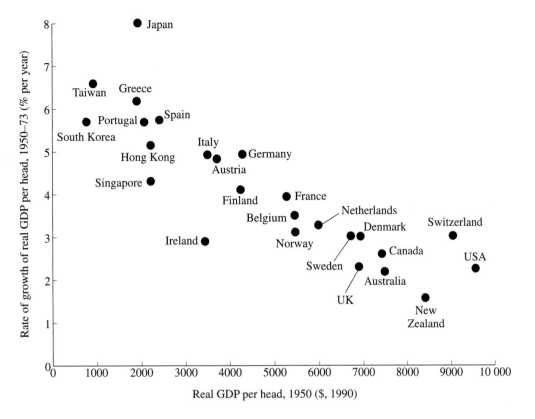

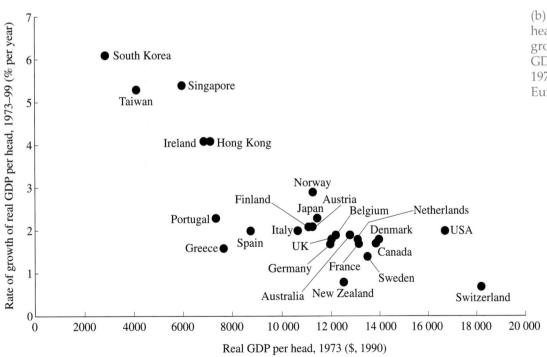

Figure 20.3 Growth performance and 'catch-up'
(a) Real GDP per head, 1950, and growth rate of real GDP per head, 1950–73, Western European countries

(b) Real GDP per head, 1973, and growth rate of real GDP per head, 1973–99, Western European countries

evidence of under-performance by the UK in that its growth was appreciably slower than that of many countries with similar initial income levels. This was confirmed formally by a regression of growth rates across European regions which took account of initial income levels and employment structures and found that, controlling for these factors, UK growth was about 0.5 percentage points lower than elsewhere in Europe (Crafts, 1995). Rapid catch-up growth was transitory and had greatly diminished by the 1980s when the productivity gap had become much lower.

Nevertheless, throughout the post-Second World War period labour productivity growth in both the UK and Germany has exceeded that of earlier years. This has reflected both more investment and faster technological change in societies which were devoting far more resources to education and research and development than they had in the nineteenth and early twentieth centuries. The decline in TFP growth in 1973–99 in all three countries in Table 20.10 is probably exaggerated by the increasingly problematic measurement of real GDP growth which was discussed in Section 1.2.

4.2   INCENTIVE STRUCTURES AND GROWTH

Two aspects of incentive structures matter for long-run growth performance. The first and more obvious aspect relates to the impact on investment and innovation decisions by the private sector. The second aspect concerns the actions of government and the possible conflict between seeking votes and enhancing productivity performance.

An analysis of the key factors influencing firms' decisions to invest and to innovate highlights issues relating to the ability to appropriate returns and to 'agency problems' within firms. The pay-off to an investment may in some circumstances be appropriated by another party. For example, the results of R&D may be copied, the training of skilled workers can accrue to those who poach them, returns may be taxed away or even expropriated by government. Where investment involves substantial outlays on sunk costs, fears that appropriation of returns may not be possible are likely to discourage investment.

The notion of 'agency problems' in this context relates to the difficulty that shareholders (the principals) may have in aligning the actions of managers (the agents) with their interests. In particular, reducing costs and adopting new technology as soon as it is cost-effective to do so requires considerable effort and perhaps even pain on the part of management. If it is hard for shareholders to know whether managers are working optimally on their behalf, managers may be less than diligent in pursuing improved productivity provided profits are 'adequate'. The situation is compounded if no shareholder is big and powerful enough to find it worthwhile to devote substantial resources to monitoring management.

Competition potentially plays an important role in mitigating these agency problems. This is partly because it quickly reveals to shareholders (through market share and profits) that managers could do better, and partly because it offers greater possibility of giving managers an incentive by performance-related rewards. In the typical British case where shareholding is diffuse, there is clear evidence that greater competition has a strongly positive impact on productivity growth (Nickell *et al.*, 1997). The evidence for the UK also suggests that lower market power is associated with greater innovative activity except where the market is very close to perfect competition, when its impact is more than offset by worries about appropriation (Aghion *et al.*, 2002). This underlines how damaging was the retreat from competition during the macroeconomic crisis of the 1930s which left about three-quarters of British manufacturing operating under the auspices of cartels (Broadberry and Crafts, 2001).

QUESTION

What predictions about the productivity performance of state-owned enterprises follow from the above analysis?

In general, there was little or no competition for British nationalized industries. The key issue is whether anyone had a strong incentive effectively to monitor and whether it was possible to establish credible rewards and punishments based on verifiable performance targets. The general experience, in the UK at least, is that establishing a satisfactory framework proved impossible and that productivity performance was indeed disappointing (Vickers and Yarrow, 1988). This has an important implication for stabilization policy in that it suggests the immediate post-war Labour government's strategy of attempting demand management through controlling the commanding heights of the economy and exercising direct control over investment had a big downside in its implications for productivity and is not a good blueprint for economic management (Broadberry and Crafts, 1996).

Why might governments find that votes are lost by policies that promote economic efficiency and productivity improvement? A classic case, familiar to students of international trade, reveals an important reason. Protectionism (in the form of tariffs or subsidies), a policy that cushions inefficient domestic firms, heavily rewards relatively small but well-organized and easily identified groups of producers at the expense of a large but disparate group of consumers and taxpayers for whom it is too expensive to organize a protest but whose less identifiable losses far outweigh the gains for the few. A more acute version of this problem arises in the context of technological change where productivity growth involves processes of creative destruction. New types of jobs appear, others disappear; for example, entry and exit of establishments accounted for about half of all labour productivity growth in UK manufacturing in 1980–92 (Disney *et al.*, 2000). The pain is obvious and immediate and entails unemployment while the benefits, though real, are in the future and probably not recognized by the gainers. The temptation for short-termist politicians is to intervene.

Fear that unemployment loses votes means that macroeconomic management has been a major influence on supply-side policy in the UK in the past. In particular, this has been true whenever governments have attempted to reduce the NAIRU through negotiating deals with the trade union movement aimed at wage restraint. These typically involved understandings that, for example, industrial relations or the structure of taxation or state ownership of industry were not to be reformed and that lame ducks would survive (Bean and Crafts, 1996).

4.3   MAIN THEMES

Three main points have emerged in this section:

- TFP growth is fundamental to long-run growth performance but varies both across countries and over time

- policies designed with short-term macroeconomic objectives in mind can have effects on long-run growth outcomes because they influence incentives to invest and to innovate

- short-term macroeconomic considerations can undermine supply-side reform as politicians (implicitly) trade off long-run growth against unemployment.

5   HOW GROWTH AND STABILIZATION INTERACT: CASE STUDIES ●

This section considers two historical episodes with a view to illuminating ideas discussed in the previous section. As in Section 3, there is no attempt to offer a comprehensive account but references are provided for those who wish to probe more deeply.

5.1   THE GOLDEN AGE

In Sections 1 and 4 we have seen that the years between the early 1950s and early 1970s were a time of rapid growth, low inflation and low unemployment for Western European countries. How did this happy state of affairs, the so-called Golden Age of European growth, come about and why did it not last? Should well-designed policy take credit for this economic success?

We have already seen that this was a time when productivity growth was very rapid in a period of transitory catch-up growth. The results of a cross-section econometric analysis of European growth reported by Temin (2002) confirm that this was the context of the Golden Age. Temin found that in the early years growth outcomes were dominated by reconstruction and the contraction of agriculture as economic liberalization took hold, and then in the later years were explained by the remaining productivity gap with the USA. In addition, as Table 20.11 shows, there was a sharp rise in investment as a share of GDP compared with the inter-war period. All these factors might explain why there was an interval of very rapid growth then a slow down as the once-and-for-all sources of catch-up became exhausted and investment ran into diminishing returns.

Table 20.11 Gross non-residential investment in the 1930s and 1960s (% GDP)

	1929–38	1960–73
France	12.1	17.0
Germany	9.8	17.6
Japan	13.6	26.6
Netherlands	14.0	19.8
UK	6.0	14.2

Source: van de Klundert and van Schaik, 1996

QUESTION

Table 20.11 shows a marked rise in investment in the Golden Age compared with the inter-war period. What do you think might explain this?

The context of an unusually strong catch-up growth is surely part of the explanation, since this provided an economic environment in which returns could be high. Nevertheless, the opportunity still needed to be grasped and this draws attention to the role of economic policy. Macroeconomic management played a part, though not, as was once thought, through active attempts to smooth out fluctuations via Keynesian-inspired fiscal policy. Rather the situation was characterized by the acceptance of the discipline of fixed exchange rates under the Bretton Woods agreement but with restrictions on capital mobility that allowed a degree of independence in monetary policy in a world of much more tightly regulated banking systems. There was no repeat of the egregious monetary policy errors in the world's leading economy that had been so damaging in the early 1930s. In sum, macroeconomic stability reinforced the confidence of investors (Boltho, 1982).

Another key feature of post-war Europe that underpinned both low unemployment and fast growth was the prevalence of post-war settlements that entailed a rapprochement between capital and labour after the conflicts of earlier decades. This involved deals brokered by the state to ensure wage moderation in return for high investment that achieved effective monitoring and commitment and was most successful under the auspices of centralized wage bargaining (Eichengreen, 1996). Wage restraint on the part of powerful trade unions, which meant unemployment was less important in reducing wage demands, was a key to lowering the NAIRU in this period, even in countries such as the UK where collective bargaining was more de-centralized (Broadberry, 1994). In addition, the rapid productivity growth of the period was a pleasant surprise to wage bargainers and, in the most successful countries such as Germany, easily exceeded wage aspirations in the early post-war period (Giersch et al., 1992).

By the early 1970s, all these favourable factors looked much weaker and were bringing the Golden Age to an end even before the stagflationary oil price shocks. In particular:

- the balance of productivity growth and after-tax wage aspirations was less conducive to low unemployment once catch-up growth weakened and taxes to finance welfare state social transfers rose

- the discipline of the fixed exchange rate system collapsed, destroyed by a combination of US monetary indiscipline at the end of the 1960s and the needs for realignment consequent on 20 years of rapid catch-up growth.

Policy makers were badly caught out and reacted much less strongly to incipient inflation in the early 1970s than Taylor Rules would suggest, in retrospect, that they should have.

During the Golden Age, the UK experienced rapid relative economic decline which should be seen as a failure to make as much of the opportunity for catch-up growth as other countries did. It is quite easy to point to aspects of supply-side policy that were unfortunate from the point of view of investment and productivity improvement. These included the failure to reform industrial relations, serious tax distortions, and the low priority given to promoting product market competition. Further, the overriding desire for low inflation and low unemployment constituted a crucial obstacle to reform, given the need to placate organized labour, or, put differently, the relative difficulty of achieving a social contract.

5.2   THE NEW ECONOMY IN 1990s USA

The 1990s was a period of exceptionally good macroeconomic performance in the USA in terms of inflation, unemployment and economic growth. At the heart of economic resurgence seemed to be the spread of new ICT, including computers and the Internet, which was dubbed the new economy, and seemed to many the onset of a new 'industrial revolution' (see Chapter 2). However, there was considerable uncertainty about the size of the output gap and how far the trend rate of productivity growth had increased in the 1990s. Accordingly, policy makers faced difficult decisions and non-trivial risks both of allowing the economy to overheat and of severe recession if they misread the situation.

QUESTION

> **Consider Table 20.12. What important information does it contain for the Chairman of the Federal Reserve System? What else might he have wished to know?**

Table 20.12 uses the tools of growth accounting that were set out in Section 4.1. The version used captures the embodiment of ICT in new varieties of capital. It explicitly identifies a contribution from labour quality growth that was subsumed in TFP growth in the format of Table 20.10. The striking feature of the table is the surge in labour productivity growth after 1995. In turn, this seems to owe a substantial amount

Table 20.12 Contributions to US labour productivity growth, 1974–99 (% per year)

	1974–90	1991–95	1996–99
Capital deepening	0.81	0.62	1.10
ICT capital	*0.44*	*0.51*	*0.96*
Other	*0.37*	*0.11*	*0.14*
Total factor productivity	0.33	0.48	1.16
ICT manufacture	*0.17*	*0.23*	*0.49*
Other	*0.16*	*0.25*	*0.67*
Labour quality	0.22	0.44	0.31
Labour productivity growth	1.37	1.53	2.57
Memorandum items			
ICT capital income share (%)	3.3	5.3	6.3
ICT manufacture output share (%)	1.4	1.9	2.5

Source: Oliner and Sichel, 2000; estimates refer to non-farm business sector

to an increased impact from ICT both in terms of capital deepening and TFP growth in the manufacture of ICT. There is also a strong increase in TFP growth in the rest of the economy. If these developments are taken at face value as a change in the trend rate of productivity growth, then at any point in the late 1990s the output gap was greater than would previously have been thought and so the stance of monetary policy could be more relaxed.

This raises a number of questions, however. First, in so far as there was an increased impact of ICT, for how long would it be sustained? The key driver of these developments was the phenomenal rate of increase of the power of computer chips, which was driving down the price of ICT and stimulating ICT capital-deepening besides underwriting a massive rate of TFP growth in ICT manufacture. If this were to cease to operate, future growth prospects would be undermined. Second, how should the behaviour of TFP growth in the rest of the economy be understood? An optimistic interpretation would be that the upturn reflected spillovers from ICT; that is, disembodied technological progress as the private sector gradually learnt about the possibilities that it opened up rather like the redesign of factories in the 1920s (Brynjolfsson and Hitt, 2000). A pessimistic interpretation would be that it was merely cyclical and denoted more intensive utilization of capital and labour inputs that the official data had not picked up (Gordon, 2000). In the late 1990s it was too soon to tell.

The public enthusiasm for the new economy, reflected in sky-high prices for technology stocks in the late 1990s, suggests that both firms and households were more inclined to a miracle rather than a mirage view. If so, then expectations of very rapid growth in future would underpin both consumption and investment expenditure. If, however, these expectations were suddenly perceived to have been incorrect (a mirage after all), then the correction of this error by both households and firms would entail a severe cutback of demand and the possibility of a deep recession (IMF, 2000). The subsequent collapse of technology stock prices suggests that this risk was non-trivial.

In these circumstances, how should monetary policy be conducted? It seems that the normal reliance on a Taylor Rule is hazardous because estimates of the output gap become extremely difficult. If so, more weight may have to be given to the inflation term and perhaps other indicators of economic performance. In fact, the Federal Reserve Bank appears to have acted as if it followed academic economists in trying to update its estimates of the NAIRU in the context of the changing balance between wage aspirations and productivity growth and relaxing policy accordingly, rather than amending the rule that it used (Ball and Tchaidze, 2002). In any event, it was much more alert to the possibility of misreading the output gap than policy makers had been in the 1970s.

After the boom subsided and, as always, too late for those operating in real time, academic research appeared to suggest that the optimistic interpretation was nearer to the truth at least for the late 1990s. Basu *et al.* (2001) investigated the issue of capacity utilization and concluded that, if anything, the underlying improvement in technological progress was greater than indicated by the growth accounting estimates.

5.3   A PERSPECTIVE ON THE CASE STUDIES

These episodes were basically pleasant surprises quite unlike the cases discussed in Section 3. Neither the Golden Age nor the new economy was really foreseen. In the aftermath of the Second World War, the general expectation was that, far from being on the threshold of the longest ever boom, there was a widespread fear of a return to the mass unemployment of the inter-war period. In the late 1980s, the USA seemed to be mired in a productivity slow down, notwithstanding the rapid diffusion of computers, and the US economy was widely perceived as in relative decline, about to be overtaken by Japan.

Three important points can be taken from these examples. First, it is important not to exaggerate the role of policy makers in delivering strong growth: changes in the underlying rate of TFP ultimately depend on the rate of technological progress and are outside their control. Second, poor policy, including sacrificing supply-side reform to macroeconomic short-termism, can, however, get in the way of exploiting technological opportunities when they come along, as is shown by the instructive example of Britain in the Golden Age. Third, changes in productivity trends make the design of monetary policy difficult, even when, as in the 1990s, the surprises are pleasant, because at first it is difficult to be sure what is happening.

6 CONCLUSION ••••••••••••••••••••••••••••••••

In the introduction I raised two key questions. These were 'how far is economic policy responsible for macroeconomic outcomes?' and 'what explains failures in the design of stabilization policy?' It is now time to pull together what has been learnt about these issues, offering some reflections on some of the main themes in the material that has been covered. Please regard these as claims whose validity you may wish to debate rather than definitive conclusions.

First, it is clear that technological change has profound impacts on the rate of economic growth, but technological change is not controlled by economic policy makers. Likewise, shocks to the price of oil. In this context, the best that can be done is to respond well to the new situation. However, poor policy design can make a significant difference to outcomes; for example, the UK coped much less well with the stagflation of the 1970s and took less than full advantage of the growth opportunities of the Golden Age than did West Germany.

Second, incomplete information, exogenous shocks and inadequate economic models are important reasons for macroeconomic policy failure but not the whole story. When policy is in the hands of politicians we can expect inflationary bias at best and egregious failures rooted in inability to impose fiscal and monetary discipline at worst. This suggests that it is better to delegate monetary policy to the central bank and accept that, in this area, there are limits to democratic accountability.

Third, on balance, macroeconomic policy making has improved. Inflation targeting on the basis of Taylor Rules is likely to deliver better results than, say, a return to the Gold Standard. Nevertheless, it is important to recognize that in the face of adverse shocks not only might it be impossible to deliver a good outcome but that the institutional arrangements themselves might not survive, since a return to unconstrained discretion could seem very attractive when in great difficulties.

Fourth, it does seem right to regard the achievement of a low rate of unemployment as a top policy priority. Nevertheless, it should be recognized that if this goal is pursued without regard to the consequences for incentive structures, the cost in terms of foregone productivity growth can be substantial.

ANSWERS TO EXERCISES

CHAPTER 11

Exercise 11.1

If *ex ante* investments are greater than savings then total planned spending would exceed output. Firms would be faced with falling stocks and rising order books, but unable to realize their investment plans. In order to do so firms would increase output, hiring more labour in the process. Output, employment and national income would rise until planned savings had risen to equal planned investment (provided there are underemployed resources in the economy sufficient to accommodate the necessary rise in output).

Exercise 11.2

Table 11.3 (completed)

Variable	Amount
Savings (*S*)	20 000
Investment (*I*)	25 000
Savings (*S*) – Investment (*I*)	*–5000*
Exports (*X*)	40 000
Imports (*M*)	45 000
Balance of trade	*–5000*
Government expenditure (*G*)	50 000
Taxation (*T*)	*50 000*
Budget deficit	*0*

In the absence of any net income earned from the rest of the world, it follows that:

$$(S - I) + (M - X) + (T - G) = 0$$

From the table $S - I = -5000$, $M - X = 5000$ (balance of trade $= X - M$), and hence $T - G = 0$. Thus $T = G$.

Exercise 11.3

1 The extent of base money in the economy is given by M0.

2 Yes. The extent to which M is greater than B can be gauged from comparing the size of M0 (which corresponds to base money) with the size of M1.

3   The value of the money multiplier is given by:

$$\frac{1}{(1-(1-c)(1-r))}$$

Substituting the values for c and r this is:

$$\frac{1}{(1-(0.9)(0.99))}$$

or 9.174.

Exercise 11.4

1   Recall that:

$$M = \frac{B}{(1-(1-c)(1-r))}$$

Here $B = 1000$ units, $c = 0.90$ and $r = 0.10$. The total money supply is:

$$M = \frac{1000}{(1-(0.1)(0.9))} = 1098.90$$

Note the total money supply is larger than B but the money multiplier is small since very little (10%) goes into the banking system as household deposits.

2   B is now 1500 units and we can work out as in (1) above that M is 1648.35.

CHAPTER 12

Exercise 12.1

1   If the marginal propensity to consume b is 0.9, the multiplier is 10:

$$\frac{1}{(1-b)} = \frac{1}{(1-0.9)} = \frac{1}{0.1} = 10$$

A decrease in investment spending of £10 billion would therefore lead to a fall in national income of £100 billion.

2   If the marginal propensity to consume b is 0.4, the multiplier is 1.67:

$$\frac{1}{(1-b)} = \frac{1}{(1-0.4)} = \frac{1}{0.6} = 1.67$$

A decrease in investment spending of £10 billion would now lead to a fall in national income of £16.7 billion.

CHAPTER 13

Exercise 13.1

If UK policy makers had wished to reduce unemployment a little after the rise in oil prices in 1979 had shifted the Phillips curve outwards, they could have introduced expansionary monetary and/or fiscal policies. The trade-off between inflation and unemployment implies that unemployment might have been stabilized between 4 per cent and 6 per cent by allowing inflation to accelerate towards, and perhaps even beyond, the rate at which it had peaked in 1975. Instead of moving south-easterly during 1980–83, the UK economy would have moved very steeply north-westerly along the Phillips curve.

Exercise 13.2

Figure 13.11 shows the completed version of Figure 13.6. There is a discussion of the results of this exercise in the text below Figure 13.6.

		Agents' expectations	
		do not change	fully anticipate policy
Government policy	expansionary	unemployment falls, inflation rises	unemployment unchanged, inflation rises
	contractionary	unemployment rises, inflation falls	unemployment unchanged, inflation falls

Figure 13.11 The effects of reflationary and disinflationary policies on unemployment and inflation

CHAPTER 14

Exercise 14.1

If P_w were above P_a in Figure 14.5, domestic production at world prices (indicated by the supply curve) would be greater than domestic demand ($Q_t > C_t$ on Figure 14.9). As a result, the good would be exported by the home economy. The gain in going from autarky to free trade is C. Consumers lose A + B, and firms gain A + B + C.

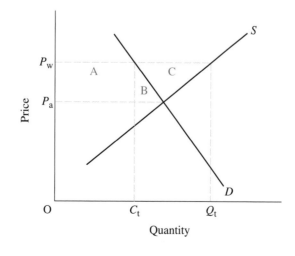

Figure 14.9 The effect of a world market price that is above the domestic market price

Exercise 14.2

A tariff raises the price of a good in the home economy above the world price. This reduces home demand below the quantity demanded at the world price. So the demand for imports (the gap between home demand and home supply at the world price) falls. Hence the supply of imports exceeds demand at the old world price. The world price must fall to reduce the quantity of imports supplied.

CHAPTER 15

Exercise 15.1

Recall the formula for the multiplier in an open economy in equation (9) from Chapter 12. This relates the change in the level of income to a change in an autonomous component of aggregate demand.

1 The first part of the question asks for the impact of new Tunisian exports of 30 000 euros on Tunisian national income when $b = 0.6$ and $m = 0$, and nothing else has changed. This latter assumption means that C, I, G, M and T are at their original levels, so the autonomous change in aggregate demand is 30 000 euros. The multiplier is

$$= \frac{1}{1-(b-m)} = \frac{1}{1-0.6} = \frac{1}{0.4} = 2.5$$

So change in $Y = 2.5 \cdot 30\ 000$ euros $= 75\ 000$ euros.

2 In this part of the question you know $M = 30\ 000$ euros, and $b = 0.6$, but $m = 0.2$. Note that M is subtracted and so the increase in imports will cause the level of national income to fall, if nothing else changes.

Change in Y

$$= \frac{1}{(1-(0.6-0.2))} \cdot -30\ 000$$

$$= \frac{1}{(1-0.4)} \cdot -30\ 000$$

$$= \frac{1}{0.6} \cdot -30\ 000$$

$$= -50\ 000$$

Exercise 15.2

1 See Figure 15.5.

2 The relationship between the seller concentration and foreign shares is shown by Figure 15.5. If the scatterplot shows an upward trend, this indicates a positive relationship between the four firm seller concentration and foreign ownership.

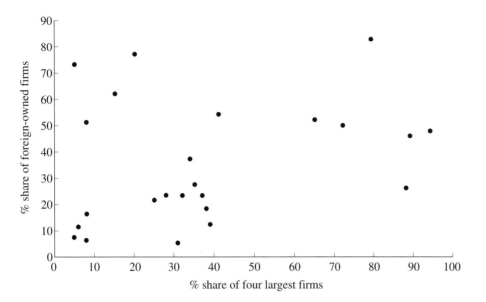

Figure 15.5
Scatterplot of seller
concentration and
foreign shares

If it appears to slope downwards, then this suggests a negative relationship
between seller concentration and foreign ownership.

The correlation coefficient between the two variables is 0.29. This, together with the
upward slope of the scatterplot, shows a positive relationship between seller
concentration and foreign ownership. That is, on average, whenever seller
concentration is high, so is the share of foreign ownership in sales.

However, the correlation coefficient is rather low, so this association is weak. You
can also see this from the scatterplot. Some sectors have high seller concentration
but low foreign shares, such as the tyres in France or textiles in the UK. Equally
some countries and sectors have high foreign shares but low seller concentration,
such as electrical appliances in Germany, Italy and France.

CHAPTER 16

Exercise 16.1

1   This is an import of goods, and so will appear as a debit item on the current
    account.

2   This is a factor income earned by residents abroad, and so will appear as a debit
    item on the current account.

3   A UK resident buying shares abroad is a capital outflow for the UK economy.
    It will be recorded as a debit item on the capital account of the balance of
    payments.

4   A UK student receiving a student grant from the EU constitutes a transfer of funds
    from abroad. It will be recorded as a credit item on the current account.

Exercise 16.2

1 The fact that the pound's real exchange rate appreciated more than its nominal exchange rate implies that UK inflation was higher than inflation in the rest of the world.

2 An appreciation of the pound's nominal exchange rate at the same time as a depreciation of its real exchange rate would imply that UK inflation was lower than inflation in the rest of the world.

Exercise 16.3

1 If a country's income growth is consistently above that of its trading partners, its demand for imports will outstrip its trading partners' demands for exports, and its exchange rate will therefore depreciate.

2 The experience of rapidly growing countries with customarily strong currencies such as Germany might be explained in terms of the competitiveness of its internationally traded manufactured goods, particularly, in view of the strong currency, the non-price aspects of competitiveness.

Exercise 16.4

1 A sudden switch in tastes away from domestic exports would shift the demand curve for the domestic currency to the left, causing the exchange rate to depreciate in the absence of intervention. In order to peg the exchange rate, the authorities would have to buy the domestic currency in sufficient quantities to keep the demand curve in its original position.

2 If world inflation surged ahead of domestic inflation, the price competitiveness of internationally traded domestic output would increase and, other things being equal:

(a) foreign demand for exports would increase, shifting the demand curve for the domestic currency to the right, and

(b) domestic demand for imports would fall, shifting the supply curve of the domestic currency to the left.

Both of these changes would cause the exchange rate to appreciate without intervention. In order to peg the exchange rate, the authorities would have to sell the domestic currency in sufficient quantities to shift the supply curve to the right of its original position.

Exercise 16.5

Here are my one sentence summaries.

1 (a) Since exchange rate movements change import and export prices, fixed exchange rates reduce the risks associated with international trade.

(b) Fixed exchange rates reduce instability caused by speculation on the foreign exchange market.

2 (a) Since flexible exchange rates automatically correct deficits and surpluses on the balance of payments, the authorities are free to pursue domestic macroeconomic goals such as growth and jobs.

  (b) Flexible exchange rates protect the economy from external shocks.

3 (a) Importers may win as well as lose through exchange rate movements.

  (b) Stability may be better achieved by allowing speculation to move currencies towards their equilibrium values.

4 (a) The balance of payments under fixed exchange rates acts as a constraint on governments by curbing irresponsible fiscal policies.

  (b) Some external influences may benefit the economy and so it should not be insulated against them.

CHAPTER 17

Exercise 17.1

Investment involves expenditure undertaken in the present that is intended to yield benefits in the future. The first two expenditures fit this category, although it should be noted that most expenditures on research and development and on education are not included as investment in the national income accounts. It could also be argued that health expenditure yields present and future benefits, and so should be regarded as investment.

A payment into a pension fund is regarded as savings and the acquisition of financial assets that will help to pay future pensions.

Exercise 17.2

The present value of the investment over all five years would be:

$$PV = \frac{£3000}{1.15} + \frac{£3000}{(1.15)^2} + \frac{£3000}{(1.15)^3} + \frac{£3000}{(1.15)^4} + \frac{£3000}{(1.15)^5} = £10\ 056$$

So the net present value of the investment is £10 056 – £10 000 = £56 and the investment is just worth doing at a 15 per cent rate of discount.

Exercise 17.3

Your present value for the investment will now be discounted by 4 per cent rather than 6 per cent.

Your returns in the first year will be $\frac{£700}{1.04}$ = £673.08

Returns in the second year will be $\frac{£900}{(1.04)^2}$ = £832.10

Returns in the third year will be $\dfrac{£900}{(1.04)^3} = £800.10$

Returns in the fourth year will be $\dfrac{£1000}{(1.04)^4} = £854.80$

So the present value of the sum of all returns = £3160.08. This is less than £7000. You would still not invest in the plane.

Exercise 17.4

Table 17.2 (completed) The multiplier and the accelerator

Period	Output	Change in output	Total capital	Net investment	Change in investment
1	100	0	200	0	–
2	110	10	220	20	20
3	140	30	280	60	40
4	200	60	400	120	60
5	290	90	580	180	60
6	380	90	760	180	0
7	380	0	760	0	–180

1   Period 2: According to the accelerator model, a rise in output of 10 units will require net investment equal to the capital–output ratio times the change in output, that is, $2 \times 10 = 20$. The desired capital stock changes to 2 times output = 220, and net investment has risen from 0 to 20.

2   Period 3: The increase in investment in period 2 leads to an increase in output in period 3. As the multiplier is 1.5 the increase in output is 30 (20×1.5), and this will lead to an increase in output from 110 to 140. The desired capital stock rises to 280 and net investment to 60 (= 280 – 220), with an increase in investment of 40.

Period 4: The increase in investment in period 3 leads to an increase in output in period 4. With a multiplier of 1.5 the increase in output is 60 (40×1.5), and this will lead to an increase in output from 140 to 200. The desired capital stock rises to 400 and net investment to 120 (= 400 – 280), with an increase in investment of 60.

Period 5: The increase in investment in period 4 leads to an increase in output in period 5 of 90 and output of 290. The desired capital is 580, net investment is 180 but investment increases by 60.

Period 6: The increase in investment in period 5 leads to an increase in output of 90, and a level of output of 380 in period 6. The desired capital stock rises to 760 and net investment remains at 180, and the increase in net investment is zero.

Period 7: The downturn begins! With no increase in net investment in the previous period, there is no increase in output. The desired capital stock remains unchanged, and net investment falls to zero. In the next period, output will fall to 380 – 270 = 110.

3 The above example reveals an important point about the accelerator model, namely that increases in investment occur only if output increases at an increasing rate. Thus, in period 6, although there is an increase in output, this increase is equivalent to the increase that occurred in period 5 and there is no change in investment.

CHAPTER 18

Exercise 18.1

A fall in the level of technology will rotate the production function downwards and, if the saving rate remains unchanged, will lead to a fall in gross investment for any given level of capital per worker. This will cause a fall in the capital stock per worker, capital reduction, until required investment is once again equal to saving per worker (gross investment). Hence, a one-off fall in the level of technology will decrease the amount of capital per worker and decrease the steady-state level of output per worker, but it will not affect the long-run growth rate. This will happen not only because the capital per worker has fallen but also because the deterioration in technology has decreased the amount each worker can produce with a given level of capital.

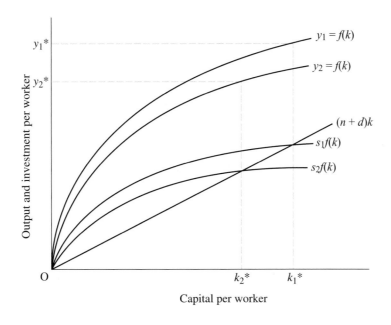

Figure 18.10 A fall in the level of technology

Exercise 18.2

The growth accounting equation is:

  rate of growth of output = rate of growth of technology (TFP) + rate of growth of inputs

1 From the information given, you can calculate that:

  rate of growth of inputs = (0.4) 8% + (0.6) 6% = 6.8%

The rate of growth of technology is 3%. So the rate of growth of output is 9.8%.

2   The rate of growth of output per worker is:

rate of growth of output – rate of growth of labour force = 9.8% – 6% = 3.8%

3   The rate of growth of capital per worker is:

rate of growth of capital – rate of growth of population = 8% – 6% = 2%

CHAPTER 20

Exercise 20.1

1   Whatever the public expects, it is always better for the government to have inflation. If the public expects zero inflation, then (reading down the left side) the pay-off for the government is 0 if actual inflation is zero and 1 if actual inflation is high. If the public expects high inflation, then (reading down the right side) the pay-off for the government is −2 if actual inflation is zero and −1, not so bad, if actual inflation is high. Inflation is therefore preferred by the government in both cases.

2   If the government's preferred option is to have inflation, then no one would believe a promise by the government not to create inflation, because it is always in the government's interest to break such a promise.

3   In the Barro–Gordon model, it is rational for the public to expect the government to create inflation because they know that inflation is the government's dominant strategy. In this case, the outcome is the bottom right-hand cell (−1, 0) with high expected inflation and high actual inflation.

REFERENCES

SERIALS

Economic Trends, London, The Stationery Office for Office for National Statistics (monthly).

OECD Economic Outlook, Paris, Organization for Economic Co-operation and Development (twice yearly).

United Kingdom Balance of Payments (The Pink Book), London, The Stationery Office for Office for National Statistics (annual).

United Kingdom National Accounts (The Blue Book), London, The Stationery Office for Office for National Statistics (annual).

OTHER REFERENCES

Abrams, F. and Astill, J. (2001) 'Story of the Blues', *Education Guardian*, 29 May.

Aghion, P., Bloom, N., Blundell, R., Griffith, R. and Howitt, P. (2002) *Competition and Innovation: An Inverted U Relationship*, NBER Working Paper No.9269, Cambridge, Mass., National Bureau of Economic Research.

Artis, M.J. and Taylor, M.P. (1989) 'Exchange rates, interest rates, capital controls and the European Monetary System: assessing the track record' in Giavazzi, F., Micossi, S. and Miller, M. (eds) *The European Monetary System*, Cambridge, Cambridge University Press.

Arulampalam, W. (2001) 'Is unemployment really scarring? Effects of unemployment experiences on wages', *The Economic Journal*, vol.111, November, pp.F585–606.

Arulampalam, W., Gregg, P. and Gregory, M. (2001) 'Unemployment scarring', *The Economic Journal*, vol.111, November, pp.F577–84.

Atkinson, A. (1999) *Is Rising Income Inequality Inevitable? A Critique of the Transatlantic Consensus*, WIDER annual lectures 3, Helsinki, World Institute for Development and Economics Research.

Baldwin, R.E. and Martin, P. (1999) *Two Waves of Globalisation: Superficial Similarities, Fundamental Differences*, NBER Working Paper No.6904, Cambridge, Mass., National Bureau of Economic Research.

Ball, L. (1993) 'How costly is disinflation? The historical evidence', *Business Review*, Federal Reserve Bank of Philadelphia, November–December.

Ball, L. and Mankiw, N.G. (1994) 'Asymmetric price adjustment and economic fluctuations', *Economic Journal*, vol.104, pp.247–61.

Ball, L. and Tchaidze, R. (2002) *The Fed and the New Economy*, NBER Working Paper No.8785, Cambridge, Mass., National Bureau of Economic Research.

Bank of England, *Notes on Monetary Policy*, at www.bankofengland.co.uk (accessed September 2002).

Bank of International Settlements (1992) *Annual Report*, Basle, BIS.

Barro, R.J. and Gordon, D. (1983) 'A positive theory of monetary policy in a natural-rate model', *Journal of Political Economy,* vol.91, pp.589–610.

Basu, S., Fernald, J. and Shapiro, M. (2001) *Productivity Growth in the 1990s: Technology, Utilization, or Adjustment?*, NBER Working Paper No.8359, Cambridge, Mass., National Bureau of Economic Research.

Baumol, W.J. and Blinder, A.S. (1988) *Economics: Principles and Policy,* New York, Harcourt Brace Jovanovich.

Bean, C. and Crafts, N.F.R. (1996) 'British economic growth since 1945: relative economic decline ... and renaissance?' in Crafts, N.F.R. and Toniolo, G. (eds), pp.131–72.

Becker, G. (1962) 'Investment in human capital: a theoretical analysis', *Journal of Political Economy,* vol.70, pp.9–44.

Berg, A. (1999) *The Asian Crisis: Causes, Policy Responses and Outcomes*, IMF Working Paper No.99/138.

Bernanke, B.S. (1983) 'Non-monetary effects of the financial crisis in the propagation of the Great Depression', *American Economic Review,* vol.73, pp.257–76.

Bernanke, B.S. and Carey, K. (1996) 'Nominal wage stickiness and aggregate supply during the Great Depression', *Quarterly Journal of Economics*, vol.111, pp.853–84.

Bhaduri, A. (1986) *Macroeconomics: The Dynamics of Commodity Production*, New Delhi, Oxford University Press.

Blanchard, O.J. (1983) 'Price asynchronisation and price inertia' in Dornbusch, R. and Simonsen, M. (eds) *Inflation, Debt and Indexation*, Cambridge, Mass., MIT Press.

Blanchflower, D.G. and Oswald, A.J. (2001) *Well-being Over Time in Britain and the USA,* Warwick Economic Research Paper No.616.

Blomstrom, M. and Kokko, A. (1998) 'Multinational corporations and spillovers', *Journal of Economic Surveys*, vol.12, no.3, pp.247–77.

Boltho, A. (1982) 'Growth' in Boltho, A. (ed.) *The European Economy: Growth and Crisis*, Oxford, Oxford University Press, pp.9–37.

Bordo, M. (1993) 'The Bretton Woods International Monetary System: an historical overview' in Bordo, M. and Eichengreen, B. (eds) *A Retrospective on the Bretton Woods System*, Chicago, University of Chicago Press, pp.3–98.

Boskin, M., Dulberger, E., Gordon, R., Griliches, Z. and Jorgenson, D. (1996) 'Toward a more accurate measure of the cost of living', Final Report to US Senate Finance Committee.

Bowen, H., Leamer, E. and Sveikauskas, L. (1987) 'Multi-country, multi-factor tests of the factor abundance theory', *American Economic Review,* vol.77, pp.791–809.

Bowles, S. (1985) 'The production process in a competitive economy: Walrasian, Neo-Hobbesian and Marxian models', *American Economic Review,* vol.75, pp.16–36.

Boyer, G. and Hatton, T. (2002) 'New estimates of British unemployment, 1870–1913', *Journal of Economic History,* vol.62, pp.643–75.

Briault, C. (1995) 'The costs of inflation', *Bank of England Quarterly Bulletin*, February, pp.33–45.

Broadberry, S.N. (1994) 'Why was unemployment in postwar Britain so low?', *Bulletin of Economic Research*, vol.46, pp.241–61.

Broadberry, S.N. (1998) 'How did the United States and Germany overtake Britain? Sectoral analysis of comparative productivity levels, 1870–1990', *Journal of Economic History*, vol.58, pp.375–407.

Broadberry, S.N. and Crafts, N.F.R. (1992) 'Britain's productivity gap in the 1930s: some neglected factors', *Journal of Economic History*, vol.52, pp.531–58.

Broadberry, S.N. and Crafts, N.F.R. (1996) 'British economic performance and industrial policy in the early postwar period', *Business History*, vol.38, pp.65–91.

Broadberry, S.N. and Crafts, N.F.R. (2001) 'Competition and innovation in 1950s Britain', *Business History*, vol.43, pp.97–118.

Broome, J. (1992) *Counting the Costs of Global Warming*, Cambridge, White Horse Press.

Brown, G. (2000) Speech given to the British Chamber of Commerce National Conference, 5 April, at http://www.treasury.gov.uk/newsroom_and_speeches/press/2000/press_49_00.cfm (accessed January 2002).

Bruno, M. (1995) 'Does inflation really lower growth?', *Finance and Development*, vol.32, pp.35–8.

Bruno, M. and Easterly, W. (1998) 'Inflation crises and long-run growth', *Journal of Monetary Economics*, vol.41, pp.3–26.

Brynjolfsson, E. and Hitt, L.M. (2000) 'Beyond computation: information technology, organizational transformation and business performance', *Journal of Economic Perspectives*, vol.14, no.4, pp.23–48.

Budget Report (2000) 'The economy', Chapter B at http://www.treasury.gov.uk/Budget/Budget_2000/Budget_Report/bud_bud00_chapb.cfm? (accessed January 2002).

Burnside, C., Eichenbaum, M. and Rebelo, S. (1999) *Prospective Deficits and the Asian Currency Crisis*, World Bank Policy Research Working Paper No.2174.

Cafaro, P. (2001) 'Thoreau, Leopold and Carson: toward an environmental virtue ethics', *Environmental Ethics*, vol.23, pp.3–17.

Calomiris, C. and Wilson, B. (1998) *Bank Capital and Portfolio Management: The 1930s Capital Crunch and the Scramble to Shed Risk*, NBER Working Paper No.6649, Cambridge, Mass., National Bureau of Economic Research.

Cameron, G., Proudman, J. and Redding, S. (1999) *Technology Transfer, R&D, Trade, and Productivity Growth*, CEP Discussion Paper No.428, London, Centre for Economic Performance.

Capie, F. and Collins, M. (1983) *The Interwar British Economy: A Statistical Abstract*, Manchester, Manchester University Press.

Caprio, G. (1998) *Banking on Crises: Expensive Lessons from Recent Financial Crises*, World Bank Policy Research Working Paper No.1979.

Carter, M. and Maddock, R. (1984) *Rational Expectations: Macroeconomics for the 1980s*, London, Macmillan.

Chadha, B., Masson, P.R. and Meredith, G. (1992) 'Models of inflation and the costs of disinflation', *IMF Staff Papers*, vol.39, pp.395–431.

Clare, A.D. and Thomas, S.H. (1993) 'Relative price variability and inflation in an equilibrium price misperceptions model', *Economic Letters*, vol.42, pp.51–7.

Clemens, M.A. and Williamson, J.G. (2001) *A Tariff-growth Paradox? Protection's Impact on the World Around 1875–1997*, NBER Working Paper No.8459, Cambridge, Mass., National Bureau of Economic Research.

Corbett, J. and Vines, D. (1999) 'The Asian crisis: lessons from the collapse of financial systems, exchange rates and macroeconomic policy' in Agenor, P.-R., Miller, M. and Vines, D. (eds) *The Asian Financial Crisis: Causes, Contagion, Consequences*, Cambridge, Cambridge University Press, pp.67–110.

Crafts, N.F.R. (1995) 'The Golden Age of economic growth in postwar Europe: why did Northern Ireland miss out?', *Irish Economic and Social History*, vol.22, pp.5–25.

Crafts, N.F.R. (1997) 'The Human Development Index and changes in standards of living: some historical comparisons', *European Review of Economic History*, vol.1, pp.299–322.

Crafts, N.F.R. (2002) *Britain's Relative Economic Decline, 1870–1999*, London, Institute of Economic Affairs.

Crafts, N.F.R. and O'Mahony, M. (2001) 'A perspective on UK productivity performance', *Fiscal Studies*, vol. 22, pp.271–306.

Crafts, N.F.R. and Toniolo, G. (eds) (1996) *Economic Growth in Europe Since 1945*, Cambridge, Cambridge University Press.

Crosse, J. (2000) 'It's a kind of magic', *VM: The Vauxhall Magazine*, London, Mediamark Publishing Ltd.

Daly, H.E. (1973) *Towards a Steady State Economy*, San Francisco, W.H. Freeman.

Dawson, G. (1992) *Inflation and Unemployment: Cause, Consequences and Cures*, Aldershot, Edward Elgar.

Dawson, G. (2002) 'The costs of reducing inflation' in Vane, H. and Snowdon, B. (eds) *An Encyclopaedia of Macroeconomics*, Aldershot, Edward Elgar.

Disney, R., Haskel, J. and Heden, Y. (2000) *Restructuring and Productivity Growth in UK Manufacturing*, Centre for Economic Policy Research Discussion Paper No.2643.

Dollar, D. and Collier, P. (2001) *Globalisation, Growth and Poverty: Building an Inclusive Economy*, Oxford, Oxford University Press.

Dollar, D. and Kray, A. (2001) *Trade, Growth and Poverty*, Policy Research Working Paper No.2199, Washington, DC, World Bank.

Driver, C. (1998) 'The case of fixed investment' in Buxton, T., Chapman, P. and Temple, P. (eds) *Britain's Economic Performance* (2nd edn), London, Routledge.

Easterlin, R. (2000) 'The worldwide standard of living since 1800', *Journal of Economic Perspectives*, vol.14, no.1, pp.7–26.

Easterlin, R. (2001) 'Income and happiness: towards a unified theory', *Economic Journal*, vol.111, pp.465–84.

Eichengreen, B. (1992) *Golden Fetters*, Oxford, Oxford University Press.

Eichengreen, B. (1996) 'Institutions and economic growth: Europe after World War II' in Crafts, N.F.R. and Toniolo, G. (eds), pp.38–72.

Eichengreen, B. and Sachs, J. (1985) 'Exchange rates and economic recovery in the 1930s', *Journal of Economic History*, vol.45, pp.925–46.

Environmental Finance (2001) 'Trading carbon: market solutions to climate change' (Special COP 7 Supplement), October, pp.I–XX.

Feenstra, R.C. (1999) 'Facts and fallacies about foreign direct investment' in Feldstein, M. (ed.) *International Capital Flows*, NBER Conference Report, Chicago, University of Chicago Press.

Feinstein, C.H. (1972) *National Income, Expenditure and Output of the United Kingdom, 1855–1965*, Cambridge, Cambridge University Press.

Fischer, S. and Modigliani, F. (1975) 'Towards an understanding of the real effects and costs of inflation', *Weltwirtschaftliches Archive*, vol.114, pp.81–99.

Fishwick, F. (1982) *Multinational Companies and Economic Concentration in Europe*, Aldershot, Gower.

Friedman, M. (1968) 'The role of monetary policy', *American Economic Review*, vol.58, pp.1–17.

Friedman, M. (1977) *Inflation and Unemployment: The New Dimension of Politics*, IEA Occasional Paper No.51, London, Institute of Economic Affairs.

Fry, M. (1995) *Money, Interest and Banking in Economic Development*, Baltimore, Johns Hopkins University.

Georgescu-Roegen, N. (1971) *The Entropy Law and the Economic Process*, Cambridge, Mass., Harvard University Press.

Giersch, H., Paque, K.-H. and Schmieding, H. (1992) *The Fading Miracle*, Cambridge, Cambridge University Press.

Gilder, G. (1989) *Microcosm: The Quantum Revolution in Economics and Technology*, New York, Simon and Schuster.

Goldstein, M., Kaminsky, G. and Reinhart, C. (2000) *Assessing Financial Vulnerability*, Washington, DC, Institute for International Economics.

Gordon, R.J. (2000) 'Does the New Economy measure up to the great inventions of the past?', *Journal of Economic Perspectives*, vol.14, no.4, pp.49–74.

Green, F. (2001) 'It's been a hard day's night: the concentration and intensification of work in late twentieth-century Britain', *British Journal of Industrial Relations*, vol.39, pp.53–80.

Greenaway, D., Morgan, W. and Wright, P. (1997) 'Trade liberalisation and growth in developing countries: some new evidence', *World Development*, vol.25, no.11, pp.1885–92.

Gregg, P. (2001) 'The impact of youth unemployment on adult unemployment in the NCDs', *The Economic Journal*, vol.111, November, pp.F626–53.

Gregory, M. and Jukes, R. (2001) 'Unemployment and subsequent earnings: estimating scarring among British men 1984–94', *The Economic Journal*, vol.111, November, pp.F607–25.

Greyson, J. (1996) 'The Natural Step: developing a consensus on criteria for a sustainable economy', *Renew: Technology for a Sustainable Future*, Network for Alternative Technology and Technology Assessment (NATTA)/The Open University, Milton Keynes.

Griffith, R., Redding, S. and Van Reenan, J. (2000) *Mapping the Two Faces of R&D: Productivity Growth in a Panel of OECD Industries*, Institute for Fiscal Studies Working Paper W00/02, London, Institute for Fiscal Studies.

Grossman, R.S. (1994) 'The shoe that didn't drop: explaining banking stability during the Great Depression', *Journal of Economic History*, vol.54, pp.654–82.

Grubb, M., with Vrolijk, C. and Brack, D. (1999) *The Kyoto Protocol: A Guide and Assessment*, London, Earthscan/The Royal Institute of International Affairs.

Haldane, A. and Quah, D. (1999) *UK Phillips Curves and Monetary Policy*, at http://econ.lse.ac.uk/~dquah/ (accessed September 2002).

Hall, T.E. and Ferguson, J.D. (1998) *The Great Depression*, Ann Arbor, University of Michigan Press.

Hicks, J.R. (1939) *Value and Capital*, Oxford, Clarendon Press.

Hirsch, F. (1976) *The Social Limits to Growth*, Cambridge, Mass., Harvard University Press.

Hobsbawm, E. (1982) *Industry and Empire*, Harmondsworth, Penguin.

Holtfrerich, C.-L. (1983) *The German Inflation, 1914–1923*, Berlin, de Gruyter.

Houghton, J. (1997) *Global Warming: The Complete Briefing*, Cambridge, Cambridge University Press.

Hume, D. (1906) *A Treatise of Human Nature*, Selby-Bigge, A.H. (ed.), Oxford, Oxford University Press (first published 1739–40).

Humphrey, T. (1986) *From Trade-offs to Policy Ineffectiveness: A History of the Phillips Curve*, Richmond, Va., Federal Reserve Bank of Richmond.

Hutton, W. (1995) *The State We're In*, London, Vintage.

IMF (2000) *World Economic Outlook*, Washington, DC, International Monetary Fund.

Jenkins, R. (1983) 'Comparing foreign subsidiaries and local firms in LDCs: theoretical issues and empirical evidence', *Journal of Development Studies*, vol.26, no.2.

Jones, C. (1995) 'R&D based models of economic growth', *Journal of Political Economy*, vol.103, pp.759–84.

Jones, C. (2001) *Introduction to Economic Growth*, London, Norton.

Junankar, P.N. (1985) *Costs of Unemployment*, Brussels, Commission of European Community.

Kaldor, N. (1958) 'Capital accumulation and economic growth', Chapter 10 in Lutz, F.A. and Hague, D.C. (eds) (1961) *The Theory of Capital*, London, Macmillan.

Kalecki, M. (1954) 'The theory of economic dynamics' in Osiatynski, J. (ed.) (1990) *Collected Works of Michal Kalecki, Volume 1 – Capitalism: Business Cycles and Full Employment*, Oxford, Clarendon Press.

Keynes, J.M. (1936) *The General Theory of Employment, Interest and Money*, London, Macmillan.

Landes, D.S. (1998) *The Wealth and Poverty of Nations: Why Are Some So Rich and Others So Poor?*, New York, W.W. Norton.

Layard, R., Nickell, S. and Jackman, R. (1994) *The Unemployment Crisis*, Oxford, Oxford University Press.

Leontief, W.W. (1953) 'Domestic production and foreign trade: the American capital position re-examined', *Proceedings of the American Philosophical Society*, vol.97, pp.332–49.

Leopold, A. (1970) *A Sand County Almanac: With Essays on Conservation from Round River*, New York, Ballantine Books.

Lindert, P.H. and Williamson, J.G. (2001) *Does Globalisation Make the World More Unequal?*, NBER Working Paper No.8228, Cambridge, Mass., National Bureau of Economic Research.

Lucas, R. (1993) 'Making a miracle', *Econometrica*, vol.61, no.2, pp.251–72.

Lutz, M.A. (1999) *Economics for the Common Good: Two Centuries of Social Economic Thought in the Humanistic Tradition*, London, Routledge.

Maddison, A. (1983) *Two Crises: Latin America and Asia, 1929–38 and 1973–83*, OECD, Paris.

Maddison, A. (1987) 'Growth and slowdown in advanced capitalist economies: techniques of quantitative assessment', *Journal of Economic Literature*, vol.25, pp.649–98.

Maddison, A. (1991) *Dynamic Forces in Capitalist Development*, Oxford, Oxford University Press.

Maddison, A. (1995) *Monitoring the World Economy, 1820–1992*, OECD, Paris.

Maddison, A. (2001) *The World Economy: A Millennial Perspective*, OECD, Paris.

Mankiw, G. (1990) 'A quick refresher course in macroeconomics', *Journal of Economic Literature*, vol.XXVIII, no.4, pp.1645–60.

Milanovic, B. (2002) 'True world income distribution, 1988 and 1993: first calculation based on household surveys alone', *The Economic Journal*, vol.112, no.476, pp.51–92.

Minford, A.P.L. and Peel, D. (1983) *Rational Expectations and the New Macroeconomics*, Oxford, Martin Robertson.

Mishkin, F.S. (1999) *Lessons from the Asian Crisis*, NBER Working Paper No.7102, Cambridge, Mass., National Bureau of Economic Research.

Mitchell, B.R. (1988) *British Historical Statistics*, Cambridge, Cambridge University Press.

Murgatroyd, L. and Neuburger, H. (1997) 'A household satellite account for the UK', *Economic Trends*, vol.527, pp.63–71.

Muth, J.F. (1961) 'Rational expectations and the theory of price movements', *Econometrica*, vol.29, pp.315–35.

Nelson, E. and Nikolov, K. (2001) *UK Inflation in the 1970s and 1980s: The Era of Output Gap Mismeasurement*, Bank of England Working Paper No.148.

Nelson, R.R. and Wright, G. (1992) 'The rise and fall of American technological leadership: the postwar era in historical perspective', *Journal of Economic Literature*, vol.30, pp.1931–64.

Newell, A. and Symons, J. (1988) 'The macroeconomics of the interwar years: international comparisons' in Eichengreen, B. and Hatton, T.J. (eds) *Interwar Unemployment in Historical Perspective*, Dordrecht, Kluwer Academic Publishers, pp.61–96.

Nickell, S. (1996) 'Competition and corporate performance', *Journal of Political Economy*, vol.104, pp.724–26.

Nickell, S., Nicolitsas, D. and Dryden, N. (1997) 'What makes firms perform well?', *European Economic Review*, vol.41, pp.783–96.

Nordhaus, W.D. (2000) 'New directions in national economic accounting', *American Economic Review Papers and Proceedings*, vol.90, pp.259–63.

OECD (2000) *Policy Brief: EMU One Year On*, Paris, OECD.

OECD (2001) *Labour Force Statistics*, Paris, Organization for Economic Co-operation and Development.

Office for National Statistics (2002) at www.statistics.gov.uk/statbase/TSDtimezone.asp (accessed September 2002).

Okun, A. (1970) 'Potential GNP: its measurement and significance' (appendix) in *Political Economy of Prosperity*, Washington, DC, Brookings Institution.

Oliner, S.D. and Sichel, D.E. (2000) 'The resurgence of growth in the late 1990s: is information technology the story?', *Journal of Economic Perspectives*, vol.14, no.4, pp.3–22.

Orphanides, A. and Solow, R.M. (1990) 'Money, inflation and growth' in Friedman, B. M. and Hahn, F.H. (eds) *Handbook of Monetary Economics, Vol. 1*, Amsterdam, North Holland.

Oulton, N. (1995) 'Supply side reform and UK economic growth: what happened to the miracle?', *National Institute Economic Review*, vol.154, pp.53–69.

Pearce, D.W. and Warford, J.J. (1993) *World Without End: Economics, Environment and Sustainable Development*, Oxford, Oxford University Press.

Phelps, E.S. (1967) 'Phillips curves, expectations of inflation and optimal unemployment over time', *Economica*, vol.34, pp.254–81.

Phillips, A.W. (1958) 'The relationship between unemployment and the rate of change of money wage rates in the United Kingdom 1861–1957', *Economica*, vol.24, pp.283–99.

Pugh, P. and Garratt, C. (2000) *Introducing Keynesian Economics*, Cambridge, Icon Books.

Puttnam, R. (2001) *Bowling Alone*, New York, Simon & Schuster.

Ramey, G. and Ramey, V.A. (1995) 'Cross country evidence on the link between volatility and growth', *American Economic Review*, vol.85, pp.1138–51.

Rodrik, D. (1996) 'Understanding policy reform', *Journal of Economic Literature*, vol.34, pp.9–41.

Rodrik, D. (1999) 'Democracies pay higher wages', *Quarterly Journal of Economics*, vol.114, no.3, pp.707–38.

Romer, C. (1992) 'What ended the Great Depression?', *Journal of Economic History*, vol.52, pp.756–84.

Romer, P. (1990) 'Endogenous technological change', *Journal of Political Economy*, vol.98, pp.S71–102.

Rosenbaum, E.F. (2000) 'What is a market? On the methodology of a contested concept', *Review of Social Economy*, vol.LVIII, no.4, pp.455–82.

Rosewell, B. (2001) 'GHG trading: easier than you think', *Environmental Finance* (Special COP 7 Supplement), October, pp.I–XX.

Sadiq, A.T. and Bolbol, A.A. (2001) 'Capital flows, FDI and technology spillovers: evidence from Arab countries', *World Development*, vol.29, no.12, pp.2111–25.

Sala-i-Martin, X. (1997) 'I just ran two million regressions', *American Economic Review*, vol.87, no.2, pp.178–83.

Samuelson, P.A. (1969) 'The way of an economist' in Samuelson, P.A. (ed.) *International Economic Relations; Proceedings of the Third Congress of the International Economics Association*, London, Macmillan, pp.1–11.

Sargent, T.J. (1986) *Rational Expectations and Inflation*, New York, Harper & Row.

Say, J.-B. (1803) *A Treatise on Political Economy*, Philadelphia, Pa., Lippincott, Grambo.

Schneider, F. (2000) 'The increase of the size of the shadow economy of 18 OECD countries: some preliminary explanations', paper presented to the Annual Public Choice Meetings, Charleston, South Carolina.

Schneider, F. and Enste, D.H. (2000) 'Shadow economies: size, causes, and consequences', *Journal of Economic Literature*, vol.38, pp.77–114.

Schumacher, E.F. (1973) *Small is Beautiful: A Study of Economics as if People Mattered*, London, Blond & Briggs.

Selzer, I.M. (2001) 'Thoughts on competition policy', *Lectures on Regulatory and Competition Policy*, London, The Institute of Economic Affairs.

Sen, A.K. (1976) 'Rational fools: a critique of the behavioural foundations of economic theory', *Philosophy and Public Affairs*, vol.6, Summer, pp.317–44.

Sen, A.K. (1987) *On Ethics and Economics*, Oxford, Basil Blackwell.

Sen, A.K. (1999) *Development as Freedom*, Oxford, Oxford University Press.

Solow, R. (1956) 'A contribution to the theory of growth', *Quarterly Journal of Economics*, vol.70, pp.65–94.

Solow, R. (1957) 'Technical change and the aggregate production function', *Review of Economics and Statistics*, vol.39, no.3, pp.312–20.

Taylor, J.B. (1994) *Goals, Guidelines and Constraints Facing Monetary Policymakers*, Boston, Federal Reserve Bank of Boston.

Temin, P. (1976) *Did Monetary Forces Cause the Great Depression?*, New York, Norton.

Temin, P. (2002) 'The Golden Age of European growth reconsidered', *European Review of Economic History*, vol.6, pp.3–22.

Temple, J. (1999) 'The New Growth evidence', *Journal of Economic Literature*, vol.37, no.1, pp.112–56.

Temple, J. (2000) 'Inflation and growth: stories short and tall', *Journal of Economic Surveys*, vol.14, pp.395–426.

UNCTAD (1998) *World Investment Report, 1998: Trends and Determinants*, Geneva, UNCTAD.

UNCTAD (2001) *World Investment Report, 2001: Promoting Linkages*, Geneva, UNCTAD.

US Bureau of the Census (1960) *Historical Statistics of the United States*, Washington, DC.

van de Klundert, T. and van Schaik, A. (1996) 'On the historical continuity of the process of economic growth' in van Ark, B. and Crafts, N.F.R. (eds) *Quantitative Aspects of Postwar European Economic Growth*, Cambridge, Cambridge University Press, pp.388–414.

Vickers, J. and Yarrow, G. (1988) *Privatization: An Economic Analysis*, Cambridge, Mass., MIT Press.

Victor, D. (2001) *After Kyoto: Politics, Economics and the Struggle to Slow Global Warming*, Princeton, Princeton University Press.

Wade, R. (2001) 'Winners and losers', *The Economist*, 26 April.

WCED (World Commission on Environment and Development) (1987) *Our Common Future*, Oxford, Oxford University Press.

Webb, S.B. (1986) 'Fiscal news and inflationary expectations in Germany after World War I', *Journal of Economic History*, vol.46, pp.769–94.

Webb, S.B. (1989) *Hyperinflation and Stabilization in Weimar Germany*, Oxford, Oxford University Press.

World Bank (1993) *The East Asian Miracle*, New York, Oxford University Press.

World Bank (2001) *World Development Indicators*, Washington, DC, World Bank.

World Bank (2002) *World Development Indicators* (CD-ROM), Washington, DC, World Bank.

Yuengert, A.M. (2001) 'Rational choice with passion: virtue in a model of rational addiction', *Review of Social Economy*, vol.LIX, no.1, pp.1–21.

ACKNOWLEDGEMENTS

Grateful acknowledgement is made to the following sources for permission to reproduce material in this book.

CHAPTER 13

Illustration

Page 378: Pugh, P. and Garratt, C., *Introducing Keynesian Economics* (2000).

CHAPTER 14

Figures

Figure 14.2: Baldwin, R.E. and Martin, P., *NBER Working Papers*, January 1999, no.6904, Mohr Siebeck; *Figure 14.3:* Clemens, M.A. and Williamson, J.G., *NBER Working Papers*, September 2001, no.8459, © the authors.

CHAPTER 15

Figures

Figures 15.1 and 15.2: © Sarah Herman, 2002; *Figure 15.3:* Atkinson, A.B., *WIDER Annual Lectures 3*, November 1999, The United Nations University, World Institute for Development and Economics Research; *Figure 15.4:* Jones, C.I. (1998) *Introduction to Economic Growth*, W.W. Norton.

Tables

Table 15.1(b): UNCTAD, 1998; *Table 15.5:* Reprinted from *World Development*, vol.25, Greenaway, D. and Morgan, W., *Trade Liberalisation and Growth in Developing Countries: Some New Evidence*, pp.1887–8. Copyright 1997, with Elsevier Science; *Table 15.6:* Dollar, D. (2001) *Globalisation, Growth and Poverty: Building an Inclusive World Economy*, World Bank.

CHAPTER 16

Tables

Table 16.1: Bank of International Settlements Annual Report, 1992, Bank of International Settlements, Basle; *Table 16.2: United Kingdom Balance of Payments (The Pink Book)*, 2001. Crown copyright material is reproduced with the permission of the Controller of HMSO.

CHAPTER 18

Gavin Cameron would like to thank Padraig Dixon, Jonathan Temple and Kamakshya Trivedi for helpful comments on various drafts of Chapter 18, and Tehmina Khan for excellent research assistance.

Tables

Table 18.1: Temple, J. (1999) 'New Growth evidence', *Journal of Economic Literature,* vol.37. American Economic Association; *Table 18.3:* Easterlin, R. (2000) 'The worldwide standard of living since 1800', *Journal of Economic Perspectives*, vol.14, issue 1. American Economic Association.

CHAPTER 19

Figures

Figure 19.1: Popperfoto; *Figure 19.2:* AKG; *Figure 19.4:* Courtesy of Vauxhall Magazine.

CHAPTER 20

Nicholas Crafts would like to thank Dudley Baines and Peter Law for helpful comments on an earlier draft of Chapter 20.

Tables

Table 20.1: Maddison, A., 'The world economy: a millennial perspective', *Development Centre Seminars*, OECD; *Table 20.6:* Schneider, F., 'The increase of the size of the shadow economy', *EPCS 2000*; *Table 20.12:* Oliner, S. and Sichel, D. (2000) 'Contributions to labour productivity growth in the non-farm business sector 1974–1999', *Journal of Economic Perspectives*, vol.14, no.4.

INDEX

Page numbers in **bold** refer to definitions given in the margin.

Index by Janet Dudley.